■ Moving Beyond Self-Interest

Moving Beyond Self-Interest

Perspectives from Evolutionary Biology,
Neuroscience, and the Social Sciences

EDITED BY

Stephanie L. Brown
R. Michael Brown
Louis A. Penner

OXFORD
UNIVERSITY PRESS

Oxford University Press, Inc., publishes works that further Oxford University's objective of excellence in research, scholarship, and education.

Oxford   New York
Auckland   Cape Town   Dar es Salaam   Hong Kong   Karachi   Kuala Lumpur
Madrid   Melbourne   Mexico City   Nairobi   New Delhi   Shanghai   Taipei   Toronto

With offices in
Argentina   Austria   Brazil   Chile   Czech Republic   France   Greece   Guatemala   Hungary
Italy   Japan   Poland   Portugal   Singapore   South Korea   Switzerland   Thailand
Turkey   Ukraine   Vietnam

Published by Oxford University Press, Inc.
198 Madison Avenue, New York, New York 10016
www.oup.com

Oxford is a registered trademark of Oxford University Press, Inc.

Library of Congress Cataloging-in-Publication Data

Moving beyond self-interest : perspectives from evolutionary biology, neuroscience,
and the social sciences / edited by Stephanie L. Brown, R. Michael Brown, Louis A. Penner.
    p. cm.
Includes bibliographical references and index.
ISBN 978-0-19-538810-7 (hbk) 1. Helping behavior. 2. Compassion. 3. Behavior evolution.
I. Brown, Stephanie L. II. Brown, R. Michael. III. Penner, Louis A., 1943-
BF637.H4M69 2011
155.9'2—dc22   2010048059

9 8 7 6 5 4 3 2 1

Printed in the United States of America on acid-free paper

■ *To my sister, Michelle, who inspires me to learn and grow.*

—Stephanie Brown

■ *To Gordie Hamilton: World War II veteran, camp counselor, Boy Scout leader, high school teacher, camping program director, and beloved father figure to thousands of young men and women. Thank you for expecting, both firmly and compassionately, that we move beyond self-interest, and for showing us how to do it.*

—Michael Brown

■ *To my brother Jerry: His life was an exemplar of going beyond self-interest and caring for and giving to other people.*

—Louis Penner

■ FOREWORD

■ TWAS BAD BIOLOGY THAT KILLED THE ECONOMY

> Policeman: *"Well, Denham, the airplanes got him."*
> Denham: *"Oh no, it wasn't the airplanes. Twas beauty killed the beast."*
> King Kong (1933)

The volume in front of us asks why we care for others, a question often phrased in terms of the altruism versus selfishness dichotomy. I am a biologist, hence familiar with the "puzzle of altruism," as it is often called, which is that one's own survival and reproduction should get priority over those of others. Why be altruistic if you could be selfish? The more I think about this question, however, the more problematic the whole underlying dichotomy becomes.

Admittedly, there are many puzzles to be found in animal and human behavior, but one of the most striking and most common forms of altruism, which is mammalian maternal care, is not one of them. Biologists have absolutely no trouble explaining how it might have evolved, as it benefits the female's own progeny. We also know that it comes with built-in rewards, such as the oxytocin release and good feelings associated with nursing. This maternal "caregiving system" is considered in some detail in essays by Numan (Chapter 6) and Brown, Brown, and Preston (Chapter 5), and its relevance for understanding human prosocial acts in response to need is evident throughout *Moving Beyond Self-Interest*. If maternal care served as template for empathy and altruism in other human domains, as many now think, the sharp dividing line between selfishness and altruism becomes blurred to the point that we need to start looking for new paradigms. This is what the present volume tries to accomplish for human relations.

A new way to approach human relations has important implications for the larger view of society and the economy—which this volume tries to explore. Here, too, altruism has been considered a "puzzle," and anathema to human nature. Some ideologues have taken this to mean that we should not even appeal to kindness, that the latter does not really belong in a healthy society. Could this line of thinking—ranging from Ayn Rand to Alan Greenspan—be one of the underlying causes of recent shocks to the world economy?

■ THE SELFISHNESS ASSUMPTION

The CEO of Enron—now in prison—happily applied 'selfish gene' logic to his human capital, thus creating a self-fulfilling prophecy. An avowed admirer of Richard Dawkins's gene-centric view of evolution, Jeffrey Skilling mimicked natural selection by ranking his employees on a one-to-five scale representing the best (one) to the worst (five). Anyone with a ranking of five got axed, but not without first having been humiliated on a website featuring his or her portrait. Under this so-called 'Rank & Yank' policy, people proved perfectly willing to slit one another's throats, resulting in a corporate atmosphere marked by appalling dishonesty within and ruthless exploitation outside the company.

Thus, in assuming that the human species is driven by greed and fear, the CEO produced employees driven by these very motives. Enron imploded under the mean-spirited weight of his policies, offering a preview of what was in store for the world economy as a whole.

The deeper problem, however, was the view of human nature. The book of nature is like the Bible: people read into it what they like, from tolerance to intolerance and from altruism to greed. It's good to realize, though, that if biologists call genes selfish, this doesn't mean that genes actually are. Genes can't be any more 'selfish' than a river can be 'angry' or sun rays 'loving'. Genes are little chunks of DNA. At most, they are 'self-promoting', because successful genes help their carriers spread more copies of themselves.

Since evolution advances by elimination, it is indeed a ruthless process. Yet its *products* don't need to be ruthless at all, a point driven home by two of the editors of the present volume (Brown & Brown) in their theoretical work on social bonds and altruism—"Selective Investment Theory"—the conceptual catalyst for *Moving Beyond Self-Interest*. Many animals survive by being social and sticking together, which implies that they can't follow the right-of-the-strongest principle to the letter: the strong need the weak. This applies equally to our own species, at least if we give humans a chance to express their cooperative side. Like Skilling, too many economists and politicians ignore and suppress this side. They model human society on the perpetual struggle that they believe exists in nature, which is actually no more than a projection. Obviously, competition is part of the picture, but humans can't live by competition alone.

Lovers of open competition can't resist invoking evolution. The e-word can be found in the infamous 'greed speech' of Gordon Gekko, the corporate raider played by Michael Douglas in the 1987 movie *Wall Street*:

> "The point is, ladies and gentleman, that 'greed'—for lack of a better word—is good. Greed is right. Greed works. Greed clarifies, cuts through and captures the essence of the evolutionary spirit."

The evolutionary spirit? This competition-is-good-for-you logic has been extraordinarily popular ever since Ronald Reagan and Margaret Thatcher reassured us that the free market would take care of all of our problems. Since the 2008 economic meltdown, this view has obviously been under debate, since the "invisible hand" of the market clearly did not steer things in the right direction by itself. The logic may have been great, but its connection to reality was poor. As Adam Smith already understood, pure individualism is not what we have been made for. Empathy (or as Smith called it: sympathy) and solidarity are very much part of our evolution, and not just a recent part, but age-old capacities that we share with other mammals.

■ LESSONS FROM PROSOCIAL PRIMATES

Many great advances in society—democracy, equal rights, social security—have come about thanks to what used to be called 'fellow feeling'. The French revolutionaries chanted of *fraternité*, Abraham Lincoln appealed to the bonds of sympathy and Theodore Roosevelt glowingly spoke of fellow feeling as "the most important factor in producing a healthy political and social life".

The ending of slavery is particularly instructive. On his trips to the south, Abraham Lincoln had seen shackled slaves, an image that kept haunting him, as he wrote to a friend. Such feelings motivated him and many others to fight slavery. Or take the current healthcare debate, in which empathy plays a prominent role—influencing the way in which we respond to the misery of people who have been turned away by the system or lost their insurance. Consider the term itself—it is not called health 'business', but health 'care', thus stressing human concern for others.

Human nature obviously can't be understood in isolation from the rest of nature, and this is where biology comes in. Looking at our species, we see a creature of flesh and blood with a brain that, albeit three times larger than a chimpanzee's, doesn't contain any new parts. Superior our intellect may be, but we have no basic wants or needs that cannot also be observed in our close relatives. Like us, they strive for power, enjoy sex, want security and affection, kill over territory and value trust and cooperation. Yes, we use cell phones and fly airplanes, but our psychological make-up is essentially that of a social primate.

Without claiming other primates as moral beings, it is not hard to recognize the pillars of morality in their behavior. These pillars are summed up in our golden rule, which transcends the world's cultures and religions. "Do unto others as you would have them do to you" brings together empathy (attention to others' feelings) and reciprocity (if others follow the same rule, you will be treated well). Human morality could not exist without empathy and reciprocity, tendencies increasingly found in our fellow primates.

For example, after one chimpanzee has been attacked by another, a bystander will go over to embrace the victim gently until he or she stops yelping. The tendency to console is so strong that Nadia Kohts, a Russian scientist who raised a juvenile chimpanzee a century ago, said that if her charge had escaped to the roof of her house, there was only one way to get him down. Holding out food would not do the trick: the only way would be for her to sit down and sob, as if she were in pain. The young ape would rush down from the roof to put an arm around her. The empathy of our closest relative exceeds its desire for a banana.

Consolation has been studied extensively based on hundreds of cases, as it is a common, predictable behavior among apes. Similarly, reciprocity is visible when chimpanzees share food specifically with those who have recently groomed them or supported them in power struggles. Sex is often part of the mix. Wild males have been observed to take great risk raiding papaya plantations to obtain the delicious fruits for fertile females and get copulations in return. Chimps know how to strike a deal.

There is also evidence for prosocial tendencies and a sense of fairness. Chimpanzees voluntarily open a door to give a companion access to food, and capuchin monkeys seek rewards for others even if they themselves gain nothing from it. We demonstrated this by placing two monkeys side by side: separate, but in view. One of them needed to barter with us with small plastic tokens. The critical test came when we offered them a choice between two differently colored tokens with different meanings: one token was 'selfish', the other 'prosocial'. If the bartering monkey picked the selfish token, it received a small piece of apple for returning it, but its partner got nothing. The prosocial token, on the other hand, rewarded both monkeys equally at the same time. The monkeys developed an overwhelming preference for the prosocial token.

We repeated the procedure many times with different pairs of monkeys and different sets of tokens, and found that the monkeys kept picking the prosocial option. This was not based on fear of possible repercussions, because we found that the most dominant monkeys (who have least to fear) were in fact the most generous. More likely, helping others is self-rewarding in the same way that humans feel good doing good.

In other studies, primates will happily perform a task for cucumber slices until they see others being rewarded with grapes, which taste so much better. They become agitated, throw down their measly cucumbers and go on strike. A perfectly fine vegetable has become unpalatable simply as a result of seeing a companion get something better. I have to think of this reaction each time I hear criticism of the bonuses on Wall Street.

Despite so much evidence of prosocial tendencies in other primates, revealing hints of a deeper moral order, many people prefer to ignore this work and instead view their nature as "red in tooth and claw". There is never any doubt about continuity between humans and other animals with respect to negative behavior: when humans maim and kill each other, we are quick to call them 'animals', but we prefer to claim noble traits for ourselves. When it comes to the study of human nature, this is a losing strategy, however, as it excludes about half of our background—the prosocial half. Short of divine intervention, this more attractive side of our behavior is also the product of evolution, a view increasingly supported by animal research as well as by contributors to the present volume.

■ EMPATHY

Everyone is familiar with the way mammals react to our emotions and the way we react to theirs. This creates the sort of bond that makes millions of us share our homes with cats and dogs rather than iguanas and turtles. The latter are just as easy to keep, yet lack the empathy that we need to get attached.

Animal studies on empathy are on the rise, including studies into how rodents are affected by the pain of others. Laboratory mice become more sensitive to pain once they have seen another mouse in pain. Pain contagion occurs between mice from the same home box, but not between mice that don't know each other. This is a typical bias that is also true of human empathy: the closer we are to a person, and the more similar we are to them, the more easily empathy is aroused.

Many chapters in this volume touch on the way empathy operates in human society, and some, like Decety's (Chapter 7), clearly link human empathic abilities to our evolutionary background as social animals.

Empathy relates to basic body mimicry. This is where it starts—not in the higher regions of imagination or in the ability to reconstruct consciously how we would feel if we were in someone else's place. It began with the synchronization of bodies: running when others run; laughing when others laugh; crying when others cry; or yawning when others yawn. Most of us have reached the incredibly advanced stage at which we yawn even at the mere mention of yawning, but this is only after lots of face-to-face experience.

Yawn contagion works in other species, too. At Kyoto University, investigators showed apes in the laboratory the videotaped yawns of wild chimps. Soon, the lab chimps were yawning like crazy. With our own chimps, we have gone one step further. Instead of showing them real chimps, we play three-dimensional animations of an ape-like head going through a yawn-like motion. In response to the animated yawns, our apes yawn with maximal opening of the mouth, eye-closing and head-rolling, as if they are going to fall asleep at any moment.

Yawn contagion reflects the power of unconscious synchrony, which is as deeply ingrained in us as in many other animals. Synchrony is expressed in the copying of small body movements, such as a yawn, but also occurs on a larger scale, involving travel or movement. It is not hard to see its survival value. You're in a flock of birds and one bird suddenly takes off. You have no time to figure out what's going on so you take off at the same instant. Otherwise, you may be lunch.

Mood contagion serves to coordinate activities, which is crucial for any travelling species (as most primates are). If my companions are feeding, I decide to do the same, because once they move off, my chance to forage will be gone. The individual who doesn't stay in tune with what everyone else is doing will lose out, as he or she cannot rest while the others are moving or move while the others are foraging.

Natural selection has produced highly social and cooperative animals, which rely on one another for survival. On its own, a wolf cannot bring down large prey, and chimpanzees in the forest are known to slow down for companions who cannot keep up due to injuries or sick offspring. So, why accept the assumption of cut-throat nature when there is ample proof to the contrary?

■ THE LURE OF BAD BIOLOGY

Bad biology exerts an irresistible attraction. Many think that competition is what life is all about, or believe that it is desirable for the strong to survive at the expense of the weak. They describe evolution—or at least their cardboard version of it—as an almost heavenly process. John D. Rockefeller concluded that the growth of a large business "is merely the working out of a law of nature and a law of God", and Lloyd Blankfein, chairman and CEO of Goldman Sachs—the biggest money-making machine in the world—recently depicted himself as merely "doing God's work".

We tend to think that the economy was killed by irresponsible risk-taking, a lack of regulation or a bubbling housing market, but the problem goes deeper. Those were just the little airplanes circling King Kong's head. The ultimate flaw was the lure of bad biology and a gross simplification of human nature due to confusion about how natural selection operates and what kind of creatures it has produced. This misunderstanding has led to a denial of what binds people together to the point that society itself has sometimes been seen as an illusion. As Margaret Thatcher put it: "There is no such thing as society—there are individual men and women, and there are families."

Economists should reread their father figure, Adam Smith, who saw society as a huge machine. Its wheels are polished by virtue, whereas vice causes them to grate. The machine just won't run smoothly without a strong community sense in every citizen. Smith frequently mentioned honesty, morality, sympathy and justice, seeing them as essential companions to the invisible hand of the market. His views were based on our being a social species, born in a community with responsibilities towards the community.

Instead of falling for ideas about nature that are simply untrue, why not pay attention to what we actually know about human nature and the behavior of our near relatives? The message from biology is that we are group animals: intensely social, interested in fairness and cooperative enough to have taken over the world. Our great strength is precisely our ability to *overcome* competition. Why not design societies that play to this strength? Smith, Brown, and Rigdon (Chapter 15), and Le Grand (Chapter 16) underscore this point, arguing that mainstream economic models used to inform social policy are uninformed by the idea that humans have been designed by evolution to care for others, not just for themselves. These authors make concrete proposals to design policies that reinforce the social sensitivities and proclivities bestowed upon us by evolution.

The fundamental yet rarely asked question is why natural selection designed our brains so that we're in tune with our fellow human beings and feel distress at their distress, pleasure at their pleasure. If exploitation of others were all that mattered, evolution should never have got into the empathy business. Yet it did, and it is about time we end a misrepresentation of human nature that has promoted excessive amounts of mistrust, cynicism, and egoism in human society.

Frans B. M. de Waal

Frans de Waal is C. H. Candler Professor of Psychology at Emory University and the director of the Living Links Center at the Yerkes National Primate Research Center. He is the author of eight popular books, including *Chimpanzee Politics* and *Our Inner Ape*. His latest book, *The Age of Empathy*, is published by Harmony Books.

▪ PREFACE

▪ STEPHANIE L. BROWN, R. MICHAEL BROWN, AND
LOUIS A. PENNER

A human being is a part of the whole, called by us "Universe," a part limited in time and space. He experiences himself, his thoughts and feelings, as something separated from the rest—a kind of optical delusion of his consciousness. This delusion is a kind of prison for us, restricting us to our personal desires and to affection for a few persons nearest to us. Our task must be to free ourselves from this prison by widening our circle of compassion to embrace all living creatures and the whole of nature in its beauty. Nobody is able to achieve this completely, but the striving for such achievement is in itself a part of the liberation and a foundation for inner security.

—(Albert Einstein, 1949, *quoted in Chou, 1980*)

Our volume, entitled *Moving Beyond Self-Interest,* is a collection of essays written by leading scientists in psychology, evolutionary biology, neuroscience, political science, and social policy that addresses the topic of *how* individuals become motivated to care for others. As such, the contents of this volume may contain clues for how we, as human beings, might follow Einstein's advice to widen "our circle of compassion." If there is one theme that unites the essays in this volume, it is that the essayists have dispensed with the assumption that all of human experience can be reduced to self-interest—what Einstein referred to as an "optical delusion" or "prison." What emerges from the resulting essays is that humans are united by a common motivational system, with an identifiable brain architecture, that moves us to care for others, not just ourselves. In several of the essays that follow, this common system is referred to by many as a "caregiving system," with the understanding that it is a product of natural selection, that its development and expression are consequences of a dynamic and ongoing interplay between genotype and environment, and that it functions to provide security and other resources to those in need.

▪ PART ONE: INTRODUCTION

Chapter 1: Background and Historical Perspective. Our volume is not only evolutionary in the biological sense, but in thought, moving beyond perspectives that reduce all behavior to self-interest. Accordingly, our first chapter provides a historical context for evaluating and interpreting this shift in thought. After a brief introduction to philosophical perspectives on altruism, the essay describes evolutionary theories of altruistic behavior, from Darwin to the present, in some detail, and continues with a discussion of theories of altruistic motivation generated by social and developmental psychologists. The essay concludes with a call to action from social psychologists Berscheid and Collins (2000), chiding social scientists for neglecting the motivational basis of caregiving and urging them to close this gap, not only for obvious scientific reasons but also for the sake of those in society who suffer the effects of inadequate caregiving. We echo their sentiments and their sense of urgency.

■ PART TWO: FOUNDATIONS OF CAREGIVING

In Part II of our volume, scholars representing the disciplines of evolutionary biology, social and developmental psychology, and neuroscience describe how natural selection might have favored the evolution of other-directed motivation (Krebs), how other-directed motivation in the form of a "caregiving system" interacts with the attachment system (Mikulincer & Shaver), and how other-directed motivation and attachment are woven together, and made possible, by the parasympathetic nervous system (Porges & Carter). First, Krebs describes an arguably defining feature of many forms of caregiving—altruism—differentiating between biological and psychological altruism, and describing the likely evolutionary origins of each. Mikulincer and Shaver provide a much-needed extension of Bowlby's caregiving system, arguing that an important function of the system is to provide a secure base for others, and suggesting that the effectiveness of this function is influenced by individual differences in attachment. Finally, Porges and Carter identify evolutionary developments in the parasympathetic nervous system that provide a foundation for all mammalian social behavior, and they discuss the importance of neuropeptides (e.g., oxytocin) in orchestrating social behavior, including their role in producing beneficial effects of caregiving on physiology, behavior, and health.

■ PART THREE: THE NEUROSCIENCE OF CAREGIVING MOTIVATION

In Part III scholars in neurobiology and affective neuroscience describe new developments in understanding the neurophysiological basis of caregiving motivation. S. Brown, R. Brown, and Preston present a theory of caregiving motivation based on mammalian models of parental nurturance, including implications for regulating stress and promoting physical health. Then Numan describes in some detail his animal model of maternal care, and explains how the model can be extended to other social behaviors, especially human cooperation and competition. Decety, also using an evolution-based neuroscience approach, shows how perspective taking and the ability to differentiate self from other affect our ability to appreciate another's pain and distress. Finally, Swain reviews brain circuits that underlie parental and romantic love, and argues that these circuits may also affect risk and resiliency to various forms of psychopathology.

■ PART FOUR: THE PSYCHOLOGY OF CAREGIVING MOTIVATION

Using an evolutionary perspective, Bugental, Beaulieu, and Corpuz begin Part IV by suggesting that parental investment in children can vary depending on resource availability and physical cues to children's health. Penner, Harper, and Albrecht focus on parents of children with pediatric cancer and show that those parents who experience the highest levels of empathic concern (as opposed to distress) are the most effective caregivers. Schulz and Monin describe the costs and benefits of caring for someone who is disabled or seriously ill, and Gruber and Keltner explore links between a likely caregiving system motivational mechanism—compassion— and psychopathology. Crocker and Canevello conclude from their research that the system that directs compassion to others can also produce well-being for the self—"a foundation for inner security." Finally, Berscheid identifies semantic and conceptual obstacles to articulating and exploring the caregiving-love construct in the context of interpersonal relationships.

■ PART FIVE: IMPLICATIONS FOR ECONOMICS, POLITICS, AND SOCIAL POLICY

The essays in Part V focus on possible points of contact between new models of caregiving motivation and economics, political science, and social policy development. Smith, S. Brown, and Rigdon describe how insights from this volume might be used to inform current debates in economics, including controversies over how to maximize utility. Le Grand argues that large-scale, government-administered social policies are inextricably linked to underlying assumptions about human nature, and considers implications of an understanding of caregiving motivation for policy change in the area of social service delivery. In conclusion, Kullberg and Singer argue that acknowledging the caregiving system and appreciating its evolutionary origins and neurophysiological foundations might enhance social science accounts of human social evolution, and better explain problematic aspects of contemporary politics—"national identity and conflict, and the willingness of citizens to fight, kill, and die for their countries in war."

■ REFERENCES

Peter Y. Chou, *Albert Einstein & the Wisdom Mudra* (1980). Quote from *The New York Times*, March 29, 1972.

ACKNOWLEDGMENTS

Many of us take for granted that kindness, concern for others, empathy, cooperation, and self-sacrificing behavior are distinguishing, even defining qualities of human nature. But until recently, behavioral scientists, by and large, have downplayed these qualities or reduced even the loftiest forms of other-directed, prosocial acts to raw self-interest. Our book—*Moving Beyond Self-Interest*—is not intended to displace self-interest accounts of human prosociality, but to complement them. New and merging theoretical and empirical developments, across a variety of scientific disciplines, lend credence to the idea that human nature is not only self-serving, but other-serving as well. The essays in this volume describe some of these new developments, exploring not only antecedents and consequences of caring for and helping others, but also neurophysiological motivational mechanisms that may drive such behavior—what many have referred to as the "caregiving system".

Our book is the legacy of a project—*Developing Alternatives to Self Interest (DASI)*—supported by the Center for Advancing Research and Solutions for Society (CARSS) at the University of Michigan. The DASI project, co-conceived with Jennifer Crocker (contributor to this volume), provided an opportunity for scholars from a variety of disciplines and institutions to share ideas and findings from concurrent investigations of other-focused motivation and behavior. We owe a debt of gratitude to David Featherman, director of CARSS, who provided support not only for the DASI initiative, but also for the book itself. Through the help of CARSS we were able to pay authors a modest stipend for their contributions, and hold an authors' conference to extract common themes from diverse research programs that span developmental, clinical, and social psychology; evolutionary biology; affective and behavioral neuroscience; economics; political science; and social policy. It was through the generous support of CARSS that we were able to turn our shared insights into a product that may be useful to others who have struggled with fundamental issues related to the motivation for human social behavior. It is our hope that insights from this book may be used in some way to address some of society's most troublesome problems, including family strife and the undermining of extended family networks, war, destruction of the environment, and ongoing and seemingly insurmountable challenges to the poor, sick, disabled, victimized, and otherwise disenfranchised people of the world.

Stephanie Brown would like to acknowledge the intellectual contributions of husband and social psychologist Dylan Smith, who provided insightful comments and feedback on all facets of the present volume, throughout its development; Barbara Fredrickson and Amiram Vinokur for their outstanding mentorship; and Randolph Nesse and Douglas Kenrick for their challenging comments, many of which helped refine ideas presented in this volume. Stephanie Brown would also like to recognize the scientific contributions of C. Sue Carter, Frans de Waal,

Stephen Porges, and Michael Numan, whose work, considered together, paints a novel, other-directed picture of humankind—the *raison d'être* of this volume. Finally, Stephanie Brown would like to acknowledge Robert C. Bolles (1928-1994). His undergraduate History of Psychology course at the University of Washington helped her discover the value of paradigmatic approaches in psychology, and his research served as a model for integrating biology and human social behavior.

Michael Brown acknowledges his wife, Norma L. Brown, a psychologist in private practice and long-time collaborator in research. Her support, feedback, and patience knew no bounds. She made essential contributions to theoretical ideas that provided impetus for the present volume, made concrete suggestions for developing the book, and, on occasion, served as a fourth (unheralded) editor. Michael Brown also owes a debt of gratitude to biologist Paul Cook—entomologist and avid evolutionist, former instructor, mentor, and co-author. Working with Paul demonstrated that connecting the *how* with the *why* of behavior was possible, challenging, and downright intriguing. Although he is deceased, his imprint is manifested in our volume.

Louis Penner would like to acknowledge his productive personal and professional collaboration with his wife, Teri Albrecht. Dr. Albrecht is the principal investigator on a National Cancer Institute grant to fund the study of caregiving in pediatric cancer, and she has been a source of wisdom and insight. Louis Penner would also like to acknowledge the colleagues who, over the years, have helped shape his thinking about and research on prosocial behavior. These include Bill Graziano, Jack Dovidio, Jane Piliavin, and Dave Schroeder. Finally, Louis Penner would like to recognize the pioneering work of people such as Dan Batson, John Darley, Nancy Eisenberg, Bibb Latané, Samuel and Pearl Oliner, and Irving Piliavin, who inspired him and many other social psychologists to try to understand why humans are motivated to help one another.

All three editors gratefully acknowledge grant support received from the National Science Foundation and the National Institutes of Health. An NIMH career award (K01 MH065423-01), together with NSF grants to Stephanie Brown (0719629; 90820609), supported data collection and theoretical work that were pivotal in developing the present volume. Grant support from the National Cancer Institute (RO 1 CA 100027-03; 1RO1CA138981-01A1) supported Louis Penner's investigations of caregiving in families of pediatric cancer patients. Note that the views and opinions expressed in this volume do not necessarily represent the views of the NIH or NSF.

Finally, we wish to thank the editorial staff at Oxford University Press for their invaluable assistance and patience, especially editors Lori Handelman and Abby Gross, and editorial assistant Joanna Ng. Lori had faith in our project from the beginning. She not only recognized the importance of an other-directed approach to understanding human nature, but also was well versed in the theory, research, and issues related to this approach. Abby ensured there were no hitches as we transitioned from developmental to production phases of the book. And Joanna made certain that nagging problems or details were not left untended.

CONTENTS

■ CONTRIBUTORS

Terrance L. Albrecht
Department of Family Medicine and
    Public Health Sciences
Karmanos Cancer Institute
Wayne State University
Detroit, Michigan

David A. Beaulieu
Department of Psychology
Tomball College
Tomball, Texas

Ellen Berscheid
Department of Psychology
University of Minnesota
Minneapolis, Minnesota

Stephanie L. Brown
Department of Preventive Medicine
State University of New York at
    Stony Brook
Stony Brook, New York
Institute for Social Research
University of Michigan
Ann Arbor, Michigan

R. Michael Brown
Department of Psychology
Pacific Lutheran University
Tacoma, Washington

Daphne B. Bugental
Department of Psychology
University of California, Santa Barbara
Santa Barbara, California

C. Sue Carter
Department of Psychiatry
College of Medicine
University of Illinois at Chicago
Chicago, Illinois

Amy Canevello
Department of Psychology
University of North Carolina
Charlotte, North Carolina

Randy Corpuz
Department of Psychology
University of California, Santa
    Barbara
Santa Barbara, California

Jennifer Crocker
Department of Psychology
The Ohio State University
Columbus, Ohio

Jean Decety
Departments of Psychology and
    Psychiatry
University of Chicago
Chicago, Illinois

June Gruber
Department of Psychology
Yale University
New Haven, Connecticut

Felicity W. K. Harper
Department of Family Medicine and
    Public Health Sciences
Karmanos Cancer Institute
Wayne State University
Detroit, Michigan

Dacher Keltner
Department of Psychology
University of California, Berkeley
Berkeley, California

Dennis L. Krebs
Department of Psychology
Simon Fraser University
Burnaby, British Columbia,
    Canada

Judith S. Kullberg
Department of Political
    Science
Eastern Michigan University
Ypsilanti, Michigan

Julian Le Grand
Department of Social Policy
The London School of Economics
    and Political Science
London, England

Mario Mikulincer
School of Psychology
Interdisciplinary Center
Herzliya, Israel

Joan K. Monin
Division of Chronic Disease
    Epidemiology
School of Public Health
Yale University
New Haven, Connecticut

Michael Numan
Department of Psychology
Boston College
Chestnut Hill, Massachusetts

Louis A. Penner
Department of Family Medicine and
    Public Health Sciences
Karmanos Cancer Institute
Wayne State University
Detroit, Michigan
The Institute for Social Research
University of Michigan
Ann Arbor, Michigan

Stephen W. Porges
Department of Psychiatry
College of Medicine
University of Illinois at Chicago
Chicago, Illinois

Stephanie D. Preston
Department of Psychology
University of Michigan
Ann Arbor, Michigan

Mary L. Rigdon
Departments of Psychology and
    Economics
Rutgers University—New Brunswick
Piscataway, New Jersey

Richard Schulz
University Center for Social and Urban
    Research
University of Pittsburgh
Pittsburgh, Pennsylvania

Phillip R. Shaver
Department of Psychology
University of California, Davis
Davis, California

J. David Singer (1925–2009)
Most recently:
Department of Political Science
University of Michigan
Ann Arbor, Michigan.

Dylan M. Smith
Department of Preventive Medicine
State University of New York at
    Stony Brook
Stony Brook, New York

James E. Swain
Department of Psychiatry
University of Michigan
Ann Arbor, Michigan

■ PART ONE
Introduction

1 Background and Historical Perspective

■ R. MICHAEL BROWN, LOUIS A. PENNER, AND
STEPHANIE L. BROWN

Our goal in this chapter is to provide readers with background information that helps illuminate and lend perspective to the essays in this volume. We begin with an introductory discussion of the term "caregiving," and then we consider important people, ideas, events, and findings that are pivotal to the appreciation and advancement of scientific approaches to understanding the motivation behind human caregiving.

■ WHAT IS CAREGIVING?

In this volume our contributors articulate independent lines of thinking and research that converge on a model or models of human *caregiving*. Experts in social and developmental sciences have argued that such an effort is long overdue (e.g., Berscheid & Collins, 2000). But what do scientists and practitioners mean by "caregiving"? In contemporary culture, caregiving is often equated with helping behavior—activities designed to aid or assist individuals in need. But caregiving can take on special, usually restricted meanings, depending on who is using the term. For example, for many clinicians and health care professionals, caregiving means helping those with physical or psychological disabilities. The focus is typically on informal care—care that is most often provided by family members. To developmental psychologists and child care professionals, caregiving refers to parental investment in offspring. To attachment theorists—typically developmental or social psychologists—caregiving means providing security to children, spouses, or other relationship partners in need (e.g., Bowlby, 1969; George & Solomon, 1999; Mikulincer & Shaver, 2005, this volume; Shaver & Hazan, 1987; Shaver, Hazan, & Bradshaw, 1988).

In the present volume, the term caregiving can encompass all of the aforementioned domains, but is not restricted to them. Caregiving is simply helping those in need, be they our own children or parents, sick or disabled friends, loved ones or spouses, comrades in a foxhole, or victims of natural (or unnatural) disasters.

Not surprisingly, scientific interest in caregiving and its motivation is rooted in philosophical thought, especially ideas that address the phenomenon of *altruism*. As Krebs (this volume) notes, altruism means different things to different disciplines, and sometimes to different individuals within the same discipline (West, Griffin, & Gardner, 2006). For evolutionary biologists, altruism is a form of cooperation or helping behavior that benefits the recipient at some cost to the helper. The cost may be minimal, as in taking an extra few minutes to help a roommate in need. Or it may be high, as in risking injury or death to save a drowning child. In each case there is a cost to the helper because resources (time, energy, or safety) that could enhance the helper's own individual fitness (reproduction of offspring), directly or indirectly, are redirected to others, facilitating *their* fitness. For many social psychologists, however, altruism refers to a person's motivation. Altruists intend to benefit another person, regardless of the costs involved, and whether or not there is a reward, or expectation of a reward, for doing so.

Although it would be misleading to equate all helping behavior with altruism, it is reasonable to argue that caregiving activities often fit the biological definition of altruism, and many professional caregivers at least report that their attempts to help others are altruistically motivated (Rhoades & McFarland, 1999). Accordingly, understanding and appreciating contemporary theory and research on caregiving, including the essays in this volume, may be enhanced by a consideration of the history of scientific inquiries into altruism.

■ THE SCIENCE OF CAREGIVING IN HISTORICAL PERSPECTIVE

Appreciation of altruistic behavior and motivation in Western thought can be traced to the early Greeks (Zanker, 1996), and exhortations regarding altruism are found throughout the long history of religious thought worldwide—for example, in Hinduism, Buddhism, Judaism, Islam, and Christianity (Neusner & Chilton, 2005). But the characterizations of altruism that were influential in the biological and social sciences are more recent, emerging during the 19th century with the French philosopher Auguste Comte.

The Dawn of Scientific Research on Altruism

Auguste Comte (1798–1857)

Comte is perhaps best known for his positivistic philosophy, elaborating and transforming earlier ideas from Francis Bacon, George Berkeley, and David Hume into an empirical foundation for science, and indeed for human decision making. Comte also contributed a history and taxonomy of science, and is considered a seminal force in shaping the discipline of sociology. Most important for our purposes, Comte apparently coined the term altruism, characterizing it as unselfish sacrificing for the benefit of others (Martineau, 1896). He championed altruism as a moral and societal imperative, legitimized it as an area of scientific inquiry, and argued that it was innate. He drew a sharp contrast between altruism and egoism:

> Personality, characterized by egoism, conflicts with sociality, or altruism, and each individual undergoes three stages of human life: (1) the personal (self-love); (2) the domestic (love of family); and (3) the social, or one that achieves the 'subordination of self-love to social feeling. (Comte, 1908, p. 101, as cited in Millon, Grossman, & Meager, 2004)

Comte's insistence that altruism is selfless and his distinction between altruistic and egoistic instincts set the stage for debates over the selfish vs. selfless nature of other-regarding behavior, debates restricted neither to metaphysics nor to the late 19th and early 20th centuries (e.g., Batson, Sager, Garst, Kang, Rubchinsky, & Dawson, 1997; Cialdini, Brown, Lewis, Luce, & Neuberg, 1997). Also, it is interesting to note that Comte saw "domestic" love, even maternal caregiving, as potentially self-serving, but believed it provided a template for altruism and altruistic motives (e.g., sympathy) directed to those outside the family. Finally, Comte's characterization of altruism as the subordination of self-love to social feeling inspired, or at least foreshadowed, scientific interest in the self-vs.-other motivational struggles associated with altruistic decision making (e.g., Batson, Batson,Todd, Brummett, Shaw, & Aldeguer, 1995; S. L. Brown & Brown, 2006; Cosmides & Tooby, 2000; Sober & Wilson, 1998).

Charles Darwin (1809–1882)

Charles Darwin's contributions to our understanding of all things living were, of course, nothing short of earthshaking when first published a little over 150 years ago, and they continue to generate scientific, philosophical, and religious aftershocks today. Darwin's keen observational sense missed little in nature, including altruism. For example, in a notebook entry written May 5, 1839, he remarked on the self-vs.-other motivational conflict associated with providing maternal care to offspring: "In a dog we see a struggle between its appetite, or love of exercise and its love of its puppies: The latter generally soon conquers, & the dog probably thinks no more of it" (cited in Gruber & Barrett, 1974). In *The Descent of Man* (1871), Darwin provided examples illustrating species continuity in affection, especially maternal affection, and observed that altruism (including defense and protection) is directed preferentially toward kin, but not exclusively so. In discussing "the moral sense," Darwin argued that "it is fundamentally identical with the social instincts" and that its foundation lay not in selfishness but in operating "for the general good of the community" (p. 801). Darwin clearly recognized important benefits to the self that were consequences of operating for the good of the community. But he saw no need to reduce altruistic acts to "the base principle of selfishness . . . unless indeed the satisfaction which every animal feels when it follows its proper instincts, and the dissatisfaction felt when prevented, be called selfish" (pp. 832–833).

Darwin thought that altruism, whether directed toward relatives or strangers, was made possible by the social instincts (emotions) of sympathy and love, which themselves could be products of natural selection, likely derived from more fundamental parental and filial "affections." Evolutionary thinkers during the latter half of the 20th century gave little attention to the possibility that benevolence toward strangers is an evolutionary derivative of parental nurturance. For those who modeled human altruism toward strangers, its evolution was something of an enigma. After all, even a few selfish individuals could undermine a population of altruists in short order. Not surprisingly, the relevant literature is replete with detailed accounts of hypothesized mechanisms to resist exploitation (e.g., Cosmides & Tooby, 1992; S. L. Brown & Brown, 2006). Recently, however, there appears to be renewed interest in Darwin's original idea that parental and family "affections" may have driven the evolution of altruism both within and outside the family (e.g., Clutton-Brock, 2002; Hrdy, 2005).

In *The Expression of the Emotions in Man and Animals*, Darwin (1872) spent some time characterizing manifestations of the two emotions associated with altruistic behavior—love and sympathy. He observed that facial expressions such as smiling and a desire for physical contact often accompany love and "tender feelings," while sadness and tears sometimes accompany feelings of sympathy. But very different feelings could be aroused if the person we love or sympathize with requires our immediate assistance. Even a caring mother's "gentle smile and tender eyes" could change at a moment's notice in response to threat, replaced, for example, by less savory emotions:

> No emotion is stronger than maternal love. . . . But let anyone intentionally injure her infant, and see what a change! how she starts up with threatening aspect, how her eyes sparkle and her face reddens, how her bosom heaves, nostrils dilate, and heart beats; for anger, and not maternal love, has habitually led to action. (Darwin, 1872, p. 1304)

In this passage Darwin recognizes that at least some forms of altruistic intervention require negative emotion as a motivating force. Reading between the lines, he also seems to have exposed a dark side to strong interpersonal bonds. While they appear to facilitate loving care within a group (the family, in Darwin's example), intense social bonds can also be associated with lowered thresholds for fearful, angry, and violent interactions between groups, a possibility that has received renewed attention from recent evolutionarily informed inquiries (e.g., S. L. Brown & Brown, 2006; Choi & Bowles, 2007; Schaller & Neuberg, 2008).

Some have argued that the evolution of altruism by means of natural selection—"survival of the fittest"—is an oxymoronic concept. How can there be a heritable basis for altruism if, by their very nature, altruists are predisposed to sacrifice themselves for others? Darwin recognized the problem:

> It is extremely doubtful whether the offspring of the sympathetic and benevolent parents, or those which were the most faithful to their comrades, would be reared in greater number than the children of selfish and treacherous parents of the same tribe. He who was ready to sacrifice his life, as many a savage has been, rather than betray his comrades, would often leave no offspring to inherit his noble nature. The bravest men, who were always willing to come to the front in war, and who freely risked their lives for others, would on an average perish in larger number than other men. Therefore, it seems scarcely possible . . . that the number of men gifted with such virtues, or that the standard of their excellence, could be increased through natural selection, that is, by the survival of the fittest. (Darwin, 1871, p. 870)

Darwin did more than acknowledge the potential problem altruism and other seemingly self-defeating traits posed for his theory. For example, in the first edition of *On the Origin of Species* (1859) he considered the challenge to his theory posed by the existence of female worker ants, whose activities enhance the reproductive success of their queen (and survival of the colony), apparently at a cost to their own reproduction (they are sterile). How could natural selection have preserved traits like sterility? Darwin's proposed solution was that selection could act on families, not just individuals. E. O. Wilson (1975) elaborates:

> To save his own theory, Darwin introduced the idea of natural selection operating at the level of the family rather than of the single organism. In retrospect, his logic seems impeccable. If some of the individuals of the family are sterile and yet important to the welfare of fertile relatives, as in the case of insect colonies, selection at the family level is inevitable. With the entire family serving as the unit of selection, it is the capacity to generate sterile but altruistic relatives that becomes subject to genetic evolution. (pp. 117–118)

Darwin's observation that natural selection need not be restricted to the individual and could result in traits that were advantageous to families as well as to the "community" presaged 20th-century evolutionary theories of kin selection (Hamilton, 1964) and group selection (Wright, 1945; Wynne-Edwards, 1962; D. S. Wilson & Sober, 1994). Darwin also anticipated Robert Trivers's (1971) evolutionary account of reciprocal altruism, speculating that selective improvements in proximate cognitive mechanisms—"reasoning powers and foresight"—would lead an individual to learn from experience that "if he aided his fellow-men, he would commonly receive aid in return" (Darwin, 1871, p. 870).

Finally, Darwin allowed for the possibility that in some cases altruism may best be understood as a "mistaken instinct," as happens when a bird "will feed the deserted young even of distinct species" (1871, p. 1082). Nowadays, some evolutionary biologists (e.g., Dawkins, 1989) refer to this and other examples of evolutionarily puzzling kindness (e.g., adoption) as "misfires." The idea is that algorithms underlying cooperation and sacrifice evolved in ancestral environments in which the vast majority of recipients would have been family members or potential reciprocators. These algorithms misfire in an altered environment composed of perfect strangers. As Dawkins puts it, altruistic behavior "has been shaped under the conditions that normally prevail in nature, and in nature strangers are not normally found in your nest" (p. 101).

Other Evolutionary Theorists

There were other 19th- and early 20th-century thinkers who stimulated scientific interest in altruism and, by extension, prosocial behavior generally. Included are contemporaries or near contemporaries of Darwin. A major proponent and interpreter of Darwin's ideas, and the first to construct a psychology based on Darwinian notions, *Herbert Spencer* (1820–1903) derived his views of altruism from Comte, defining it as "all action which, in the normal course of things, benefits others instead of benefiting self" (Spencer, 1904, p. 201) and arguing that altruism is as fundamental to the human organism as egoism, and that "self-sacrifice . . . is no less primordial than self-preservation" (Spencer, 1904, p. 203). Spencer also held that altruism can be conscious or unconscious and, in accord with Darwin (and some of the contributors to this volume), that parental and family altruism are likely progenitors of altruistic acts that benefit those outside the family.

Thomas Huxley (1825–1895) and **Peter Kropotkin** (1842–1921) were notable for their opposing views on the role of altruism in evolution and in society. Huxley, a self-taught and respected comparative anatomist, referred to himself as "Darwin's bulldog," an apt name for this staunch defender of all things Darwinian. Like Spencer, Huxley saw "nature red in tooth and claw," emphasizing the ongoing competition and struggle for existence that provides grist for the evolutionary mill: "The animal world is on about the same level as a gladiator's show . . . the strongest, the swiftest, and the cunningest live to fight another day" (Huxley, 1899, pp. 199–200). For Huxley, there was no room for altruism in this dog-eat-dog world, save for within the relatively safe confines of the family.

Kropotkin, a Russian prince perhaps best known for his advocacy of anarchism, was dismayed and repulsed by Huxley's dark account of nature. Kropotkin's travels and observations had convinced him that the struggle for existence—one of Darwin's preexisting conditions for natural selection—was more about animals fighting to survive the challenges imposed by harsh physical environments than about tooth and claw fights to the death amongst themselves. A passage from his book *Mutual Aid* (1902) makes the point:

> Two aspects of animal life impressed me most during the journeys which I made in my youth in Eastern Siberia and Northern Manchuria. One of them was the extreme severity of the struggle for existence which most species of animals have to carry on against an inclement Nature; the enormous destruction of life which periodically results from natural agencies; and the consequent paucity of life over the vast territory which fell under my observation. And the other was, that even in those few spots where animal life teemed in abundance, I failed to find—although I was eagerly looking for it—that bitter struggle for the means of existence, among animals belonging to the same species, which was considered by most Darwinists (though not always by Darwin himself) as the dominant characteristic of struggle for life, and the main factor of evolution. (p. 4)

Kropotkin concluded that natural selection favored cooperation over competition, because the former helped individual animals and the groups to which they belong survive the rigors of their environments.

The Huxley–Kropotkin dispute brought into sharp focus the self-interested vs. other-regarding qualities of social animals, especially humans. Huxley's cynicism regarding altruism took hold, influencing thinking in both the biological and social sciences. But while the social sciences, operating in a virtual evolutionary vacuum, downplayed altruism or explained it away by reducing it to self-interest, evolutionary biologists could not ignore the possibility that altruism was as fundamental to the nature of social animals as egoism.

Beyond Darwin

Evolutionary thinkers would spend much of the 20th century trying to solve mathematically and scientifically the problem Darwin had recognized as potentially fatal to his theory: How could altruistic traits, which by definition work against the survival and reproduction of the altruist, possibly have evolved?

Group Selection

One possible solution to the paradox is that despite their costs to individual fitness, altruistic traits have evolved because they benefited the groups to which individuals belonged—for example, families (kin groups), local populations (demes), or species. Indeed, Darwin suggested that the costs of altruism might be offset if the recipients of altruistic acts were family members, an apparent endorsement of the possibility of group selection. In the simplest case, families composed of at least some individuals who are self-sacrificing would outcompete (i.e., reproduce more than) groups composed entirely of selfish individuals, making possible the perpetuation of altruistic traits. As Dugatkin (2006) has noted, the biologist Sewall Wright extended this logic in a formal model of group selection in 1945. In contrast to Darwin, Wright argued that group selection for altruism could occur even if group members were unrelated. As Dugatkin puts it:

> Even though some organisms may pay a price for cooperative or altruistic behavior, this sort of behavior can still evolve if groups with more (unrelated) cooperators outcompete groups with fewer (unrelated) cooperators. For example, imagine a cluster of human groups. In some groups, individuals patrol the group's territory and guard against intruders and predators. Such guards are altruistic in the sense that they pay a price—they may be killed or injured during their duties—but everyone in the group benefits by their presence. If two groups start out at the same time but differ in the number of altruists (guards) within them, the group with many guards will, on average, have a higher survival rate per member than those with fewer guards. As such, group selection models predict that guarding behavior can evolve even though it has a potential cost associated with it. (p. 50)

Wright's ideas on group selection received little attention, but nearly two decades later a simpler, less mathematical, and example-rich endorsement of group selection stimulated a good deal of controversy. The ethologist V. C. Wynne-Edwards (1962) argued that selection at the level of the individual, which Darwin had emphasized, could not account for the evolution of social mechanisms that tend to limit reproduction, such as territorial behaviors and dominance hierarchies in a variety of animal species. Wynne-Edwards considered such mechanisms to be altruistic in the sense that they functioned as reproductive restraints, lowering the classical Darwinian fitness of individuals within a local population but benefiting the larger group by reducing population density and thereby preventing the population from exhausting its limited resources. This can be seen in the example of territorial behavior, summarized succinctly by J. L. Brown (1975, p. 132):

1) Territorial behavior limits population density.
2) Limitation of population density curtails reproduction (prevents over-population).
3) Curtailment of reproduction prevents permanent reduction or extinction of the food supply.
4) Populations having such "self-regulatory" properties survive longer than those lacking them (through population selection), causing the evolutionary fixation of behavioral traits that benefit the population by limiting it at safe levels.

The Wynne-Edwards revival of the group as the unit of selection for the evolution of altruistic traits created a stir and met with immediate negative reactions. For example, although George Williams (1966) recognized the theoretical plausibility of group selection accounts of the evolution of altruism, he argued that the Wynne-Edwards proposal hinged on an unrealistic assumption, namely, that selection between groups for altruism would somehow have to outpace selection for selfish genes within a group. He also argued that the mere presence of a group benefit—presumably due to the altruism of its members—does not constitute evidence for group selection. John Maynard Smith (1976) generated a mathematical model (the "haystack" model) that showed how group selection for altruism could occur despite intense selection for selfishness within a group. But for his model to work, it would be essential that groups of individuals remain isolated for periods of time (as though they were inhabiting separate haystacks), then all come together and mix, then return to isolated groups, and so on. Maynard Smith concluded that although the haystack model was a plausible means of selecting for altruism at the level of the group, the model's requirements were so restrictive and unrealistic that for all practical purposes group selection for altruism was not likely a strong evolutionary force in nature. These criticisms resonated with evolutionary biologists, dealing a temporary knockout blow to group selection.

Gene Selection and the Hamiltonian Revolution

William Hamilton (1936–2000), a young biologist trained at University College, London, and the London School of Economics, provided a rationale for the evolution of altruism that was not dependent on principles of group selection. As Krebs (this volume) notes, Hamilton demonstrated mathematically that the costs entailed in helping others could be offset so long as those helped are related genetically to the helper (Hamilton, 1964). To be sure, others before Hamilton (including Darwin) had noted the close connection between altruistic behavior and kinship. For example, the biologist J. B. S. Haldane (1955)observed that to ensure the perpetuation of a rare gene for altruism, it would make more sense for the carrier to risk death to save his own drowning child than it would to save, say, a first cousin. When asked whether it would be worth sacrificing one's life for one's brothers, Haldane (1974) replied, "Yes, for three brothers, five uncles or nine first cousins."

Haldane had captured the essence of *inclusive fitness*, namely, that the evolutionary fate of a trait (e.g., altruism) depends not only on the transmission of its underlying genes from parent to offspring via sexual reproduction (personal or classical fitness), but also on helping others reproduce who carry copies of those same genes. Helping a sibling reproduce may be as effective as leaving a single offspring, since genetic relatedness between siblings is on average the same as between parent and offspring (50%). In other words, the chances of sharing a gene for altruism are the same for parent and child and for brother and sister: 0.5. Helping a first cousin reproduce would be less effective, because the chance that the gene would be shared is substantially less at 0.125. Haldane knew these things, but it was Hamilton who provided the precise mathematical formulation for inclusive fitness theory and tied it explicitly to the evolution of social traits, especially altruism. Hamilton's logic is captured in the simple inequality $c < rb$—Hamilton's Rule—where c represents reproductive costs incurred by the altruist, b the reproductive benefits that accrue to the recipient of the altruistic act, and r the degree of genetic relatedness between altruist and recipient.

Hamilton's 1964 papers were nothing short of revolutionary, though it took several years before they were formally recognized as such by mainstream evolutionary biology. Hamilton's Rule shifted the focus of evolution to selection at the level of the gene (as opposed to the individual, or the group), seemingly resolving the paradox of the evolution of altruism raised by Darwinian individual selection without requiring the stringent and more complicated assumptions of group selection. With the aid of luminaries like Maynard Smith (1976), Williams (1966), and later Richard Dawkins (1989), it was now possible to discern at a glance both the logical difficulties and unrealistic assumptions of the Wynne-Edwards version of the evolution of altruism and the elegant appeal of the Hamiltonian alternative. The new emphasis on gene selection eliminated the Wynne-Edwards version of group selection as a viable account of the evolution of altruism for much of the remainder of the 20th century.

Extending Gene Selection Accounts of the Evolution of Altruism

As Darwin thought and Hamilton proved, altruism can evolve so long as altruists direct their assistance to close biological relatives. What is surprising, however, is that humans in particular have a propensity for giving to and even sacrificing for unrelated individuals. Hamilton's kin selection theory could explain benevolence to strangers if, as is likely, we evolved in relatively small kin groups and only later migrated toward much larger and genetically heterogeneous populations. The idea is that in the latter groups, mechanisms for triggering altruistic behavior are "fooled" into responding to unrelated individuals as if they were kin—a misfire.

But it is also possible that the evolution of human altruism and other forms of cooperation did not stop once we made the transition from kin groups to larger ones consisting largely of unrelated individuals. Trivers (1971, 1985) made this very point and used it as a launchpad for another, now widely accepted argument—the theory of *reciprocal altruism*. As the name implies, the theory holds that natural selection would favor acts of altruism directed toward unrelated individuals, even strangers, so long as the recipients of these acts reciprocated at a later point in time. The theory assumes the existence of opportunities for reciprocation and mechanisms for detecting potential cheaters, those who take without giving back.

Extending the Theory of Reciprocal Altruism

Despite supporting evidence for the theory of reciprocal altruism, some critics have argued that in the real world, or at least the one imagined for our ancestors, conditions that would make reciprocity a strong evolutionary force are too restrictive to be realistic (e.g., Dessalles, 1999). These concerns stimulated alternative accounts—the theories of *indirect reciprocity*, *strong reciprocity*, and *costly signaling*.

These theories focus not on the recipient of the altruistic act but on an audience that discovers directly or through reputation the identities of those who engage in altruistic acts. The evolution of altruism among unrelated individuals depends on audience members cooperating with reputed altruists—indirect reciprocity (Alexander, 1987; Nowak & Sigmund, 1998); punishing those who fail to cooperate with altruists—strong reciprocity (Fehr & Fischbacher, 2003; Fehr & Gächter, 2002; Gintis, 2000; Gintis, Bowles, Boyd, & Fehr, 2003); or mating selectively with those who can afford to advertise costly altruistic traits, as in the case of wealthy philanthropists—costly signaling (Dessalles, 1999; Gintis, Smith, & Bowles, 2001; Zahavi, 1995, 1997).

Integrating Gene-Centered Accounts of the Evolution of Altruism

More recent extensions of gene-centered accounts of the evolution of altruism include proposals by two teams working independently—evolutionary biologist Gil Roberts and colleagues (Roberts, 2005; Roberts & Atkinson, 2003) and psychologists Stephanie and Michael Brown (2006), editors of this volume. Both theories are based on a common prerequisite for the evolution of costly giving to others—fitness interdependence, a state that exists when a potential helper's reproductive success is tied to that of a person in need. Using a game theoretic paradigm, Roberts demonstrated mathematically that cooperation could evolve in a population under conditions of fitness interdependence, even when helpers and recipients are unrelated and in the absence of reciprocity. Brown and Brown argued that social bonds formed between individuals who were interdependent constituted natural selection's solution to the central problem posed by high-cost altruism: how to give without being taken (i.e., exploited). They provided considerable evidence from ethology, neuroscience, and psychology that cues for fitness interdependence are important for the formation of social bonds, which in turn reduce conflicts between self-interest and other-regarding motives, facilitating altruistic responses.

The concept of fitness interdependence provides a means of integrating theories of altruism directed to kin (kin selection) and theories of altruism directed to unrelated individuals. As Roberts (2005) puts it, altruism based on fitness interdependence "can therefore potentially provide a much sought-after mechanism for achieving cooperation without relatedness, reciprocation, punishment . . . or policing" (p. 907).

Reviving and Extending Group Selection Accounts of Altruism

Refined versions of group selection explanations of the evolution of altruism began surfacing in the 1990s, articulated passionately by evolutionary biologist David Sloan Wilson and philosopher Eliot Sober (e.g., Sober & Wilson, 1998; Wilson & Sober, 1994). These advocates acknowledged the validity of critiques of earlier group selection models, but noted that their own newer models provided a basis for group selection of altruism despite the threat of its undoing from selfish individuals within a population. Wilson and others argued, for example, that groupings within a population are not necessarily spatially defined or fixed (as earlier critiques had implied); they can arise and change in any number of ways based on things like kinship and behavioral similarity—so-called trait groups. In the case of altruism, all that is required is that individuals prefer to interact with like-minded individuals—altruist with altruist, egoist with egoist. They argued further that in the case of humans, cultural norms related to altruism are conducive to group selection: They reduce variability within groups and increase differences between groups. These arguments have been expanded and repackaged under the rubric of "multilevel selection," since supporters of selection at the level of the group do not deny the possibility or importance of selection at other levels (e.g., gene, individual, or colony).

The Psychology of Altruism

In stark contrast to evolutionary biology, psychology has a relatively short history of interest in prosocial behavior generally, and altruism in particular. This is understandable in view of 19th- and early 20th-century psychology's almost exclusive focus on sensation, perception, and conscious experience, and the subsequent domination of American psychology by behavioral (stimulus–response) approaches to learning, which began in the early 1900s (Pavlov, Watson, Thorndike), extended through the 1930s and '40s (Tolman, Hull), and continued well into the 1960s and '70s (Spence, Guthrie, Skinner, Bandura). These theories were important in the formulation and testing of models of animal and human learning, but for our purposes they were important in another way. Some highly influential learning theorists—most notably Watson and Skinner—discouraged the use of hypothetical constructs as explanations for observable behaviors. Attributing behavior to internal motives was considered unnecessary and often ridiculed, and social motives like altruism were not exempt from this prohibition. Thus it is hardly surprising that early theories that suggested there were such things as innate altruistic motives (e.g., McDougall, 1908) had little or no impact once the behaviorist revolution was underway (Batson & Shaw, 1991).

Theories of motivation, where one would think prosocial emotions and behavior might get some consideration, focused mainly on generating and prioritizing needs and motives (e.g., Maslow's hierarchy of needs) or on elucidating hypothetical constructs presumed important in learning—expectancies, needs, drives, drive reduction, drive induction, goals, and incentives (as in Tolman's theory and the Hull–Spence framework). And classic theories of emotion were, for the most part, arguments over the causal status of emotional experience relative to bodily indicators of physiological arousal (e.g., a racing heart): Does a racing heart produce the emotional experience of fear (James–Lange)? Are fear and a racing heart both concomitant reactions to selected sensory input (Cannon–Bard)? Or is fear a consequence of a particular cognitive interpretation of the racing heart (Schacter–Singer)? The emphasis in these theories, and in the emotion literature generally, was on so-called negative emotions (e.g., fear and anger), and this state of affairs has only begun to change in recent years (e.g., Cohn, Fredrickson, Brown, Mikels, & Conway, 2009; Fredrickson, 2003; Haidt, 2003).

Social Psychology Perspectives

Social psychologists were somewhat more receptive than learning theorists to the notion that unobservable constructs such as thoughts and feelings could be used to explain and understand observable behaviors, but paid little attention to altruism or prosocial actions. One reason for this was the widespread belief that human behavior is primarily determined by "rational choices" that attempt to maximize an individual's welfare (Jost, 2010). There were, of course, voices of dissent, who argued for the study of other-oriented phenomena such as a desire for social justice. Among these voices were such luminaries as Kurt Lewin, Gordon Allport, and Solomon Asch. Indeed, in 1959 Asch argued that social psychologists should study "the vectors that make it possible for people to think and care and work for others" (p. 372). While, as Jost (2010) noted, this comment presaged subsequent research on altruism, social psychologists who agreed with Lewin, Allport, and Asch did not actually study prosocial behaviors or motives but rather focused on finding solutions to pressing social problems of the time, such as prejudice and intergroup conflict.

Increased attention on prosocial behavior came a few years later and was due almost solely to a single event—the well-publicized fatal stabbing of Kitty Genovese in 1964, in which individuals who might have helped her failed to do so. Almost immediately social psychologists launched a concerted effort to understand the bystander effect, or "bystander apathy" (Dovidio, 1984). The resulting studies produced a good deal of important information on situational determinants of helping behavior (Krebs, 1970) but did not really address whether altruistic motives might underlie such behavior. Instead, early models or theories of why people act prosocially rather explicitly rejected altruism as a cause of such actions because, as before, they could not accept the notion of truly selfless behaviors. As Piliavin and Charng (1990) put it:

> For a long time, it was intellectually unacceptable to raise the question of whether "true" altruism could exist. Whether one spoke to a biologist, a psychologist, a psychiatrist, a sociologist, an economist, or a political scientist the answer was the same: Anything that appears to be motivated by a concern for someone else's needs will, under closer scrutiny, prove to have ulterior selfish motives. (p. 28)

Things began to change in the 1980s with the publication of work by C. Daniel Batson, a collaborator in earlier research on bystander apathy (Darley & Batson, 1973). Batson's model of altruism focused on those conditions that constitute altruistic motivation, especially empathy, but it is important to reiterate that Batson's conceptualization of altruism differs in some substantial ways from that of the evolutionary biologists. For Batson (Batson, 1998; Batson & Shaw, 1991) altruism refers not to the prosocial act per se but to the underlying motive for the act: "Altruism is a motivational state with the ultimate goal of increasing another's welfare." (Batson & Shaw, 1991 p. 108). Thus according to Batson, the costs or potential benefits of the action are not the key elements of altruism; the critical element is what motivates a person to act prosocially.

It can be argued that Batson's major contribution was what mathematicians might call a counterproof. He demonstrated, in contrast to theories of the time, that under certain conditions humans may be totally motivated by the welfare of another. That is, he showed that altruistic motives do exist. Further, he showed that the intention to help can also be driven by factors that lie beyond self-interest, most notably, *empathy*, a term translated from the German *Einfühlung* into English at the turn of the 20th century by psychologist Edward Titchener (1867–1927), Wilhelm Wundt's prolific student. Batson distinguished between potential helpers' imagining how the person in need feels (empathy, or *empathic concern*) and how they, the helpers, would feel in the same situation, which can result in both empathic concern and *personal distress* (see also Penner, Harper, & Albrecht and Decety, this volume).

From Batson's perspective, and buttressed by a good deal of research, it is empathic concern that produces true altruistic (selfless) motivation; personal distress results in egoistic attempts to reduce the distress. Batson's insistence that true altruism is possible, empathically mediated or otherwise, has not gone unchallenged (Cialdini et al., 1997; Maner, Luce, Neuberg, Cialdini, Brown, S., & Sagarin., 2002), but since the late 1980s his empathy–altruism hypothesis and supporting arguments and data have continued to resonate with and influence social psychologists (Dovidio Piliavin, Schroeder, & Penner, 2006; Penner, Harper, & Albrecht, this volume; Penner, Dovidio, & Piliavin, 2005) and, more recently, others ranging from social workers (e.g., Gerdes & Segal, 2009) to neuroscientists (Decety, this volume; Lamm, Batson, & Decety, 2007).

Altruism in Children

Observations of even very young children—those in their second year of life—reveal that they show concern for others and engage in sharing (e.g., Rheingold, Hay, & West, 1976), so it should not be surprising that developmental psychologists have shown considerable interest in understanding the development and motivation of prosocial behavior. Well before Batson's pivotal empathy–altruism hypothesis gained traction in social psychology, Martin Hoffman (1978), influenced by Jean Piaget, proposed a theory of empathy linked to stages of cognitive development, and gave empathy causal status in influencing altruistic responding (see Hoffman, 2000, for an updated version of this theory). His idea was that empathy—"an affective response more appropriate to someone else's situation than to one's own" (Hoffman, 1982, p. 281)—is an innate response that develops in concert with children's changing understandings of self and others as distinct entities: Infants can and often do respond to the cries of other infants with cries of their own (emotional contagion), but do not possess the cognitive wherewithal to understand the difference between themselves and others. As toddlers, infants begin to appreciate the self–other distinction but exhibit a relatively egoistic understanding of what it takes to comfort another in distress, which is to say, whatever it takes to comfort them (e.g., a favorite blanket). With increasing cognitive development, sensitivity to the needs of others and attempts to help reduce their distress become less egocentric. At its apex, the development of empathy makes possible helping that is responsive not only to the immediate situation faced by another but also to that person's life circumstances.

Results of pioneering studies conducted by Radke-Yarrow, Zahn-Waxler, and colleagues (Radke-Yarrow & Zahn-Waxler, 1984; Zahn-Waxler, Radke-Yarrow, Wagner, & Chapman, 1992) generally supported Hoffman's argument that both empathic responding and prosocial behavor increase with age during childhood. Although there have been reports that the relationship between empathy and prosocial behavior is modest (Underwood & Moore, 1982), especially for younger children, the magnitude of the relationship depends in part on the methods used to assess empathy (Eisenberg & Miller, 1987).

Nancy Eisenberg and colleagues have extended Hoffman's ideas in two ways. First, Eisenberg & Strayer (1987) have argued, not unlike Batson, that empathy can develop into either sympathy or personal distress. Sympathy, an other-oriented affective response, can foster attempts to help others and serve to inhibit aggression (Eisenberg, 2005; Eisenberg, Fabes, & Spinrad, 2006). Personal distress, by contrast, is self-focused and leads to attempts to reduce one's own (as opposed to another's) negative arousal.

Second, consistent with Hoffman's (1981) idea that empathy is biologically based, but unlike Batson, Eisenberg and colleagues have offered a *dispositional* account of the relationship between empathy and prosocial behavior (Eisenberg, Fabes, Guthrie, & Reiser, 2000). These investigators hypothesize that there are consistent and stable individual differences that govern how empathy will influence prosocial behavior. More specifically, young children skilled at regulating their emotions—the use of "effortful control"—can overcome self-oriented negative emotions, be sympathetic, and engage in prosocial behavior; those who are ineffective at emotional self-regulation are less likely to do so. Relevant data suggest that these individual differences reflect not only genetic differences in temperament, but also their interaction with parental patterns of emotional expressivity (Valiente et al., 2004).

Parental Altruism

Long before Hoffman, Eisenberg, and others began their developmental investigations of empathy and altruism in children, John Bowlby, a British psychoanalyst by training, set in place a theory that was predicated on the existence of a system that would motivate parents to provide sensitive and effective caregiving to their children. Bowlby's (1969) *attachment theory* was a well-specified template—inspired by ethology, comparative psychology, and cybernetics—offering to explain how and why infants form affectional bonds to their parents.

Bowlby's basic idea was that infants come into the world equipped by evolution with behaviors that function to ensure proximity to their caregivers—so-called attachment behaviors, such as grasping, looking, rooting, sucking, crying, and smiling. According to Bowlby, these and other reflexive schemes signal the infant's location and needs to caregivers and elicit caregiving responses (and ultimately protection) from them. But what motivates parents to respond appropriately to their infants' signals? Bowlby hypothesized that a complementary *caregiving system* supplied the impetus for sensitive parenting, and that the goals of the attachment and caregiving systems are essentially the same—to protect an individual from harm (see Mikulincer & Shaver, this volume). Threats to a child's survival, for instance, activate her attachment system, which in turn produces behaviors (e.g., crying or following) designed to ensure proximity to the parent or other attachment figure. Activation of a parental caregiving system produces a set of complementary responses "designed to promote proximity and comfort when the parent perceives that the child is in real or potential danger" (Cassidy, 1999, p. 10).

Unfortunately, Bowlby spent considerably more time explaining how infants come to love their caregivers than how parents are motivated to care for their children. And with only a handful of exceptions (e.g., George & Solomon, 1999; Mikulincer & Shaver, 2005, this volume; Shaver & Hazan, 1987; Shaver et al., 1988), the vast majority of attachment researchers have followed suit; systematic and self-sustaining efforts to articulate and empirically explore the motivational architecture of the caregiving system have been few and far between. Social psychologists Berscheid and Collins (2000) made this point over a decade ago in a commentary that needs no updating, except for its urgency:

> Lack of attention to the caregiving side of the attachment theoretical equation has been evident for some time. . . . The neglect of caregiving in the very domain in which one would expect it to receive a full-court press, both theoretically and empirically, has been puzzling. It has been puzzling not only for scientific reasons but for practical reasons as well. Popular recognition of the perilous position of many infants and young children as a result of inadequate caregiving has increased in recent years. Teenage pregnancy, single motherhood, dual career families, marital dissolution, fragmentation of the extended kinship network, and drug and alcohol abuse are among the many factors that have been frequently implicated by politicians, social commentators, and others for the failure of many children in the United States to receive the care they need. Thus, it is especially curious that widespread societal concern has not moved the swelling army of attachment researchers to examine the caregiving construct. (p. 107)

Clearly, answers to the question of what motivates giving are incomplete. But like Berscheid and Collins, we, along with other contributors to this volume, are convinced that the time is right for mounting a serious and integrative effort to delineate the particulars of the motivational system or systems that make sensitive caregiving—whether directed to children, parents, siblings, friends, lovers, comrades, or complete strangers—possible and probable.

■ RECENT TRENDS: TOWARD A PARADIGM SHIFT?

New lines of theory and research are emerging and merging, promising to complete the process of moving the behavioral and social sciences beyond exclusive preoccupation with self-interest explanations of altruism and other forms of prosocial behavior. This venture crosses traditional disciplinary boundaries—integrating evolution and neuroscience with new formulations in the affective sciences, social psychology (basic and applied), and developmental psychology (basic and applied); and suggesting new directions for other social science disciplines, especially economics and political science. In our view, these developments—described in the essays that follow—hold enormous potential for illuminating the positive side of human nature, improving relationships (interpersonal, societal, and global), and addressing successfully some of the most vexing problems ever to confront our species.

■ REFERENCES

Alexander, R. D. (1987). *Biology of moral systems.* New York, NY: Aldine de Groyter.

Asch, S. E, (1959). A perspective on social psychology. In S. Koch (Ed.), *Psychology: A study of a science.* (Vol. 3, pp. 363–383). New York, NY: McGraw-Hill.

Batson, C. D. (1987). Prosocial motivation: Is it ever truly altruistic? *Advances in Experimental Social Psychology, 20,* 65–122.

Batson, C. D. (1998). Altruism and prosocial behavior. In D. Gilbert, S. Fiske, & G. Lindzey (Eds.), *The handbook of social psychology* (4th ed., Vol. 2, pp. 282–316). New York, NY: McGraw-Hill.

Batson, C. D., Batson, J. G., Todd, R. M., Brummett, B. H., Shaw, L. L., & Aldeguer, C. M. R. (1995). Empathy and the collective good. *Journal of Personality and Social Psychology, 68,* 619–631.

Batson, C., Sager, K., Garst, E., Kang, M., Rubchinsky, K. & Dawson, K. (1997). Is empathy-induced helping due to self–other merging? *Journal of Personality and Social Psychology, 73,* 495–509.

Batson, C. D., & Shaw, L. L. (1991). Evidence for altruism: Toward a pluralism of prosocial motives. *Psychological Inquiry, 2,* 107–192.

Berscheid, E., & Collins, W. A. (2000). Who cares? For whom and when, how, and why? *Psychological Inquiry, 11,* 107–109.

Bowlby, J. (1969). *Attachment and loss: Vol. I. Attachment.* New York, NY: Basic Books.

Brown, J. L. (1975). *The evolution of behavior.* New York, NY: Norton.

Brown, S. L., & Brown, R. M. (2006). Selective Investment Theory: Recasting the functional significance of close relationships. *Psychological Inquiry, 17,* 1–29.

Cassidy, J. (1999). The nature of the child's ties. In J. Cassidy & P. R. Shaver (Eds.), *Handbook of attachment: Theory, research, and clinical applications* (pp. 3–20). New York, NY: Guilford.

Choi, J.-K., & Bowles, S. (2007). The coevolution of parochial altruism and war. *Science, 318,* 636–640.

Cialdini, R. B., Brown, S. L., Lewis, B. P., Luce, C., & Neuberg, S. L. (1997). Reinterpreting the empathy–altruism relationship: When one into one equals oneness. *Journal of Personality and Social Psychology, 73,* 481–494.

Clutton-Brock, T. (2002). Breeding together: Kin selection and mutualism in cooperative vertebrates. *Science, 296,* 69–72.

Cohn, M. A., Fredrickson, B. L., Brown, S. L., Mikels, J. A., & Conway, A. M. (2009). Happiness unpacked: Positive emotions increase life satisfaction by building resilience. *Emotion, 9,* 361–368.

Cosmides, L., & Tooby, J. (1992). Cognitive adaptations for social exchange. In J. Barkow, L. Cosmides, & J. Tooby (Eds.), *The adapted mind: Evolutionary psychology and the generation of culture* (pp. 163–228). New York, NY: Oxford University Press.

Cosmides, L., & Tooby, J. (2000). Evolutionary psychology and the emotions. In M. Lewis & J. M. Haviland-Jones (Eds.), *Handbook of emotions* (2nd ed., pp. 91–215). New York, NY: Guilford.

Darley, J. M., & Batson, C. D. (1973). From Jerusalem to Jericho: A study of situational and dispositional variables in helping behavior. *Journal of Personality and Social Psychology, 27*, 100–108.

Darwin, C. (1859). *On the origin of species by means of natural selection; or, the preservation of favoured races in the struggle for life.* London, England: John Murray.

Darwin, C. (1871). The descent of man, and selection in relation to sex. In E. O. Wilson (Ed.), *From so simple a beginning: The four great books of Charles Darwin* (pp. 783–1248). New York, NY: Norton.

Darwin, C. (1872). The expression of the emotions in man and animals. In E. O. Wilson (Ed.), *From so simple a beginning: The four great books of Charles Darwin* (pp. 1276–1477). New York, NY: Norton.

Dawkins, R. (1989). *The selfish gene.* New York, NY: Oxford University Press.

Dessalles, J. L. (1999). Coalition factor in the evolution of non-kin altruism. *Advances in Complex Systems, 2*, 143–172.

Dovidio, J. F. (1984). Helping behavior and altruism: An empirical and conceptual overview. In L. Berkowitz (Ed.), *Advances in experimental social psychology* (Vol. 17, pp. 361–427). New York, NY: Academic Press.

Dovidio, J., Piliavin, J., Schroeder, D., & Penner, L. (2006). *The social psychology of prosocial behavior.* Mahwah, NJ: Lawrence Erlbaum.

Dugatkin, L. A. (2006). *The altruism equation.* Princeton, NJ: Princeton University Press.

Eisenberg, N. (2005). Age changes in prosocial responding and moral reasoning in adolescence and early adulthood. *Journal of Research on Adolescence, 15*, 235–260.

Eisenberg, N., Fabes. R. A., Guthrie, I. K., & Reiser, M. (2000). Dispositional emotionality and regulation: their role in predicting quality of social functioning. *Journal of Personality and Social Psychology, 78*, 136–157.

Eisenberg, N., Fabes, R. A., & Spinrad, T. L. (2006). Prosocial development. In W. Damon (Series Ed.) & N. Eisenberg (Vol. Ed.), *Handbook of child psychology* (6th ed., pp. 646–718). New York, NY: John Wiley & Sons.

Eisenberg, N., & Miller, P. A. (1987). The relation of empathy to prosocial and related behaviors. *Psychological Bulletin, 101*, 91–119.

Eisenberg, N., & Strayer, J. (1987). Critical issues in the study of empathy. In. N. Eisenberg & J. Strayer (Eds.). *Empathy and its development* (pp. 3–13). New York, NY: Cambridge University Press.

Fehr, E., & Fischbacher, U. (2003). The nature of human altruism. *Nature, 425*, 785–791.

Fehr, E., & Gächter, S. (2002). Altruistic punishment in humans. *Nature, 415*, 137–140.

Fredrickson, B. L. (2003). The value of positive emotions. *American Scientist, 91*, 330–335.

George, C., & Solomon, J. (1999). Attachment and caregiving: The caregiving behavioral system. In J. Cassidy & P. R. Shaver (Eds.), *Handbook of attachment: Theory, research, and clinical applications* (pp. 649–670). New York, NY: Guilford.

Gerdes, K. A., & Segal, E. A. (2009). A social work model of empathy. *Advances in Social Work, 10*, 114–127.

Gintis, H. (2000). Strong reciprocity and human sociality. *Journal of Theoretical Biology, 206*, 169–179.

Gintis, H., Bowles, S., Boyd, R., & Fehr, E. (2003). Explaining altruistic behavior in humans. *Evolution and Human Behavior, 24*, 153–172.

Gintis, H., Smith, E. H., & Bowles, S. (2001). Costly signaling and cooperation. *Journal of Theoretical Biology, 213*, 103–119.

Gruber, H. E., & Barrett, P. H. (1974). *Darwin on man.* New York, NY: Dutton.

Haidt, J. (2003). The moral emotions. In R. J. Davidson, K. Scherer, & H. H. Goldsmith (Eds.), *Handbook of affective sciences* (pp. 852–870). Oxford, England: Oxford University Press.

Haldane, J. B. S. (1955). Population genetics. *New Biology, 18,* 34–51.

Haldane, J. B. S. (1974). I'd lay down my life for two brothers or eight cousins. *New Scientist, 8,* 325.

Hamilton, W. D. (1964). The genetic evolution of social behavior: I and II. *Journal of Theoretical Biology, 7,* 1–52.

Hoffman, M. L. (1978). Empathy, its development and prosocial implications. In C. B. Keasey (Ed.). Nebraska Symposium on Motivation (Vol. 25, pp. 169–218). Lincoln: University of Nebraska Press.

Hoffman, M. L. (1981). Is altruism part of human nature? *Journal of Personality and Social Psychology, 40,* 121–137.

Hoffman, M.L. (1982). Development of prosocial motivation: Empathy and guilt. In N. Eisenberg (Ed.), *The development of prosocial behavior* (pp. 281–338). New York, NY: Academic Press.

Hoffman, M. L. (2000). *Empathy and moral development: Implications for caring and justice.* New York, NY: Cambridge University Press.

Hrdy, S. B. (2005). Evolutionary context of human development: The cooperative breeding model. In C. S. Carter, L. Ahnert, K. E. Grossman, S. B. Hrdy, M. E. Lamb, S. W. Porges, & N. Sachser (Eds.), *Attachment and bonding: A new synthesis* (pp. 9–32). Cambridge, MA: MIT Press.

Huxley, T. H. (1899). *Evolution and ethics and other essays.* New York, NY: D. Appleton & Company.

Jost, J. (2010) Social justice: History, theory, and research. In S. Fiske, D. Gilbert, & G. Lindzey (Eds.), *Handbook of social psychology: Vol. 2* (5th ed., pp. 1122–1165). Hoboken, NJ: John Wiley & Sons.

Krebs, D. (1970). Altruism: An examination of the concept and a review of the literature. *Psychological Bulletin, 73,* 258–302.

Kropotkin, P. (1902). *Mutual aid: A factor of evolution.* London, England: William Heinemann.

Lamm, C., Batson, C. D., & Decety, J. (2007). The neural substrate of human empathy: Effects of perspective-taking and cognitive appraisal. *Journal of Cognitive Neuroscience, 19,* 42–58.

Maner, J. K., Luce, C. L., Neuberg, S. L., Cialdini, R. B., Brown, S., & Sagarin, B. J. (2002). The effects of perspective taking on motivations for helping: Still no evidence for altruism. *Personality and Social Psychology Bulletin, 28,* 1601–1610.

Martineau, H. (Ed.). (1896). *The positive philosophy of Auguste Comte.* London, England: George Bell & Sons.

Maynard Smith, J. (1976). Group selection. *Quarterly Review of Biology, 51, 277–283.*

McDougall, W. (1908). *An introduction to social psychology.* New York, NY: Luce.

Mikulincer, M., & Shaver, P. R. (2005). Attachment security, compassion, and altruism. *Current Directions in Psychological Science, 14,* 34–38.

Millon, T. M., Grossman, S. D., & Meager, S. E. (2004). *Masters of the mind: Exploring the story of mental illness from ancient times to the new millennium.* Hoboken, NJ: Wiley.

Neusner, J., & Chilton, B. (Eds.). (2005). *Altruism in world religions.* Washington, DC: Georgetown University Press.

Nowak, M., & Sigmund, K. (1998). Evolution of indirect reciprocity by image scoring. *Nature, 393,* 573–576.

Penner, L. A., Dovidio, J. F., Piliavin, J. A., & Schroeder, D. A. (2005). Prosocial behavior: Multilevel perspectives. *Annual Review of Psychology, 56,* 365–392.

Piliavin, J. A., & Charng, H. (1990). Altruism: A review of recent theory and research. *Annual Review of Psychology, 16,* 27–65.

Radke-Yarrow, M., & Zahn-Waxler, C. (1984). Roots, motives, and patterns in children's prosocial behavior. In E. Staub, D. Bar-Tal, J. Karylowski, & J. Reykowski (Eds.), *Development and maintenance of prosocial behavior* (pp. 81–99). New York, NY: Plenum.

Rheingold, H. L., Hay, D. F., & West, M. J. (1976). Sharing in the second year of life. *Child Development, 47,* 1148–1158.

Rhoades, D. R., & Mcfarland, K. F. (1999). Caregiver meaning: A study of caregivers of individuals with mental illness. *Health and Social Work, 24,* 291–299.

Roberts, G. (2005). Cooperation through interdependence. *Animal Behaviour, 70,* 901–908.

Roberts, G., & Atkinson, N. (2003). *Cooperation through interdependence.* Paper presented at the meeting of the Human Behavior and Evolution Society, Lincoln, NE.

Schaller, M., & Neuberg, S. L. (2008). Intergroup prejudices and intergroup conflicts. In C. Crawford & D. L. Krebs (Eds.), *Foundations of evolutionary psychology* (pp. 399–412). Mahwah, NJ: Lawrence Erlbaum.

Shaver, P., & Hazan, C. (1987). Being lonely, falling in love: Perspectives from attachment theory. *Journal of Personality and Social Psychology, 2,* 105–124.

Shaver, P. R., Hazan, C., & Bradshaw, D. (1988). Love as attachment: The integration of three behavioral systems. In R. J. Sternberg & M. L. Barnes (Eds.), *The psychology of love* (pp. 68–99). New Haven, CT: Yale University Press.

Sober, E., & Wilson, D. S. (1998). *Unto others: The evolution and psychology of unselfish behavior.* Cambridge, MA: Harvard University Press.

Spencer, H. (1904). *The principles of ethics (Volume 1).* New York, NY: D. Appleton & Company.

Trivers, R. L. (1971). The evolution of reciprocal altruism. *Quarterly Review of Biology, 46,* 35–57.

Trivers, R. (1985). *Social evolution.* Menlo Park, CA: Benjamin/Cummings.

Underwood, B., & Moore, B. (1982). Perspective-taking and altruism. *Psychological Bulletin, 91,* 143–173.

Valiente, C., Eisenberg, N., Fabes, R. A., Shepard, S. A., Cumberland, A., & Losoya, S. H. (2004). Prediction of children's empathy-related responding from their effortful control and parents' expressivity. *Developmental Psycholology, 40,* 911–926.

West, S. A., Griffin, A. S., & Gardner, A. (2006). Social semantics: Altruism, cooperation, mutualism, strong reciprocity and group selection. *Journal of Evolutionary Biology, 20,* 415–432.

Williams, G. C. (1966). *Adaptation and natural selection.* Princeton, NJ: Princeton University Press.

Wilson, D. S., & Sober, E. (1994). Re-introducing group selection to the human behavioral sciences. *Behavioral and Brain Sciences, 17,* 585–654.

Wilson, E. O. (1975). *Sociobiology: The new synthesis.* Cambridge, MA: Harvard University Press.

Wright, S. (1945). Tempo and mode in evolution: A critical review. *Ecology, 26,* 415–419.

Wynne-Edwards, V. C. (1962). *Animal dispersion in relation to social behaviour.* Edinburgh, UK: Oliver & Boyd.

Zahavi, A. (1995). Mate selection—a selection for handicap. *Journal of Theoretical Biology, 53,* 205–214.

Zahavi, A. (1997). *The handicap principle: A missing piece of Darwin's puzzle.* New York, NY: Oxford University Press.

Zahn-Waxler, C., Radke-Yarrow, M., Wagner, E., & Chapman, M. (1992). Development of concern for others. *Developmental Psychology, 28,* 126–136.

Zanker, G. (1996). *The heart of Achilles: Characterization and personal ethics in the Iliad.* Ann Arbor: University of Michigan Press.

■ PART TWO

Foundations of Caregiving

2 How Altruistic by Nature?

■ DENNIS L. KREBS

Debates about the human capacity for altruism are prominent in the history of ideas. Are people capable of behaving in genuinely altruistic ways, or are apparent acts of altruism disguised forms of selfishness? I became interested in this question as an adolescent after reading Freud's *Interpretation of Dreams*. My initial take on the issue was that humans are fundamentally selfish by nature and that attributions of altruism are products of self-deception. In graduate school, I noticed that social psychology textbooks contained chapters on aggression, but not on positive forms of social behavior. My search for psychological research on altruism eventuated in the publication of a review of the literature. While I was working on that review, a lecturer from the biology department of my university, Robert Trivers, looked me up, told me that he was working on a model of how altruism could evolve biologically, and asked for a copy of my paper. (Trivers describes this exchange in his collected works: Trivers, 2002.) We exchanged drafts and became friends. I found Trivers's paper on the evolution of reciprocal altruism far more relevant to the question of how altruistic humans are by nature than my paper was, and developed an interest in evolutionary theory that grew throughout the years.

■ THE DEFINITIONAL ISSUE

A rule should guide all discussions of altruism: Before one states a position, one must define the construct. It is distressing to contemplate how often people who engage in debates about the human capacity for altruism use the word to refer to different phenomena.

Altruism has been defined in two main ways. First, it has been defined as acts that have the *effect or consequence* of benefiting a recipient at a cost to a donor. Variations within this category are defined mainly by different kinds of costs and benefits. Second, altruism has been defined in terms of the *intentions and motives* of actors, as acts that are aimed at improving the welfare of recipients as an end in itself and not as a means of improving the welfare of the donor. Variations within this category are defined mainly by different kinds of welfare.

In the first half of this chapter I review evidence that dispositions to behave in ways that increase the chances of recipients surviving and reproducing, at a cost to the survival and reproductive success of the donor, have evolved in humans and other animals. I will refer to such dispositions as *biologically altruistic*. In the second half I review evidence that some evolved mental mechanisms give rise to altruistic motives and intentions. I will refer to the behaviors that flow from such motives and intentions as *psychologically altruistic*.

■ THE EVOLUTION OF BIOLOGICAL ALTRUISM

Evolutionary theorists define altruism in terms of behaviors that have the effect of increasing the fitness of recipients and diminishing the fitness of donors. This type of altruism has been called "evolutionary altruism" (Batson, 2000; Sober & Wilson, 1998), but I believe that it is more appropriately characterized as biological altruism. Evidence of biological altruism is important because it threatens Darwin's theory of evolution. If, as Darwin assumed, natural selection is mediated by the survival of the fittest individuals, and if, by definition, behaving altruistically diminishes the fitness of individuals, then dispositions to behave in altruistic ways should not evolve. For this reason, Darwin viewed evidence that social insects engage in self-sacrificial altruism as potentially fatal to his theory.

In the face of an apparent inconsistency between Darwin's theory of evolution and evidence that some animals behave in ways that increase the fitness of others at a cost to their fitness, something had to give. Either animals could not, on the laws of evolution, possess a capacity for biological altruism, or the principles of evolution that were inconsistent with the evolution of altruism had to be revised. Neo-Darwinian evolutionary theorists opted for the second alternative, thereby significantly refining Darwin's theory.

The Evolution of Biologically Altruistic Behaviors through Kin Selection

Our understanding of the process of evolution and animals' capacity for altruism was revolutionized when theorists redefined biological evolution in terms of the selection of genes, as opposed to the selection of individuals. Modern evolutionary theorists view individuals as vehicles designed by natural selection to transport copies of their genes to future generations. Individuals can accomplish this in the biologically selfish ways that everybody understands, by competing with other individuals for resources that foster their survival and reproductive success. In addition, however, individuals can propagate replicas of their genes by sacrificing their biological welfare for the sake of others who possess identical copies of their alleles. In a seminal paper, Hamilton (1964) explained how a genetically based disposition to sacrifice one's life to save the lives of those to whom one is related by common descent (i.e., one's kin) could evolve through "kin selection." Note that although such a disposition qualifies as biologically altruistic, it is genetically selfish: It increases the number of copies of one's genes that one contributes to future generations, at a cost to the genes' alleles.

Researchers have produced evidence that many social species, including humans, are disposed to help their kin (Trivers, 1985), even when the physical and hedonic costs of helping are very high (Burnstein, 2005). The more highly related people are to those who need help, the more pain they are willing to endure to assist them (Kurland & Gaulin, 2005). Wang (2002) has found that people who are faced with decisions about helping groups of relatives in perilous situations tend to identify with the group as a whole and adopt a "live or die together" type of decision rule. In a real-life study, vacationers who were trapped in burning buildings in a vacation complex in England risked their lives to locate and assist their relatives (Sime, 1983).

The Expansion of Kin-Selected Altruism

Hamilton (1964) argued that biological altruism could evolve if the fitness costs to donors were less than the fitness benefits to recipients times their degree of relatedness: $c < br$. On this decision-making rule, humans would have evolved to help only a narrow range of recipients, namely, those to whom they were related by common descent, and they would be disposed to help them only when the genetic benefits to those relatives outweighed the genetic costs to themselves. Fortunately for human nature, however, the mental mechanisms that instantiate Hamilton's decision-making rule are not perfectly designed. People are not capable of determining precisely how closely related they are to those in need of help, or of correctly anticipating the fitness costs and fitness benefits of behavioral choices. People must rely on cues to genetic relatedness, such as familiarity and phenotypic similarity, and they must invoke imperfect, best-bet behavioral strategies. Ironically perhaps, the more imperfectly that mechanisms for recognizing kin and for reckoning costs and benefits are designed, the more biologically altruistic we would expect humans and other animals to be. Indeed, if kin-recognition mechanisms "misfire" in modern environments (in which, for example, people interact with many more individuals who are familiar to them and similar to their relatives than early humans did), these mechanisms may induce them to behave in ways that are maladaptive genetically because they induce them to assist people who do not possess copies of their altruism-coding genes.

The Evolution of Reciprocal Altruism

In 1971 Trivers explained how dispositions to exchange goods and services with others could evolve if both parties gained fitness benefits. Following the publication of Trivers article, biologists searched for evidence in the animal kingdom of what Trivers called "reciprocal altruism" but found much less than they expected. Some scientists have accounted for the rareness of reciprocal altruism by suggesting that only a few species possess the cognitive abilities necessary to engage in fitness-increasing social exchanges—abilities such as individuals' capacity to remember who has helped them, the capacity to calculate the value of the assistance they received, and the wherewithal to engage in exchanges that produce mutual gains (Hauser, Chen, Chen, & Chuang, 2003).

The Expansion of Reciprocal Altruism

Humans' capacity for language enables them to engage in expanded systems of reciprocity by making commitments such as "If you give me what I need now, I will repay you (with interest) in the future; if I help you and you fail to pay me back, I will get even with you." As expressed by Nesse (2001), "commitment is fundamentally different from kin selection and reciprocity. . . . A commitment is an act or signal that gives up options in order to influence someone's behavior by changing incentives or expectations. . . . Some commitments . . . are pledges to act in ways that will be contrary to obvious self-interest" (p. 13). Even though those who renege on their commitments may come out ahead in the short term, they may lose in the long term through a loss in credibility. The long-term value of a good reputation tends to outweigh the short-term costs of maintaining it.

Several investigators have demonstrated that people are more inclined to sacrifice their interests for those with whom they have formed enduring social bonds than we would expect if they engaged in concrete tit-for-tat forms of reciprocity (Shackelford & Buss, 1996). People often make ongoing sacrifices for friends in need, with no expectation of immediate returns (Simpson & Campbell, 2005), and may feel offended when their friends adopt an "exchange orientation" and offer to pay them back (Clark & Mills, 1993). Tooby & Cosmides (1996) suggested that mental mechanisms that dispose people to help their friends evolved because it is in people's adaptive interest to suffer the relatively small costs of helping friends over long periods of time if such acts increase the probability of their friends being there for them when their fitness is in serious jeopardy. Put another way, it pays off for people to invest in their friends as insurance policies to foster their own long-term security and fitness.

Related to the idea that individuals can increase their fitness by helping others, animals that form enduring partnerships—whether with members of the opposite sex or the same sex—may operate as a unit, helping each other build shelters, produce and rear offspring, fend off predators, and defend territory (Ellis, 1998). In such cases it is in each individual's interest to uphold the partner's welfare, because this upholds the welfare of the fitness-enhancing unit of which the individual is a part. In a similar vein, inasmuch as individuals' fitness is dependent on the vitality of the groups of which they are members, it may be in their biological interest to make short-term sacrifices to uphold the long-term welfare of their groups.

The Evolution of Biologically Altruistic Behaviors through Selective Investments in Others

Brown and Brown (2006) have integrated accounts of the evolution of altruism under one overriding principle: It pays off biologically for individuals to invest selectively in those on whom their fitness is dependent. "From the perspective of selective investment theory, the key to understanding the evolution of altruism is not whether a potential altruistic recipient carries copies of the altruist's genes, or whether the recipient is likely to be a reciprocal altruist, but rather the direction and magnitude of the correlation between the reproductive success of potential altruists and their recipients" (Brown & Brown, 2006, p. 9) Brown and Brown argue that behaving altruistically toward those with whom one has formed social bonds constitutes a long-term investment that reaps return benefits when the fitness of helpers is tied to the fitness of recipients through shared genes or through shared interests.

How Biologically Altruistic Are Return-Benefit Forms of Altruism?

If dispositions to help one's kin are biologically altruistic (but not genetically altruistic, because they induce individuals to behave in ways that propagate replicas of their genes), what is the status of dispositions to engage in concrete reciprocity, to keep prosocial commitments, to help friends, and to invest selectively in those with whom one's fitness is interdependent? Later I will argue that the mental mechanisms that mediate such behaviors may well give rise to psychologically altruistic motives. Here I want to point out that if the "altruistic" behaviors in question produce ultimate gains in individual fitness, they do not meet the criteria for biological (or genetic) altruism. Even though the two behaviors that constitute concrete reciprocity—the original helping act and the act of reciprocating it—may be biologically altruistic when considered out of context (because each act temporarily increases the recipient's fitness at a cost to the donor's fitness), the reciprocal exchange produces net biological benefits for both parties. On the other hand, when biological benefits over the lifetime are sacrificed to preserve the benefits to one's kin (as could be true in the case of fitness interdependence based on common genes), behaviors aimed at helping others could be said to be examples of biological altruism. To the extent that helping one's friends, keeping one's commitments, and investing in those with whom one's fitness is interdependent are biologically costly in the short run but provide fitness benefits in the long run, the mechanisms that regulate these forms of conduct evolved because they produced ultimate gains in personal fitness. In accounting for the evolution of mechanisms that give rise to these forms of "altruism" in terms of ultimate adaptive benefits to the individuals who engage in them, evolutionary theorists implicitly acknowledge that these types of behavior are not biologically altruistic.

The Evolution of Biologically Altruistic Behaviors in Modern Societies

The forms of altruism practiced by humans in large, complex societies are unique in the animal kingdom. Modern humans contribute to the public good, donate to charity, help strangers anonymously, repay people whom they never expect to see again, resist the temptation to free ride, and suffer the costs of punishing free riders who fail to fulfill their social obligations. Accounts of how dispositions to behave in these ways evolved have generated a great deal of controversy among evolutionary theorists. Some theorists have argued that these types of altruism evolved through individual-level forms of natural selection and therefore are biologically selfish. Other theorists have argued that they evolved through cultural group selection (the selection of groups that share altruism-inducing beliefs and customs), which renders them biologically altruistic.

The Evolution of Biologically Altruistic Behaviors through Indirect Reciprocity.

Representing the first camp, Alexander (1987) has suggested that at a critical juncture in the evolution of the human species, early humans began to form intermediate-sized tribes, and when this happened, systems of direct reciprocity expanded into systems of indirect reciprocity in which individuals who helped members of their groups were paid back by third parties who selected them as exchange partners. When humans developed large technological nations with socially imposed monogamy, private property, laws, and so on, systems of indirect reciprocity generated increasingly large returns. Alexander (1987) suggests that "in such a milieu . . . a modicum of indiscriminate altruism would arise as social investments because of benefits to individuals being viewed as altruists" (p. 192). He goes on to argue that "general acceptance of indiscriminate altruism and general acceptance of its beneficial effects result in a society with high social utility. This encouragement and acceptance is expected to occur partly because of the likelihood, much of the time, that nearly everyone benefits from living in a unified society and partly because individuals gain from inducing indiscriminate altruism in others" (pp. 192–193).

As discussed, accounts of the evolution of altruism based on individual-level selection take the altruism out of biological altruism, because they posit eventual return benefits. In recent years, a group of evolutionary theorists has argued that genuinely altruistic dispositions have evolved in large-scale societies—not through individual selection that produces return benefits in the long run, but through group-level processes that select dispositions to suffer biological costs for the sake of one's group (Richerson & Boyd, 2005). Such theorists argue that findings from research on large groups establishes that many forms of altruism could not "have a self-interested function, all possibility of return effects having been removed. Instead, they must have been selected to benefit the group or appeared by some process of cultural diffusion" (Trivers, 2006, p. 79).

The Evolution of Biologically Altruistic Behaviors through Gene–culture Coevolution

Richerson and Boyd (2005) agree with traditional evolutionary theorists that "ancient" social instincts that evolved through kin selection and reciprocity dispose people to behave in altruistic ways in small groups. However, they argue that the culturally defined tribes and large-scale systems of cooperation created by humans during the Pleistocene era mediated the cultural group selection of "tribal instincts" qualitatively different from the social instincts that evolved earlier through individual-level selection. These theorists assert that the new tribal instincts became "superimposed onto human psychology without eliminating those that favor friends and kin" (Richerson & Boyd, 2005, p. 215). Tribal instincts dispose people to identify with in-groups that are distinguished by symbolic markers, to abide by culturally created rules and norms that uphold their groups, and to punish those who violate the norms. In contrast to ancient instincts evolved through kin selection and reciprocity, tribal instincts may be both biologically and genetically altruistic: "Our social instincts hypothesis requires that cultural group selection be strong enough to counter individualistically motivated selfish decision making in order to favor tribal-scale cooperation" (Richerson & Boyd, 2005, p. 192).

Traditional evolutionary theorists have reacted in two ways to gene–culture coevolutionary accounts of the evolution of altruism in modern societies. First, they have advanced evidence that gene–culture coevolutionary theorists have underestimated the benefits that individuals may obtain by upholding large-scale systems of cooperation in which they interact selectively and conditionally with other cooperators and reject those who behave selfishly. Second, they have accounted for evidence that humans engage in costly forms of biological and genetic altruism in terms of the automatic, subconscious activation of mental mechanisms that evolved through individual selection in small groups of early humans. These theorists argue that "our psychology simply fails to optimize behavior in evolutionarily novel circumstances (such as laboratory experiments or big cities) and better reflects the constraints of the environments in which our psychological mechanisms for cooperation evolved, environments characterized by small groups of extended kin, few strangers, strong hierarchies and lasting reputations" (Johnson, Price, & Takezawa, 2008, p. 9).

To summarize the discussion to this point, I have distinguished between consequence-based and motive-based conceptions of altruism, explained that evolutionary theorists define altruism in terms of the fitness consequences of behaviors, and argued that some of the helping behaviors that evolutionary theorists characterize as altruistic do not really qualify as biologically altruistic because they produce long-term benefits for those who engage in them. I turn now to a discussion of motive-based forms of altruism.

■ THE EVOLUTION OF ALTRUISTIC MOTIVES

In contrast to evolutionary theorists, laypeople do not tend to define altruism in terms of the consequences of helping behaviors. Most people hold that to qualify as altruistic, an act must stem from altruistic motives and intentions. For example, most people would consider those who try to help others and fail through no fault of their own more altruistic than those who benefit others unintentionally while trying to exploit them. As mentioned, altruism that is defined in terms of people's motives and intentions has been called "psychological altruism" (Batson, 2000; Sober & Wilson, 1998).

When humans and other animals benefit others at immediate costs to themselves, are they motivated to improve the welfare of recipients as an end in itself or are they helping others in order to improve their own welfare? To evaluate people's capacity for psychological altruism, we must get inside their heads, identify the proximate mental mechanisms and psychological states that induce them to help others, and determine the types of goals they are trying to achieve. I consider this one of the most significant and challenging research questions in the study of human caregiving. If the terminal goal of a helping behavior is to improve the welfare of a recipient, then it qualifies as psychologically altruistic; if the terminal goal is to improve the welfare of the donor, then it does not (Batson, 2000).

In addressing the implications of evolutionary theories of altruism for human caregiving, it is important to note that nothing in accounts of the evolution of consequence-based forms of altruism precludes the possibility that the mechanisms that dispose individuals to help others generate genuinely altruistic motives, even if the helping behaviors end up producing return benefits. Proximate mental mechanisms that motivate people to help others as an end in itself could improve the helpers' welfare and increase their fitness, even though this is not what the helpers were trying to do, and altruistic motives could be by-products of mechanisms that, on balance, increased the fitness of our ancestors.

■ PROXIMATE SOURCES OF ALTRUISTIC MOTIVES

Many kinds of mental mechanisms could induce people to sacrifice their immediate interests for the sake of others. People could help their kin, their friends, members of their groups, and strangers whom they will never meet again for all kinds of reasons. In the next section I consider the proximate sources of helping behaviors whose motivational sources have been investigated most extensively—those that give rise to impulsive helping in emergencies, sympathetic and empathic helping, and the disposition to support one's group.

Altruistic Impulses

In *Descent of Man*, Darwin (1874) argued that some social instincts dispose individuals to behave in psychologically altruistic ways. He argued that "it is probable that [such] instincts are persistently followed from the mere force of inheritance, without the stimulus of pleasure or pain. . . . Hence, the common assumption that men must be impelled to every action by experiencing some pleasure or pain may be erroneous" (p. 102). For example,

> Under circumstances of extreme peril, as during a fire, when a man endeavors to save a fellow-creature without a moment's hesitation, he can hardly feel pleasure; and still less has he time to reflect on the dissatisfaction which he might subsequently experience if he did not make the attempt. Should he afterwards reflect over his own conduct, he would feel that there lies within him an impulsive power widely different from a search after pleasure or happiness; and this seems to be the deeply planted social instinct. (p. 117)

Contemporary research on bystander intervention has supported Darwin's conclusions. According to Piliavin, Dovidio, Gaertner, & Clark (1981), when people categorize an event as an extreme emergency, they experience a "fight or flight" reaction that induces them to narrow their attention, focus on the plight of the victim, truncate the processing of further information, and help without thinking. "Cost considerations become peripheral and not attended to" (p. 239). Perception of similarity to the victim slowers the threshold for this reaction. Thinking about and analyzing the situation—mediated by higher mental processes—reduces the probability of helping. Piliavin et al. speculated that "there may be an evolutionary basis for. . . . impulsive helping" (p. 180).

Empathy and Sympathy

A large number of studies have found that feelings of empathy and sympathy dispose people to help others (see Batson, 1991; de Waal, 2008; Hoffman, 2000). Some investigators have argued that empathy and sympathy engender psychologically altruistic motives, but others have argued that people are motivated to help those with whom they empathize and sympathize to relieve their own vicariously experienced pain or to achieve other self-serving goals.

Darwin (1874) took a position on this issue. He disputed the claim that sympathetic behaviors are aimed at "reliev[ing] the suffering of another, in order that our own painful feelings may be at the same time relieved," because this account fails to explain "the fact that sympathy is excited, in an immeasurably stronger degree, by a beloved, than by an indifferent person" (p. 103). The social psychologist Batson (1991) and his colleagues have examined this issue experimentally.

Batson hypothesized that when people focus on the plight of others in need, they may react in one of two ways. First, they may experience an egoistic state of "personal distress," which they can reduce either by helping the person in need or in other ways, such as looking away and leaving the scene. Alternatively, people may experience "an other-oriented emotional response . . . called empathy, sympathy, compassion, etc." that engenders "a motivational state with the ultimate goal of increasing another's welfare" (Batson, 2000, pp. 207–208). De Waal (2008) has argued that personal distress stems from a primitive core of empathy and is readily apparent in other animals, whereas empathic concern stems from later-evolved mental mechanisms and is rare in the animal kingdom (see also Decety, this volume).

Batson and his colleagues conducted a large number of studies designed to determine whether empathy engenders egoistic or altruistic motives. The basic design involved inducing participants to empathize with a person in need, then providing them with an opportunity to reduce their vicariously experienced distress or achieve other selfish goals in less costly ways than by helping the person with whom they were empathizing. For example, in one study they provided participants with the opportunity to relieve the distress engendered by seeing someone in pain by leaving the scene, and in other studies they provided participants with convenient nonaltruistic ways of elevating their mood, making a good impression, and justifying selfish choices. Batson and his colleagues consistently found that when people are in an empathic state, they seek to help those with whom they empathize as an end in itself, as opposed to wanting to help them instrumentally in order to achieve egoistic goals. Not everyone, however, has been convinced by their findings (see Cialdini et al., 1987; Sober & Wilson, 1998).

Tribal Instincts

Social psychologists such as Tajfel and Turner (1985) have found that people automatically identify with groups to which they have been assigned, even on an arbitrary basis, and feel disposed to help members of their groups. Richerson and Boyd (2001) attribute such dispositions to the tribal instincts discussed earlier, which they view as similar to "the principles in the Chomskyan linguists' 'principles and parameters' . . . of language. . . . The innate principles furnish people with basic predispositions, emotional capacities, and social skills that are implemented in practice through highly variable cultural institutions, the parameters" (p. 191).

As noted, Richerson and Boyd have asserted that because tribal instincts evolved through cultural group selection, they are biologically altruistic. Are the states engendered by these instincts psychologically altruistic, or are people motivated to uphold their groups to improve their own welfare? Clearly, people could be motivated to uphold their groups to promote their long-term security, to enhance their reputations, to try to get to Heaven, and so on. In addition, inasmuch as people identify with groups, it could be argued that the efforts they expend to uphold them are psychologically selfish, because their behaviors are directed at improving the welfare of the "me" in "we."

Investigators have attempted to decipher the motives underlying group-upholding behaviors by determining whether people engage in such behaviors when they do not reap personal benefits or when the personal costs of upholding groups outweigh the gains. Several investigators have concluded that people are naturally disposed to uphold the collective interests of their groups as an end in itself, at great costs to themselves, rather than upholding their groups' interests as a means of promoting their own interests (see Dawes, van de Kragt, & Orbell, 1988, for a review of the evidence). The most obvious example is probably soldiers' willingness to sacrifice their lives for the sake of their units during wars.

Moral Emotions

Several evolutionary theorists have argued that a set of "moral emotions" has evolved in the human species whose function is to motivate people to help others and to uphold the social orders of their groups, even when it is immediately costly to do so. For example, theorists have suggested that feelings of gratitude motivate people to help those who have helped them (McCullough, 2008), feelings of guilt motivate people to make amends (Moll, di Oliveira-Souza, Zahn, & Grafman, 2008), and feelings of forgiveness induce individuals to repair damaged social relations (McCullough, 2008).

Psychologists and neuroscientists have begun to identify the stimuli that activate moral emotions and to map the neural circuits and hormonal correlates associated with them. For example, Moll et al. (2008) have found that gratitude "is elicited by detecting a good outcome to oneself, attributed to the agency of another person, who acted in an intentional manner to achieve the outcome" (p. 16). These theorists have suggested that "gratitude is associated with a feeling of attachment to the other agent and often promotes the reciprocation of favors. . . . Activated brain regions include the ventral striatum, the OFC [orbitofrontal cortex], and the anterior cingulate cortex" (p. 16).

Several theorists have suggested that moral emotions produce psychologically altruistic motivational states, even though the behaviors to which they give rise pay off in the end. For example, Frank (2001) has argued that emotional reactions such as gratitude and guilt motivate people to honor their commitments, even when it is immediately costly to do so. Even though the long-term benefits of honoring commitments outweigh the immediate costs of keeping them, the emotions that dispose people to honor their commitments do not motivate them to achieve these long-term goals. Rather, they motivate them to behave in psychologically altruistic ways. As expressed by Frank (2001), "the commitment model is a tentative first step in the construction of a theory of unopportunistic behavior. It challenges the self-interest model's portrayal of human nature in its own terms by accepting the fundamental premise that material incentives ultimately govern behavior. Its point of departure is the observation that persons *directly* motivated to pursue self-interest are often for that reason doomed to fail. They fail because they cannot solve commitment problems. These problems can often be solved by persons known to have abandoned the quest for maximum material advantage" (p. 256). Brown and Brown (2006) make a similar point with respect to selective investments in others.

Sophisticated Mental Abilities

If you asked people to select the mental mechanisms that they consider the most promising sources of altruistic motivation, the top candidates probably would be those that give rise to uniquely human cognitive abilities such as the ability to reason. I have reviewed research demonstrating that primitive impulses and emotional states may dispose people to behave in psychologically altruistic ways. Darwin (1874) suggested that although humans share such instincts and emotions with other animals, humans' unique intellectual abilities enable them to engage in forms of altruism qualitatively different from those displayed by any other animal.

There is no question that as intellectual abilities evolved in the human species, people became better able to understand when others need help and to figure out effective ways of helping them. However, it is unclear whether such "cold" cognitive abilities engender altruistic motives. People could understand that others need help and figure out the best way to help them, but not feel motivated to do anything about it. Damasio (1994) has found that people suffering from certain brain injuries are able fully to understand what they ought to do without experiencing the desire to behave accordingly.

To account for the role that higher mental abilities play in the generation of altruistic motives, we must explain how they interact with more primitive mental mechanisms. De Waal (2008) has advanced a model of the evolution of empathy that offers an exemplary account of the ways in which early-evolved and later-evolved mental mechanisms give rise to psychologically altruistic motives and structure altruistic behaviors.

In de Waal's model, "empathy covers all the ways in which one individual's emotional state affects another's, with simple mechanisms at its core and more complex mechanisms and perspective-taking abilities at its outer layers. Because of the layered nature of the capacities involved, we speak of the Russian doll model, in which higher cognitive levels of empathy build upon a firm, hard-wired basis. . . . [which] serves to motivate behavioral outcomes" (p. 11).

De Waal reviews evidence that animals that lack perspective-taking abilities may experience the distress of others vicariously. However, "for an individual to move beyond being sensitive to others toward an explicit other-orientation requires a shift in perspective. The emotional state induced in oneself by the other now needs to be attributed to the other instead of the self" (de Waal, 2008, p. 9).

De Waal cites evidence that apes, humans, elephants, and dolphins are able to recognize themselves in mirrors, that this ability is correlated with perspective-taking abilities in humans, and that animals that possess self-recognition abilities engage in "targeted helping," defined as "help that is fine-tuned to another's specific situation and goals" (p. 9).

Developmental psychologists have accounted for the acquisition of empathy in a manner that parallels de Waal's evolutionary account. For example, Hoffman (2000) has identified four stages in the acquisition of empathy, mediated by the development of increasingly sophisticated perspective-taking abilities. In the first stage infants are capable only of experiencing "global distress" in response to immediate signs of distress in others, whereas in the last stage adults may experience empathy for disadvantaged groups or classes of people that they have never observed directly. Like de Waal, Hoffman argues that sophisticated forms of empathy are necessary for sophisticated forms of altruism.

■ CONCLUSION

There are two main types of altruism—one defined in terms of the consequences of helping behaviors, and the other defined in terms of the motives and intentions of those who help others. Although some of the consequence-defined types of helping behavior that evolutionary theorists have labeled altruistic are biologically selfish, evolutionary theorists have explained how behaviors that increase the fitness of recipients at a cost to the fitness of actors can evolve through kin selection and gene–culture coevolution. Defined in this manner, we can safely conclude that the capacity to behave in biologically altruistic ways has evolved in the human species, rendering humans conditionally altruistic by nature.

Most people define altruism in terms of the motives and intentions of those who sacrifice their interests for the sake of others. Although the evolved mechanisms that induce people to help others may sometimes—even often—engender instrumentally selfish motives, a growing body of evidence suggests that some of the proximate mechanisms that induce people to help their kin, their friends, those who have helped them, and members of their groups produce genuinely altruistic motives. Following a review of relevant literature, Piliavin and Charng (1990) conclude that a "paradigm shift" has begun in psychology, "away from the earlier position that behavior that appears to be altruistic must, under closer scrutiny, be revealed as reflecting egoistic motives. Rather, theory and data now being advanced are more compatible with the view that true altruism—acting with the goal of benefiting another—does exist and is a part of human nature" (p. 27).

■ REFERENCES

Alexander, R. D. (1987). *The biology of moral systems*. New York, NY: Aldine de Gruyter.

Batson, C. D. (1991). *The altruism question: Toward a social-psychological answer*. Hillsdale, NJ: Erlbaum.

Batson, C. D. (2000). Unto others: A service . . . and a disservice. *Journal of Consciousness Studies, 7*, 207–210.

Brown, S. L., & Brown, M. (2006). Selective investment theory: Recasting the functional significance of close relationships. *Psychological Inquiry, 17,* 30–59.

Burnstein, E. (2005). Altruism and genetic relatedness. In D. Buss (Ed.), *The handbook of evolutionary psychology* (pp. 528–551). Hoboken, NJ: Wiley.

Cialdini, R. B., Schaller, M., Houlihan, D., Arps, J., Fultz, J., & Beaman, A. L. (1987). Empathy-based helping: Is it selflessly or selfishly motivated? *Journal of Personality and Social Psychology, 52,* 749–758.

Clark, M. S., & Mills, J. (1993). The difference between communal and exchange relationships: What it is and is not. *Personality and Social Psychology Bulletin, 19,* 684–691.

Damasio, A. R. (1994). *Decartes' error: Emotion, reason, and the human brain.* New York, NY: Grosset/Putnam.

Darwin, C. (1874). *The descent of man and selection in relation to sex.* New York, NY: Rand, McNally & Company.

Dawes, R., van de Kragt, A. J. C., & Orbell, J. M., (1988). Not me or thee but we: The importance of group identity in eliciting cooperation in dilemma situations: Experimental manipulations. *Acta Psychologica, 68,* 83–97.

de Waal, F. B. M. (2008). Putting the altruism back in altruism. *Annual Review of Psychology, 59,* 279–300.

Ellis, B. J. (1998). The partner-specific investment inventory: An evolutionary approach to individual differences in investment. *Journal of Personality, 66,* 383–442.

Frank, R. H. (2001). Cooperation through emotional commitment. In R. Nesse (Ed.) *Evolution and the capacity for commitment* (pp. 57–76). New York, NY: Russell Sage Foundation.

Hamilton, W. D. (1964). The evolution of social behavior. *Journal of Theoretical Biology, 7,* 1–52.

Hauser, M. D., Chen, M. K., Chen, F., & Chuang, E. (2003). Give unto others: Genetically unrelated cotton-top tamarin monkeys preferentially give food to those who altruistically give food back. *Proceedings of the Royal Society of London. Series B, Biological Sciences 270,* 2363–2370.

Hoffman, M. (2000). *Empathy and moral development: Implications for caring and justice.* Cambridge, UK: Cambridge University Press.

Johnson, D. D. P., Price, M. E., & Takezawa, M. (2008). Renaissance of the individual: Reciprocity, positive assortment, and the puzzle of human cooperation. In C. Crawford & D. L. Krebs (Eds.), *Foundations of Evolutionary Psychology* (pp. 331–352). New York, NY: Taylor & Francis.

Kurland, J. A., & Gaulin, S. J. C. (2005). Cooperation and conflict among kin. In D. Buss (Ed.), *The handbook of evolutionary psychology* (pp. 447–482). Hoboken, NJ: Wiley.

McCullough, M. E. (2008). *Beyond revenge: The evolution of the forgiveness instinct.* San Francisco: Jossey-Bass.

Moll, J., di Oliveira-Souza, R., Zahn, R., & Grafman, J. (2008). The cognitive neuroscience of moral emotions. In W. Sinnott-Armstrong (Ed.), *Moral psychology: The neuroscience of morality: Emotion, brain disorders, and development* (pp. 1–18). Cambride MA: The MIT Press.

Nesse, R. M. (2000). How selfish genes shape moral passions. In L. D. Katz (Ed.), *Evolutionary origins of morality: Cross-disciplinary perspectives* (pp. 227–231). Thorverton, UK: Imprint Academic.

Nesse, R. M. (2001). (Ed.), *Evolution and the capacity for commitment* . New York, NY: Russell Sage Foundation.

Piliavin, J., & Charng, H. (1990). Altruism—A review of recent theory and research. *Annual Review of Sociology, 16,* 27–65.

Piliavin, J. A., Dovidio, J. F., Gaertner, S. L., & Clark, R. D. (1981). *Emergency intervention*. New York, NY: Academic Press.

Richerson, P. J., & Boyd, R. (2001). The evolution of subjective commitment: A tribal instincts hypothesis. In R. Nesse (Ed.) *Evolution and the capacity for commitment* (pp. 186–219). New York, NY: Russell Sage Foundation.

Richerson, P. J., & Boyd, R. (2005). *Not by genes alone: How culture transformed human evolution*. Chicago, IL: University of Chicago Press.

Shackelford, T. K., & Buss, D. M. (1996). Betrayal in mateships, friendships, and coalitions. *Personality and Social Psychology Bulletin, 22*, 1151–1164.

Sime, J. D. (1983). Affiliative behavior during escape to building exits. *Journal of Experimental Psychology, 3*, 21–41.

Simpson, J. A., & Campbell, L. (2005). Methods of evolutionary sciences. In D. M. Buss (Ed.), *The handbook of evolutionary psychology* (pp. 119–144). Hoboken, NJ: Wiley.

Sober, E., & Wilson, D. S. (1998). *Unto others: The evolution and psychology of unselfish behavior*. Cambridge, MA: Harvard University Press.

Tajfel, H., & Turner, J. C. (1985). The social identity theory of intergroup behavior. In S. Worchel & W. G. Austin (Eds.), *Psychology of intergroup relations* (pp. 7–24). Chicago: Nelson-Hall.

Tooby, J., & Cosmides, L. (1996). Friendship and the banker's paradox: Other pathways to the evolution of adaptations for altruism. *Proceedings of the British Academy, 88*, 119–143.

Trivers, R. L. (1971). The evolution of reciprocal altruism. *Quarterly Review of Biology, 46*, 35–57.

Trivers, R. (1985). *Social evolution*. Menlo Park, CA: Benjamin Cummings.

Trivers, R. (2002). *Natural selection and social theory: Selected papers of Robert Trivers*. Oxford, UK: Oxford University Press.

Trivers, R. (2006). Reciprocal altruism: 30 years later. In P. M. Kapeler & C. P. van Schaik (Eds.), *Cooperation in primates and humans* (pp. 67–84). New York, NY: Springer-Verlag.

Wang, X. T. (2002). A kith-and-kin rationality in risky choices: Empirical examinations and theoretical modeling. In F. Salter (Ed.), *Risky transactions: Trust, kinship, and ethnicity* (pp. 47–70). Oxford, UK: Berghahn.

3 Adult Attachment and Caregiving

Individual Differences in Providing a Safe Haven and Secure Base to Others

■ MARIO MIKULINCER AND PHILLIP R. SHAVER

Over the past two decades, we have been working to develop Bowlby's (1982) and Ainsworth's (Ainsworth, Blehar, Waters, & Wall, 1978) attachment theory into a general theory of adult personality and behavior in social relationships (see Mikulincer & Shaver, 2007, for a review). Attachment theory was first developed as a way of understanding human infants' emotional attachments to their parents and other caregivers, and the first measures of individual differences in attachment behavior were designed to study infant–mother interactions in the laboratory. Several investigators subsequently developed ways to assess attachment patterns and states of mind in adults (e.g., Hazan & Shaver, 1987, with numerous replications and extensions reviewed by Mikulincer & Shaver, 2007; see Hesse, 2008, on the Adult Attachment Interview). Meanwhile, attachment theory itself has been greatly expanded to address issues that have arisen in studies of adults.

While we were extending Bowlby's theory into the realm of adult attachment, the Fetzer Institute, a private foundation, issued a call in 2001 for research proposals on compassion and altruism. We became aware of this request while one of us (Mikulincer) was in the process of publishing a multistudy paper on attachment security and compassionate responses to others' suffering in the *Journal of Personality and Social Psychology* (Mikulincer et al., 2001) and the other (Shaver) was exploring the meaning of compassion and loving-kindness in Buddhist writings. This synchronicity encouraged us to write a research proposal on attachment, compassion, and altruism which resulted in a three-year research project, several articles and book chapters, and a theoretical elaboration of Bowlby's original conception of the caregiving behavioral system. We have since gone on to study social motivation more generally in terms of parallel behavioral systems in the domains of attachment, exploration, caregiving, affiliation, sex, and power (Mikulincer & Shaver, 2006).

In this essay we focus on what we have learned about the two behavioral systems that govern support seeking and support provision: the attachment and caregiving systems. Bowlby (1982) hypothesized that the attachment system governs one person's (e.g., an infant's) reliance on another person (e.g., a parent) for protection and support, especially when the former feels fear or needs help. Bowlby hypothesized that the caregiving system is the motivational heart of a parent's (or other adult's) response to a child's distress or need for support or assistance. In our opinion (and the opinions of influential theorists such as Batson, 2010), this system is also the core of all empathic, compassionate reactions to another person's needs (Shaver, Mikulincer, & Shemesh-Iron, 2010).

We begin by explaining the behavioral system construct in more detail and show how individual differences in a person's attachment system affect the functioning of the caregiving system. We review examples from the literature on attachment, focusing on what attachment theorists call providing a "safe haven" for others in distress. We then describe the few studies that have addressed how individual differences in attachment affect what theorists call providing a "secure base" for others' exploration and self-development. Finally, we outline some new studies on this issue.

■ A BEHAVIORAL SYSTEMS PERSPECTIVE ON ATTACHMENT AND CAREGIVING

Although Bowlby (1973, 1980, 1982), the originator of attachment theory, focused primarily on the formation of attachment bonds in childhood, he also suggested how evolution has shaped brain mechanisms that govern other kinds of human behavior (e.g., exploration, parental caregiving, and sexual mating). In the process he borrowed from ethology the concept of *behavioral system*, a species-specific neural program that organizes an individual's behavior in ways that increase the likelihood of survival and reproductive success. Each behavioral system is organized around a particular goal (e.g., attaining a sense of security or learning about a novel object or aspect of the environment) and includes a set of interchangeable, functionally equivalent behaviors that constitute the *primary strategy* of the system for attaining its goal (e.g., proximity seeking or empathically understanding another person's needs). These behaviors are automatically triggered, or "activated," by stimuli or situations that make a particular goal salient (e.g., loud noises that signal danger). The behaviors are terminated, or "deactivated," by other stimuli or outcomes that signal attainment of the desired goal. Each behavioral system also includes cognitive operations that facilitate goal attainment and excitatory and inhibitory neurological links with other systems.

Bowlby (1973) believed that although behavioral systems are innate, experience shapes their parameters and strategies in various ways, resulting in systematic individual differences. According to Bowlby, the residues of such experiences are stored in the form of *working models of self and others*—mental representations that guide future attempts to attain a behavioral system's goal. With repeated use, these models become automatic and are important sources of within-person continuity in behavioral system functioning throughout development.

The Attachment Behavioral System

Bowlby (1982) stated that the biological function of the attachment system is to protect individuals (especially during infancy and childhood, but later in life as well) from danger by assuring that they maintain proximity to loving and supportive others (*attachment figures*). The proximal goal of the system is to attain a subjective sense of protection or security (called "felt security" in an influential paper by Sroufe & Waters, 1977), which normally terminates the system's activation. The goal of attaining security is made salient by perceived threats and dangers, which drive people to seek actual or symbolic proximity to attachment figures. According to Ainsworth et al. (1978), during infancy, attachment system activation includes nonverbal expressions of need and desire for proximity, as well as observable behavior aimed at restoring and maintaining actual proximity. In our extension of the theory to adult attachment (Mikulincer & Shaver, 2004), the primary attachment strategies in adulthood do not necessarily involve actual proximity-seeking behavior, but can also include conscious or unconscious mental representations of past experiences with supportive attachment figures, which we have been able to measure in various ways.

An abiding inner sense of attachment security (based on actual experiences) promotes general faith in other people's good will; a sense of being loved, esteemed, understood, and accepted by relationship partners; and optimistic beliefs about one's ability to handle frustration and distress. Bowlby (1988) considered attachment security to be a mainstay of mental health and social adjustment throughout life. A host of cross-sectional and longitudinal studies support this view (see J. A. Feeney, 2008, and Mikulincer & Shaver, 2007, for reviews).

However, when attachment figures are not reliably available, responsive, and supportive, individuals fail to attain a sense of attachment security and are likely to construct negative working models, experience heightened worries about self-protection and lovability, and adopt strategies of affect regulation (which Cassidy & Kobak, 1988, called *secondary attachment strategies*) other than appropriate proximity seeking. Attachment theorists (e.g., Cassidy & Kobak, 1988; Mikulincer & Shaver, 2007) emphasize two such secondary strategies: hyperactivation and deactivation of the attachment system. Hyperactivation is manifested in energetic attempts to gain greater proximity, support, and protection, combined with a lack of confidence that it will be provided. Deactivation of the system involves inhibition of proximity-seeking tendencies, denial of attachment needs, maintenance of emotional and cognitive distance from others, and compulsive reliance on oneself as the only dependable source of comfort and protection.

When studying these secondary strategies during adolescence and adulthood, attachment researchers have focused mainly on a person's *attachment style*—the chronic pattern of relational cognitions and behaviors that results from a particular history of attachment experiences (Fraley & Shaver, 2000). Initially, attachment research was based on Ainsworth et al.'s (1978) three-category typology of attachment patterns in infancy—secure, anxious, and avoidant—and on Hazan and Shaver's (1987) conceptualization of similar adult styles in romantic relationships. Subsequent studies (e.g., Brennan, Clark, & Shaver, 1998) revealed, however, that attachment styles are more appropriately conceptualized as regions in a two-dimensional space. The first dimension, *avoidant attachment*, reflects the extent to which people distrust their relationship partners' good will, deactivate their own attachment systems, and strive to maintain behavioral independence and emotional distance from partners. The second dimension, *anxious attachment*, reflects the degree to which people worry that their partners will not be available in times of need and therefore engage overzealously in proximity seeking. People who score low on both insecurity dimensions are said to be secure or securely attached. The two dimensions can be measured with reliable and valid self-report scales and are associated in theoretically predictable ways with mental health, adjustment, and relationship quality (Mikulincer & Shaver, 2007).

The Caregiving Behavioral System

Bowlby (1982) asserted that human beings are born with a capacity to provide protection and support to others who are either chronically dependent or temporarily in need. These behaviors, he said, are organized by a caregiving behavioral system. This system emerged over the long course of evolution because it increased the inclusive fitness (Hamilton, 1964) of humans by increasing the likelihood that children, siblings, and tribe members with whom a person shared genes would survive to reproductive age and produce and rear viable offspring. According to this logic, the proliferation of individuals' genes depends not only on their own reproductive success (based on transmitting genes through sexual reproduction) but also on the extent to which others who share copies of their genes reproduce.

Although the caregiving system presumably evolved primarily to increase the viability of an individual's own offspring and close relatives, it may also have been more generally adapted to respond to the needs of other tribe members. Today, through educational elaboration, it can be extended to include genuine concern for anyone in need. Although most of us probably care more, and more easily, for people to whom we are closely related, either psychologically or genetically, we can direct our caregiving efforts to all suffering human beings. Just as attachment-related motives, once they became universally present in our psychological repertoire, can affect a wide variety of social processes, caregiving motives can be applied more broadly than to one's immediate genetic relatives.

Following this reasoning, we (Shaver et al., 2010) proposed that if a person's caregiving system develops under favorable social circumstances, then compassion, empathy, loving-kindness, and generosity become common reactions to other people's needs. However, if the caregiving system develops under unfavorable circumstances, such as an absence of parental modeling, training, and support or interactions with parents that engender insecurities and worries, a child is likely to become less compassionate and less empathic to other people's needs and suffering.

Bowlby (1982) described the goal of the caregiving system as reducing other people's suffering, protecting them from harm, and fostering their growth and development (e.g., Collins, Guichard, Ford, & Feeney, 2006; George & Solomon, 2008; Gillath, Shaver, & Mikulincer, 2005). That is, the system is designed to serve two major functions: to meet another person's needs for protection and support in times of danger or distress (Bowlby called this "providing a safe haven"), and to support others' exploration, autonomy, and growth when exploration is safe and desirable (Bowlby called this "providing a secure base for exploration"). From this perspective, the goal of the care seeker's attachment system—to maintain a safe haven and secure base—is also the aim of the care provider's caregiving system. When a caregiver's behavioral system is activated by a person who needs help, the system's primary strategy is to perceive the needy individual's problem accurately and provide effective help. When this help is successful, the caregiver's caregiving system is satisfied and, for the moment, deactivated.

According to Collins et al. (2006), the caregiving system is likely to be activated (a) when another person seeks help in coping with danger, stress, or discomfort (safe-haven needs), or (b) when someone needs or can use help with projects or tasks that might increase the person's knowledge, skills, and personal development (secure-base needs or goals). In either case, effective caregiving involves accurate empathy and empathic concern for another person's feelings, needs, and projects. Collins et al. described optimal caregiving in terms of two qualities emphasized by previous attachment researchers (e.g., Ainsworth et al., 1978): sensitivity (being attuned to and accurately interpreting others' signals of need) and responsiveness (validating others' needs, perceptions, and feelings; respecting their beliefs and values; and providing useful assistance and support; Reis & Shaver, 1988).

Although Bowlby (1982) assumed that everyone is born with the potential to become an effective care provider, the functioning of the caregiving system depends on several factors. Effective caregiving can be impaired by feelings, beliefs, and concerns that dampen or conflict with motivation to help or with sensitivity and responsiveness. It can also be impaired by deficits in social skills, fatigue, and problems in emotion regulation that cause caregivers to feel overwhelmed by a needy other's pain or to wish to distance themselves physically, emotionally, or cognitively from the person's problems and distress (Collins et al., 2006).

Interplay of the Attachment and Caregiving Systems

Bowlby (1982) noticed that activation of the attachment system can interfere with the caregiving system. Potential caregivers may feel that obtaining safety and care for themselves is more urgent than providing a safe haven or secure base for others. At such times, people are likely to be so focused on their own vulnerability that they lack the mental resources to attend sensitively to others' needs. Only when a sense of attachment security is restored can a potential caregiver perceive others to be not only potential sources of security and support but worthy human beings who themselves need and deserve sympathy and support.

Reasoning along these lines, attachment theorists (e.g., Gillath, Shaver, & Mikulincer, 2005; Kunce & Shaver, 1994; Mikulincer & Shaver, 2007; Shaver & Hazan, 1988) hypothesized that attachment security provides an important foundation for optimal caregiving. Moreover, being secure implies (given the theory) that a person has witnessed, experienced, and benefited from effective care by generous attachment figures, which provides a model to follow when occupying the caregiving role. And because secure individuals are comfortable with intimacy and interdependence (Hazan & Shaver, 1987), they can allow other people to approach them for help and express feelings of vulnerability and need (Lehman, Ellard, & Wortman, 1986). Secure individuals' confidence concerning other people's good will makes it easier for them to construe others as deserving sympathy and support, and their positive model of self allows them to feel confident about their ability to handle another person's needs while effectively regulating their own emotions. (See Eisenberg, 2010, for evidence that emotional dysregulation in the face of another's suffering is one cause of inadequate helping.)

Individuals with an anxious or avoidant attachment style are likely to have difficulty providing effective care (Collins et al., 2006; George & Solomon, 2008; Shaver & Hazan, 1988). Although those who suffer from attachment anxiety may have some of the qualities necessary for effective caregiving (e.g., willingness to experience and express emotions and comfort with psychological intimacy and physical closeness), their habitual focus on their own distress and unsatisfied attachment needs may siphon important mental resources away from attending accurately and consistently to others' needs. Moreover, their strong desire for closeness and approval may cause them to become intrusive or overly involved, blurring the distinction between another person's welfare and their own. Attachment anxiety can color caregiving motives with egoistic desires for acceptance, approval, and gratitude, which can impair sensitivity and lead to what Kunce and Shaver (1994) called *compulsive caregiving.*

Avoidant individuals' lack of comfort with closeness and negative working models of other people may also interfere with optimal caregiving. Their discomfort with expressions of need and dependence may cause them to back away rather than get involved with someone whose needs are strongly expressed. As a result, avoidant individuals may attempt to detach themselves emotionally and physically from needy others, feel superior to those who are vulnerable or distressed, or experience disdainful pity rather than empathic concern. In some cases, avoidant people's cynical or hostile attitudes and negative models of others (Mikulincer & Shaver, 2007) may transform sympathy or compassion into schadenfreude, or gloating.

In the remainder of this chapter, we review studies that test these theoretical ideas about the interplay of attachment and caregiving motives and processes. Most of the studies focus on ways in which attachment security or insecurity shapes a person's responses to others' distress. Less research has focused on ways in which attachment insecurities may bias responses to someone who could use support for exploration and personal development. That is, we know more about the effects of attachment-related processes on providing a safe haven for someone in need than we know about their effects on providing a secure base for a person's pursuit of goals other than safety. In the next section, we briefly review evidence concerning links between attachment insecurities and the provision of a safe haven for others. We then present past and new research findings concerning associations between attachment insecurities and the provision of a secure base for others' pursuit of goals other than safety.

■ ATTACHMENT INSECURITIES AND INADEQUATE PROVISION OF A SAFE HAVEN

Research has confirmed that attachment insecurities interfere with providing a safe haven for someone in distress. In the parent–child domain, for example, Belsky, Rovine, and Taylor (1984) found that avoidant mothers responded much less supportively than secure mothers when their infants were distressed and needed comforting. In a study of maternal sensitivity, Haft and Slade (1989) found that secure mothers were more attuned to their babies' needs than were insecure mothers. Avoidant mothers ignored their infants' negative affect, and anxious mothers attuned inconsistently to their infants' negative affect. These different reactions are thought by attachment theorists to be two of the main causes of the infants' specific kinds of insecure attachment. The avoidant infants have been discouraged from expressing needs, and anxious infants have been rewarded, on a partial reinforcement schedule, for strident expressions of need that capture their mothers' unreliable attention.

Crowell and Feldman (1991) video-recorded mothers' behavior when their children were exposed to an attachment-related threat—separation from mother in a laboratory setting. Secure mothers (assessed with the Adult Attachment Interview; see Hesse, 2008) were more affectionate toward their children and prepared them better for the separation than insecure mothers did. Moreover, whereas avoidant mothers showed little emotion toward their children, anxious mothers were highly distressed, making it more difficult for their children to recover from the separation. In another example of an opportunity for parents to provide a safe haven for their children, Goodman, Quas, Batterman-Faunce, Riddlesberger, and Kuhn (1997) asked parents to describe their interactions with their children after the children had just undergone a threatening and painful medical procedure. Secure parents (assessed with a self-report questionnaire) were more likely than insecure parents to physically comfort the child and discuss the procedure thoroughly. In a related study, Edelstein et al. (2004) videotaped parents' behavior when their children received an inoculation at an immunization clinic. More avoidant parents, as measured with a self-report scale, were coded by judges as less responsive to their distressed children than secure ones.

Attachment-related individual differences in providing a safe haven for dating partners or spouses have also been studied. Several investigators have found that secure individuals are more likely than their anxious or avoidant counterparts to provide safe-haven support to a partner in distress (e.g., B. C. Feeney & Collins, 2001; J. A. Feeney, 1996; J. A. Feeney & Hohaus, 2001; Kunce & Shaver, 1994). Moreover, individuals who score high on anxious attachment also score higher on measures of compulsive caregiving, reflecting their over involvement with partners' problems and their tendency to create more problems for partners rather than solve the one at hand (e.g., Kunce & Shaver, 1994).

Insecure people's nonoptimal care for romantic or dating partners has also been observed in laboratory experiments (e.g., Collins & Feeney, 2000; B. C. Feeney & Collins, 2001; Rholes, Simpson, & Orina, 1999; Simpson, Rholes, & Nelligan, 1992; Simpson, Rholes, Orina, & Grich, 2002). For example, Simpson et al. (1992) unobtrusively videotaped dating couples while the female member of each couple waited to undergo a stressful procedure. Secure men noticed their partners' worries and provided more emotional support and more supportive verbal comments when their partners showed higher levels of distress. In contrast, men who scored high on avoidance actually provided less support when their partners' distress increased. Collins and Feeney (2000) videotaped dating couples while one member of the couple disclosed a personal problem to the other. Among participants who were assigned the role of caregiver (listening to a partner's disclosures), the attachment-anxious ones were coded by judges as less supportive, less responsive, and more negative toward the distressed partner than participants who scored low on attachment anxiety.

There is also evidence that the effects of attachment security on the provision of a safe haven extend beyond close relationships and can be observed in reactions to needy and distressed strangers. For example, Mikulincer et al. (2001) found that experimentally heightening the sense of attachment security (e.g., by subliminally presenting names of security-enhancing attachment figures on a computer screen) increased compassionate responses to a suffering other. They also found that whereas higher scores on avoidant attachment were negatively associated with empathic reactions to others' suffering, higher scores on the anxiety dimension were associated with reports of greater personal distress.

Mikulincer, Shaver, Gillath, and Nitzberg (2005, Studies 1 and 2) examined the decision to help or not help a person in distress. Participants watched a confederate while she performed a series of aversive tasks. As the study progressed, the confederate appeared to become increasingly distressed, and participants were given an opportunity to take her place, in effect sacrificing themselves for the welfare of another. Shortly before being exposed to the confederate's seeming distress, participants were primed with representations of attachment security (the name of a participant's security provider) or neutral representations (the name of a familiar person who was not an attachment figure). As compared to the neutral priming manipulations, security priming increased participants' self-reports of compassion and willingness to take the distressed person's place. No interaction was found between security priming and participants' attachment orientations.

■ ATTACHMENT INSECURITIES AND INADEQUATE PROVISION OF A SECURE BASE

The studies reviewed in the previous section, as well as others we do not have space to describe, clearly indicate that attachment insecurities, as predicted, interfere with the sensitive and effective provision of safety, support, and comfort to others who are distressed and in need. As mentioned, effective caregivers should also, according to attachment theory, be able to support other people's exploration and personal growth or development. According to Bowlby (1988), an important part of effective caregiving is the provision of a secure base from which another person can "make sorties into the outside world" (p. 11) with confidence that he or she can return for assistance and comfort should obstacles arise. A secure base can allow a person to take sensible risks, engage in challenging activities, and pursue new goals. There is accumulating evidence that the provision of a secure base has beneficial effects on recipients' mental heath and social adjustment (e.g., Deci, La Guardia, Moller, Scheiner, & Ryan, 2006; B. C. Feeney, 2004; Schultheiss, Kress, Manzi, & Glasscock, 2001; Vansteenkiste, Simons, Lens, Sheldon, & Deci, 2004).

Do attachment insecurities hamper the provision of a secure base? Are insecurely attached individuals less willing or able to provide a secure base for others' exploration, autonomy, and growth? Recent findings from our and others' laboratories are beginning to suggest that attachment insecurities—anxiety and avoidance—do interfere with providing a secure base for an interaction partner's exploration.

In an unpublished study, B. C. Feeney (2005) asked participants to complete self-report scales tapping attachment insecurities, provision of a secure base to a dating partner, and motives for providing (or not providing) a secure base to the partner. More avoidant people reported being less available and responsive when their dating partners engaged in exploratory activities or pursued important personal goals, whereas more anxious people reported more intrusive behavior that interfered with a partner's exploratory activities. In addition, avoidant people reported more egoistic reasons for providing a secure base (e.g., to get something explicit in return), and their reasons for not helping reflected their aversion to interdependence (e.g., not wanting to be responsible for the partner or not wanting to encourage the partner's dependence). Anxiously attached adults gave egoistic reasons for helping—reasons that reflected unmet desires for closeness and security (e.g., to gain a partner's approval or to increase the partner's commitment to the relationship). When asked why they sometimes chose not to provide a secure base for their partners, anxious individuals attributed their reluctance to worries that the partners' independent pursuits might weaken the relationship.

In a recent series of studies conducted in collaboration with us, Sofer-Roth (2008) assessed attachment-related differences in responses to romantic partners' disclosure of their happiness, successes, and achievements. In the first study, Sofer-Roth examined relations between attachment insecurities and ways in which people reacted to a partner's happiness. For this purpose, 160 Israeli undergraduates (91 women and 69 men), each of whom was involved in a romantic relationship, completed the Experiences in Close Relationships inventory (ECR; Brennan et al., 1998), which measures attachment anxiety and avoidance, and a 29-item scale created specifically for this study to assess responses to a partner's happiness. Participants were asked to recall a specific situation in which their partners told them or expressed happiness about successes or achievements, and to rate the extent to which they reacted with each of the feelings, thoughts, and behaviors described in the scale. The 29 items were generated in a previous study in which 48 Israeli undergraduates answered open-ended questions about their reactions to a romantic partner's happiness.

A factor analysis revealed that the 29 items could be organized in terms of four factors, which together accounted for 53.8% of the item variance. The first factor included 11 items tapping secure-base provisions (e.g., "I admired him/her for how successful he/she was," "I complimented and praised him/her"). The second factor included 8 items indicating jealousy (e.g., "I was jealous because I wasn't a part of the happy event"), fear (e.g., "I was afraid that I would have to struggle or compete for his/her time"), and insecurity (e.g., "I felt less confident about the future of our relationship"). The third factor included 5 items indicating disapproval or criticism (e.g., "I expressed my feeling that it wasn't such a happy event," "My reaction ruined his/her happiness"), and the fourth factor included 5 items indicating envy (e.g., "I felt inferior to my partner," "Somehow it didn't seem fair that he/she has all the talents or luck").

Avoidant attachment correlated negatively with the secure-base provision factor and positively with the envy factor. Although attachment anxiety was not inversely associated with providing a secure base, it was positively related to disapproval/criticism, jealousy/fear, and envy. That is, both forms of attachment insecurity predisposed people to react in ways that could be expected to reduce a partner's happiness and discourage further exploration. These associations remained significant after controlling for relationship satisfaction, so they seem to be reflections of the participants' attachment patterns, not of their relationships.

In a second study, Sofer-Roth (2008) examined whether the observed attachment-related differences also affect marital relationships and can be extended beyond general self-reports to behavioral observations of couple interactions and to daily reactions to a partner's expressions of happiness. Sofer-Roth asked members of 55 newlywed couples to independently complete the ECR inventory, participate in a video-recorded laboratory interaction, and complete daily diary questionnaires.

For the video-recorded interaction, one partner (the *disclosing* partner) completed a battery of personality tests and received feedback that he or she was highly competent in abstract thinking, responsibility/accountability, adaptability, and coping resources. Following this positive feedback, the disclosing partner was reunited with his or her partner, and the couple was asked to wait alone in a room for 5 minutes. During this time their interaction was video-recorded, and later two judges independently rated (a) the extent to which disclosing partners expressed happiness about the positive feedback they received and (b) the extent to which their partners listened attentively to the disclosures and expressed happiness, admiration, boredom, criticism, or envy. Results indicated that after the disclosing partner's expressed happiness was statistically controlled for, avoidant participants were rated as more bored and less likely to listen attentively to the disclosing partner or express happiness and admiration. Anxious participants reacted to partners' disclosures of happiness with envy.

Partners also independently completed a diary questionnaire each evening for 14 days. Each indicated independently whether something good (outside of the relationship itself) had happened that day to the other partner that caused that partner to feel good. If such an event had occurred, participants provided a brief description of it and rated their responses to their partners' good moods using 20 of the 29 items from the questionnaire described earlier. The findings were compatible with those from the more general questionnaire study. More avoidant participants were less likely to provide a daily secure base for their partners, and more anxious participants were more likely to react with disapproval/criticism, jealousy/fear, and envy. These patterns appeared for both husbands and wives and remained statistically significant even after controlling for relationship satisfaction and other traits (e.g., self-esteem, neuroticism, and extroversion).

■ CONCLUDING REMARKS

Attachment theory and research make a compelling case for viewing caregiving motivation and behavior in terms of one of several behavioral systems proposed by Bowlby (1982) in his comprehensive framework for studying social motives and close social relationships. Because he was primarily interested, as were his psychoanalytic contemporaries, in parent–child relationships, he viewed the attachment behavioral system mostly in terms of its observable features in infants and young children. And he viewed the caregiving behavioral system mostly in terms of its observable features (and concomitant subjective states) in parents of infants and young children.

One of our goals has been to extend Bowlby's conceptions of these two behavioral systems into a framework for studying motives and behavior in close relationships of all kinds across the life span. In the present chapter, we have shown how the attachment and caregiving systems interrelate and how individual differences in attachment affect caregiving of two kinds—providing a safe haven for a person in distress and providing a secure base for another's exploration and personal development. The findings to date raise interesting applied questions: Would interventions designed to increase attachment security cause parents, teachers, physicians, nurses, and therapists to be more compassionate and effective caregivers? Should professional caregivers and foster parents be screened for attachment security? The findings encourage us to pursue several additional issues, such as the contribution of secure interactions with parents during infancy and early childhood to the development of empathy, compassion, and effective caregiving; the personality and situational barriers that may interfere with the beneficial effects of security on caregiving; and the beneficial effects of good caregiving on the functioning of a person's attachment system and the creation of mutually satisfying close relationships.

■ REFERENCES

Ainsworth, M. D. S., Blehar, M. C., Waters, E., & Wall, S. (1978). *Patterns of attachment: Assessed in the Strange Situation and at home.* Hillsdale, NJ: Erlbaum.

Batson, C. D. (2010). Empathy-induced altruistic motivation. In M. Mikulincer & P. R. Shaver (Eds.), *Prosocial motives, emotions, and behavior: The better angels of our nature* (pp. 15–34). Washington, DC: American Psychological Association.

Belsky, J., Rovine, M., & Taylor, D. C. (1984). The Pennsylvania Infant and Family Development Project: II. The development of reciprocal interactions in the mother–infant dyad. *Child Development, 48,* 706–717.

Bowlby, J. (1973). *Attachment and loss: Vol. 2. Separation: Anxiety and anger.* New York: Basic Books.

Bowlby, J. (1980). *Attachment and loss: Vol. 3. Sadness and depression.* New York: Basic Books.

Bowlby, J. (1982). *Attachment and loss: Vol. 1. Attachment* (2nd ed.). New York: Basic Books. (Orig. ed. 1969)

Bowlby, J. (1988). *A secure base: Clinical applications of attachment theory.* London: Routledge.

Brennan, K. A., Clark, C. L., & Shaver, P. R. (1998). Self-report measurement of adult attachment: An integrative overview. In J. A. Simpson & W. S. Rholes (Eds.), *Attachment theory and close relationships* (pp. 46–76). New York: Guilford Press.

Cassidy, J., & Kobak, R. R. (1988). Avoidance and its relationship with other defensive processes. In J. Belsky & T. Nezworski (Eds.), *Clinical implications of attachment* (pp. 300–323). Hillsdale, NJ: Erlbaum.

Collins, N. L., & Feeney, B. C. (2000). A safe haven: An attachment theory perspective on support seeking and caregiving in intimate relationships. *Journal of Personality and Social Psychology, 78,* 1053–1073.

Collins, N. L., Guichard, A. C., Ford, M. B., & Feeney, B. C. (2006). Responding to need in intimate relationships: Normative processes and individual differences. In M. Mikulincer & G. S. Goodman (Eds.), *Dynamics of romantic love: Attachment, caregiving, and sex* (pp. 149–189). New York: Guilford Press.

Crowell, J. A., & Feldman, S. S. (1991). Mothers' working models of attachment relationships and mother and child behavior during separation and reunion. *Developmental Psychology, 27,* 597–605.

Deci, E. L., La Guardia, J. G., Moller, A. C., Scheiner, M. J., & Ryan, R. M. (2006). On the benefits of giving as well as receiving autonomy support: Mutuality in close friendships. *Personality and Social Psychology Bulletin, 32,* 313–327.

Edelstein, R. S., Alexander, K. W., Shaver, P. R., Schaaf, J. M., Quas, J. A., Lovas, G. S., & Goodman, G. S. (2004). Adult attachment style and parental responsiveness during a stressful event. *Attachment and Human Development, 6,* 31–52.

Eisenberg, N. (2010). Empathy-related responding: Links with self-regulation, moral judgment, and moral behavior. In M. Mikulincer & P. R. Shaver (Eds.), *Prosocial motives, emotions, and behavior: The better angels of our nature* (pp. 129–148). Washington, DC: American Psychological Association.

Feeney, B. C. (2004). A secure base: Responsive support of goal strivings and exploration in adult intimate relationships. *Journal of Personality and Social Psychology, 87,* 631–648.

Feeney, B. C. (2005). *Individual differences in secure base support provision: The role of attachment style, relationship characteristics, and underlying motivations.* Unpublished manuscript, Carnegie Mellon University, Pittsburgh, PA.

Feeney, B. C., & Collins, N. L. (2001). Predictors of caregiving in adult intimate relationships: An attachment theoretical perspective. *Journal of Personality and Social Psychology, 80,* 972–994.

Feeney, J. A. (1996). Attachment, caregiving, and marital satisfaction. *Personal Relationships, 3,* 401–416.

Feeney, J. A. (2008). Adult romantic attachment: Developments in the study of couple relationships. In J. Cassidy & P. R. Shaver (Eds.), *Handbook of attachment: Theory, research, and clinical applications* (2nd edition, pp. 456–481). New York: Guilford Press.

Feeney, J. A., & Hohaus, L. (2001). Attachment and spousal caregiving. *Personal Relationships, 8,* 21–39.

Fraley, R. C., & Shaver, P. R. (2000). Adult romantic attachment: Theoretical developments, emerging controversies, and unanswered questions. *Review of General Psychology, 4,* 132–154.

Fredrickson, B. L. (2001). The role of positive emotions in positive psychology: The broaden-and-build theory of positive emotions. *American Psychologist, 56,* 218–226.

George, C., & Solomon, J. (2008). The caregiving system: A behavioral-system approach to parenting. In J. Cassidy & P. R. Shaver (Eds.), *Handbook of attachment: Theory, research, and clinical applications* (2nd edition, pp. 833–856). New York: Guilford Press.

Gillath, O., Shaver, P. R., & Mikulincer, M. (2005). An attachment-theoretical approach to compassion and altruism. In P. Gilbert (Ed.), *Compassion: Conceptualizations, research, and use in psychotherapy* (pp. 121–147). London: Brunner-Routledge.

Goodman, G. S., Quas, J. A., Batterman-Faunce, J. M., Riddlesberger, M. M., & Kuhn, J. (1997). Children's reactions to and memory for a stressful event: Influences of age, anatomical dolls, knowledge, and parental attachment. *Applied Developmental Science, 1,* 54–75.

Haft, W., & Slade, A. (1989). Affect attunement and maternal attachment: A pilot study. *Infant Mental Health Journal, 10,* 157–172.

Hamilton, W. D. (1964). The genetic evolution of social behavior. *Journal of Theoretical Biology, 7,* 1–52.

Hazan, C., & Shaver, P. R. (1987). Romantic love conceptualized as an attachment process. *Journal of Personality and Social Psychology, 52,* 511–524.

Hesse, E. (2008). The Adult Attachment Interview: Protocol, method of analysis, and empirical studies. In J. Cassidy & P. R. Shaver (Eds.), *Handbook of attachment: Theory, research, and clinical applications* (2nd ed., pp. 552–598). New York: Guilford Press.

Kunce, L. J., & Shaver, P. R. (1994). An attachment-theoretical approach to caregiving in romantic relationships. In K. Bartholomew & D. Perlman (Eds.), *Advances in personal relationships* (Vol. 5, pp. 205–237). London, England: Kingsley.

Lehman, D. R., Ellard, J. H., & Wortman, C. B. (1986). Social support for the bereaved: Recipients' and providers' perspectives of what is helpful. *Journal of Consulting and Clinical Psychology, 54,* 438–446.

Main, M., Kaplan, N., & Cassidy, J. (1985). Security in infancy, childhood, and adulthood: A move to the level of representation. *Monographs of the Society for Research in Child Development, 50,* 66–104.

Mikulincer, M., Gillath, O., Halevy, V., Avihou, N., Avidan, S., & Eshkoli, N. (2001). Attachment theory and reactions to others' needs: Evidence that activation of the sense of attachment security promotes empathic responses. *Journal of Personality and Social Psychology, 81,* 1205–1224.

Mikulincer, M., & Shaver, P. R. (2004). Security-based self-representations in adulthood: Contents and processes. In W. S. Rholes & J. A. Simpson (Eds.), *Adult attachment: Theory, research, and clinical implications* (pp. 159–195). New York: Guilford Press.

Mikulincer, M., & Shaver, P. R. (2006). The behavioral systems construct: A useful tool for building an integrative model of the social mind. In P. A. M. van Lange (Ed.), *Bridging social psychology* (pp. 279–284). Mahwah, NJ: Erlbaum.

Mikulincer, M., & Shaver, P. R. (2007). *Attachment in adulthood: Structure, dynamics, and change.* New York: Guilford Press.

Mikulincer, M., Shaver, P. R., Gillath, O., & Nitzberg, R. A. (2005). Attachment, caregiving, and altruism: Boosting attachment security increases compassion and helping. *Journal of Personality and Social Psychology, 89,* 817–839.

Reis, H. T., & Shaver, P. R. (1988). Intimacy as an interpersonal process. In S. Duck (Ed.), *Handbook of research in personal relationships* (pp. 367–389). London: Wiley.

Rholes, W. S., Simpson, J. A., & Orina, M. M. (1999). Attachment and anger in an anxiety-provoking situation. *Journal of Personality and Social Psychology, 76,* 940–957.

Schultheiss, D. E. P., Kress, H. M., Manzi, A. J., & Glasscock, J. M. J. (2001). Relational influences in career development: A qualitative inquiry. *Counseling Psychologist, 29,* 214–239.

Shaver, P. R., & Hazan, C. (1988). A biased overview of the study of love. *Journal of Social and Personal Relationships, 5,* 473–501.

Shaver, P. R., & Mikulincer, M. (2002). Attachment-related psychodynamics. *Attachment and Human Development* [Special Issue: The psychodynamics of adult attachments: Bridging the gap between disparate research traditions], *4,* 133–161.

Shaver, P. R., Mikulincer, M., & Shemesh-Iron, M. (2010). A behavioral systems perspective on prosocial behavior. In M. Mikulincer & P. R. Shaver (Eds.), *Prosocial motives, emotions, and behavior: The better angels of our nature* (pp. 73–91). Washington, DC: American Psychological Association.

Simpson, J. A., Rholes, W. S., & Nelligan, J. S. (1992). Support seeking and support giving within couples in an anxiety-provoking situation: The role of attachment styles. *Journal of Personality and Social Psychology, 62*, 434–446.

Simpson, J. A., Rholes, W. S., Orina, M. M., & Grich, J. (2002). Working models of attachment, support giving, and support seeking in a stressful situation. *Personality and Social Psychology Bulletin, 28*, 598–608.

Sofer-Roth, S. (2008). *Adult attachment and the nature of responses to a romantic partner's expression of personal happiness.* Unpublished doctoral dissertation, Bar-Ilan University, Ramat Gan, Israel.

Sroufe, L. A., & Waters, E. (1977). Attachment as an organizational construct. *Child Development, 48*, 1184–1199.

Vansteenkiste, M., Simons, J., Lens, W., Sheldon, K. M., & Deci, E. L. (2004). Motivating learning, performance, and persistence: The synergistic effects of intrinsic goal contents and autonomy-supportive contexts. *Journal of Personality and Social Psychology, 87*, 246–260.

4

Mechanisms, Mediators, and Adaptive Consequences of Caregiving

■ STEPHEN W. PORGES AND C. SUE CARTER

■ **INTRODUCTION AND PERSPECTIVE**

The authors of this chapter are married to each other. We began our academic careers in different research fields. Porges was trained in experimental psychology and was studying the psychophysiology of human attention. Carter was a zoologist working in animal behavior and neuroendocrinology. Sometime in the late 1990s it became apparent that although we were asking different questions and using different scientific models, we were in fact studying components of the same neural systems. After decades of marriage, we had become professionally reacquainted in the brain stem. It is in the brain stem that the circuits regulating the autonomic nervous system and endocrine function, interact, and communicate to manage the physiology of social behavior. Through our almost daily intellectual dialogue, we developed and now share a "brain stem–centric" model of social behavior. Our model, as applied in this essay, examines the neurobiology of caregiving in light of the bidirectionality between peripheral structures involved in the autonomic and endocrine systems (e.g., heart, lungs, adrenals, and gut) and brain stem nuclei. The model also incorporates an appreciation for evolutionary changes in the regulation of these structures, as well as in the regulation of higher centers in the brain.

The defining features of our view of a social nervous system focus on several brain stem structures that are regulated by ancient neurochemicals (Carter, Grippo, Pournajafi-Nazarloo, Ruscio, & Porges, 2008; Landgraf & Neumann, 2004). Thus, a necessary context for understanding the biology of sociality includes evolution and phylogeny. We will argue that like other forms of positive social behaviors, caregiving is an emergent property of the evolution of the mammalian nervous system (Porges, 1997). Knowledge of the processes that have sculpted the mammalian nervous system provides an integrated point of view on the costs and benefits of caregiving. The elements of these systems are not unique to caregiving. However, awareness of the neurophysiological systems that underlie caregiving and the related concept of social support is essential to understanding the mechanisms through which both giving and receiving can influence health and well-being.

Positive social behaviors and their neural underpinnings are essential for both reproduction and survival. Positive social behaviors also are usually reciprocal and symbiotic. Social engagement and caregiving are most readily expressed in a context of safety. Among the novel adaptations of the mammalian nervous system is an evolved "social-engagement system," which permits social behavior and social communication. The social-engagement system also serves to inhibit more primitive systems responsible for defensive reactions to threat and danger (Porges, 2001, 2003).

Understanding of the neurochemistry of the social-engagement system is aided by acknowledging that the biology of the mother–infant interaction provides a neuroendocrine prototype for mammalian sociality. Neuropeptide hormones, such as oxytocin and vasopressin, that are involved in birth and lactation as well as in the regulation of the autonomic nervous system probably evolved from primitive molecules necessary for water conservation and homeostasis. Many of the same neural and endocrine systems that permit birth, lactation, and maternal behavior have been implicated in the giving and receiving of positive experiences (Carter, 1998). However, the processes that underlie positive sociality are not limited to mother–infant interactions or to biological parent–infant relationships. Biologically unrelated individuals may express or experience caregiving (Hrdy, 2008). Knowledge of the shared neural and endocrine systems responsible for mammalian caregiving offers an important perspective on more general causes and consequences of mammalian sociality.

■ DEFINING FEATURES OF CAREGIVING INCLUDE SYMBIOSIS AND RECIPROCITY

Caregiving includes providing food, protection, or other resources. However, caregiving may extend beyond these physical elements to include emotional support for the need for affiliation and perceived safety. Most mammals, including humans and rodents, are motorically immature at birth, and caregiving is necessary to compensate for the infant's undeveloped motor and autonomic nervous systems. Due to an immature corticospinal motor system, the infant is incapable of independently obtaining food or protecting itself from a predator. Due to an immature autonomic nervous system, the infant is incapable of independent thermoregulation or ingestion and digestion of certain foods. Thus the mature nervous system of the caregiver becomes intertwined with the undeveloped nervous system of the infant to create a model of "symbiotic regulation." The caregiver becomes part of a complex feedback system supporting the biological and behavioral needs of the infant. Within this model the caregiver is not solely giving to the infant. The behaviors of the infant also trigger specific physiological processes (e.g., in autonomic and endocrine feedback circuits) that help establish strong bonds, provide emotional comfort for the caregiver, and stimulate neural systems that support the caregiver's health.

Through maturation, motor and autonomic systems change. As the infant matures, there is a transition from dependence on the caregiver for the regulation of biobehavioral processes to a greater degree of self-regulation. However, throughout the life span most mammals will continue to be dependent on others to maintain optimal well-being and state regulation (Hrdy, 2008). In some but not all mammalian species, caregiving is based on or induces selective and reinforcing emotional social relationships and bonds (Carter, 1998; Porges, 1998). When enduring bonds are present, devastating reactions to separation or loss are to be expected (Bowlby, 1988).

Caregiving may or may not be reciprocal. However, reciprocity and the spontaneous reversal of the roles of giver and receiver are positive features of strong relationships and are the optimal features of symbiotic regulation. Conversely, a lack of reciprocity often signals distressed and vulnerable relationships. The inability of an individual to enter into and maintain reciprocal social relations is a feature of several psychiatric disorders (Teicher et al., 2003).

When a mammalian mother initially interacts with her offspring, usually she has just given birth and must provide milk to nurture the newborn. The onset of maternal caregiving is normally closely associated with birth and lactation. The physical events of birth and lactation provide endocrine windows of opportunity for the establishment of strong social bonds. The hormones of birth and lactation are plausible candidates to explain the causes and beneficial effects of caregiving (Carter, 1998; Numan, 2007).

■ **THE EVOLUTION OF A CAREGIVING SYSTEM: THE TRANSITION FROM "SELF-REGULATION" TO "OTHER-REGULATION"**

Evolutionary theories attempting to explain between- and within-species variation in social behavior tend to focus on ultimate causes and assumed selection pressures. These theories are based on ancient historical events, and evidence is limited to the fossil record. Thus it can be difficult to test evolutionary theories within the context of the expressed behavior or physiology of contemporary animals. However, a phylogenetic perspective that investigates the biological and behavioral shifts from reptiles to mammals bypasses the need to focus on ancient events and may be used to illustrate several neurobiological features underlying sociality, some of which may bear on evolutionary hypotheses. For example, most behaviors associated with caregiving and prosociality in humans are seen in other mammals but not in reptiles are common. Within mammals, variations among species, individual variation, and developmental changes in social contact and caregiving provide experiments of nature. Analyses of these variations cast a new light on the neurobiology of sociality.

The phylogenetic transition from reptiles to mammals appears to be, in part, a shift from an organism capable of "self-regulation" to an organism that is dependent at certain points in development on "other-regulation." It is within this phylogenetic transition, in which regulation by others becomes adaptive, that the neurobiology of sociality emerges. The defining feature of the "other" in the mammalian model of regulation require adaptive consequences, including support and protection of the vulnerable infant.

We are not suggesting that regulation of homeostasis in humans is strictly accomplished by other-regulation. For most mammals, and especially humans, a developmental increase in self-regulation capacity parallels the development of specific features of the nervous system. With physical maturation, neural pathways from the cortex to the brain stem exhibit greater efficiency in regulating the autonomic nervous system and enable the maintenance of physiological homeostasis in both safe and dangerous situations (Porges, 2001). These maturational changes provide greater abilities to self-regulate and reduce dependence on others. However, developmental trends in self-regulation occur in a context of giving and receiving throughout the life span and thus may often involve some level of physiological dependence between individuals.

■ THE PHYLOGENY OF THE MAMMALIAN NERVOUS SYSTEM AND COMMUNICATION SYSTEMS

The phylogeny of the mammalian nervous system offers important clues to social behavior. In the transition from aquatic to terrestrial life, ancient gill (branchial) arches were co-opted to form the face and head in many species. This change has implications for how and why features of the central nervous system are inextricably linked to features of the face and the head. In modern mammals, including humans, these interconnections permit social engagement and social communication, including sucking, swallowing, facial expressions and the production and receipt of airborne vocalizations (Porges 2001, 2007). Below we describe our work on the polyvagal theory, which uses insights from phylogeny to advance hypotheses about how positive social behaviors are connected to the regulation of autonomic states.

■ THE POLYVAGAL THEORY

Overview

In essence, polyvagal theory reveals the intimate connection between social behavior and the autonomic nervous system (Porges, 2007). The mammalian nervous system cannot function without the support of visceral organs supplying oxygen and energy. The autonomic nervous system, via bidirectional pathways, regulates the viscera and conveys information upward to the hypothalamus, amygdala, and neocortex. Sensory information from the viscera contributes to what humans experience as emotion or emotional states. These emotional states, in turn, are components of the motivational systems that stimulate social engagement and allow sociality to be experienced as reinforcing. Often these emotional and motivational states involve other brain systems, including those that rely on dopamine and endogenous opioids (Numan, 2007).

Traditional views of the mammalian autonomic nervous system have divided the system into two neural circuits: one that generates a sympathetic response mobilizing energy or arousal for task demands (e.g., the fight-or-flight stress response), and one that generates a parasympathetic response directing energy for use in restorative physiological functions (e.g., promoting immune function, digestion, and cellular repair). Polyvagal theory challenges this view by suggesting that the mammalian autonomic nervous system actually retains three, not two, neural circuits, which are hierarchically organized (Porges, 1995, 1998, 2001, 2003, 2007). These three circuits include the one responsible for the sympathetic fight-or-flight response, but subdivide parasympathetic activation into (a) a vagal circuit that coordinates activity in the face and head while also promoting the regulation of restorative autonomic states above the diaphragm and (b) an evolutionarily ancient vagal circuit that regulates autonomic states below the diaphragm and permits an immobilization response to cues that the organism is in mortal danger.

These three neural circuits are expressed in a phylogenetically organized hierarchy (figure 4.1 and table 4.1). In this hierarchy of adaptive responses, the newest circuit is the branch of the parasympathetic nervous system that coordinates activity in the face and head, permitting social communication. This newer circuit is used first in response to challenges to the organism. If the newest circuit fails to provide safety, older survival-oriented circuits are recruited sequentially, with the defensive fight-or-flight response preceding the use of an immobilization response.

TABLE 4.1 *Polyvagal Theory: Phylogenetic Stages of Neural Control*

Autonomic Nervous System Component	Origin of Motor Neurons	Behavioral Functions	Autonomic Functions
Myelinated vagus (ventral vagal complex, VVC)	**Nucleus ambiguus** (NA)	**Social engagement and caregiving.** Expressed as a coordinated face–heart connection and observed as enhanced regulation of the striated muscles of the face and head and increased calming of the viscera, including active dampening of sympathetic–adrenal functions and reducing fear. The enhanced regulation of facial muscles results in greater prosody, improved listening, and greater emotional expressivity.	**Neuroprotection.** Stabilization of autonomic processes, including producing cardiac respiratory sinus arrhythmia (RSA), which protects the heart and enhances oxygenation of the brain. These functions of the autonomic nervous system, by regulating state and calming the individual, permit sociality and provide resources necessary for symbiotic and reciprocal social interactions.
Sympathetic– adrenal system (*sympathetic nervous system*)	**Spinal cord**	**Mobilization.** Active adaptations including fight-or-flight responses.	**Activation.** Increased heart rate, release of glucocorticoids and catecholamines. Production of energy, including glucose metabolism, and conversion of norepinephrine to epinephrine.
Unmyelinated vagus (*dorsal vagal complex, DVC*)	Dorsal nucleus of the vagus	**Immobilization.** Passive adaptations including death feigning and loss of consciousness.	**Conservation.** Prevalence of bradycardia (slowing the heart) and apnea (cessation of breathing). Reduced energy production.

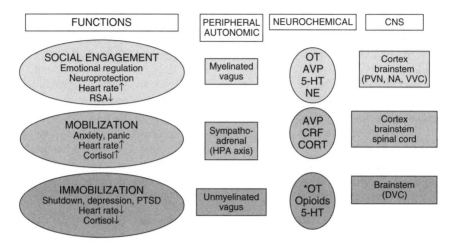

Figure 4.1 The Polyvagal Theory: Hierarchal Organization of Neuroendocrine and Autonomic Processes Implicated in Social Behavior and the Adaptive Management of Stressful Experiences. Neuropeptides, including oxytocin (OT), arginine vasopression (AVP), corticotrophin releasing factor (CRF), and endogenous opioids, as well as neurotransmitters such as serotonin (5-hydroxytryptamine, 5-HT) and norepinephrine (NE), influence behavior and emotions through direct actions on the brain as well as indirect effects on different components of the autonomic nervous system and the hypothalamic-pituitary-adrenal (HPA) axis. OT, 5-HT, and endogenous opioids, acting in the brain stem, may be protective during or against shutting down and immobilization. CNS, central nervous system; CORT, cortisol (corticosterone); DVC, dorsal vagal complex; NA, nucleus ambiguus; *OT; PTSD, posttraumatic stress disorder; PVN, paraventricular nucleus of the hypothalamus; RSA, respiratory sinus arrhythmia; VVC, ventral vagal complex.

Social behavior, social communication, and visceral homeostasis, as promoted by the newest circuit, are largely incompatible with neurophysiological states and behaviors that are regulated by circuits that support the defense strategies of both fight or flight and immobilization. Inhibition of systems that are in general defensive or protective is necessary to initiate social engagement and to allow positive social behaviors. Conversely, positive social behaviors may be inhibited during prolonged periods of adversity. However, systems that support sociality, because they are intertwined with restorative physiological states, also may be protective against the costly or destructive effects of *chronic* fear or stress. Below we expand on the mechanics of these three distinct neural circuits, which are described in the polyvagal theory.

The Vagus Nerve

Of particular importance to mammalian social behavior and to polyvagal theory is the parasympathetic component of the autonomic nervous system, especially the vagus (10th cranial) nerve, which consists of afferent (sensory) and efferent (motor) components. The afferent component transmits information concerning the status of visceral organs (e.g., heart, lungs, and gut) to the brain. The efferent component consists of two branches that influence the activities of these organs. The *unmyelinated* vagus primarily regulates organs below the diaphragm (e.g., the gut), while the *myelinated* vagus regulates organs above the diaphragm (e.g., heart and lungs). However, both branches of the vagus influence the heart, although the pacemaker (i.e., sino-atrial node) is regulated predominantly by the myelinated vagus. The neural regulation of the pacemaker by the myelinated vagal circuit functions as a rapid neural mechanism to coordinate metabolic resources with the behavioral demands of a rapidly changing physical and social environment (Porges, 2007).

The unmyelinated component of the vagus, which permits slowing of the heart (bradycardia), originates in the dorsal motor nucleus of the vagus (also known as the dorsal vagal complex, DVC). The unmyelinated vagus is shared by mammals with other vertebrates (e.g., reptiles, amphibia, and fish). The phylogenetically more recent myelinated branch originates in the nucleus ambiguus of the ventral vagal complex, allowing rapid interaction between the brain and viscera. The myelinated vagus stabilizes cardiovascular function and is responsible for *respiratory sinus arrhythmia* (RSA), a rise and fall in heart rate associated with phases of breathing: Usually heart rate increases with inspiration and decreases with expiration. RSA, sometimes called *vagal tone* or *cardiac vagal tone*, is an index of the dynamic influence of the myelinated vagus on the heart. The term "vagal tone" might be misleading, since there may be vagal influences to the heart via the unmyelinated vagus that would not be reflected in RSA. Because RSA reflects reduced influences of the myelinated vagus on the heart, when it is depressed, heart rate quickly accelerates. Recovery of RSA reflects the reestablishment of influence of the myelinated vagus on the heart (see Porges, 2007), yielding a physiological state that would promote social behavior. RSA, reflecting the dynamic influence of the myelinated vagus, is cardioprotective and directly implicated in cortical oxygenation. Measures of RSA are predictive of and probably permissive for health and longevity in humans. For example, RSA predicts mortality after a heart attack (Kleiger, Miller, Bigger, & Moss, 1987).

Of particular importance to mammalian social behavior, the myelinated vagus is associated in the brain stem with cranial nerves that innervate the face and head. Thus, the myelinated vagal functions are coordinated with the neural regulation of the larynx and pharynx to coordinate sucking, swallowing, and breathing with vocalizations. The muscles of the human face, especially those of the upper face involved in subtle emotional expressions, have projections from this system, which may be particularly important in social communication during face-to-face interactions.

■ NEUROANATOMICAL EVOLUTION AND SOCIAL COGNITION

The comparatively modern processes that supply oxygen to the large primate cortex coevolved with the emergence of higher levels of cognitive functions (Porges, 2001, 2007). The expanding mammalian cortex in general, and specific sensory and neuroanatomical changes in particular, set the stage for human cognition, speech, and more elaborate forms of caregiving beyond the maternal–infant interaction. For example, in contrast to their reptilian ancestors, mammals evolved auditory systems that enabled them to respond to airborne acoustic signals, an important requisite for increasingly complex modes of social interaction. And phylogenetic transitions in brain stem areas that regulate the vagus intertwined with areas that regulate the striated muscles of the face and head. The result of this transition was the emergence of a capability for a dynamic social-engagement system with social-communication features (e.g., head movements, production of vocalizations, and a selective ability to hear conspecific, i.e., same species, vocal communication.) Concurrently and in support of these anatomical changes, the new mammalian myelinated vagus emerged. The myelinated vagus could inhibit the sympathetic nervous system and the hypothalamic-pituitary-adrenal (HPA) axis, effectively making it possible to inhibit mobilization (fight-or-flight) responses. This inhibitory feature of the autonomic nervous system allowed animals to engage in high levels of social interaction, including nurturance of the young, and to engage other conspecifics in a prosocial manner without triggering defensive behaviors, while maintaining a calm physiological and behavioral state.

The phylogenetic transition from reptiles to mammals also resulted in a face–heart connection, in which the striated muscles of the face and head were regulated in the same brain stem areas that evoked the calming influence of the myelinated vagus. The striated muscles of the face and head are involved in social cueing (e.g., facial expressions, vocalizations, listening, and head gesture). Such cues serve as "trigger" stimuli to feature detectors in the nervous system that detect risk and safety in the environment (see the next section). The expanded mammalian cortex also demands high levels of oxygen. Oxygenation of the cortex in mammals is accomplished in part through the same adaptations of the autonomic nervous system that permit elaborate forms of reciprocal sociality. The systems that support the oxygenation of the neocortex, including terrestrial lungs and a four-chambered heart, also are regulated in part by the myelinated branch of vagus nerve.

This synergism of neural mechanisms in mammals down regulated defensive systems and promoted proximity by providing social cues (e.g., intonation of vocalization, facial expressivity, posture, and head gesture) that the organism was not in a physiological state that promoted aggressive and dangerous behaviors. Detection of these social cues allowed for symbiotic regulation of behavior and the elaboration of reciprocal caregiving. These same systems provided setting conditions under which social behaviors could have a significant impact on cognition and health. In the human nervous system specific features of person-to-person interactions are innate triggers of adaptive biobehavioral systems, which in turn can support health and healing. Conversely, the absence of social interactions or conditions of social adversity may lead to maladaptive behaviors and illness.

■ NEUROCEPTION AND THE SOCIAL MANAGEMENT OF THREAT AND DANGER

The integrated functions of the myelinated vagus permit the expression of positive emotions and social communication. However, the nervous system is constantly assessing the environment as safe, dangerous, or life threatening. For example, components of the autonomic nervous system regulate the muscles of the middle ear, permitting the extraction of human voices from background noises that may include the very high- or very low-frequency sounds that signal danger. Under conditions of threat or fear RSA is reduced, heart rate increases, and social communication is compromised. Through a process of "neuroception" specific neural circuits are triggered that may support defensive strategies.

As discussed above, defensive strategies may involve either active coping (i.e., fight-or-flight responses) or passive coping (i.e., immobilization responses). The fight-or-flight system allows mobilization and permits the organism to engage in active or instrumental behaviors that facilitate coping. This system is supported by the sympathoadrenal systems, for example, by the release of catecholamines and glucocorticoids, which increase available energy. Under conditions such as inescapable danger or other forms of extreme stress, mobilization strategies may be inhibited. Defensive strategies are then characterized by passive coping, including immobility. Under more severe conditions many systems may be shut down, including those dependent on the neocortex. In these circumstances animals may show death-feigning or "helplessness" behaviors.

The unmyelinated vagus tends to slow the heart, consistent with a reptilian adaptive strategy of freezing and conserving energy in the face of danger. However, mammals, with their large cortices, cannot maintain clear cognition and consciousness without relatively high concentrations of oxygen. Thus prolonged decelerations of the heart can lead to unconsciousness and eventually death. Mechanisms exist for protecting the heart and brain from shutting down at several levels within the body. As described below, among these are the neural effects of peptide hormones.

■ NEUROCHEMISTRY AND THE SOCIAL NERVOUS SYSTEM

Neuropeptides regulate sociality, emotion, and the autonomic nervous system. Social behaviors are supported and coordinated by both endocrine and autonomic processes. The complex networks of biochemical systems necessary for reproduction and homeostasis also are implicated in social behavior (Carter et al., 2008). Given the energetic demands of social interactions, it is not surprising that the same neurotransmitters that are involved in social behavior also regulate the autonomic nervous system. Two mammalian hormones/neuromodulators—oxytocin (OT) and arginine vasopressin (AVP)—have been shown to be of particular importance to birth, lactation, and maternal behavior as well as sociality. There is increasing evidence that the functions of these same molecules, and especially OT, are central to the causes and consequences of positive social behaviors, including sensitivity to social cues in others and constructs such as trust and caregiving (Heinrichs, von Dawans, & Domes, 2009).

OT and AVP are small neuropeptides that differ from each other in only two of nine amino acids (Landgraf and Neumann, 2004). OT is produced primarily in hypothalamic nuclei, including the supraoptic nucleus (SON) and paraventricular nucleus (PVN). AVP is also synthesized in the PVN, SON, and other brain regions implicated in the regulation of emotional behaviors and of circadian rhythms. AVP also is abundant—especially in males—in the amygdala, bed nucleus of the stria terminalis, and lateral septum, brain regions of particular importance to social and emotional regulation and self-defense (DeVries & Panzica, 2006).

OT and AVP are transported from the SON and PVN to the mammalian posterior pituitary, where they are released into the bloodstream and act as hormones on peripheral targets such as the uterus and mammary tissue. Within the brain, these same chemicals also serve as neuromodulators, affecting a broad range of neural processes (Landgraf & Neumann, 2004). Both OT and AVP are capable of moving throughout the central nervous system, probably by passive diffusion.

Receptors for OT and AVP are found in various brain areas implicated in social behavior (Gimpl & Fahrenholz, 2001). In contrast to most biologically active compounds, OT appears to have only one form of receptor. AVP has at least three distinct receptor subtypes, with separable functions. However, the OT peptide also may affect the AVP receptors and vice versa.

The neuroanatomy of the OT system allows a coordinated effect on behavior, autonomic functions and peripheral tissues. In some cases AVP and OT have opposite functions, possibly because they are capable of acting as antagonists to each other's receptors, while in other cases these peptides have similar effects. Dynamic interactions between OT and AVP may in turn regulate physiology and behavior, allowing shifts between positive social behaviors and defensive states (Viviani & Stoop, 2008).

■ EVOLUTION OF OXYTOCIN AND VASOPRESSIN

It is likely that the essential elements upon which sociality are based arose from physiological processes fundamental to the need to conserve water and minerals. Among these are adaptations allowing the transition from aquatic to terrestrial life, including internal fertilization, and eventually pregnancy and placental reproduction. Although AVP is also known as the "antidiuretic hormone," both OT and AVP influence kidney function in adults, in general conserving water and minerals. The capacity to maintain or reabsorb water was a critical element in the evolution of terrestrial mammals. The capacity for internal fertilization and the development of the placenta and lactation required a well-developed water regulation system. This shift also provided a protective environment for offspring before and after birth, and the emergence of contemporary versions of the neocortex and cognition.

Genes for the synthesis of OT and AVP are very ancient, estimated to be over 700 million years old (Donaldson & Young, 2008). These genes existed before the split between vertebrates and invertebrates. The original molecular structure from which the peptides evolved, believed to be vasotocin, differs from OT and AVP by only one amino acid. Vasotocin is found in mammalian fetuses, although its expression is reduced at the time of birth.

The specific coding sequences that define OT and AVP may have emerged more than once, but in their current form probably evolved around the time that mammals first emerged. OT, through its functions in birth and lactation, assists in maternal nurturing of a comparatively immature infant (Brunton & Russell, 2008; Numan, 2007). The capacity of OT to induce uterine contractions may have allowed the expansion of the human skull and cortex, and eventually cognition. These changes in turn allowed the elaboration of human speech and other forms of social communication that rely on cognitive function.

■ NEUROPEPTIDES INFLUENCE AUTONOMIC FUNCTIONS THROUGH EFFECTS ON THE BRAIN STEM

The PVN of the hypothalamus (including cells that synthesize OT and AVP) is an important site of convergence for neural communication coordinating endocrine and cardiovascular responses to various forms of challenge (Michelini, Marcelo, Amico, & Morris, 2003). At the level of the PVN, OT may influence both the HPA axis and autonomic functions. The presence of oxytocin receptors in the brain stem region known as the dorsal vagal complex (DVC). The DVC, contains the dorsal nucleus of the vagus) has been verified by autoradiography in rodents (Gimpl & Fahrenholz, 2001). The amygdala, with connections to cortex as well as hypothalamus and lower brain stem, integrates cognitive and emotional responses. The amygdala also contains OT and AVP as well as their receptors, and projections to and from the central nucleus of the amygdala may be critical determinants of emotional reactivity (Viviani & Stoop, 2008). Thus the central nucleus of the amygdala is one site (among several) where shifts from positive to negative emotions may be managed. According to this model, OT working within the amygdala may down regulate reactivity, while AVP acting in the extended amygdala and lateral septum (especially in males) might upregulate emotional reactivity, vigilance, and defensiveness. These processes explain in part the capacity of OT to down regulate activity in the amygdala (as measured by fMRI), especially under conditions of fear or emotional dysregulation (Meyer-Lindenberg, 2008). AVP plays a complex role in behavior through effects on blood pressure and heart rate, as well as on the sympathoadrenal axis and parasympathetic functions. Both the AVP peptide and AVP V1a receptors have been identified in the central nucleus of the amygdala, and both are implicated in the regulation of brain stem areas including the myelinated vagus, with source nuclei in the brain stem region known as the ventral vagal complex. That region, where OT-containing processes have been observed, is necessary for RSA.

Receptors for both OT and AVP are found in pathways regulating the myelinated vagus. However, oxytocin receptors are particularly abundant in the DVC, which regulates the unmyelinated vagus. As described above, the unmyelinated vagus can slow the heart and trigger clinical bradycardia. Under normal conditions the myelinated vagal system (including RSA) restrains the unmyelinated vagus, protecting this system from stopping the heart (Porges, 2007). Under extremely stressful conditions, such as birth, OT may (by acting on neural targets including the DVC) protect the autonomic nervous system from reverting to this more primitive vagal system, which could lead to shutting down and reduced emotional, social, and cognitive function. Evolutionary changes in functions of neuropeptides, including OT and AVP, allowed the mammalian birth process

(Brunton & Russell, 2008) and, in turn, the coordination of mammalian cognition and social behaviors.

▪ NEUROPEPTIDES AND THE MANAGEMENT OF STRESSFUL EXPERIENCES

The hypothalamus, and especially the PVN, is an important site of convergence for neural communication relating stress, affective disorders, and cardiovascular regulation to social behavior. Thus it is not surprising that OT influences the HPA axis and autonomic function (Carter, 1998; Viviani & Stoop, 2008). This peptide plays a central role in autonomic tone, as OT-deficient mice show disruptions in sympathovagal balance and an impaired ability to manage stress (Michelini et al., 2003). With regard to endocrine function, OT generally suppresses the activity of the HPA axis (Neumann, 2008).

Oxytocinergic projections from the PVN to key brain stem regions are important in cardiovascular control. The presence of OT binding sites in the DVC has been verified via autoradiography in several species (Gimpl & Fahrenholz, 2001), and OT increases the excitability of vagal neurons. In addition, OT receptors in the brain stem have been shown to modulate baroreflex control of heart rate by facilitating the bradycardic response to pressor challenges. Thus under optimal conditions systems that rely on OT may modulate and constrain over arousal, allowing optimal management of challenges as well as permitting social engagement and caregiving (Porges, 2007).

Peripheral OT administration is able to reduce heart rate and blood pressure (Michelini et al., 2003). The protective effects of OT may be most readily observed in the face of adversity or a stressful environment. For example, in socially monogamous prairie voles (Carter, DeVries, & Getz, 1995) exogenous OT ameliorated isolation-induced changes in behavior and heart rate (Grippo, Trahanas, Zimmerman, Porges, & Carter, 2009). Prairie voles isolated from their social partners for a period of weeks displayed elevated heart rate before, during, and after a social stressor. This effect was blocked by peripheral injections of OT, despite the fact that OT levels are in some cases already heightened during isolation. This suggests that while *endogenous* increases in OT are not sufficient to ameliorate isolation-induced changes in autonomic function, supplementation with *exogenous* OT may have measurable effects. In paired animals, supplementation of OT did not lower heart rate. Thus at least some of the beneficial actions of OT may become apparent only under conditions of adversity.

Centrally released OT can counter the defensive behavioral strategies associated with stressful experiences. OT also may inhibit the central effects of AVP and other adaptive peptides, such as corticotropin-releasing factor, which plays a major role in the HPA axis (Neumann, 2008).

Generally, but not always, the effects of endogenous OT are neuroprotective. We have found in studies done in prairie voles that intense stressors (such as restraint or exposure to a social intruder) can release OT and AVP. Milder stressors, such as handling, increase blood levels of AVP, but not usually OT. Exposure to an infant also may transiently release OT, especially in reproductively naive males.

Infant exposure concurrently blocks stress-induced increases in adrenal steroids and has the capacity to facilitate subsequent pair-bond formation (Carter et al., 2008). These and many other examples support the general hypothesis that OT plays a critical role in the management of stressful experiences while also facilitating social behavior.

Animal research suggests that OT affects the immune system, acting during development to "educate" the thymus. OT can also be a powerful anti-inflammatory agent, both in vivo and in vitro. For example, OT can restore tissue following exposure to burns, protect against sepsis, and reduce the response to pathogens. At comparatively high levels endogenous OT may promote wound healing, humans, as in other mammals (Gouin et al., 2010). These functions of OT could provide another set of mechanisms through which caregiving, under conditions that allow the release of OT, might protect and heal both those who give and those who receive nurture.

■ PUTTING THE PIECES TOGETHER: THE SOCIAL-ENGAGEMENT SYSTEM

As discussed above, pathways from the five cranial nerves that control the muscles of the face and head are critical to human social behavior. Collectively, these motor pathways are labeled as *special visceral efferents*. The special visceral efferent pathways regulate the muscles of mastication (e.g., in ingestion), muscles of the middle ear (e.g., in listening to vocalizations), muscles of the face (e.g., in emotional expression), muscles of the larynx and pharynx (e.g., in vocal prosody and intonation), and muscles controlling head tilt and turning (e.g., in gesture) (figure 4.2). The source nuclei of the circuits regulating the striated muscles of the face and

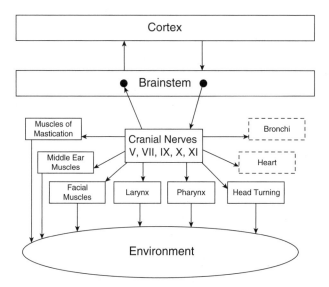

Figure 4.2 Efferent pathways of the mammalian social-engagement system.

head interact in the brain stem with the source nucleus of the myelinated vagus; together these form an *integrated social-engagement system*. This system, in interaction with neurohormonal mechanisms, provides the neural structures and substrates involved in social and emotional behaviors and ties these systems to the rest of the body and thus to health.

■ MAMMALIAN SOCIAL COMMUNICATION AND THE EVOLUTION OF SOCIAL COGNITION

Positive forms of communication, including speech and other vocalizations, are typically components of successful caregiving. Vocalizations also convey information regarding physiological state. For example, infant cries are indicators of health state and also can elicit caregiving. The coordinated regulation of social communication and visceral systems helps to explain the relationship between positive social experiences and health.

Shared neural pathways underlie social communication and visceral functions such as the regulation of the cardiovascular, digestive, and immune systems. Both heart rate and the acoustic features of vocalizations are parallel outputs of the integrated social-engagement system. For example, through the myelinated vagus the brain stem regulates vocal communication (i.e., pathways controlling breath and laryngeal and pharyngeal muscles) as well as heart rate (Porges, 2007).

Thus features of acoustic vocalizations can reflect vagal regulation of the heart. For example, vocal prosody (acoustic variation perceived as melodic vocal intonations) and heart rate variability (i.e., RSA) are parallel and modulated outputs of the social-engagement system (Porges & Lewis, 2009). A depressed social-engagement system is characterized by low variability in both heart rate (i.e., low-amplitude RSA through the myelinated vagus) and vocal intonations (i.e., lack of prosody). Human voices that lack prosody fail to attract or interest others and are perceived as reflecting emotionally detached or boring individuals. In contrast, an optimally functioning social-engagement system will have features of high heart rate variability (i.e., high-amplitude RSA) and greater modulation of vocal intonation (i.e., high prosody). Lack of prosody is a risk factor similar to lack of heart rate variability, and both may be used as indications of health risk. (Vocal prosody may be synchronized with other rhythmic features of autonomic function as well.)

Collectively, the muscles of the face and head function as filters that regulate the valence of social stimuli (e.g., observing facial features and listening to vocalizations) and determinants of engagement with the social environment (Porges, 2003). The neural control of these muscles determines social experiences by changing facial features (especially in humans and other primates), modulating laryngeal and pharyngeal muscles to regulate intonation of vocalizations (prosody), and coordinating both facial and vocal motor tone with respiratory actions. In addition, the frequency of breathing is encoded into the phrasing of vocalizations, which—independent of the content of speech—may express meaning. For example, urgency may be conveyed by short phrases associated with short exhalations (i.e., rapid breathing) while calmness may be conveyed by long phrases associated with long exhalations (i.e., slow breathing) (Porges & Lewis, 2009). The origins of these coordinated functions are most readily appreciated in the context of the evolution of neuroanatomical mechanisms for social engagement and social communication.

■ SEX DIFFERENCES IN THE SOCIAL-ENGAGEMENT SYSTEM

Sex differences in the capacity to nurture or be nurtured are frequently observed and often debated. Women are more likely to give direct nurture, sometimes through their rolea as spouses or parents, or in a professional capacity, such as nursing. In men (including in animals) nurturance may be expressed through less direct "caregiving" behaviors, such as defense or protection of the family or resources.

Culture and experience play an important role in the development, expression, and maintenance of sex differences. However, it is likely that male–female differences in the capacity to nurture also are based in part on biology, which may in turn influence sexually dimorphic behavioral traits and states (Carter, Boone, Pournajafi-Nazarloo, & Bales, 2009).

Gonadal steroid hormones and their receptors can affect sex differences, especially in early development. In addition, sex differences in endogenous neuropeptides, such as OT and AVP, or their receptors could influence sexually dimorphic social behaviors. For example, differential exposure to estrogen across the life span might be expected to enhance the availability of OT. Increased OT in turn might allow individuals to expression higher levels of sociality. However, remarkably little research has addressed these questions, and at least in blood, OT often does not differ between males and females. In addition, both the effects of estrogen and OT are context dependent (Grippo et al., 2009). Thus other systems, including the hormones of the HPA and gonadal axes, and autonomic states associated with activation or mobilization may influence the consequences of OT, whether of endogenous or exogenous origin.

AVP levels in blood also do not reliably differ between the sexes. However, a male bias does exist in *central* AVP, especially in a neural axis that includes the amygdala, bed nucleus of the stria terminalis, and lateral septum (De Vries & Panzica, 2006). This system is important for determining reactions to negative and positive stimuli and may help to explain disorders, including autism, that are highly sexually dimorphic and characterized by differences in social behavior and emotional reactions to stressful experiences. For example, males may be more inclined to show high levels of vigilance or territorial defensiveness, and dysregulation of this system might create vulnerabilities associated with male-biased disorders such as autism (Carter, 2007). As described above, the effects of AVP also can be dynamically influenced by OT and vice versa (Viviani & Stoop, 2008).

Social experiences are likely to be major factors regulating the synthesis of OT, AVP, and their receptors (Carter et al., 2009). Thus, the social history of an individual may be translated into an ontogenetic recalibration of neuropeptidergic functions, with potential consequences for both physiology and behavior. Developmental exposure to exogenous OT or AVP also can have lifelong consequences. In many cases males and females show differential responses to exogenous peptides, also with the potential to modify behavioral patterns across the life span. It seems likely that epigenetic changes in peptides and their receptors are one of the mechanisms through which social experiences are converted into long-lasting individual differences. Social behaviors, including alloparenting, (care of young by nonparents) are especially sensitive to social and hormonal experiences in early life. Thus the fundamental components of caregiving may have evolved with the capacity to be modified by early experiences, gender, and also by hormones, such as OT and AVP, that are capable of regulating sociality and emotional reactivity in later life.

Based upon our understanding of the properties of these biological systems, it is likely that hormonal states can influence behavioral responses, with effects on behavioral or emotional states associated with perception of safety or threat. These systems, including hormonal and autonomic pathways, also may be "tuned" by early experiences, such as a history of good parenting or alternatively neglect or abuse (Teicher et al., 2003). For example, positive early experiences could facilitate access to the social-engagement system, enable a more "cognitive" approach to problems, and concurrently allow some individuals to be particularly resilient in the face of challenge. Alternatively, a history of abuse or neglect might create a vulnerability to emotional hyperreactivity or even shutdown in the face of threat.

■ CLINICAL IMPLICATIONS OF THE SOCIAL-ENGAGEMENT SYSTEM

Contemporary medicine, especially over the last century, has focused on mechanisms of disease. Medical advances have been largely technical. The natural mechanisms underlying health and healing remain remarkably poorly understood. Our work advances a new perspective for medicine by suggesting that person-to-person interactions that trigger neural circuits promoting calm physiological states can contribute to health, healing, and growth processes (Harris, 2009). Threatening interactions, on the other hand, trigger defensive strategies associated with physiological states supporting mobilization (e.g., fight-or-flight behaviors) or immobilization (e.g., behavioral shutdown, syncope, or death feigning). As described above, the nervous system is constantly assessing the environment as being safe, dangerous, or life threatening. Through this process of neuroception, neural circuits are triggered that will either support health and healing or support defensive strategies of fight-flight or shutdown. Neuroception involves brain structures, including the amygdala, that can be modulated by neuropeptides including OT and AVP. Under optimal conditions, person-to-person interactions can be innate triggers within the human nervous system for adaptive biobehavioral systems that support health and healing. Both the giving of and receiving of care or love has the capacity to protect, heal, and restore. The mechanisms underlying these processes are only now becoming apparent.

In the context of caregiving, the quality of the person-to-person interactions between caregivers and those being cared for is critical. Often this involves contingent and "appropriate" gesture, facial expression, prosody, proximity, and touch.

In addition to specific clinical treatments, social support and social-engagement behaviors by friends and relatives may be capable of reversing illness and maintaining health. It is likely that OT is important to the positive consequences of social support, possibly through effects on the autonomic nervous system and immune system. For example, in humans that immune responses to an endobacterial challenge can be significantly blocked by concurrent treatment with OT (Clodi et al., 2008).

■ **SUMMARY**

As a species, humans are highly social mammals, dependent on others for survival and reproduction. Under optimal conditions this dependency is both symbiotic and reciprocal. The evolved neural, autonomic, and endocrine underpinnings of sociality are shared with other species, permitting a cross-species analysis of the processes responsible for sociality. Awareness of the neurobiology of social engagement offers insights into human concepts such as social support and caregiving, which in turn can be associated with good health and recovery from illness. These systems are integrated throughout the body, including at the level of the brain stem, where hormones such as OT and AVP influence behavior, the autonomic nervous system, and the immune system. Projections between these ancient systems and more modern brain structures, including the cortex, act to generate diffuse and sometimes powerful feelings or emotions. The same neuroendocrine and autonomic systems that permit high levels of social behavior and social bonds regulate the management of stressful experiences and the capacity of the mammalian body to heal itself. However, the activities of brain stem and autonomic systems are context dependent. In a context of safety or comparatively mild stressors, the release of OT and the involvement of the myelinated vagus may down regulate defensive systems and promote reciprocal social interactions, with the consequence of enhanced opportunities for symbiotic regulation to support health and restorative processes. In the context of chronic stress or fear, the actions of these same adaptive systems might have consequences that interfere with both the establishment of social behavior and the body's ability to heal and restore. We believe that knowledge of the evolutionary origins and neurobiology of sociality provides a contextual perspective for understanding both the causes and consequences of mammalian caregiving behaviors.

■ **REFERENCES**

Bowlby, J. (1988.). *A secure base: Parent–child attachment and healthy human development.* New York, NY: Basic.

Brunton, P. J. & Russell, J. A. (2008). The expectant brain: Adapting for motherhood. *Nature Reviews Neuroscience, 9,* 11–25.

Carter, C. S. (1998). Neuroendocrine perspectives on social attachment and love. *Psychoneuroendocrinology, 23,* 779–818.

Carter, C. S. (2007). Sex differences in oxytocin and vasopressin: Implications for autism spectrum disorders? *Behavioural Brain Research, 176,* 170–186.

Carter, C. S., Boone, E. M., Pournajafi-Nazarloo, H., & Bales, K. L. (2009). The consequences of early experiences and exposure to oxytocin and vasopressin are sexually-dimorphic. *Developmental Neuroscience, 31,* 332–41.

Carter, C. S., DeVries, A. C., & Getz, L. L. (1995). Physiological substrates of mammalian monogamy: The prairie vole model. *Neuroscience and Biobehavioral Reviews, 19,* 303–314.

Carter, C. S., Grippo, A. J., Pournajafi-Nazarloo, H., Ruscio, M. G., & Porges, S. W. (2008). Oxytocin, vasopressin and social behavior. *Progress in Brain Research, 170,* 331–336.

Clodi, M., Vila, G., Geyeregger, R., Riedl, M., Stulnig, T.M., Struck, J., . . . Luger, A. (2008). Oxytocin alleviates the neuroendocrine and cytokine response to bacterial endotoxin in healthy men. *American Journal of Physiology: Endocrinology and Metabolism, 295,* E686–E691.

De Vries, G. J., & Panzica, G. C. (2006). Sexual differentiation of central vasopressin and vasotocin systems in vertebrates: Different mechanisms, similar endpoints. *Neuroscience, 138,* 947–955.

Donaldson, Z. R., & Young, L. J. (2008). Oxytocin, vasopressin and neurogenetics of sociality. *Science, 322,* 900–904.

Gimpl, G., & Fahrenholz, F. (2001). The oxytocin receptor system: Structure, function and regulation. *Physiological Reviews, 81,* 629–683.

Gouin, J. P., Carter, C. S., Pournajafi-Nazarloo, H., Glaser, R., Malarkey, W. B., Loving, T. J., . . . Kiecolt-Glaser, J. K. (2010). Marital behavior, oxytocin, vasopressin and wound healing. *Psychoneuroendocrinology 35,* 1082–1090

Grippo, A. J., Trahanas, D. M., Zimmerman, R. R., II, Porges, S. W., & Carter, C. S. (2009). Oxytocin protects against isolation-induced autonomic dysfunction and behavioral indices of depression. *Psychoneuroendocrinology, 34,* 1542–1553.

Harris, J. C. (2009). Toward a restorative medicine—the science of care. *Journal of the American Medical Association, 301,* 1710–1712.

Heinrichs, M., von Dawans, B., & Domes, G. (2009). Oxytocin, vasopressin and human social behavior. *Frontiers in Neuroendocrinology, 30,* 548–557.

Hrdy, S. B. (2008). *Mothers and others: The evolutionary origins of mutual understanding.* , Cambridge, MA: Belknap Press, Harvard University.

Kleiger, R. E., Miller, J. P., Bigger, J. T., Jr., & Moss, A. J. (1987). Decreased heart rate variability and its association with increased mortality after acute myocardial infarction. *American Journal of Cardiology, 59,* 256–262.

Landgraf, R., & Neumann, I. D. (2004). Vasopressin and oxytocin release within the brain: A dynamic concept of multiple and variable modes of neuropeptide communication. *Frontiers in Neuroendocrinology, 25,* 150–176.

Meyer-Lindenberg, A. (2008). Impact of prosocial neuropeptides on human brain function. *Progress in Brain Research, 170,* 463– 470.

Michelini, L. C., Marcelo, M. C., Amico, J., & Morris, M. (2003). Oxytocin regulation of cardiovascular function: Studies in oxytocin-deficient mice. *American Journal of Physiology: Heart and Circulatory Physiology, 284,* H2269–H2276.

Neumann, I. D. (2008). Brain oxytocin: A key regulator of emotional and social behaviours in both females and males. *Journal of Neuroendocrinology, 20,* 858–865.

Numan, M. (2007). Motivational systems and the neural circuitry of maternal behavior in the rat. *Developmental Psychobiology, 49,* 12–21.

Porges, S. W. (1995). Orienting in a defensive world: Mammalian modifications of our evolutionary heritage. A Polyvagal Theory. *Psychophysiology, 32,* 301–318.

Porges, S. W. (1997). Emotion: An evolutionary by-product of the neural regulation of the autonomic nervous system. *Annals of the New York Academy of Sciences, 807,* 62–77.

Porges, S. W. (1998). Love: An emergent property of the mammalian autonomic nervous system. *Psychoneuroendocrinology, 23*, 837–861.

Porges, S. W. (2001). The Polyvagal Theory: Phylogenetic substrates of a social nervous system. *International Journal of Psychophysiology, 42*, 123–146.

Porges, S. W. (2003). Social engagement and attachment: A phylogenetic perspective. *Annals of the New York Academy of Sciences 1008*, 31– 47.

Porges, S. W. (2007). The polyvagal perspective. *Biological Psychology, 74*, 116–143.

Porges, S. W., & Lewis, G. F. (2009). The polyvagal hypothesis: Common mechanisms mediating autonomic regulation, vocalizations, and listening. In S. M. Brudzynsk (Ed.), *Handbook of mammalian vocalizations: An integrative neuroscience approach* (pp. 255–264). Amsterdam: Academic Press.

Teicher, M. H., Andersen, S. L., Polcari, A., Anderson, C. M., Navalta, C. P., & Kim, D. M. (2003). The neurobiological consequences of childhood maltreatment. *Neuroscience and Biobehavioral Reviews, 27*, 33–44.

Viviani, D., & Stoop, R. (2008). Opposite effects of oxytocin and vasopressin on the emotional expression of the fear response. *Progress in Brain Research, 170*, 207–218.

PART THREE

The Neuroscience of Caregiving Motivation

5 The Human Caregiving System

A Neuroscience Model of Compassionate Motivation and Behavior

■ STEPHANIE L. BROWN, R. MICHAEL BROWN, AND STEPHANIE D. PRESTON

The human tendency to provide care to others, over a long period of time, and even in the absence of reciprocity, attracted the attention of the first two authors as psychologists trained to consider how behavior is shaped by reinforcement. How is it that individuals come to pair the costs of helping another person with reward for the self? We viewed actions that involve the sustained allocation of resources to someone other than the self as a scientific mystery. As a father–daughter team—developmental psychologist and social psychologist, respectively—S. L. Brown and R. M. Brown became interested in using evolutionary theory to explain the motivation to help others. We were unable to reconcile insights generated from evolutionary biology with models used in psychology and economics to describe human motivation. After considerable reflection and analysis, we decided to abandon an assumption that is pervasive in the social sciences—that all social behavior can be reduced to the pursuit of rewards and benefits for the self, and to general impulses that compel individuals to seek pleasure and avoid pain (S. L. Brown & Brown, 2006; R. M. Brown & Brown, 2007, 2006). As an alternative, we entertained the hypothesis that a dedicated neurobiological system, independent of but interacting with pleasure–pain systems, drives individuals to prioritize and promote the well-being of others—under certain, well-specified conditions. In this essay, we have teamed up with third author, a biological psychologist, to delineate what this dedicated neurobiological system might look like.

■ WHAT DO WE MEAN BY SACRIFICE AND ALTRUISM?

As an example of the type of behavior that we are hoping to explain, we start with parenting. Motivational accounts of parenting that invoke self-interest—the standard maximize rewards–minimize costs calculus—are, at the very least, strained. Although parents may experience pleasurable states generally and feelings of love specifically (Swain, this volume), these emotions are not always revealed in surveys of parent mood or in reports of parent marital satisfaction. For example, some studies show that parents experience no elevation of mood when taking care of their children (Kahneman Krueger, Schkade, Schwarz, & Stone, 2004). And considerable data from studies of marital happiness show that the early years of marriage, and in particular the transition to parenting, are characterized by declining relationship satisfaction (Linville et al., 2010).

These data suggest that parenting, however rewarding, generates significant costs. Indeed, as parents of young children, many of us give up sleep, sex, and freedom to become vigilant protectors and promoters of someone other than ourselves. And for some of us, this heavy investment continues for a lifetime. This level of sacrifice may explain why our children do not always elevate our mood and why marital satisfaction can be elusive. If anticipation of reward (or other forms of self-interest) are to explain the motivation to parent, they must demonstrate the ways in which the benefits of parenting outweigh its significant costs. So far, this has not happened.

Even if one could make a case that parenting occurs in anticipation of the rewards it generates, what about other examples of caregiving? For instance, if a loved one becomes ill or gets injured, some of us give up a career, social life, mating opportunities, or financial security to spend months or years taking care of the person in need. What are the underlying rewards that motivate that level of sacrifice?

Perhaps the most challenging examples of sacrificial behaviors for reward-based models are found outside the realms of parenting and caring for sick family members or loved ones. Dramatic instances of self-sacrifice include so-called altruistic suicides (Durkheim, 1951), in which individuals intentionally end their lives, ostensibly (at least in some cases) to relieve the burden they perceive they place on others (deCatanzaro, 1986; R. M. Brown et al., 2009; Joiner, 2005). And we are all familiar with instances of heroic sacrifice in combat (Wong, Kolditz, Millen, & Potter, 2003), in which soldiers risk injury or death to save their comrades. The motivation for such behavior is difficult to explain in terms of the pursuit of benefits, pleasure, or preferences. On the contrary, these behaviors require individuals to forgo immediate and future pleasure and reward in favor of certain pain, injury, and perhaps even death.

■ AN EVOLUTIONARY THEORY OF SACRIFICE

We developed Selective Investment Theory as an alternative way to explain the motivational basis for instances of sacrifice and costly, long-term investment in others. According to the theory, social bonds—the glue of close relationships—provide access to a motivational architecture that enables individuals to suppress their own self-preservation goals and preferences when necessary in order to prioritize and promote the well-being of another person. This view of social bonds represents a departure from traditional reward-based, learning models of close relationships (e.g., attachment theory or learning theory), which emphasize the importance of using relationship partners to meet individual needs.

Considering the significant costs of helping others on a sustained basis (Krebs, this volume; Shulz & Monin, this volume; Penner, Harper, & Albrecht, this volume), our theory also suggests that social bonds are formed selectively, under conditions referred to as positive "fitness interdependence." In essence, positive fitness interdependence is a state of linked reproductive success between two or more individuals in which increases in one person's fitness result in increases in the fitness of the other or others. As we discuss in our elaboration of Selective Investment Theory (S. L. Brown & Brown, 2006), individuals can be interdependent if they share genes, as in the case of blood relatives, or if they are linked to one another for outcomes and resources that affect survival and reproduction. Cues for positive fitness interdependence include, for example, perceptions of phenotypic similarity, familiarity, common threat, and shared emotions, as well as circumstances such as sexual intercourse that create a positive linkage in fitness-related outcomes.

States of positive fitness interdependence are an appealing prerequisite for forming social bonds and behaving altruistically because attempts to exploit or otherwise decrease the fitness of one individual result in a comparable decrease in the fitness of the other. In ancestral conditions that were likely marked by high degrees of fitness interdependence, exploitation of a common resource would have been lethal not only to the altruist but also to the "cheater." Thus we have argued that exploitation could not have been selected for under states of positive fitness interdependence, which provides a genetic safety net for behaving altruistically. From the vantage point of our theory, social bonds, based on positive fitness interdependence, are proximate (motivational) causes of costly, long-term investment in others.

In our first published presentation of selective investment theory (S. L. Brown & Brown, 2006), we did not flesh out the motivational system that mediates between social bonds and caring for and helping others, other than to hypothesize that it is rooted in the evolution of parental care. We now address this omission, turning attention to what we and others have referred to as a "caregiving system"— the neurophysiological circuitry that allows cues for interdependence and social bonds (and other selected stimuli) to drive cognitions, emotions, and behaviors that propel us beyond self-interest.

■ THE CAREGIVING SYSTEM: A THEORETICAL FRAMEWORK

We propose that a dedicated neurobiological system, shaped by evolution to direct maternal care (S. L. Brown & Brown, 2006; Numan, 2006), is selectively recruited in both humans and nonhumans to motivate many forms of helping behavior, including costly long-term investment in others. Below we describe our caregiving system framework, including functional and evolutionary requirements of such a system, as well as candidate brain regions, hormones, and neural circuits that may be capable of directing the motivation to help others.

Our model proposes that perceptions of another's need for help interact with relationship variables and available resources to influence both caregiving motivation and behavior (figure 5.1). The medial preoptic area (MPOA) of the hypothalamus is responsible for activating caregiving motivation in response to these need, relationship, and resource inputs. This other-related and resource-related information also outputs to other motivational centers, including those that generate reward-based and avoidance-driven impulses that can conflict with caregiving motivation. Helping behavior is released through inhibition of these competing impulses.

Sensitivity to Need

At a minimum, an effective and evolutionarily adaptive caregiving system must be sensitive to cues for distress or need in others (Preston & Brown, 2011 submitted). Although overt distress, solicitation, or other cues for need may not be necessary for activating caregiving motivation, helping behavior that is not attuned to the needs of the recipient risks compromising the inclusive fitness of the helper. For example, a mother who sees a lion approaching her toddler must register the threat to her child in addition to the threat to herself. This sensitivity component is a commonsense requirement for any caregiving system and was a centerpiece of Bowlby's (1969) ideas. Indeed, attachment researchers, beginning with Ainsworth, Bell, and Stayton (1972), have highlighted caregiver sensitivity, but mainly in terms of its effects on the security of infant attachments. Until recently there has been little theoretical or empirical emphasis on determinants of such sensitivity in humans (but see Collins, Guichard, Ford, & Feeney, 2006).

Animal research, on the other hand, has not only documented the importance of need detection in provisioning offspring but also suggested mechanisms by which this happens. Species studied include insects (Kőlliker, Chuckalovcak, Haynes, & Brodie, 2006), birds (Budden & Wright, 2001; Kilner & Johnstone, 1997; Wright & Leonard, 2002), and nonhuman primates (Ueno & Matsuzawa, 2004; Warneken, Hare, Melis, Hanus, & Tomasello, 2007), but the most detailed and extensive neurophysiological data come from rodents (for extensive reviews see Lonstein & Morrell, 2007; Numan, 2006, 2007, this volume; Numan & Insel, 2003; Rosenblatt, 1992).

The rodent data suggest that caregiving motivation is directed within the hypothalamus, which is generally known to regulate homeostatic states such as body temperature, weight, blood pressure, and fluid and electrolyte balance

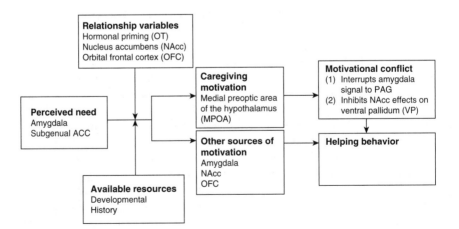

Figure 5.1 A Biological Framework for Studying the Caregiving System. Brain regions, hormones, and circuits are described under each variable in the model. ACC, anterior cingulate cortex; OT, oxytocin; PAG, periaqueductal gray.

(Molavi, 1997). In the context of maternal care, the MPOA and the surrounding ventral bed nucleus of the stria terminalis (vBST) are thought to act as a "switch" that turns on maternal motivation, influencing sensorimotor integration to facilitate active, voluntary maternal responses such as pup retrieval and nest building (Numan, 2006, p. 164). Evidence that the hypothalamus may become active in response to cues for need in others comes from studies of the amygdala and the subgenual anterior cingulate cortex (sgACC), both of which have been implicated in helping behavior (Moll et al., 2006; Numan, 2006), perceiving need in others (Lorberbaum et al., 1999, 2002), and influencing hypothalamic processes, including activation of the MPOA (Diorio, Viau, & Meaney, 1993; Numan, 2006).

The Motivation to Help

Data from rodent studies indicate that the MPOA/vBST directs maternal behavior in two ways: by increasing approach motivation and by inhibiting avoidance motivation that would interfere with providing help to another. The MPOA/vBST must be intact for normal maternal behavior to occur (Numan & Insel, 2003). For example, damage to the MPOA/vBST interferes with active maternal responses to the pup, such as pup retrieval, but does not interfere with passive maternal responses such as huddling and nursing (e.g., Jacobson, Terkel, Gorski, & Sawyer, 1980, Terkel, Bridges, & Sawyer, 1979). Moreover, damage to the MPOA/vBST does not impair motor behavior, sexual behavior, hoarding, activity levels, body weight, or temperature regulation, which are also under the control of the hypothalamus (reviewed in Numan, 2006). These data suggest that the MPOA/vBST is specialized for active maternal care and that the motivation for maternal care can be disassociated from the motivation to engage in other types of motor behaviors, including those that are reward based, such as sexual activity.

Inhibiting Impulses that Compete with Providing Care

An effective caregiving system must be capable of resolving motivational conflict that undermines the allocation of valuable resources to those in need (S. L. Brown & Brown, 2006; R. M. Brown & Brown, 2006). The caregiving system we have proposed can deal with such conflicts in at least two ways. We first consider how it could directly inhibit the *motivation* to seek rewards for the self, as originally hypothesized by S. L. Brown and Brown (2006). Studies of the interaction of maternal motivation and reward processes described below support this possibility.

Inhibition of Reward-Seeking Motivation?

A closer look at the rodent model of maternal care reveals that MPOA-directed caregiving motivation might be accomplished via inhibitory processes in the nucleus accumbens (NAcc), a group of subcortical, dopaminergic neurons located near the septum with inputs from and outputs to components of the limbic system. The NAcc plays a critical role across species in mediating reward-based behavior, including the development and expression of food preferences, sexual behavior,

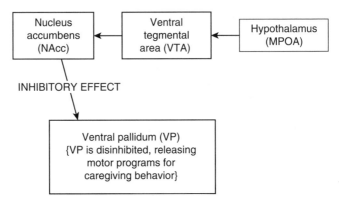

Figure 5.2 MPOA-directed inhibition of reward motivation.

and drug and chemical addiction (Swain, this volume). The NAcc receives inputs from the prefrontal cortex via the ventral tegmental area (the origin of dopaminergic neurons), and from limbic structures, including the MPOA. The NAcc outputs to the ventral pallidum (VP), which in turn plays a role in orchestrating motor programs involved in caregiving (figure 5.2).

The NAcc has both inhibitory (D1) and excitatory (D2) dopamine receptors, and there is evidence that dopamine activation of D1-like receptors is important in facilitating maternal behavior (Numan, Numan, Pliakou, et al., 2005a) and in maintaining (but not forming) monogamous pair bonds in prairie voles (Aragona et al., 2006; Aragona & Wang, 2009). If NAcc–VP reward circuits are inhibited at the same time maternal behavior is facilitated (via input from the MPOA), then it is possible that NAcc-mediated reward processes are not driving maternal behavior.[1]

If human caregiving can be characterized by MPOA inhibition of the NAcc, then perhaps this inhibitory process is experienced as a shift in motivation—away from addictive or consumptive types of motivation (e.g., drugs, sex, food, money, or alcohol), toward allocating resources to others in need. Indeed, a variety of studies have shown the importance of inhibiting the NAcc for other goal-directed behaviors (e.g., Stratford and Kelley, 1999; reviewed in Numan, 2006). And some studies demonstrate that maternal behavior can still occur despite lesions to the NAcc (e.g., Numan, Numan, Schwarz, et al., 2005b). This work indicates that the NAcc is not always necessary for active, voluntary types of maternal behavior such as pup retrieval.

Avoiding Avoidance

The second way that engagement of a caregiving system may lead to suppression of competing, self-maximizing motives is by minimizing the projected costs to the self of helping behavior. To go back to our earlier example, a lion that approaches a mother who is some distance from her toddler would likely trigger competing impulses in the mother—behaviors aimed at saving the child may be in opposition to behaviors triggered by the mother's own fight-or-flight response. In this situation, an effective caregiving system would inhibit the behavioral response to the threat to the mother's survival while facilitating protection of her child.

Data from rodents are entirely consistent with this possibility. In the animal model, the MPOA appears to motivate helping behavior in part by inhibiting the fear-based (avoidance) response to the novel pup stimuli. After the threat or need stimulus is perceived and activates the amygdala, inhibition of the avoidance response by the MPOA is theorized to occur by suppressing projections from the amygdala to the periaqueductal gray (PAG), the command center for mobilizing sympathetic activation (Numan, 2006).

Additional support for the possibility that caregiving behavior occurs via inhibition of the competing avoidance (stress) response is offered by studies (e.g., Fleming et al., 1980) showing that damage to either the medial amygdala or PAG, which would interfere with the avoidance response, facilitates caregiving behavior in virgin females. Furthermore, there are substantial interconnections between the MPOA and PAG, which are thought to be inhibitory and some parts of the PAG express Fos-protein synthesis (indicating inhibition) during maternal behavior (Lonstein & Stern, 1997).

Further evidence in favor of a linkage between helping behavior and inhibition of the stress response comes from studies of the hormonal correlates of helping behavior. For example, oxytocin (OT), which has been shown to stimulate altruistic behavior in humans and nonhumans (including maternal behavior, reviewed in S. L. Brown & Brown, 2006), decreases activity in the hypothalamic-pituitary-adrenal (HPA) axis (Carter, 1998), blood pressure, and cortisol, and delays withdrawal from heat and mechanical stimuli (Uvnas-Moberg, 1997, 1998a, 1998b).

In humans, evidence indicates that helping others is indeed associated with reduced stress or accelerated recovery from stress. Helping behavior predicts faster recovery from depressive symptoms that accompany spousal loss (S. L. Brown, Brown, et al., 2008) and buffers the effect on mortality of exposure to stressful life events (Poulin, Brown, Dillard, & Smith, 2011, submitted).

In summary, this body of research is consistent with the possibility that a motivational system that responds selectively to the needs of others must compete with the system or systems that help individuals seek rewards and respond to threats to self-preservation. In humans, resolution of this motivational conflict may be accomplished by inhibiting addictive or consumptive reward-seeking motivation and by inhibiting fear/avoidance motivation (S. L. Brown & Brown, 2006; Numan, 2006). Importantly, an intimate connection between helping behavior and stress regulation may explain why helping others has been shown repeatedly to be associated with better health and longevity (Post, 2007).

Responding Selectively to Bonded Targets

Another critical requirement for an effective caregiving system is to provide givers some degree of protection against exploitation. This assumption is fundamental to virtually all contemporary accounts of the evolution of altruism that focus on implications of selection at the level of the gene as opposed to selection at the level of the group (e.g., Alexander, 1987; S. L. Brown & Brown, 2006; Hamilton, 1964; Trivers, 1971; Zahavi, 1995, 1997). Accordingly, any evolved mammalian caregiving system should be particularly responsive not only to cues for need but also to cues that indicate the risk of exploitation. We hypothesize that to limit the threat of exploitation, caregiving neural circuitry is modulated by cues for fitness interdependence, social bonds based on fitness interdependence, and cues that signal another person's vulnerability (indicating to potential givers that the person in need is in no position to exploit them). Below we describe how OT, interdependence, and social bonds may modulate access to caregiving neural circuitry.

Neuroendocrine Modulation of the Caregiving System

OT is causally related to helping behavior and stress regulation (S. L. Brown & Brown, 2006, Carter, 1998) and has receptors throughout the maternal caregiving circuit (Brunton & Russell, 2008). OT is selectively released in nonhumans and humans under circumstances that suggest fitness interdependence, for example, birth, breast-feeding, and sexual behavior (Carter, 1998); among humans OT has been associated with trust (Zak et al., 2004).

OT has been hypothesized to be the hormonal basis of social bonds, love, and affiliation (Carter, 1998) because it can facilitate bonding behaviors such as grooming, the formation of partner preferences, and the exploration of novel environments which indicates that the social bond provides a secure base. Despite its apparent role in establishing social bonds and the onset of maternal behavior, OT is not essential for the maintenance of maternal behavior. OT antagonists, antibodies to OT, and lesions of OT-producing neurons can interfere with maternal care only *before* it has been established (Carter, 1998; Numan and Corodimas, 1985). This implies that OT does not directly mediate postpartum maternal behavior (e.g., Numan, 1990), but rather that it may be needed to prime the MPOA in order to inhibit the typical fear-based avoidance response of virgin rat females to pups and facilitate the release of caregiving behaviors (Numan, 2006).

Recognizing Bonded Partners

That OT is not essential for sustaining maternal responses suggests that it may produce changes in brain regions that activate caregiving neural circuitry, possibly through pairing the recognition of a bonded partner with activation of neural circuitry for maternal care. We are intrigued by the possibility that connections between the orbital frontal cortex (OFC) and hypothalamus[2] allow the OFC to modulate access to subcortical hypothalamic circuitry. The basis for this hypothesis lies in how properties of the OFC make it a candidate brain region for facilitating bond formation, maintenance, and dissolution.

The medial OFC stores emotional and visceral experiences of social memories (Ongür and Price, 2000), a function that is essential for the formation and maintenance of social bonds (S. L. Brown and Brown 2006). The OFC is also important for odor discrimination (Tanabe et al., 1975; Zatorre & Jones-Gotman, 1991), which is well established as important in triggering maternal responsiveness in nonhuman mammals (Numan, 2006). The ability of the OFC to code for stimulus specificity (Zald and Kim, 1996) derives from its bimodal cells that respond to multiple sensory inputs from a single stimulus. These neurons make the OFC an ideal mechanism for helping individuals code, recognize, and discriminate trustworthy, bonded, or interdependent partners.

Cells in the OFC are also noteworthy because they alter their firing with changes in motivational state. For example, some cells in the OFC will fire in response to food when an animal is hungry but not when it is satiated (Rolls et al., 1989). Although the OFC is not essential for many reinforcement tasks, Zald and Kim (1996) write that it "appears to be essential in situations where the affective value of a stimulus changes" (p. 252). This characteristic of the OFC could help individuals navigate new relationships, altering patterns of neuronal firing as strangers become acquaintances, friends, and loved ones or as former relationship partners become estranged. Thus the OFC could detect important changes in the status of social bonds (and the likelihood of exploitation) and help mediate the caregiving system's responses to such changes.

Effects of lesions to the ventromedial OFC in human patients provide evidence for its role in coordinating the establishment and dissolution of social bonds. If the OFC can alter social bonds, then damage to this area should disrupt social behavior. Indeed, patients with damage to the ventromedial OFC show reduced autonomic activity with exposure to socially meaningful stimuli (Damasio et al., 1990).

To summarize, there is sufficient evidence to show that social bonds and helping behavior share neurohormonal features, and some evidence that the underlying neural circuitry is also similar. The OFC may code for specific individuals and memories, coordinate different responses to the same social stimuli, and trigger the release of OT. Research not reviewed here further implicates the OFC in rational thought and decision-making processes, including decisions about whether to help another person (Preston & de Waal, in press). Because of this, we hypothesize that activation in the OFC may determine whether helping behavior is motivated by the caregiving system or by a deliberate cost–benefit analysis. Eisler and Levine (2002) offer a similar proposal, suggesting that the OFC releases caring capacities and prevents their inhibition by emotional stress, stimuli, and beliefs.

Selective Engagement as a Function of Resource Availability

As discussed above, providing care for others can be inherently costly, risking exploitation, resource depletion, or even death. Given these threats, the caregiving system should be sensitive to the helper's potential to provide resources, and access to the system should be limited to instances in which helpers have sufficient resources to invest. Cues that enable individuals to track their own resource-providing potential may include early developmental experiences that alter the landscape of the caregiving system. For example, the adequacy of maternal care in infancy influences the development of neuroendocrine responses to stress (Liu et al., 1997). Early exposure to stress in the form of maternal separation, loss, abuse, or neglect results in changes to brain morphology and neurochemistry and may alter the expression of genes that influence anxiety and mood disorders (Sanchez, Ladd, & Plotsky, 2001). These findings are consistent with the possibility that unpredictable parental investment dysregulates the stress response in infants, thereby interfering with the normal development of their caregiving neural circuitry. Consequently, as adolescents and adults, such individuals may turn out to be hypersensitive to cues for danger or exploitation and reluctant to invest heavily in others unless there is good evidence that the situation is safe and resources are adequate.

■ CONCLUSIONS

The evidence we have reviewed is compatible with the existence of a dedicated neurobiological system for giving care to others, not readily reducible (at a neurological level) to anticipation of reward or avoidance of pain. The existence of such a system poses a critical challenge to dominant views in psychology and the behavioral sciences that rely on concepts such as rational self-interest or psychological hedonism to explain social behavior. Our framework has implications for a wide variety of phenomena, including providing a mechanism to explain the health benefits of helping others (e.g., Brown, Nesse, Vinokur, & Smith, 2003; S. L. Brown, Smith, et al., 2009). Hormones involved in caregiving, such as OT and progesterone (e.g., S. L. Brown, Fredrickson, et al., 2009) can be neuroprotective, and restorative in terms of the implications for physical health (Heaphy & Dutton, 2006). Moreover, the ability of caregiving system motivation to enhance stress regulation may decrease individuals' exposure to harmful levels of stress hormones such as cortisol.

Science is only beginning to understand the neurobiological substrates of helping behavior and interpersonal relationships. However, even a glimpse into these systems illuminates a critical divide between assumptions of human behavior used to construct social policy (e.g., rational self-interest) and the neural architecture that was shaped by evolution to ensure the organism's role in promoting the survival and reproductive success of others. It is our hope that by advancing a biological framework for the study of the caregiving system, we can take steps towards bridging this divide.

■ NOTES

1. S. L. Brown and Preston interpret these results differently (see Preston & Brown, 2011). Whereas Brown suggests that animal models of maternal care can be used to hypothesize the inhibition of reward-seeking motives in humans, Preston considers NAcc involvement in the caregiving circuit to be evidence that helping behavior in humans is mediated by reward-seeking drives mediated by the NAcc.

2. The hypothalamus is heavily interconnected with the anterior cingulate cortex (especially the subgenual area of the ACC) and the medial OFC. Interconnections to the hypothalamus become less dense as projections originate from more lateral cortical areas, with the fewest interconnections in the lateral prefrontal cortex (Kringelbach & Rolls, 2004).

■ REFERENCES

Ainsworth, M. D. S., Bell, S. M., & Stayton, D. J. (1972). Individual differences in the development of some attachment behaviors. *Merrill-Palmer Quarterly, 18*, 123–143.

Alexander, R. D. (1987). *Biology of moral systems*. Seattle, WA: University of Washington Press.

Aragona, B. J., Liu, Y., Yu, Y. J., Curtis, J. T., Detwiler, J. M., Insel, T. R., & Wang, Z. (2006). Nucleus accumbens dopamine differentially mediates the formation and maintenance of monogamous pair bonds. *Nature Neuroscience, 9,* 133–139.

Aragona, B. J., & Wang, Z. (2009). Dopamine regulation of social choice in a monogamous rodent species. *Frontiers in Behavioral Neuroscience, 3,* 1–11.

Bowlby, J. (1969). Disruption of affectional bonds and its effects on behavior. *Journal of Contemporary Psychotherapy, 2,* 75–86.

Brown, R. M. & Brown, S. L. (2006). SIT stands and delivers: A reply to the commentaries. *Psychological Inquiry, 17,* 60–74.

Brown, R. M., & Brown, S. L. (2007). Towards uniting the behavioral sciences with a gene-centered approach to altruism. *Behavioral and Brain Sciences, 30,* 19–20.

Brown, S. L., & Brown, R. M. (2006). Selective Investment Theory: Recasting the functional significance of close relationships. *Psychological Inquiry, 17*(1): 1–29.

Brown, S. L., Brown, R. M., House, J. S., & Smith, D. M. (2008). Coping with spousal loss: The potential buffering effects of self-reported helping behavior. *Personality & Social Psychology Bulletin 34*: 849–861.

Brown, S. L., Fredrickson, B. L., Wirth, M., Poulin, M., Meirer, E., Heaphy, E., . . . Schultheiss, O. (2009). Closeness increases salivary progesterone in humans. *Hormones and Behavior, 56,* 108–111.

Brown, S. L., Nesse, R. M., Vinokur, A. D., & Smith, D. M. (2003). Providing social support may be more beneficial than receiving it: Results from a prospective study of mortality. *Psychological Science 14*(4), 320–327.

Brown, S. L. Smith, D. M., Schulz, R., Kabeto, M., Ubel, P., Yee, J., Kim, C. & Langa, K. (2009). Caregiving and decreased mortality in a national sample of older adults. *Psychological Science, 20,* 488–494.

Brunton, P., & Russell, J. (2008). The expectant brain: adapting for motherhood. *Nature Reviews Neuroscience, 9,* 11–25.

Budden, A. E., & Wright, J. (2001). Begging in nestling birds. In V. Nolan, Jr. & C. F. Thompson (Eds.), *Current Ornithology* (Vol. 16, pp. 83–118). New York, NY: Plenum Press.

Carter, C. S. (1998). Neuroendocrine perspectives on social attachment and love. *Psychoneuroendocrinology, 23,* 779–818.

Collins, N. L., Guichard, A. C., Ford, M. B., & Feeney, B. C. (2006). Responding to need in intimate relationships: Normative processes and individual differences. In M. Mikulincer & G. S. Goodman (Eds.), *Dynamics of romantic love: Attachment, caregiving, and sex* (pp. 149–189). New York, NY: Guilford Press.

Damasio, A. R., Tranel, D., & Damasio, H. (1990). Individuals with sociopathic behavior caused by frontal damage fail to respond autonomically to social stimuli. *Behavioural Brain Research 41*(2), 81–94.

deCatanzaro, D. (1986). A mathematical model of evolutionary pressures regulating self-preservation and self-destruction. *Suicide and Life-Threatening Behavior, 16,* 166–181.

Diorio, D., Viau, V., & Meaney, M. J. (1993). The role of the medial prefrontal cortex (cingulate gyrus) in the regulation of hypothalamic-pituitary-adrenal responses to stress. *Journal of Neuroscience, 13,* 3839–3847.

Durkheim E. (1951). *Suicide: A study in sociology.* New York, NY: The Free Press.

Eisler, R., & Levine, D. S. (2002). Nurture, nature, and caring: We are not prisoners of our genes. *Brain and Mind, 3,* 9–52.

Fleming, A. S, Vaccarino, F,, & Luebke C. (1980). Amygdaloid inhibition of maternal behavior in the nulliparous female rat. *Physiol Behav, 25,* 731–743.

Hamilton, W. D. (1964). The genetic evolution of social behavior: I and II. *Journal of Theoretical Biology, 7,* 1–52.

Heaphy, E. D., & Dutton, J. E. (2006). Positive Social Interactions and the Human Body at Work: Linking Organizations and Physiology. *Academy of Management Review, 33,* 137–162.

Jacobson, C. D., Terkel, J., Gorski, R. A., & Sawyer, C. H. (1980). Effects of small medial preoptic area lesions on maternal behavior: Retrieving and nest building in the rat. *Brain Research, 194,* 471–478.

Joiner, T. (2005). *Why people die by suicide.* Cambridge, MA: Harvard University Press.

Kahneman, D., Krueger, A. B., Schkade, D. A., Schwarz, N., & Stone, A. (2004). A survey method for characterizing daily life experience: The day reconstruction method. *Science, 306* (5702), 1776–1780.

Kilner, R, & Johnstone, R. A. (1997). Begging the question: Are offspring solicitation behaviours signals of need? *Trends in Ecology and Evolution, 12,* 11–15.

Kölliker, M. J., Chuckalovcak, J. P., Haynes, K. F., & Brodie, E. D., III. (2006). Maternal food provisioning in relation to condition-dependent offspring odours in burrower bugs (*Sehirus cinctus*). *Proceedings of the Royal Society of London, Series B, 273,* 1523–1528.

Kringelbach, M. L., & Rolls, E. T. (2004). The functional neuroanatomy of the human orbitofrontal cortex: Evidence from neuroimaging and neuropsychology. *Progress in Neurobiology 72*(5): 341–372.

Linville, D., Chronister, K., Dishion, T., Todahl, J., Miller, J., Shaw, D., . . . Wilson, M. (2010). Longitudinal analysis of parenting practices, couple satisfaction, and child behavior problems. *Journal of Marital Family Therapy, 36,* 244–255.

Liu, D., Diorio, J., Tannenbaum, B., Caldji, C., Francis, D., Freedman, A., et al., & Meaney, M. J. (1997). Maternal care, hippocampal glucucorticoid receptors, and hypothalamic-pituitary-adrenal response to stress. *Science, 277,* 1659–1662.

Lonstein, J. S., & Morrell, J. I. (2007). Neuroendocrinology and neurochemistry of maternal motivation and behavior. In A. Lajtha & J. D. Blaustein (Eds.), *Handbook of neurochemistry and molecular neurobiology* (3rd ed., pp. 195–245). Berlin, Germany: Springer-Verlag.

Lonstein, J. S. & Stern, J. M. (1997). Role of the midbrain periaqueductal gray in maternal nurturance and aggression: C-fos and electrolytic lesion studies in lactating rats. *Journal of Neuroscience, 17,* 3364–3378.

Lorberbaum, J. P., Newman, J. D., Dubno, J. R., Horwitz, A. R., Nahas, Z., Teneback, C. C., et al. & George, M. S. (1999). Feasibility of using fMRI to study mothers responding to infant cries. *Depression and Anxiety, 10*(3), 99–104.

Lorberbaum, J., Newman, J. D., Horwitz, A. R., Dubno, J. R., Lydiard, R. B., Hamner, M. B., et al. & George, M. S. (2002). A potential role for thalamocingulate circuitry in human maternal behavior. *Biological Psychiatry, 51*(6), 431–445.

Molavi, D. W. (1997). *Neuroscience tutorial: Hypothalamus and autonomic nervous system.* St. Louis, MO: Washington University School of Medicine, 1997. (http://thalamus.wustl.edu/course/hypoANS.html)

Moll, J., Krueger, F., Zahn, R., Pardini, M., de Oliveira-Souza, R., & Grafman, J. (2006). Human fronto-mesolimbic networks guide decisions about charitable donation.

Proceedings of the National Academy of Sciences of the United States of America, 103(42), 15623–15628.

Numan, M. (1990). Long-term effects of preoptic area knife cuts on the maternal behavior of postpartum rats. *Behavioral and Neural Biology, 53*(2), 284–290.

Numan, M. (2006). Hypothalamic neural circuits regulating maternal responsiveness toward infants. *Behavioral an Cognitive Neuroscience Reviews, 5*(4), 163–190.

Numan, M. (2007). Motivational systems and the neural circuitry of maternal behavior in the rat. *Developmental Psychobiology, 49*(1), 12–21.

Numan, M., & Corodimas, K. P. (1985). The effects of paraventricular hypothalamic lesions on maternal behavior in rats. *Physiology and Behavior, 35*(3), 417–425.

Numan, M., & Insel, T. R. (2003). *The neurobiology of parental behavior.* New York, NY: Springer

Numan, M., Numan, M. J., Pliakou, N., Stolzenberg, D. S., Mullins, O. J., Murphy, J. M., & Smith, C. D. (2005). The effects of D1 or D2 dopamine receptor antagonism in the medial preoptic area, ventral pallidum, or nucleus accumbens on the maternal retrieval response and other aspects of maternal behavior in rats. *Behavioral Neuroscience, 119*, 1588–1604.

Numan, M., Numan, M. J., Schwarz, J. M., Neuner, C. M., Flood, T. F., & Smith, C. D. (2005). Medial preoptic area interactions with the nucleus accumbens–ventral pallidum circuit and maternal behavior in rats. *Behavioral and Brain Research, 158*, 53–68.

Ongür, D., & Price, J. L. (2000). The organization of networks within the orbital and medial prefrontal cortex of rats, monkeys and humans. *Cerebral Cortex, 10*, 206–219.

Post, S. G. (Ed.). (2007). *Altruism and health: Perspectives from empirical research.* New York, NY: Oxford University Press.

Poulin, M., Brown, S., Dillard, A., & Smith, D. (2011 *Health benefits of helping behavior: Stress-buffering as a potential mechanism.* Manuscript submitted for publication.

Preston, S. D., & Brown, S. L. (submitted). *The ultimate and proximate bases of active altruism.* Manuscript submitted for publication.

Preston, S. D., & de Waal, F. B. M (2011). Altruism. In J. Decety & J. Cacioppo (Eds.), *Handbook of social neuroscience.* New York: Oxford University Press.

Rolls, E. T., Sienkiewicz, Z. J., & Yaxley, S. (1989). Hunger modulates the responses to gustatory stimuli of single neurons in the caudolateral orbitofrontal cortex of the macaque monkey. *European Journal of Neuroscience, 1*, 53–60.

Rosenblatt, J. S. (1992). Hormone–behavior relations in the regulation of maternal behavior. In J. B. Becker, S. M. Breedlove, & D. Crews (Eds.), *Behavioral endocrinology* (1st ed., pp. 219–259). Cambridge, MA: MIT Press/Bradford Books.

Sanchez, M., Ladd, C., & Plotsky, P. (2001). Early adverse experience as a developmental risk factor for later psychopathology: Evidence from rodent and primate models. *Development and Psychopathology, 13*, 419–449.

Stratford, T. R., & Kelley, A. E. (1999). Evidence of functional relationship between NAcc shell and lateral hypothalamus subserving the control of feeding behavior. *Journal of Neuroscience, 19*, 11040–11048.

Tanabe, T., Lino, M., & Takaqi, S. F. (1975). Discrimination of odors in olfactory bulb, pyriform-amygdaloid areas, and orbitofrontal cortex of the monkey. *Journal of Neurophysiology, 38*, 1284–1296.

Terkel, J., Bridges, R. S., & Sawyer, C. H. (1979). Effects of transecting lateral neural connections of the medial preoptic area on maternal behavior in the rat: Nest building, pup retrieval and prolactin secretion. *Brain Research, 169*, 369–380.

Trivers, R. L. (1971). The evolution of reciprocal altruism. *Quarterly Review of Biology, 46*, 35–57.

Ueno, A., & Matsuzawa, T. (2004). Food transfer between chimpanzee mothers and their infants. *Primates, 45*, 231–239.

Uvnas-Moberg, K. (1997). Physiological and endocrine effects of social contact. *Annals of the New York Academy of Sciences, 807*, 146–163.

Uvnas-Moberg, K. (1998a). Antistress pattern induced by oxytocin. *News in Physiological Sciences, 13*, 22–25.

Uvnas-Moberg, K. (1998b). Oxytocin may mediate the benefits of positive social interaction and emotions. *Psychoneuroendocrinology, 23*, 819–835.

Warneken, F., Hare, B., Melis, A. P., Hanus, D., & Tomasello, M. (2007). Spontaneous altruism by chimpanzees and young children. *PLoS Biology, 5*, 1414–1420.

Wong, L., Kolditz, T. A., Millen, R. A., & Potter, T. M. (2003). *Why they fight: Combat motivation in the Iraq War.* Carlisle Barracks, PA: Strategic Studies Institute.

Wright, J., & Leonard, M. L. (2002). *The evolution of nestling begging: Competition, cooperation & communication.* Dordrecht, The Netherlands: Kluwer Academic Press.

Zahavi, A. (1995). Mate selection—a selection for handicap. *Journal of Theoretical Biology, 53*, 205–214.

Zahavi, A. (1997). *The handicap principle: A missing piece of Darwin's puzzle.* New York, NY, Oxford University Press.

Zak, P. J., Kurzban, R., & Matzner, W. (2004). The neurobiology of trust. *Annals of the New York Academy of Sciences, 1032*, 224–227.

Zald, D. H., & Kim, S. W. (1996). Anatomy and function of the orbital frontal cortex, II: Function and relevance to obsessive–compulsive disorder. *Journal of Neuropsychiatry, 8*(3), 249–261.

Zatorre, R. J., & Jones-Gotman, M. (1991). Human olfactory discrimination after unilateral frontal or temporal lobectomy. *Brain, 114*(part A), 71–84.

6 Neural Circuits Regulating Maternal Behavior

Implications for Understanding the Neural Basis of Social Cooperation and Competition

■ MICHAEL NUMAN

In this essay I want to show how maternal-behavior research, which is my area of expertise, can help us understand sociality in a broader context.

But how did I become interested in the study of maternal behavior? As an undergraduate at Brooklyn College, I read a chapter by Daniel Lehrman (1961) on the role of hormones in the parental behavior of birds and mammals and I was entirely captivated. The chapter beautifully showed the richness and complexity of the mechanisms regulating parental behavior. Here was a natural behavior that was necessary for reproductive success, that was affected by genes and hormones, but that also had a developmental course that allowed for the influence of experiential factors. After reading that chapter, I became preoccupied with the question of how experience, genetics, and hormones could modify the brain so that an organism's responsiveness to infants could change.

I have spent my entire career investigating these issues. Initially, I did not consider the broader implications of maternal-behavior research for social behavior in general. This understanding emerged over time and contributes to the ideas in this essay. By understanding the neural underpinnings of maternal behavior, one delves into the neurobiological factors that influence core human characteristics involved in social bonding, nurturing behavior, and love. In this too-violent world, the factors that give rise to these prosocial characteristics are worthy of our full attention.

What are the neural mechanisms that determine whether individuals cooperate or compete with other members of their species? In other words, what neural mechanisms determine whether perceived social stimuli are assigned a positive or a negative valence by the perceiver, with positive social stimuli activating neural pathways that cause contact-seeking behaviors, acceptance, caregiving, and other prosocial behaviors, while negative social stimuli activate pathways that cause avoidance, rejection, competition, or even attack (antisocial behaviors)? These questions form the overarching issue of this essay, which focuses on the neurobiological mechanisms that shift an individual away from antisocial behaviors and toward prosocial behaviors.

My research concerns the neurobiology of maternal caregiving motivation in rodents, and in this essay I will show how hormonal, genetic, and experiential (learning) factors, by modifying the way the brain works, can switch a female rat away from antisocial and toward prosocial responding to infant stimuli. The rodent research will form a foundation to help us understand the opposing neural mechanisms that mediate either social competition or cooperation in humans and the variety of factors that can operate on these mechanisms so that prosocial responding is favored. My perspective follows that set forth by Pfaff (2007) in his outstanding book *The Neurobiology of Fair Play*, where he argues that the neural circuits underlying complex prosocial behaviors, such as cooperation and reciprocal altruism, are likely to be based on the core circuits that underlie sexual and maternal motivation.

For a variety of species, it is clear that social stimuli can be processed by either an aversion/rejection neural network or an attraction/acceptance neural network. In social ants, pheromones or odors released by individuals elicit acceptance responses from other colony members, but these same individuals would be attacked by members of other ant colonies of the same species. These colony odors are learned by worker ants during early adulthood (Hölldobler & Wilson, 2009). Therefore, if a young ant is switched from its natal colony to an alien colony early in life, it will subsequently attack members of its native colony. Somewhat similarly, in humans, much of our social world is divided into in-group and out-group members. We tend to react in a more positive social manner to our in-group, while we have the potential to be violent toward out-group individuals. Within human populations, cognitive factors play an important role in determining how social stimuli are processed and evaluated. Political ideologies and religious views are powerful manipulators of our social reactivity, suggesting that cognitive mechanisms can influence the way socioemotional neural circuits process social stimuli.

■ MATERNAL BEHAVIOR AS A MODEL SYSTEM

In most adult nulliparous (virgin) female mammals, infant stimuli elicit avoidance, rejection, or attack responses (Numan & Insel, 2003). This is the case for both rats and sheep, the species on which most of the research on the biology of maternal behavior has been performed. At birth, however, female rats and sheep will accept and care for, rather than reject, infants presented to them, and hormonal events associated with the termination of pregnancy are involved in stimulating this maternal motivation (Numan & Insel, 2003). These findings from typical virgin and lactating mammals have given rise to the idea that hormones stimulate maternal behavior at birth by acting on the brain to depress rejection and avoidance responses toward young while facilitating neural circuits that regulate approach and acceptance responses (Numan, 2006, 2007; Numan & Insel, 2003; Numan & Sheehan, 1997; Rosenblatt & Mayer, 1995). The important point is that the same stimulus, an infant of one's species, can be processed by either acceptance circuits or aversion circuits, depending on the female mammal's internal state.

My research program has tried to relate approach–avoidance models of motivated behavior, which describe the switching or transition of behavior from avoidance and rejection to approach and attraction, to their neural underpinnings, using the neurobiology of maternal behavior in rats as an exemplar (Numan, 2006: Numan & Insel, 2003; Numan & Sheehan, 1997). The hypothalamus, amygdala, and nucleus accumbens (all of which are subcortical structures involved in emotional and motivated behavior) play dominant roles in my neural models. Others have offered neural models of motivated behavior along similar lines, proposing that amygdala output regulates avoidance or withdrawal from stimuli, the nucleus accumbens regulates approach responses, and the prefrontal cortex (PFC) modulates the output of these two subcortical regions (Ernst & Fudge, 2009). The PFC is sometimes referred to as the executive controller of behavior, and it is involved in planning movements and emotional regulation (rational control of emotionality). Given that the PFC is involved in mediating the effects of cognition on behavior, such models show how cognitive factors could influence subcortical neural circuits controlling socioemotional responses. In this essay, I will expand and develop these models to show how the nervous system can react to the same stimulus in either a positive or negative way. An important advance will be to show that different neural populations in the amygdala are involved in either negative or positive social behaviors.

■ NEURAL CIRCUITS REGULATING MATERNAL RESPONSIVENESS IN RATS

The hypothalamus is a subcortical brain structure that is significantly involved in regulating basic motivational and emotional states such as hunger and thirst, sexual and parental motivation, and aggression and fear. The hypothalamus is affected by external sensory stimuli and the organism's internal state, and its outputs influence how an organism responds to biologically significant stimuli (Numan, 2006; Swanson, 1987). The medial preoptic area (MPOA) is located in the front part of the hypothalamus and is essential for maternal behavior: It is responsive to both hormonal and infant-related stimuli, and as I will show, its neural connections to other brain areas allow maternal behavior to occur (Numan & Insel, 2003). In a variety of species, depression of normal MPOA function disrupts maternal behavior. In addition, pregnancy hormones act locally on MPOA neurons to stimulate maternal behavior. Based on this evidence, it can be proposed that in the typical female mammal, the hormones associated with the end of pregnancy gain access to the brain and alter the functioning of particular MPOA neurons. Such hormonally primed MPOA neurons now respond to infant-related stimuli such that MPOA neural projections inhibit aversion- and withdrawal-related circuits and excite approach and acceptance circuits (Numan, 2006).

The Amygdala and Maternal Behavior

The amygdala is a subcortical structure in the limbic system that is buried under the temporal lobe of the brain. The amygdala contains different neural populations, each of which has unique projections to other parts of the brain. As a result, different parts of the amygdala are involved in different functions. Stimuli from pups elicit rejection and withdrawal responses from virgin female rats by activating the medial part of the amygdala (Numan, 2006; Numan & Insel, 2003). In fact, lesions or destruction of this "aversion" area of the medial amygdala can actually facilitate maternal behavior in virgin rats. Such a process fits with the large body of evidence that indicates that the amygdala regulates fearful and defensive responses (Amaral, 2002; LeDoux, 1996). However, the amygdala can also assign a positive valence to incoming sensory stimuli and can regulate approach and other positive attraction responses (Belova, Paton, & Salzman, 2008; Costafreda, Brammer, David, & Fu, 2008; Lai, Ramiro, Yu, & Johnston, 2005; Paton, Belova, Morrison, & Salzman, 2006). Lesions to the lateral amygdala disrupt maternal behavior in postpartum rats (Numan, 2006; Numan et al., 2010). Therefore the hormonal events of late pregnancy appear to change the way the brain processes stimuli from pups. It can be proposed that in virgin females, stimuli from pups activate amygdala neurons that are part of an aversion circuit, while for the postpartum female, such stimuli activate other amygdala neurons whose projections are part of an attraction circuit.

Evidence from my laboratory (Sheehan, Paul, Amaral, Numan, & Numan, 2001) suggests that in naïve virgin female rats, pup stimuli activate medial amygdala neurons that project to the anterior hypothalamic nucleus (AHN), which in turn projects to a part of the midbrain called the periaqueductal gray (PAG). PAG projections to the lower brain stem and spinal cord are known to influence reflex-like defensive and withdrawal responses. But why do pup stimuli promote approach responses, rather than rejection responses, in hormonally primed lactating females? One proposal (Numan, 2006; Numan & Insel, 2003) is that once MPOA neurons are primed by hormones they can respond to diverse pup stimuli, and MPOA outputs then exert two important effects: they inhibit the aversion system and excite an attraction/acceptance system. The projections from MPOA neurons to the AHN and PAG (Numan & Numan, 1997) could be one route through which the MPOA depresses the aversion circuit. But how might the MPOA neurons excite the attraction/acceptance system? As will be outlined below, the lateral part of the amygdala sends neural projections to a part of the brain called the nucleus accumbens–ventral pallidum circuit (NA–VP circuit). This nuclear group has been shown to control attraction and approach responses to biologically significant stimuli, and the MPOA appears to promote attraction and acceptance behavior by facilitating the processing of pup stimuli that are relayed to the NA–VP circuit by the lateral amygdala (and other parts of the brain). Figure 6.1 shows diagrams of these neural models.

The Mesolimbic Dopamine System and Goal-Directed Motivated Responses: A Component of the Attraction Circuit

The mesolimbic dopamine (DA) system originates from midbrain neurons in the ventral tegmental area (VTA), and the NA–VP circuit is a major forebrain region to which it projects. DA action on the NA–VP circuit facilitates the processing of sensory input that arrives there from the amygdala and other areas. The mesolimbic DA system has often been said to regulate reward-seeking behavior (Berridge & Robinson, 1998). A rewarding stimulus is one that attracts us and that, once we obtain it, gives us pleasure. A rewarding stimulus can also reinforce or strengthen those behaviors that were successful in obtaining the desired stimulus. Berridge and Robinson (1998) have made the convincing case that DA action at the level of

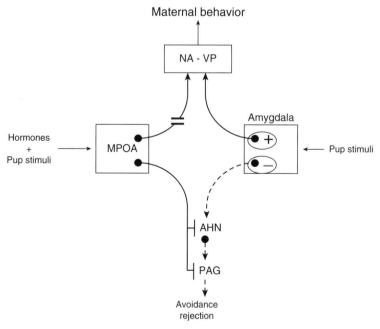

Figure 6.1 Proposed Neural Circuits Regulating Maternal Behavior in Rats. Pup stimuli reaching the amygdala can activate neural circuits that lead to either positive (+) maternal responses (approach to and acceptance of pups) or the negative (−) responses of avoidance and rejection of pups, depending on the female's internal state. Circuits shown in dashed lines are active in naïve virgin females, while circuits shown in solid lines are active in postpartum females. A virgin female avoids pups because negative amygdala circuits, which project to the anterior hypothalamic nucleus (AHN) and periaqueductal gray (PAG), are activated. It is proposed that postpartum females respond in a positive manner to infants because the hormone-primed medial preoptic area (MPOA) inhibits the AHN and PAG avoidance pathway and facilitates the ability of the nucleus accumbens–ventral pallidum circuit (NA–VP) to process pup stimuli arriving from positive amygdala neural inputs. Neural circuits ending in an arrow are excitatory, and those ending in a bar are inhibitory. The circuit from MPOA to NA–VP has a break in it because the details of the circuit are not fully described. (This description is presented in Figure 6.2.) For simplicity, we have shown the NA–VP as only receiving positive inputs from the amygdala and only being involved in prosocial acceptance responses. In fact, the situation is more complicated (see Faure, Reynolds, Richard, & Berridge, 2008).

the NA–VP circuit promotes attraction and approach responses to rewarding stimuli. Such approach responses are sometimes referred to as appetitive or goal-directed motivated responses.

Therefore, when the mesolimbic DA system is active, it increases an organism's responsiveness to biologically significant social and nonsocial stimuli, such as mating partners, infants, and food (Numan, 2006; Numan & Stolzenberg, 2008). This kind of analysis led Mogenson (1987) to refer to DA input to the NA–VP circuit as the "limbic motor system," since these brain areas and connections are involved in translating sensory inputs processed through the limbic system into behavioral reactivity toward the corresponding stimuli. This model not only shows how amygdala output can influence voluntary reward-seeking behavior as a result of being processed through the NA–VP circuit; it also shows how the amygdala's effectiveness can be modulated by DA release into NA–VP.

But what activates DA release into the NA–VP circuit? That depends on the particular motivated behavior. For maternal behavior, research shows that MPOA projections to the VTA, which activate DA input to the NA–VP circuit, constitute a route through which the MPOA promotes active maternal caregiving responses by allowing the NA–VP to react to pup stimuli inputs carried by amygdala attraction circuits (Numan, 2006; Numan & Stolzenberg, 2008, 2009). Figure 6.2 shows the details of this neurocircuitry. My proposal is that for nulliparous females, pup stimuli activate amygdala aversion circuits, while in postpartum females, MPOA output inhibits these aversion circuits and promotes activity in attraction/acceptance circuits (Numan, 2006). Such proposals are important because it describes in a concrete way how changes in internal state (the transition from the virgin to the postpartum female) can alter the way the same external stimuli are processed.

The Role of Oxytocin and other Neuromodulatory Factors

Although the output of the MPOA is essential for maternal responsiveness, several other factors interact with MPOA output to promote optimal maternal caregiving motivation. Oxytocin (OT) is a neuropeptide that is both a hormone (released from the pituitary gland) and a neurotransmitter/neuromodulator (released at synapses in the brain). In addition to projecting to the pituitary, neurons in the paraventricular nucleus of the hypothalamus project to a variety of brain regions, allowing OT to be released into the maternal brain at the time of birth.

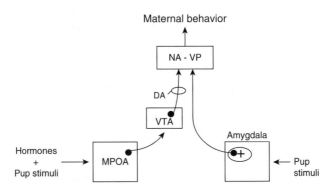

Figure 6.2 The Proposed Neural Circuit Through Which the Medial Preoptic Area (MPOA) Promotes Positive Maternal Responses. The hormone-primed MPOA is shown to activate the ventral tegmental area (VTA), which gives rise to dopamine (DA) neural input to the nucleus accumbens–ventral pallidum circuit (NA–VP). DA release into NA–VP promotes maternal behavior in response to pup stimuli arriving from positive amygdala circuits. Neural circuits ending in an arrow are excitatory.

Importantly, OT receptors (OTRs) are located in the MPOA, VTA, NA, and amygdala, and OT has been shown to act on the MPOA, VTA, and NA to facilitate the onset of maternal behavior (Numan & Insel, 2003; Numan & Stolzenberg, 2009). OT also exerts anxiolytic effects, decreasing fearfulness and anxiety, by acting on the amygdala (Numan & Insel, 2003). Therefore, OT release into the mother's brain may play a coordinating neuromodulatory role, promoting activity in attraction/acceptance circuits and decreasing activity in central aversion circuits. A recent study has found that serotonin neurons in the raphe nucleus (located in the brain stem) express OTRs and that some of the anxiolytic effects of OT may be mediated through serotonin release (Yoshida et al., 2009). Since the raphe nucleus projects to medial parts of the amygdala, it is possible that serotonin release into the amygdala, mediated by OT, is one of the ways that OT depresses the aversion system. A large body of evidence shows that serotonin neural systems decrease anxiety, fearfulness, defensiveness, and aggression and that serotonin exerts these effects by acting at the level of the amygdala, hypothalamus, and PFC (Holmes, 2008; Meyer-Lindenberg et al., 2006; New et al., 2004). OT, by affecting serotonin systems, can therefore have widespread effects.

The PFC projects strongly to the amygdala. One of the effects of this projection is to regulate emotional reactions by decreasing the amygdala's responsiveness to aversive and threatening stimuli (Rosenkranz, Moore, & Grace, 2003; Sotres-Bayon, Cain, & LeDoux, 2006). The PFC not only influences amygdala function but also projects to the NA–VP circuit (Wright & Groenewegen, 1995) and to the MPOA (Simerly & Swanson, 1986). Therefore, it is in a strategic position to exert modulatory effects on both aversion and acceptance neural networks. Recent work indicates that the PFC plays a role in regulating the organization of maternal responses in postpartum rats (Afonso, Sison, Lovic, & Fleming, 2007). However, more work needs to be done to establish whether the PFC is essential for the transition from infant avoidance to infant acceptance, which forms the basis of the onset of maternal behavior in rats and other species (Numan & Insel, 2003). The significance of the potential role of the PFC is that it would allow cortical cognitive processes to influence subcortical emotional processing.

Experiential Influences on the Neural Circuitry of Maternal Behavior: Effects on Appetitive and Aversion Circuits

The attraction/acceptance and aversion/rejection circuits we have been discussing are not fixed or rigid circuits turned on or off by hormones or neuropeptides, but have been shown to be plastic and modifiable by experience. The important general point is that learning processes can influence whether social stimuli activate aversion or attraction circuits. Virgin female rats avoid pups, and first-time mother rats require hormonal stimulation to show adequate maternal behavior. Once a female rat acquires maternal experience, however, her future maternal behavior becomes less dependent on hormonal stimulation (Numan, 2006; Numan & Insel, 2003; Numan & Stolzenberg, 2009). This effect has been referred to as *maternal memory*. It appears that interacting with pups and showing maternal behavior permanently modifies the influence of pup stimuli such that their access to the aversion circuitry is decreased while their access to attraction circuits is potentiated. DA release into the NA–VP circuit during maternal behavior in first-time females appears essential for the development of maternal memory (Parada, King, Li, & Fleming, 2008). Perhaps this DA release in some way facilitates the ability of pup stimuli to activate the appetitive NA–VP circuits. Therefore, the neural circuits that promote the initial onset of maternal behavior (MPOA projections to the VTA that cause DA release into the NA) appear to provide a mechanism that "emancipates" maternal circuits from endocrine control.

Not only can adult maternal experience modify the way the maternal brain processes infant-related stimuli, but early life experiences can also have dramatic effects on the way the brain ultimately deals with social stimuli. A large body of evidence indicates that organisms exposed to early life stresses, including maternal abuse and neglect, show increased anxiety, fearfulness, impulsive aggression, and poor maternal behavior in adulthood (Kaffman & Meaney, 2007). Early primate work by Harlow's group (Ruppenthal, Arling, Harlow, Sackett, & Suomi, 1976) showed that rhesus monkeys raised without their mothers were anxious and highly stress reactive and showed poor maternal behavior toward their own offspring. Maestripieri (2005) has shown that rhesus monkeys that are abused by either their biological mothers or foster mothers develop an abusive phenotype to their own offspring in adulthood. These results conform to human data showing that children who are abused or neglected by their parents tend to become abusive or neglectful parents themselves (Champagne, 2008; Kaffman & Meaney, 2007; Numan & Insel, 2003). Therefore, early adverse experiences can have long-term developmental effects that increase the activity of central aversion circuits and decrease the activity of prosocial attraction circuits necessary for maternal behavior. Maestripieri et al. (2006) report that rhesus monkeys that experienced high levels of abuse and rejection from their mothers had lower cerebrospinal fluid levels of serotonin.

Even normal variations in maternal behavior in rodents can have developmental effects on offspring. In comparison to pups raised by attentive mothers, those raised by less attentive mothers develop a more fearful phenotype and also show less attentive maternal behavior to their own offspring (Champagne, 2008; Kaffman & Meaney, 2007). Being raised by a less attentive mother has been shown to influence the development of the amygdala and the MPOA in rats: The amygdala is under less inhibition by γ-aminobutyric acid (GABA, a major inhibitory neurotransmitter), and the MPOA has fewer estrogen and OT receptors. What these results suggest is that lower levels of maternal caregiving, even when this maternal behavior is within the normal range and all young survive to weaning, can increase aversive amygdala output and decrease appetitive MPOA output in the affected offspring, and that these neural changes can affect the development of emotionality and maternal behavior in those offspring.

Environmental interventions that occur after a period of less-than-adequate maternal care appear capable of reversing some of its effects. Harlow's group (Ruppenthal et al., 1976; Numan & Insel, 2003) found that if rhesus monkeys raised without mothers were raised in a peer group, their subsequent maternal behavior and emotionality improved compared with those who did not enter a peer group. Champagne and Meaney (2007) showed that the behavioral and neural effects of being raised by less attentive mothers could be partially reversed by exposing the young to an enriched social environment during the post weaning period.

Finally, genetic factors have been found to interact with early life experiences to affect the development of attraction and aversion circuits. Rats from the Flinders sensitive line, which has been used as a genetic model of depression, show deficits in maternal behavior and in DA release in the NA (Friedman, Berman, & Overstreet, 2006; Lavi-Avnon, Yadid, Overstreet, & Weller, 2005, Lavi-Avnon et al., 2008). Similarly, Carola et al. (2008) report that a genotype that affects serotonin transmission exacerbates the effects of poor maternal care on the development of anxiety and stress reactivity in mice. Analogous results have been reported for humans and nonhuman primates (Caspi et al., 2002; Weder et al., 2009).

■ GENERALIZATIONS BEYOND MATERNAL BEHAVIOR: NONHUMAN ANIMALS

To what extent can we use the aversion–attraction neural systems analysis of maternal behavior to understand other social behaviors? Do the core circuits underlying maternal behavior form the foundation upon which other prosocial neural circuits are built? I would like to suggest that this is the case, and consider below several supportive examples.

Sexual Motivation

We have argued that MPOA projections to the VTA, which activate mesolimbic DA input to the NA–VP circuit, are part of an attraction/acceptance circuit regulating maternal responsiveness. MPOA neurons are also positively involved in male and female sexual motivation. It is possible that MPOA projections to VTA regulate the prosocial approach and contact behaviors underlying all forms of reproductive and parental behavior. It remains to be determined whether distinct MPOA microcircuits represent each behavior or whether the MPOA plays a more general function in the regulation of reproductive, parental, and other prosocial behaviors (see Newman, 1999; Numan, 2006; Numan & Insel, 2003; Stolzenberg & Numan, 2011).

Long-Term Pair Bonding

An important aspect of social behavior in certain mammals is the formation of long-term social bonds or attachments. Most mammals have polygynous mating systems (one male mates with several females), and males and females only come together socially to mate, after which the female rears the young on her own. However, some mammals, including humans, are relatively monogamous and form long-term bonds between male and female mating partners such that they prefer each other as social companions even when they are outside the mating context. Research indicates that evolutionary forces that affect the genotype of a species can influence the chemical architecture of the brain, with concomitant effects on social behavior. Vole species have been the primary subjects in this research (see Ross et al., 2009; Young & Wang, 2004). The prairie vole is a species where males and females form relatively permanent bonds after mating. Experimental results show that OT action on the NA–VP circuit is essential for pair-bond formation in female prairie voles. DA release into the NA, which occurs during mating, coacts with OT action in the NA–VP to facilitate the formation of the pair bond. Since the MPOA is important for sexual motivation, it is possible that as in maternal behavior, MPOA projections to the VTA are involved in stimulating DA release into the NA–VP during mating in voles. An interesting idea for the formation of pair bonds is as follows (see Young & Wang, 2004): Sensory input from the mating partner reaches the NA–VP circuit via positively valent amygdala neurons, and DA action on the NA–VP facilitates approach and acceptance behaviors. As a result of the concomitant effects of OT action on the NA–VP circuit, these neural connections from the amygdala to the NA–VP circuit are strengthened or consolidated, allowing sensory input from the mating partner to gain selective access to NA–VP approach and acceptance circuits. Thus in the future, even outside the mating context, individuals that mated together in the past will be attracted to one another.

Another vole species, the montane vole, does not form pair bonds. Males and females come together to mate but separate afterwards. Although DA is released into the NA–VP region of this species during mating, OTRs are not highly localized in this region. Differences in the expression of OTRs in different vole species have been linked to variations within the OTR gene. A lower OTR distribution in the NA–VP neurons that form part of the attraction/acceptance circuit may account for the fact that the neural connections between partner sensory input and NA–VP neurons are not permanently strengthened. In that case, mating behavior and continuous DA release into NA would be necessary to maintain prosocial interactions.

The mechanisms underlying pair-bond formation involve aspects of the same neural networks that are involved in maternal behavior and maternal-memory formation. With respect to the formation of maternal memory and long-term mother–infant bonds, the following can be proposed: As a result of the hormonally primed MPOA causing DA release into the NA–VP in response to pup stimuli, such stimuli may subsequently gain access to attraction circuits within the NA–VP continuum without hormone priming of the MPOA. Since OTRs are located in the rat NA, OT may interact with mesolimbic DA effects to influence maternal-memory formation (D'Cunha, King, Fleming, & Levy, 2011). An important point to gain from this analysis is that formation of pair bonds, that is, affiliative bonds between adults, may use the neural circuits underlying enduring mother–infant bonds as a foundational starting point. Such an analysis makes sense, since all mammals develop mother–infant attachments but only some mammalian species develop strong adult social bonds. In those species where such sociality would be adaptive, evolutionary forces may have appropriated and modified the maternal circuitry to develop the neural network underlying adult social bonds.

Estrogen Receptors in Amygdala and Male Prosocial Behavior

Cushing and Wynne-Edwards (2006) examined the expression of estrogen receptors (ERs) in the medial amygdala of male rodents of a variety of social and
asocial species. Testosterone secreted by the testes can be converted to estradiol in
the brain, where it can bind to ERs. Cushing and Wynne-Edwards found a correlation between low levels of ER expression and prosocial behaviors In an experimental study, Cushing, Perry, Musatov, Ogawa, and Papademetriou, (2008)
increased the expression of ERs in the medial amygdala of prairie vole males.
Males with increased ER expression showed less prosocial behavior (paternal
behavior and formation of partner preferences). These results suggest that for
these species, estradiol action at the level of medial amygdala may bias the
amygdala circuitry in favor of the aversion circuitry and away from the attraction/
acceptance circuitry.

Amygdala Activation in Both Approach and Avoidance

Finally, Lai et al. (2005) have studied social recognition in hamsters and found that
the amygdala is activated when an individual approaches a familiar hamster and
when an individual avoids a hamster that defeated it in a previous aggressive
encounter. It would be interesting to determine whether distinct amygdala neurons were activated under each condition, with one population contributing to the
proposed prosocial system and the other participating in an aversion neural network. These findings raise an additional point. In many cases, a particular social
stimulus may initially be neutral, not possessing a positive or negative valence.
However, pleasant or aversive interactions with that stimulus may influence
whether it activates approach or avoidance/defensive circuits, respectively, in the
future.

In all these examples, one can see how physiological (hormonal), genetic, and
experiential factors can all influence social responsiveness, and that aspects of the
neural circuitry involved in maternal behavior are also involved in other social
behaviors.

■ GENERALIZATIONS TO HUMAN BEHAVIOR

Can these results from studies of nonhuman animals be related to human behavior, whether cooperation, approach, and acceptance or aversion, aggression, and
competition? Research on humans suggests that the human brain contains ele-
mentary and distinct approach and withdrawal circuits that also mediate positive
and negative affect (moods and emotions) (Davidson, 2002). Figure 6.3 shows a
simplified scheme for the discussion that follows. This proposed neural model is
derived from the circuits we described above from the animal research. It shows
MPOA projections to the VTA facilitating the output of positive circuits from the
NA–VP. The amygdala can activate approach or aversion circuits. The PFC can
also have dual effects based on distinct outputs (Davidson, 2002; Wager Davidson,
Hughes, Lindquist, & Ochsner, 2008). It can increase aversion and withdrawal by

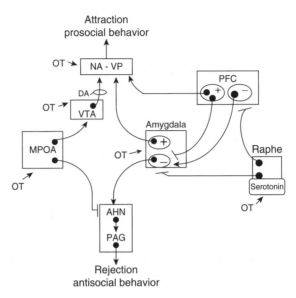

Figure 6.3 A Simplified Model of the Neural and Neurochemical Regulation of Social Behavior. This model is built upon the circuits shown in figures 6.1 and 6.2. Medial preoptic area (MPOA) projections to dopamine (DA) neurons in the ventral tegmental area (VTA) facilitate the output of NA–VP prosocial circuits. The amygdala gives rise to either prosocial (+) or antisocial (−) circuits, and the MPOA may depress the negative circuits. Distinct prefrontal cortex (PFC) circuits can either increase aversion and defensive responses by activating negative amygdala circuits or can bias the individual in the direction of prosocial behavior by inhibiting negative amygdala circuits and stimulating NA–VP output. Finally, serotonin neural pathways from the raphe nucleus and oxytocin (OT) neural inputs (derived from the paraventricular nucleus of the hypothalamus) can exert neuromodulatory influences on these neural circuits, decreasing anxiety, aggression, and competition, and facilitating approach and cooperation. In this simplified neural model, we only show descending projections from the amygdala to the anterior hypothalamic nucleus (AHN) and periaqueductal gray (PAG) as giving rise to antisocial and defensive responses. These types of responses, however, would be rather stereotyped and reflexive in nature. Other neural projections from negative amygdala regions to the cerebral hemispheres (not shown) are involved in regulating more voluntary antisocial responses. Neural circuits ending in an arrow are excitatory, and those ending in a bar are inhibitory. At the level of the amygdala, OT is shown with an arrow; it is possible for OT to promote prosocial behavior by either activating positive circuits or inhibiting negative circuits.

activating negative amygdala circuits or it can bias the brain toward approach and acceptance by inhibiting these negative circuits and stimulating NA–VP output. Finally, serotonin and OT input to these systems can exert modulatory effects, decreasing anxiety, aggression, and competition and facilitating approach and cooperation. Several pieces of evidence from the human literature support aspects of the proposed model.

Prefrontal Cortex–Amygdala Interactions: The Influence of Serotonin, Genes, and Experience

A variety of studies have indicated that dysregulation of the PFC is associated with impulsive aggression and violent crime (Best, Williams, & Coccaro, 2002). Impulsive aggression may, in part, be the result of a decreased ability of the PFC to down-regulate output from those amygdala circuits that form part of the aversion/rejection network. In a functional magnetic resonance imaging (fMRI) study, Coccaro, McCloskey, Fitzgerald, and Phan (2007) found that human subjects with intermittent explosive disorder showed increased amygdala activation and decreased PFC activation in response to angry faces in comparison with control subjects. Therefore, for these aggressive individuals, certain social stimuli may be more likely to trigger defensive circuits mediated by amygdala output. With respect to the role of serotonin in decreasing anxiety, aggression, and aversion, New et al. (2004) note that fluoxetine treatment, which stimulates serotonin synaptic transmission, decreases impulsive aggression while also increasing metabolic activity in the PFC.

There are genetic polymorphisms (different variants or alleles of a particular gene) that can affect the development of serotonin neural circuits in the brain (Buckholtz & Meyer-Lindenberg, 2008). One example is a gene that regulates the synthesis of monoamine oxidase A (MAOA), which is involved in the metabolic inactivation of serotonin and has also been associated with impulsive aggression. One variant of the MAOA gene (MAOA-L) produces less MAOA, which results in a decrease in the breakdown of serotonin. Eisenberger, Way, Taylor, Welch, & Lieberman (2007) compared MAOA-L humans with counterparts who possessed the MAOA-H allele (the high-expressing variant). MAOA-L individuals were found to have higher trait aggression and showed higher levels of social distress in a game in which social exclusion or rejection occurred. One possible explanation is that an overabundance of serotonin *during brain development* (because of decreased metabolic inactivation) results in a compensatory mechanism that downregulates the production of serotonin receptors. If this downregulation is too severe and overly compensatory, then the MAOA-L genotype may actually result in decreased serotonin neural transmission in adulthood. In an fMRI study, Meyer-Lindenberg et al. (2006) found that when subjects are shown angry or fearful faces, those with the MAOA-L genotype show increased amygdala and decreased PFC activation in comparison with MAOA-H individuals,.

With respect to the development of antisocial behavior, violence, and criminal behavior, there appears to be an interaction of genetics and environment. Early adverse experience during development (child maltreatment or abuse) was more likely to be associated with the subsequent occurrence of antisocial behavior in MAOA-L individuals than in their MAOA-H counterparts (Caspi et al., 2002; Weder et al., 2009).

Oxytocin and Human Social Behavior

In my review of nonhuman animal studies above, I emphasized the importance of OT for maternal and social behaviors and I suggested that OT neural systems can both promote activity in attraction neural systems and depress activity in aversion neural circuits. This raises the question of whether there is evidence for similar effects in humans. Feldman, Weller, Zagoory-Sharon, and Levine (2007) report that mothers who had higher blood levels of OT during pregnancy bonded more strongly to their infants during the postpartum period. They suggest that peripheral release of OT was likely to be correlated with increased central release of OT into the maternal brain and that this may have facilitated positive mother–infant interactions. Another correlational study has implications for understanding the role of OT as a possible moderator of effects of early adverse experiences on the development of social behavior. Fries, Zeigler, Kurian, Jacoris, and Pollack (2005) compared two groups of children. One group was raised normally by their biological parents, while the other group was composed of children raised in orphanages for about 17 months prior to adoption. The adopted children were studied after approximately three years in their adoptive homes. Urine samples were taken from the children after positive physical contact and social interaction with their biological or adoptive mothers. OT levels in urine increased significantly more in children interacting with their biological parents than it did in the adopted children. The implication of this study, which coincides with the rodent and primate work reviewed previously, is that early childhood neglect may impact the development of OT neural systems, which could then impact the development of social behavior. In this light, it is relevant that infants raised in orphanages can have problems with their subsequent social development (Fries et al., 2005).

Several studies have made use of intranasally applied OT, which presumably passes the blood–brain barrier, to examine the effects of OT on social behavior in humans. The human amgydala can be activated by both negative and positive social stimuli, such as angry and happy faces (Domes et al., 2007). In fMRI studies, it has been found that intranasal OT administration decreases amygdala activation to both sorts of social stimuli (Domes et al., 2007; Kirsch et al., 2005). This finding appears surprising in the context of our view that OT can both decrease aversion systems and increase attraction systems. Perhaps OT acts elsewhere in the circuits we have described (such as the NA–VP or MPOA) to influence attraction- and acceptance-type social behaviors. Further support for a role for OT in positive social behavior in humans comes from a study by Guastella, Mitchell, & Mathews (2008). Subjects who received intranasal OT or placebo were shown a series of happy, angry, or neutral faces. Twenty-four hours later they were shown a group of faces, some of which they had viewed the day before. Compared with controls, the OT-treated subjects were more likely to have remembered seeing the previously viewed happy faces, suggesting that OT neural systems may have increased the salience and processing of positive social stimuli. In a more recent study, Theodoridou, Rowe, Penton-Voak, and Rogers (2009) found that people of both sexes who received intranasal OT rated faces they had never seen before as more trustworthy and attractive than did control subjects.

I would like to end this discussion on OT and human social behavior by discussing the possible role of OT in reciprocal altruism. If you were to help another individual for the first time, you might lend a small-to-moderate amount of support. If the recipient of your support returned the favor in the future, then on subsequent interactions you might provide additional support or aid to that person. In other words, as social relationships develop, trust between individuals develops, which promotes cooperation and reciprocal altruism between them. An interesting hypothesis is that as a social bond develops between two adults, individual-specific social stimuli are likely to activate OT neural systems that promote prosocial interactions. There is some support for this interesting idea (Baumgartner, Heinrichs, Vonlanthen, Fischbacher, & Fehr, 2008). Kosfeld, Heinrichs, Zak, Fischbacher, and Fehr (2005) studied individuals as they played a trust game with a partner. The basic premise was: how much money would you (the investor) give to another person (the trustee), who was then supposed to share any gained profits with you? A problem is that the trustee could betray the investor and keep all the profits. This game was played so that the investor could not know ahead of time how the trustee would behave. Normal subjects tended to invest only a small amount of money with the trustee, while subjects administered intranasal OT tended to invest a lot of money.

In an fMRI study concerning interactions between the PFC and subcortical structures, Wager et al. (2008) obtained evidence that the PFC can not only down regulate negative emotions but also upregulate positive emotions. Subjects were shown negative or aversive images and rated their emotional responses. In some cases, when shown aversive images, subjects were asked to reappraise the image so that it would become less negative: They were asked to create a positive interpretation of the scene. Successful reappraisal, such that aversive scenes resulted in decreased negative emotional experiences, was associated with increased activity in both the PFC and the NA area. It is interesting to speculate that as in rats, in humans OT action on the amygdala decreases aversive responses, while OT action on the NA–VP circuit or MPOA promotes positive social responses. In this regard, note that OT-binding neurons have been located in the human preoptic area and VP (Loup, Tribollet, Dubois-Dauphin, & Dreifuss, 1991).

Williams Syndrome and the Development of Amygdala Socioemotional Circuits

One final group of studies is relevant to the issue of dual amygdala output circuits and social behavior. Williams syndrome (WS) is a human genetic anomaly caused by the deletion of about 20 genes from chromosome 7. Individuals with this syndrome differ from normal controls on a variety of measures (Reiss et al., 2004), one of which is a phenotype characterized by hypersociality (Jones et al., 2000). They are gregarious and empathic, show no fear of strangers, eagerly approach them, and are overfriendly toward them. Haas et al. (2009) report that in an fMRI study, WS subjects, when compared with controls, showed increased amygdala activation to positive (happy) social stimuli and decreased amygdala activation to negative (fearful) social stimuli. These changes seem to be related to social stimuli, as amygdala activation to threatening nonsocial stimuli is not decreased in WS subjects (Meyer-Lindenberg et al., 2005). Haas et al. conclude that the hypersocial behavior of WS subjects may be based on the altered development of distinct amygdala nuclei that are involved in different social functions. In other words, amygdala output that regulates prosocial behavior appears to be promoted, while that related to a social-aversion circuit appears to be damped down.

■ CONCLUSIONS

Based on my analysis of maternal behavior, I have proposed that distinct neural circuits underlie social approach and acceptance behaviors (prosocial behaviors) and social avoidance, defensive, and attack behaviors (antisocial behaviors). I have tried to broaden this view by arguing that the same social stimulus can give rise to either social cooperation or social competition (or avoidance) based on the circuits and associated affective responses that are engaged by the particular stimulus. Most important, I have shown that the way in which a social stimulus is processed and evaluated can be influenced by a variety of factors, which include internal physiological state (e.g., hormones), genetic factors, experiential influences throughout development, and cognitive factors.

Because I am a behavioral neuroscientist, I have emphasized neural systems that regulate behavior. The reader may be wondering about prosocial and antisocial *feeling* states in humans. Distinct neocortical brain circuits that receive inputs from subcortical areas most likely underlie the unique conscious feeling states that are associated with different types of social behaviors. In this regard and in relation to my neural models, note that the output of the NA–VP circuit can influence neural activity in the PFC. Furthermore, both positive and negative amygdala regions project directly or indirectly to the PFC (see figure 6.3 caption). Therefore, the PFC not only is involved in emotional regulation and movement control (through its projections to subcortical regions) but is, in all likelihood, also concerned with both positive and negative feeling states, and distinct neural circuits are probably involved in these disparate functions.

The relevance of the work I have reviewed for human social interactions is significant. The most important point is that the neural circuits that underpin positive and negative social reactivity can be modified and influenced by experiential and cognitive factors. Too much of our social world is divided into in-groups and out-groups, which can promote competition rather than cooperation between groups. To build a better social world across groups and nations, we need to emphasize our interdependence and we should promote positive interactions, tolerance, and the development of trust. Ideology and religious views are powerful manipulators of our social reactivity, undoubtedly caused by cortical–subcortical interactions that influence how social stimuli are processed. However, since political and religious views are derived from experience, they can also be changed by experience. Finally, because of the importance of early life experiences for the development of social neural circuits, we should do our best to create environments where children are raised in warm, loving, and supportive families.

■ REFERENCES

Afonso, V. M., Sison, M., Lovic, V., & Fleming, A. S. (2007). Medial prefrontal cortex lesions in the female rat affect sexual and maternal behavior and their sequential organization. *Behavioral Neuroscience, 121*, 515–526.

Amaral, D. G. (2002). The primate amygdala and the neurobiology of social behavior: Implications for understanding social anxiety. *Biological Psychiatry, 51*, 11–17.

Baumgartner, T., Heinrichs, M., Vonlanthen, A., Fischbacher, U., & Fehr, E. (2008). Oxytocin shapes the neural circuitry of trust and trust adaptation in humans. *Neuron, 58*, 639–650.

Belova, M. A., Paton, J. J., & Salzman, C. D. (2008). Moment-to-moment tracking of state value in the amygdala. *Journal of Neuroscience, 28*, 10023–10030.

Berridge, K. C., & Robinson, T. E. (1998). What is the role of dopamine in reward: Hedonic impact, reward learning, or incentive salience? *Brain Research Reviews, 28*, 309–369.

Best, M., Williams, J. M., & Coccaro, E. F. (2002). Evidence for a dysfunctional prefrontal circuit in patients with an impulsive aggressive disorder. *Proceedings of the National Academy of Sciences of the United States of America, 99*, 8448–8453.

Buckholtz, J. W., & Meyer-Lindenberg, A. (2008). MAOA and the neurogenetic architecture of human aggression. *Trends in Neurosciences, 31*, 120–129.

Carola, V., Frazzetto, G., Pascucci, T., Audero, E., Puglisi-Allegra, S., Cabib, S., . . . Gross, C. (2008). Identifying molecular substrates in a mouse model of the serotonin transporter X environment risk factor for anxiety and depression. *Biological Psychiatry, 63*, 840–846.

Caspi, A., McClay, J., Moffitt, T. E., Mill, J., Martin, J., Craig, I. W., . . . Poulton, R. (2002). Role of genotype in the cycle of violence in maltreated children. *Science, 297*, 851–853.

Champagne, F. A. (2008). Epigenetic mechanisms and the transgenerational effects of maternal care. *Frontiers in Neuroendocrinology, 29*, 386–397.

Champagne, F. A., & Meaney, M. J. (2007). Transgenerational effects of social environment on variations in maternal care and behavioral response to novelty. *Behavioral Neuroscience, 12*, 1353–1363.

Coccaro, E. F., McCloskey, M. S., Fitzgerald, D. A., & Phan, K. L. (2007). Amygdala and orbitofrontal reactivity to social threat in individuals with impulsive aggression. *Biological Psychiatry, 62*, 168–178.

Costafreda, S. G., Brammer, M. J., David, A. S., & Fu, C. H. Y. (2008). Predictors of amygdala activation during the processing of emotional stimuli: A meta-analysis of 385 PET and fMRI studies. *Brain Research Reviews, 58*, 57–70.

Cushing, B. S., Perry, A., Musatov, S., Ogawa, S., & Papademetriou, E. (2008). Estrogen receptors in the medial amygdala inhibit the expression of male prosocial behavior. *Journal of Neuroscience, 28*, 10399–10403.

Cushing, B. S., & Wynne-Edwards, K. E. (2006). Estrogen receptor-α distribution in male rodents is associated with social organization. *Journal of Comparative Neurology, 494*, 595–605.

Davidson, R. J. (2002). Anxiety and affective style: Role of the prefrontal cortex and amygdala. *Biological Psychiatry, 51*, 68–80.

D'Cunha, T. M., King, S. J., Fleming, A. S, & Levy, F. (2011). Oxytocin receptors in the nucleus accumbens shell are involved in the consolidation of maternal memory in postpartum rats. *Hormones and Behavior, 59*, 14–21.

Domes, G., Heinrichs, M., Glascher, J., Buchel, C., Braus, D. F., & Herpertz, S. C. (2007). Oxytocin attenuates amygdala responses to emotional faces regardless of valence. *Biological Psychiatry, 62*, 1187–1190.

Eisenberger, N. I., Way, B. M., Taylor, S. E., Welch, W. T., & Lieberman, M. D. (2007). Understanding the genetic risk for aggression: Clues from the brain's response to social exclusion. *Biological Psychiatry, 61*, 1100–1108.

Ernst, M., & Fudge, J. L. (2009). A developmental neurobiological model of motivated behavior: Anatomy, connectivity and ontogeny of the triadic nodes. *Neuroscience & Biobehavioral Reviews, 33*, 367–382.

Faure, A., Reynolds, S. M., Richard, J. M., & Berridge, K. C. (2008). Mesolimbic dopamine in desire and dread: Enabling motivation to be generated by localized glutamate disruptions in nucleus accumbens. *Journal of Neuroscience, 28*, 7184–7192.

Feldman, R., Weller, A., Zagoory-Sharon, O., & Levine, A. (2007). Evidence for a neuroendocrinological foundation of human affiliation. *Psychological Science, 18*, 965–970.

Friedman, E., Berman, M., & Overstreet, D. (2006). Swim test immobility in a genetic rat model of depression is modified by maternal environment: A cross-foster study. *Developmental Psychobiology, 48*, 169–177.

Fries, A. B. W., Zeigler, T. E., Kurian, J. R., Jacoris, S., & Pollack, S. D. (2005). Early experience in humans is associated with changes in neuropeptides critical for regulating social behavior. *Proceedings of the National Academy of Sciences of the United States of America, 102*, 17237–17240.

Guastella, A. J., Mitchell, P. B., & Mathews, F. (2008). Oxytocin enhances the encoding of positive social memories in humans. *Biological Psychiatry, 64*, 256–258.

Haas, B. W., Mills, D., Yam, A., Hoeft, F., Bellugi, U., & Reiss, A. (2009). Genetic influences on sociability: Heightened amygdala reactivity and event-related responses to positive social stimuli in Williams syndrome. *Journal of Neuroscience, 29*, 1132–1139.

Hölldobler, B., & Wilson, E. O. (2009). *The superorganism*. New York, NY: Norton.

Holmes, A. (2008). Genetic variation in cortico-amygdala serotonin function and risk for stress-related disease. *Neuroscience & Biobehavioral Reviews, 32*, 1293–1314.

Jones, W., Bellugi, U., Lai, Z., Chiles, M., Reilly, J., Lincoln, A., & Adolphs, R. (2000). II. Hypersociality in Williams syndrome. *Journal of Cognitive Neuroscience (Supplement), 12*, 30–46.

Kaffman, A., & Meaney, M. J. (2007). Neurodevelopmental sequelae of postnatal maternal care in rodents: Clinical and research implications of molecular insights. *Journal of Child Psychology and Psychiatry, 48*, 224–244.

Kirsch, P., Esslinger, C., Chen, Q., Meir, D., Lis, S., Siddhanti, S., . . . Meyer-Lindenberg, A. (2005). Oxytocin modulates neural circuitry for social cognition and fear in humans. *Journal of Neuroscience, 25*, 11489–11493.

Kosfeld, M., Heinrichs, M., Zak, P. J., Fischbacher, U., & Fehr, E. (2005). Oxytocin increases trust in humans. *Nature, 435*, 673–676.

Lai, W. S., Ramiro, L. L. R., Yu, H. A., & Johnston, R. E. (2005). Recognition of familiar individuals in golden hamsters: A new method and functional neuroanatomy. *Journal of Neuroscience, 25*, 11239–11247.

Lavi-Avnon, Y., Weller, A., Finberg, J. P. M., Gispan-Herman, I., Kinor, N., Stern, Y., . . . Yadid, G. (2008). The reward system and maternal behavior in an animal model of depression: A microdialysis study. *Psychopharmacology, 196*, 281–291.

Lavi-Avnon, Y., Yadid, G., Overstreet, D. H., & Weller, A. (2005). Abnormal patterns of maternal behavior in a genetic animal model of depression. *Physiology & Behavior, 84*, 607–615.

LeDoux, J. (1996). *The emotional brain*. New York, NY: Simon and Schuster.

Lehrman, D. S. (1961). Hormonal regulation of parental behavior in birds and infrahuman mammals. In W. C. Young (Ed.), *Sex and internal secretions* (pp. 1268–1382). Baltimore, MD: Williams and Wilkins.

Loup, F., Tribollet, E., Dubois-Dauphin, M., & Dreifuss, J. J. (1991). Localization of high-affinity binding sites for oxytocin and vasopressin in the human brain: An autoradiographic study. *Brain Research, 555*, 220–232.

Maestripieri, D. (2005). Early experience affects the intergenerational transmission of infant abuse in rhesus monkeys. *Proceedings of the National Academy of Sciences of the United States of America, 102*, 9726–9729.

Maestripieri, D., Higley, J. D., Lindell, S. G., Newman, T. K., McCormack, K. M., & Sanchez, M. M. (2006). Early maternal rejection affects the development of monoaminergic systems and adult abusive parenting in rhesus macaques (*Macaca mulatta*). *Behavioral Neuroscience, 120*, 1017–1024.

Meyer-Lindenberg, A., Buckholtz, J. W., Kolachana, B., Hariri, A. R., Pezawas, L., Blasi, G., . . . Weinberger, D. R. (2006). Neural mechanisms of genetic risk for impulsivity and violence in humans. *Proceedings of the National Academy of Sciences of the United States of America, 103*, 6269–6274.

Meyer-Lindenberg, A., Hariri, A. R., Munoz, K. E., Mervis, C. B., Mattay, V. S., Morris, C. A., & Berman, K. F. (2005). Neural correlates of genetically abnormal social cognition in Williams syndrome. *Nature Neuroscience, 8*, 991–993.

Mogenson, G. J. (1987). Limbic–motor integration. *Progress in Psychobiology and Physiological Psychology, 12*, 117–167.

New, A. S., Buchsbaum, M. S., Hazlett, E. A., Goodman, M., Koenigsberg, H. W., Lo, J., . . . Siever, L. J. (2004). Fluoxetine increases relative metabolic rate in prefrontal cortex in impulsive aggression. *Psychopharmacology, 176*, 451–458.

Newman, S. W. (1999). The medial extended amygdala in male reproductive behavior. *Annals of the New York Academy of Sciences, 877*, 242–257.

Numan, M., Bress, J. A., Ranker, L. R., Gary, A. J., DeNicola, A. L., Bettis, J. K., & Knapp, S. E. (2010). The importance of the basolateral/basomedial amygdala for goal-directed maternal responses in postpartum rats. *Behavioural Brain Research, 214*, 368–376.

Numan, M. (2006). Hypothalamic circuits regulating maternal responsiveness toward infants. *Behavioral and Cognitive Neuroscience Reviews, 5*, 163–190.

Numan, M. (2007). Motivational systems and the neural circuitry of maternal behavior in the rat. *Developmental Psychobiology, 49*, 12–21.

Numan, M., & Insel, T. R. (2003). *The neurobiology of parental behavior*. New York, NY: Springer.

Numan, M., & Numan, M. J. (1997). Projection sites of medial preoptic and ventral bed nucleus of the stria terminalis neurons that express Fos during maternal behavior in female rats. *Journal of Neuroendocrinology, 9*, 369–384.

Numan, M., & Sheehan, T. P. (1997). Neuroanatomical circuitry for mammalian maternal behavior. *Annals of the New York Academy of Sciences, 807*, 101–125.

Numan, M., & Stolzenberg, D. S. (2008). Hypothalamic interaction with the mesolimbic dopamine system and the regulation of maternal responsiveness. In R. S. Bridges (Ed.), *Neurobiology of the parental brain* (pp. 3–22). Burlington, MA: Academic Press.

Numan, M., & Stolzenberg, D. S. (2009). Medial preoptic area interactions with dopamine neural systems in the control of the onset and maintenance of maternal behavior in rats. *Frontiers in Neuroendocrinology, 30*, 46–64.

Parada, M., King, S., Li, M., & Fleming, A. S. (2008). The roles of accumbal dopamine D1 and D2 receptors in maternal memory in rats. *Behavioral Neuroscience, 122*, 368–376.

Paton, J. J., Belova, M. A., Morrison, S. E., & Salzman, C. D. (2006). The primate amygdala represents the positive and negative value of visual stimuli during learning. *Nature, 439*, 865–870.

Pfaff, D. W. (2007). *The neuroscience of fair play*. New York, NY: Dana Press.

Reiss, A. L., Eckert, M. A., Rose, F. E., Karchemskiy, A., Kesler, S., Chang, M., … Galaburda, A. (2004). An experiment of nature: Brain anatomy parallels cognition and behavior in Williams syndrome. *Journal of Neuroscience, 24*, 5009–5015.

Rosenblatt, J. S., & Mayer, A. D. (1995). An analysis of approach/withdrawal processes in the initiation of maternal behavior in the laboratory rat. In K. E. Hood, G. Greenberg, & E. Tobach (Eds.), *Behavioral development* (pp. 177–230). New York, NY: Garland Press.

Rosenkranz, J. A., Moore, H., & Grace, A. A. (2003). The prefrontal cortex regulates lateral amygdala neuronal plasticity and responses to previously conditioned stimuli. *Journal of Neuroscience, 23*, 11054–11064.

Ross, H. E., Freeman, S. M., Spiegel, L. L., Ren, X., Terwilliger, E. F., & Young, L. J. (2009). Variation in oxytocin receptor density in the nucleus accumbens has differential effects in affiliative behaviors in monogamous and polygamous voles. *Journal of Neuroscience, 29*, 1312–1318.

Ruppenthal, G. C., Arling, G. L., Harlow, H. F., Sackett, G. P., & Suomi, S. J. (1976). A 10-year perspective of motherless-mother behavior. *Journal of Abnormal Psychology, 85*, 341–349.

Sheehan, T. P., Paul, M., Amaral, E., Numan, M. J., & Numan, M. (2001). Evidence that the medial amygdala projects to the anterior/ventromedial nuclei to inhibit maternal behavior in rats. *Neuroscience, 106*, 341–356.

Simerly, R. B., & Swanson, L. W. (1986). The organization of neural inputs to the medial preoptic nucleus of the rat. *Journal of Comparative Neurology, 246*, 312–342.

Sotres-Bayon, F., Cain, C. K., & LeDoux, J. E. (2006). Brain mechanisms of fear extinction: Historical perspectives on the contribution of the prefrontal cortex. *Biological Psychiatry, 60*, 329–336.

Stolzenberg, D. S., & Numan, M. (2011). Hypothalamic interaction with the mesolimbic DA system in the control of the maternal and sexual behaviors in rats. *Neuroscience and Biobehavioral Reviews, 35*, 826–847.

Swanson, L. W. (1987). The hypothalamus. In A. Bjorklund, T. Hokfelt, & L. W. Swanson (Eds.), *Handbook of chemical neuroanatomy* (Vol. 5, pp. 1–124). Amsterdam, The Netherlands: Elsevier.

Theodoridou, A., Rowe, A. C., Penton-Voak, I. S., & Rogers, P. J. (2009). Oxytocin and social perception: Oxytocin increases perceived facial trustworthiness and attractiveness. *Hormones and Behavior, 56*, 128–132.

Wager, T. D., Davidson, M. L., Hughes, B. L., Lindquist, M. A., & Ochsner, K. N. (2008). Prefrontal–subcortical pathways mediating successful emotion regulation. *Neuron, 59*, 1037–1050.

Weder, N., Yang, B. Z., Douglas-Palumberi, H., Massey, J., Krystal, J. H., Gelernter, J., & Kaufman, J. (2009). MAOA genotype, maltreatment, and aggressive behavior: The changing impact of genotype at varying levels of trauma. *Biological Psychiatry, 65*, 417–424.

Wright, C. I., & Groenewegen, H. J. (1995). Patterns of convergence and segregation in the medial nucleus accumbens of the rat: Relationships of prefrontal cortical, midline thalamic, and basal amygdaloid afferents. *Journal of Comparative Neurology, 361*, 383–403.

Yoshida, M., Takayanagi, Y., Inoue, K., Kimura, T., Young, L. J., Onaka, T., & Nishimori, K. (2009). Evidence that oxytocin exerts anxiolytic effects via oxytocin receptor expressed in serotonergic neurons in mice. *Journal of Neuroscience, 18*, 2259–2271.

Young, L. J., & Wang, Z. (2004). The neurobiology of pair bonding. *Nature Neuroscience, 7*, 1048–1054.

7 Neuroscience of Empathic Responding

■ JEAN DECETY

Everywhere I look, empathy abides. If you want to sell a car, a good car salesman will be the one who has empathy. So, too, with bosses and businesspeople, parents and teachers, waiters, writers, lawyers, scientists, and politicians. Every good physician has empathy. Irrespective of the disease, when we find someone who will feel for us, we feel better. Empathy is one of those human impulses that defy easy explanation. It gets entangled with sympathy or compassion or commiseration; it submerges into altruism. Broadly, we think of empathy as the ability to feel for another person, to imagine ourselves in the same situation, enduring those same experiences and emotions. Empathy makes us cry at sad movies and rescue strangers in distress. Empathy has an impact in psychotherapies and medicine, and is associated with improved patient satisfaction and compliance with recommended treatment. That is the mystery of empathy, and that is why I became fascinated with studying the neural mechanisms that instantiate such a valuable ability.

The ability to perceive, appreciate, and respond to the affective states of another and to predict the events that will result is an important and valuable interpersonal phenomenon. Human beings are intrinsically social and their survival critically depends on social interactions with others, the formation of alliances, and accurate social judgments (Cacioppo, 2002). Humans are motivated to form and maintain positive and significant relationships (Baumeister & Leary, 1995). Human social cognitive evolution cannot be accounted for by any single factor (e.g., diet or climate), but the most important factor is the increasing complexity of hominid social groups (Bjorklund & Bering, 2003). It is therefore logical to infer that dedicated mechanisms have evolved to perceive, understand, predict, and respond to the internal states of other individuals. I will argue that empathy is not unique to humans as many of the mechanisms are shared with other mammalian species. However, humans are special in that high-level cognitive abilities such as executive function, language, and theory of mind are layered on top of phylogenetically older social and emotional capacities. These evolutionary newer aspects of information processing expand the range of behaviors that can be driven by empathy for the better (like caring for and helping out-group members or even individuals from different species) but also for the worse (such as cruelty and dehumanization).

The goal of this essay is to critically examine our knowledge about the neurophysiological underpinnings of empathy in humans. After clarifying some definitional issues, I start with a discussion of the evolutionary origins of empathy, focusing on the functions of the autonomic nervous system. Then I critically review the empirical evidence that supports the notion of shared neural circuits

---

BOX 7.1   Key Concepts

- Empathy is a construct that can be decomposed in a model that includes bottom-up processing of affective sharing and emotion awareness as well as top-down processing in which the perceiver's motivation, memories, intentions, and attitudes influence the extent of an empathic experience.
- Empathy is implemented by a network of distributed, often recursively connected, interacting neural regions, including the superior temporal sulcus, insula, medial and orbitofrontal cortices, amygdala and anterior cingulate cortex, as well as by autonomic and neuroendocrine processes implicated in social behaviors and emotional states.
- The experience of empathy can lead to sympathy, which refers to feelings of concern for the well- being of the other, which includes an other-oriented motivation.
- Empathy can also lead to personal distress, an egoistic motivation to reduce stress by withdrawing from the stressor.
- Regulation of negative arousal is crucial. Difficulty inhibiting or reducing an emotional response and excessive attention toward negative emotional information may deplete executive resources available for other aspects of self-regulation.
- Investigating dysfunction of the components of empathy provides important clues for understanding deviations that can lead to the lack of empathy and concern for others.

---

for the generation of behavior, including emotions, in oneself and for its perception from others. I emphasize recent functional neuroimaging studies of pain empathy that show a partial overlap in the neural circuits underlying the firsthand experience of pain and the observation of pain in others. Next I discuss how perspective taking and the ability to differentiate the self from the other affect our ability to appreciate the pain and distress of others. Finally, I examine how some interpersonal variables modulate empathic concern.

■ EMPATHY AND ASSOCIATED PHENOMENA

Empathy plays crucial roles in much of human social interaction and is assumed to be necessary for healthy coexistence. It is thought to have a key role in motivating prosocial behavior and providing the affective and motivational base for moral development (Decety, Michalska, & Kinzler, 2011). Philosophers and psychologists have long debated the nature of empathy and whether the capacity to share and understand other people's emotions sets humans apart from other species (de Waal & Thompson, 2005). Unfortunately, as is often the case in social sciences, empathy is a loaded term with various definitions roaming the literature (Batson, 2009). Broadly construed, empathy has been defined as an affective response stemming from the understanding of another's emotional state or condition and similar to what the other person is feeling or would be expected to feel in the given situation (Eisenberg, Shea, Carlo, & Knight, 1991). Other theorists more narrowly define empathy as one specific set of congruent emotions, those feelings that are more other-focused than self-focused (Batson, Fultz & Schoenrade, 1987).

Here, we consider empathy as a construct accounting for a sense of similarity in feelings experienced by the self and the other, without confusion between the two individuals, and that can prompt empathic conern (See Table 7.1 for definitions.)

The molar construct of empathy can be decomposed in a model that includes bottom-up processing of affective sharing and top-down processing in which the perceiver's motivation, intentions, and self-regulation influence the extent of an empathic experience (Decety, 2011; Decety, 2005; Decety & Jackson, 2004; Decety & Meyer, 2008; Eisenberg & Eggum, 2009; Hodges & Wegner, 1997). Recent cognitive neuroscience research indicates that the affective, cognitive, and regulatory aspects of empathy involve interacting yet partially non-overlapping neural circuits (figure 7.1). There is also behavioral and neuroscience evidence that the affective component of empathy develops earlier than the cognitive component. Affective responsiveness is present at an early age, is involuntary, and relies on mimicry and somato-sensorimotor resonance between other and self. For instance, newborns and infants become vigorously distressed shortly after another infant begins to cry (e.g., Dondi, Simion, & Caltran, 1999). Facial mimicry of basic emotional expressions also contributes to affective sharing, and this phenomenon starts very early in life, by approximately 10 weeks of age (Haviland & Lewica, 1987). The cognitive aspects of empathy are closely related to processes involved in theory of mind (the capacity to infer the explicit content of others' mental states such as intentions and beliefs), executive function (attention, working memory, and inhibitory control), and self-regulation. The regulation of internal emotional states and processes is particularly relevant to the modulation of vicarious emotion and the experience of empathy and sympathy. Both theory of mind and emotion regulation tap into executive function resources implemented in the prefrontal cortex (Zelazo, Carlson & Kesek, 2008), with different regions—medial

TABLE 7.1 *Empathy and Associated Phenomena: Definitions*

Term	Definition
Emotional contagion	The tendency to automatically and nonconsciously mimic and synchronize facial expressions, vocalizations, postures, and movements with those of another individual.
Empathy	An emotional response that stems from another's state and is congruent with the other's emotional state. It involves at least a minimal distinction between self and other. Empathy is not a separate emotion, but a kind of induction process by which emotions, both positive and negative, are shared. The anterior insula, medial prefrontal cortex, anterior cingulate cortex, orbitofrontal cortex with their reciprocal connections with the amygdala play a critical role in empathy.
Personal distress	An aversive state (e.g., anxiety or worry) that is not congruent with the other's state and that leads to a self-oriented, egoistic reaction.
Empathic concern	An other-oriented emotion for someone in need that produces prosocial motivation, which arises from a set of biological mechanisms that evolved to promote parental care and attachment. The neural underpinnings of concern can be found in subcortical neural systems similar to those known to regulate maternal behavior, especially the medial preoptic area of the hypothalamus.

and dorsolateral, respectively— subserving those functions through their connections with subcortical limbic and brainstem structures. The prefrontal cortex develops more slowly than other brain areas, reaching maturation only late in adolescence (Bunge, Dudukovic, Thomasson, Vaidya, & Gabrieli, 2002). It is well documented that the prefrontal cortex and its functions follow an extremely protracted developmental course, and age-related changes continue well into adolescence (Toga, Thompson & Sowell, 2006). The maturation of the prefrontal cortex allows children to use verbalizations to self-regulate their feelings and exercise inhibitory control over their thoughts, attention, and actions (Diamond, 2002).

Recent developmental neuroscience research indicates that the affective, cognitive, and regulatory aspects of empathy involve interacting yet partially non-overlapping neural circuits with distinct developmental trajectories. Functional magnetic resonance imaging (fMRI) measures reveal age-related changes in the patterns of activation and functional connectivity in individuals (aged between

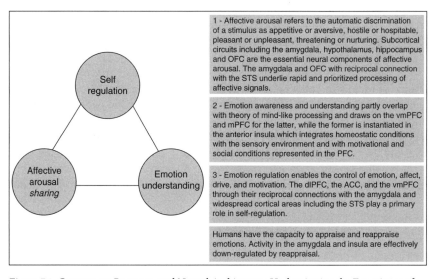

Figure 7.1 Component Processes and Neural Architecture Underpinning the Experience of Empathy. Empathy is a molar construct developed by behavioral and social scientists that, like other concepts used in social cognition, provides a means of understanding highly complex activity without needing to specify each individual action in terms of its simplest components, thereby providing an efficient approach to describing complex systems. From the model shown, it is clear that empathy is implemented by a complex network of distributed, often recursively connected, interacting neural regions including the brainsteam, limbic regions, superior temporal sulcus (STS), anterior insular cortex (AIC), medial prefrontal cortex (mPFC), ventromedial prefrontal cortex (vmPFC), and anterior cingulate cortex (ACC), as well as autonomic and neuroendocrine processes implicated in social behaviors and emotional states. Empathy is not a phenomenon of passive affective resonance with the emotions of others. Rather, goals, intentions, dispositions, context, and motivations play feedforward functions in how emotions are perceived and experienced.

7 and 38 years) when they are exposed to empathy-eliciting stimuli, reflecting a shift from a visceral emotional response critical for analyzing the affective significance of stimuli and mediated by the amygdala, posterior insula and orbitofrontal cortex to a more evaluative function that critically involves the medial prefrontal cortex and ventromedial prefrontal cortex (Decety & Michalska, 2010).

Interestingly, there is compelling evidence that prosocial behaviors, such as altruistic helping, emerge early in childhood. Infants as young as 12 months of age begin to comfort victims of distress, and at 14–18 months children display spontaneous and unrewarded helping behaviors (Warneken & Tomasello, 2009).

■ THE EVOLUTIONARY ORIGINS OF EMPATHY

Natural selection has fine-tuned the mechanisms that serve the specific demands of each species' ecology. MacLean (1985) proposed that empathy emerged with the evolution of mammals (180 million years ago). In the evolutionary transition from reptiles to mammals, three key developments were (1) nursing in conjunction with maternal care, (2) audiovocal communication for maintaining maternal–offspring contact, and (3) play. The development of this behavioral triad may have depended on the evolution of the thalamocingulate division of the limbic system, a derivative from early mammals. This division (which has no distinctive counterpart in the reptilian brain) is in turn geared in with the prefrontal neocortex, which in human beings may be inferred to play a key role in familial acculturation. When mammals developed parenting behavior, the stage was set for increased exposure and responsiveness to emotional signals of others, including signals of pain, separation, and distress. Indeed, parenting involves the protection of and transfer of energy, information to offspring. African hominoids, including chimpanzees, gorillas, and humans, share a number of parenting mechanisms with other placental mammals, including internal gestation, lactation, and attachment mechanisms involving neuropeptides such as oxytocin (Geary & Flinn, 2001).

The phylogenetic origin of behaviors associated with social engagement has been linked to the evolution of the autonomic nervous system and its relationship to emotion. According to Porges (2001), social approach or withdrawal stems from the implicit computation of feelings of safety, discomfort, or potential danger. He proposed that the evolution of the autonomic nervous system (sympathetic and parasympathetic systems) provides a means to understand the adaptive significance of mammalian affective processes, including empathy and the establishment of lasting social bonds. These basic evaluative systems are associated with motor responses that aid the adaptive responding of the organism. At this primitive level, appetitive and aversive behavioral responses are modulated by specific neural circuits in the brainstem that share common neuroarchitectures among mammals (Parr & Waller, 2007). These brain systems are genetically hardwired to enable animals to respond unconditionally to threatening or appetitive stimuli with the specific response patterns that are most adaptive to the particular species and environmental condition. The limbic system, which includes the hypothalamus, the parahippocampal cortex, the amygdala, and several interconnected areas (septum, basal ganglia, nucleus accumbens, insula, retrospenial cingulate cortex, and prefrontal cortex) is primarily responsible for emotion processing. What unites these regions are their roles in motivation and emotion, mediated by connections with the autonomic system and brainstem. The limbic system also projects to the cingulate and orbitofrontal cortices, which are involved with the evaluation and regulation of emotion, as well as decision making.

It is evident from the descriptions of comparative psychologists and ethologists that behaviors homologous to human empathy and sympathy can be observed in other mammalian species, including rodents (Langford et al., 2010). Reports on ape empathic reactions suggest that in addition to emotional connectedness, apes appreciate others' situations (de Waal, 1996). A good example is consolation, defined as reassurance behavior by an uninvolved bystander toward one of the combatants in a previous aggressive incident (de Waal & van Roosmalen, 1979). Preston and de Waal (2002) convincingly argue that empathy is not an all-or-nothing phenomenon and many forms of empathy exist between the extremes of mere agitation at the distress of others and full understanding of their predicaments. Many other comparative psychologists view empathy as a kind of induction process by which emotions, both positive and negative, are shared and by which the probabilities of similar behavior are increased in the participants. Without doubt, some components of empathy are present in other species, such as emotion contagion, which constitutes a phylogenetically ancient and basic form of intraspecies communication (see de Waal & Thompson, 2005). For example, Parr (2001) measured peripheral skin temperature in chimpanzees while they were exposed to emotionally negative video scenes. Skin temperature decreased—indicating greater negative arousal—when subjects viewed videos of conspecifics injected with needles or videos of the needles themselves, but not videos of conspecifics chasing the veterinarian. Thus when chimpanzee are exposed to meaningful emotional stimuli, they are subject to physiological changes similar to those observed during fear in humans, a response that is similar to the dispositional effects of emotional contagion (Hatfield, Rapson & Le, 2009).

In humans, the construct of empathy accounts for a more complex psychological state than the one associated with the automatic sharing of emotions. As in other species, emotions and feelings may be shared between individuals, but humans also can intentionally "feel for" and act on behalf of other people whose experiences may differ greatly from their own (Batson et al., 1991; Decety & Hodges, 2006). This phenomenon, called empathic concern or sympathy, is often associated with prosocial behaviors such as helping kin and has been considered as a chief enabling process for altruism. According to Wilson (1988), empathic helping behavior has evolved because of its contribution to inclusive genetic fitness (kin selection). In humans and other mammals, an impulse to care for offspring is almost certainly genetically hardwired. Once evolved, behavior often assumes motivational autonomy: Its motivation becomes disconnected from its ultimate goals. Thus empathy became motivationally autonomous, and humans have the ability to care not only for their offspring but also for out-group members and even animals of other species.

The emotional and social aspects of empathy and empathic concern in humans depend on ancient systems for intersubjectivity that are shared with other primates (i.e., brainstem, hypothalamus and limbic system). However, layered on top of this are higher-level (in the sense of newer) abilities involved in understanding others' mental states, language, executive functions, and more generally metacognition. These expanded the range of behaviors that can be driven by empathy. In addition, as emphasized by Harris (2000), humans can put their emotions into words, allowing them not only to express emotion but also to report on current as well as past emotions. These reports provide an opportunity to share, explain, and regulate emotional experience that is not found in other species. Conversation helps to develop empathy, for it is often where people learn of shared experiences and feelings. Moreover, this self-reflective capability (which includes emotion regulation) may be an important difference between humans and other animals (Povinelli, 2001).

Interestingly, two key regions involved in affective processing in general and empathy in particular, the anterior insula (AIC) and anterior cingulate cortex (ACC), have evolved in a singular manner in apes and humans. Cytoarchitectonic work by Allman, Watson, Tetreault, and Hakeem (2005) indicates that a population of large spindle neurons is uniquely found in the AIC and ACC of hominoid primates. Most notably, they reported a trenchant phylogenetic correlation, in that spindle cells are most numerous in aged humans; progressively less numerous in children, gorillas, bonobos and chimpanzees; and nonexistent in macaque monkeys. Craig (2007) suggested that these spindle neurons interconnect the most advanced portions of limbic sensory (AIC) and limbic motor (ACC) cortices, both ipsilaterally and contralaterally. This is in sharp contrast to the tightly interconnected and contiguous sensorimotor cortices, which are situated physically far apart as a consequence of the pattern of evolutionary development of limbic cortices. Thus the spindle neurons could enable fast, complex, and highly integrated emotional behaviors. In support of this view, convergent functional imaging findings reveal that the AIC and the ACC are conjointly activated during all human emotions. According to Craig (2002), this indicates that the limbic sensory representation of subjective feelings (in the AIC) and the limbic motor representation of volitional agency (in the ACC) together form the fundamental neuroanatomical basis for all human emotions, consistent with the definition of an emotion in humans as both a feeling and a motivation with concomitant autonomic sequelae (Rolls, 1999).

Overall, this evolutionary conceptual view is compatible with the hypothesis that advanced levels of social cognition may have arisen as an emergent property of powerful executive functioning assisted by the representational properties of language (Barrett, Henzi, & Dunbar, 2003). These higher levels operate on previous levels of organization and should not be seen as independent of or conflicting with one another. Evolution has constructed layers of increasing complexity, from nonrepresentational (e.g., emotion contagion) to representational and metarepresentational mechanisms (e.g., theory of mind and perspective taking), all of which need to be taken into account for a full understanding of human empathy.

■ SHARED NEURAL CIRCUITS BETWEEN SELF AND OTHER

It has long been suggested that empathy involves resonating with another person's unconscious affect. For instance, Ax proposed in 1964 that empathy can be thought of as an autonomic nervous system state that tends to simulate the state of another person. In the same vein, Basch (1983) speculated that because their respective autonomic nervous systems are genetically programmed to respond in a similar fashion, a given affective expression by a member of a particular species can trigger similar responses in other members of that species. This idea fits neatly with the notion of embodiment, which refers to actual bodily states and to simulations of experience in the brain's modality-specific systems for perception, action, and cognitive operations (Niedenthal et al. 2005).

The view that unconscious automatic mimicry of a target generates in the observer the autonomic response associated with that bodily state and facial expression subsequently received empirical support from behavioral and physiological studies marshaled under the perception–action coupling account of empathy (Preston & de Waal, 2002). The core assumption of the perception–action model of empathy is that perceiving a target's state automatically activates the corresponding representations of that state in the observer, which in turn activates somatic and autonomic responses. The discovery of sensorimotor neurons (called mirror neurons) provided a possible physiological mechanism for this direct link between perception and action. This unique class of cells with sensorimotor properties were first identified in the monkey ventral premotor cortex. In one of the seminal paper, Gallese and colleagues (1996) reported that approximately 17% of neurons recorded in ventral premotor area F5 of the macaque monkey responded both when the monkey executed a particular movement—for example, grasping, placing, or manipulating—and when the monkey observed someone else performing that same movement. Neurons with similar visuomotor properties were discovered later in the anterior intraparietal area (Fogassi et al., 2005) and recently in the primary motor cortex (Tkach, Reimer, & Hatsopoulos, 2007). The primary function of the mirror neurons was proposed to be related to action understanding. However, with the discovery of such cells in the primary motor cortex, it may be that mirror neurons are best interpreted as nothing more than the facilitation of the motor system via learned associations (see Decety, 2010 and Hickok, 2009, for a critical reviews).

Evidence for the existence of mirror neurons in humans is indirect and principally relies on functional neuroimaging studies that demonstrate an overlap in activation between observation and action conditions in regions homologous to the areas of the monkey brain where mirror neurons have been found. These regions include the anterior part of the inferior frontal gyrus (IFG, or pars triangularis), the ventral premotor cortex (pars opercularis), the anterior and posterior intraparietal sulcus, and an area in the lateral occipital cortex (Dinstein, Hasson, Rubin, & Heeger, 2007). In addition, transcranial magnetic stimulation (TMS) studies have demonstrated changes in the excitability of the observer's motor and premotor cortices that encode the execution of observed actions (Fadiga, Fogassi, Pavesi, & Rizzolatti, 1995). Similarly, magnetoencephalography (MEG) and electroencephalographic measurements have demonstrated suppression in the mu rhythm (8–13 Hz) over the sensorimotor cortex during the observation of action that parallels the changes detected during action production (Cheng, Yang, Lin, Lee, & Decety, 2008). It has been hypothesized that this mu rhythm reflects downstream modulation of primary sensorimotor areas by mirror neuron activity, representing a critical information-processing function translating perception into action (Pineda, 2005).

In line with a perception–action matching mechanism, a number of behavioral and electromyographic studies have demonstrated that viewing facial expressions triggers similar expressions on the viewer's own face, even in the absence of conscious recognition of the stimulus (Dimberg, Thunberg, & Elmehed, 2000; Hatfield et al., 2009). While watching someone smile, for example, observers activates at a subthreshold level the facial muscles involved in producing their own smiles. Furthermore, making a facial expression generates changes in the autonomic nervous system and is associated with feeling the corresponding emotion. In a series of experiments, Levenson, Ekman, and Friesen (1990) instructed participants to produce facial configurations for anger, disgust, fear, happiness, sadness, and surprise while heart rate, skin conductance, finger temperature, and somatic activity were monitored. They found that such voluntary facial activity produced significant levels of subjective experience of the associated emotions as well as specific and reliable autonomic measures.

The idea that the mirror neuron system is implicated in emotion perception is based mainly on studies that have reported activation in the IFG (an area homologous to the monkey ventral premotor cortex) during the observation of facial expressions of emotions (happiness, sadness, anger, disgust and surprise) and during the imitation of those expressions (e.g., Carr, Iacoboni, Dubeau, Mazziotta, & Lenzi, 2003). Leslie, Johnson-Frey, and Grafton (2004) used a paradigm in which subjects had to observe and imitate hand and face actions (smiling and frowning) using film clips. The right ventral premotor cortex was commonly activated during both observation and imitation of facial expressions. A more recent study demonstrated that even passive viewing of facial expressions activates a wide network of brain regions that were also involved in the execution of similar expressions, including the IFG and the posterior parietal cortex (van der Gaag, Minderaa, & Keysers, 2007).

However, the majority of functional neuroimaging studies have not reported activation of the IFG or other mirror neuron areas during the perception of facial expression of emotion (for meta-analyses see Murphy, Nimmo-Smith, & Lawrence, 2003; Phan, Wager, Taylor, & Liberzon, 2002). For instance, Chakrabarti and colleagues (2006) presented participants with video clips depicting happy, sad, angry and disgusted facial expressions. Only the perception of a happy expression was associated with activation of the left pars opercularis. Many studies claiming to have found mirror neuron system activation during action and emotion tasks do not have the appropriate experimental conditions to support such a claim (see Turella, Pierno, Tubaldi, & Castiello 2008, for a meta-analysis). In addition a number of studies have simply disregarded activity in all cortical areas except for the IFG and anterior intraparietal sulcus (aIPS) because these two areas are assumed to be homologous to monkey areas F5 and PF and are therefore expected to contain mirror neurons.

Using such circular reasoning, these studies have sidestepped the most important issue, which is to examine whether human mirror neurons actually exist and to characterize their physiology. This circular interpretation has been taken to such an extreme that many studies interpret any hemodynamic response in the IFG and aIPS as being due to mirror neuron activity, as if the regions consisted only of mirror neurons. Such studies both grossly ignore that mirror neurons in the monkey account for only a small minority of cells in these areas and that these areas subserve other computations, such as cognitive control and task management in the case of the right IFG (e.g., Kawashima et al., 1996; Swick, Ashley, & Turken, 2008).

The sharing of affective states may simply rely on the activation of the core affect, that is, the automatic discrimination of a stimulus—or features of a stimulus—as appetitive or aversive, hostile or hospitable, pleasant or unpleasant, threatening or nurturing (Barrett, Mesquita, Ochsner, & Gross, 2007). Subcortical circuits including the brainstem, amygdala, hypothalamus, hippocampus and orbitofrontal cortex (OFC) are the essential neural components of affective arousal. The amygdala and OFC, with reciprocal connections with the superior temporal gyrus, underlie rapid and prioritized processing of emotional signals.

To sum up, while the mirror neuron system provides a physiological mechanism for motor resonance and may play a role in mimicry and perhaps and in some aspects of emotion contagion, it seems unlikely that such a mechanism can explain emotion understanding and empathy, and certainly not empathic concern. In addition there is no evidence from neurological studies that lesions of the regions involved in the mirror neuron system lead to any dysfunction in empathy and sympathy, whereas such socio-cognitive disturbances are associated with lesions of the medial and ventromedial prefrontal cortices (e.g., Hornak et al., 2003).

■ PERCEIVING OTHERS IN PAIN

By virtue of its aversiveness, pain promotes the organism's health and integrity, to the extent that congenital absence of pain on injury significantly shortens human life (Williams, 2002). This aversive ability promotes protective or recuperative visceromotor and behavioral responses. Pain serves evolved protective functions not only by warning the suffering person but also by impelling expressive behaviors that attract the attention of others (Craig, 2009). Since pain can be an indicator of a potentially life-threatening situation, it is critical to the organism's survival.

A growing body of research demonstrates shared physiological mechanisms for the firsthand experience of pain and the perception, anticipation, or even the imagination of pain in others. The first fMRI experiment to investigate neural responses to both the firsthand experience of pain and perception of pain in others was conducted by Morrison, Lloyd, di Pellegrino, and Roberts (2004). Participants were scanned while feeling a moderately painful pinprick to the fingertips and while watching another person's hand undergo similar stimulation. Both conditions resulted in common hemodynamic activity in a pain-related area in the right dorsal ACC. Another fMRI study demonstrated that the dorsal ACC, the AIC, the cerebellum, and the brain stem were activated when healthy participants experienced a painful stimulus as well as when they observed a signal indicating that another person was receiving a similar stimulus (Singer et al., 2004). These findings were supported by an fMRI study in which participants were shown still photographs depicting right hands and feet in painful or neutral everyday-life situations and asked to imagine the level of pain that these situations would produce (Jackson, Meltzoff, & Decety, 2005). Significant activation was detected in regions involved in the affective aspects of pain processing, notably the dorsal ACC, the thalamus, and the AIC. Moreover, the level of activity within the dorsal ACC was strongly correlated with participants' mean ratings of pain attributed to the different situations.

Crying is a universal vocalization in human infants as well as in the infants of other mammals (Newman, 2007). In all studied mammals, young infants emit a species-specific cry when in distress, and mothers generally respond with caretaking behavior (Bell & Ainsworth, 1972). An fMRI study measured brain activity in healthy, breast-feeding first-time mothers with young infants while they listened to infant cries or white-noise control sounds and during a rest condition (Lorberbaum et al., 2002). When participants were exposed to the cries, signal increase was detected in the ACC, the AIC, the medial thalamus, and medial prefrontal and right OFC. Several structures thought to be important in rodent maternal behavior also displayed increased activity, including the midbrain, the hypothalamus, the dorsal and ventral striatum, and the vicinity of the lateral septal region.

Facial expressions of pain are readily understood by observers. Botvinick et al. (2005) investigated the neural response to pain expressions by performing fMRI as subjects viewed short video sequences showing faces expressing either moderate pain or no pain. In alternate blocks, the same subjects received both painful and nonpainful thermal stimulation. Facial expressions of pain were found to engage cortical areas also engaged by the firsthand experience of pain, including the ACC and AIC.

Unlike the first neuroimaging studies of pain empathy mentioned above, more recent functional MRI and MEG investigations reported significant signal change in the somatosensory cortex/posterior insula (Akitsuki & Decety, 2009, Benuzzi, Lui, Duzzi, Nichelli, & Porro, 2008; Cheng et al., 2007, 2008; Lamm, Nusbaum, Meltzoff & Decety, 2007; Lamm, Meltzoff & Decety, 2010). Neuroimaging and lesion studies have demonstrated that the somatosensory cortex/posterior dorsal insula contributes to the sensory discriminative dimension of pain (Symonds, Gordon, Bixby, & Mande, 2006). Thus the MRI and MEG results fit well with the implication of the perception–action coupling mechanism that underlies the automatic somatosensory resonance between other and self.

Summing up, current neurophysiological evidence indicates that perceiving or imagining another individual in a painful situation yields responses in the neural circuit associated with the coding of the motivational–affective and the sensory dimensions of pain in oneself. Vicariously instigated activations in the pain matrix are not necessarily specific to the emotional experience of pain, but may reflect other processes such as somatic monitoring, negative stimulus evaluation, and the selection of appropriate aversive skeletomuscular movements. Thus the shared neural representations in the affective–motivational part of the pain matrix might not be specific to the sensory qualities of pain but instead might be associated with more general survival mechanisms such as aversion and withdrawal when exposed to danger and threat. Regardless of the particular mechanism, the sharing of vicarious negative arousal provides a strong signal that can promote empathic concern in the observer.

■ PERSPECTIVE TAKING

The ability to adopt and entertain the psychological perspective of others has important adaptive value and consequences in social interaction. Well-developed perspective-taking abilities allow us to overcome our usual egocentrism and tailor our behaviors to others' expectations (Davis, Conklin, Smith, & Luce, 1996). Adopting another person's perspective involves more than simply focusing our attention on others. It involves imagining how they are affected by their situations without confusing our own feelings with theirs (Decety, 2005). For successful social interaction, and empathic understanding in particular, there must be an adjustment of the shared representations that are automatically activated through the perception–action coupling mechanism (Decety & Hodges, 2006; Decety & Sommerville, 2003). Whereas projecting one's own traits onto another does not necessitate any significant storage of knowledge about the other, empathic understanding requires incorporating characteristics of the other within the self. An essential aspect of empathic understanding is to recognize the other person as being like ourselves while maintaining a clear separation between oneself and the other. Hence mental flexibility and self-regulation are important components of empathy. One needs to calibrate one's own perspective that has been activated by the interaction with the other or even by its mere imagination. Neuroimaging experiments in healthy participants as well as lesion studies in neurological patients have demonstrated that such calibration requires the prefrontal cortical executive resources (attention, working memory, and inhibitory control) in combination with the temporoparietal junction (TPJ) (Decety & Lamm, 2007).

A number of neuroimaging studies have reported that the medial prefrontal cortex (mPFC) is specifically involved in tasks requiring the processing of information relevant to the self, such as traits and attitudes (e.g., Johnson et al., 2002). An fMRI study investigated the neural regions mediating self-referential processing of emotional stimuli and explored how these regions are influenced by the emotional valence of the verbal stimuli (Fossati et al., 2003). The self-referential condition induced bilateral activation in the dorsomedial prefrontal cortex, whereas the other-referential condition induced activation in lateral prefrontal areas. Activation in the right dorsomedial prefrontal cortex was specific to the self-referential condition regardless of word valence. The authors proposed that the right dorsomedial prefrontal cortex represents states of an emotional episodic self, which facilitates the processing of emotional stimuli with a personally relevant perspective. This proposition is in line with studies showing activations within both the left and right dorsomedial prefrontal cortex during tasks tapping theory of mind (Brunet-Gouet & Decety, 2006).

The mPFC is involved not only when we reflect on ourselves, but also when we imagine the subjective perspective of others. Mental imagery not only enables us to see the world of our conspecifics through their eyes or in their shoes but may also result in sensations similar to the other person's (Decety & Grèzes, 2006). A series of neuroimaging studies with healthy volunteers investigated the neural underpinning of perspective taking in three modes (motor, conceptual, and emotional) of self–other representations. In a first study, participants were scanned while they were asked either to imagine themselves performing everyday actions (e.g., winding up a watch), or to imagine another individual performing similar actions (Ruby & Decety, 2001). Both conditions were associated with common activation in the supplementary motor area (SMA), premotor cortex, and the TPJ region. This neural network corresponds to the shared motor representations between the self and the other. Taking the perspective of the other to simulate his or her behavior resulted in selective activation of the frontopolar cortex and right inferior parietal lobule.

In a second study, medical students were shown a series of affirmative health-related sentences (e.g., "Taking antibiotic drugs causes general fatigue") and were asked to judge their truth either according to their own perspective (as experts in medical knowledge) or according to the perspective of a layperson (Ruby & Decety, 2003). The set of activated regions recruited when the participants put themselves in the shoes of a layperson included the mPFC, the frontopolar cortex, and the right TPJ.

In a third study, participants were presented with short written sentences describing real-life situations that are likely to induce social emotions (e.g., shame, guilt, or pride) or other, emotionally neutral situations (Ruby & Decety, 2004). In one condition, they were asked to imagine how they would feel if they were experiencing these situations. In another condition, they were asked to imagine how their mothers would feel in those situations. Reaction times were prolonged when participants imagined emotion-laden situations compared with neutral ones, both from their own perspective and from the perspective of their mothers. When participants adopted their mothers' perspective, neurohemodynamic changes were detected in the frontopolar cortex, the ventromedial prefrontal cortex, the mPFC, and the right inferior parietal lobule, regardless of the affective content of the situations. Cortical regions involved in emotional processing, including the amygdala and the temporal poles, were activated in the conditions that included emotional-laden scenarios.

A more recent fMRI study used a factorial design to examine the neural correlates of self-reflection and perspective taking (D'Argembeau et al., 2007). Participants were asked to judge the extent to which trait adjectives described their own personalities (e.g., "Are you sociable?") or the personalities of a close friend (e.g., "Is Caroline sociable?") and were also asked to take a third-person perspective by estimating how the friend would make the same judgments, with the target of the judgments again being either the self (e.g., "According to Caroline, are you sociable?") or the other person (e.g., "According to Caroline, is she sociable?"). Self-referential processing (judgments targeting oneself vs. the other person) was associated with activation in the ventral and dorsal anterior mPFC, whereas perspective taking (adopting the other person's perspective rather than one's own) resulted in activation in the posterior dorsal mPFC; the interaction between the two dimensions yielded activation in the left dorsal mPFC. These findings indicate that self-referential processing and perspective taking recruit distinct regions of the mPFC and suggest that the left dorsal mPFC may be involved in decoupling a person's own perspective from other people's perspectives on oneself.

Two functional MRI studies investigated the neural mechanisms subserving the effects of perspective taking during the perception of pain in others. In one study participants looked at pictures of hands and feet in painful scenarios and were instructed to imagine and rate the level of pain perceived from the perspective of the self or another (Jackson, Brunet, Meltzoff, & Decety, 2006). Both the self and the other perspectives were associated with activation in the neural network involved in processing the affective aspect of pain, including the dorsal ACC and the AIC. However, the self perspective yielded higher pain ratings and involved the pain matrix more extensively, including the secondary somatosensory cortex, the mid-insula, and the caudal part of the AIC. Adopting the perspective of the other was associated with increased activation in the right TPJ and precuneus. In addition, distinct subregions were activated within the insular cortex for the two perspectives (anterior aspect for others and more posterior for self). These neuroimaging data highlight both the similarities and the distinctiveness of self and other as important aspects of human empathy. The experience of pain in oneself is associated with more caudal activations (within area 24), consistent with spinothalamic nociceptive projections, whereas the perception of pain in others is represented in more rostral (and dorsal) regions (within area 32). A similar rostrocaudal organization is observed in the insula, consistent with its anatomical connectivity and electrophysiological properties (Jackson, Rainville, & Decety, 2006). Painful sensations are evoked in the posterior part of the insula (and not in the anterior part) by direct electrical stimulation in neurological patients (Ostrowsky et al., 2002). Altogether, these findings are in agreement with the fact that indirect pain representations (as elicited by the observation of pain in others) are qualitatively different from the actual experience of pain.

In a second neuroimaging study, the distinction between empathic concern and personal distress was investigated more specifically using a number of behavioral measures and a set of ecological and extensively validated dynamic stimuli (Lamm, Batson, & Decety, 2007). Participants watched a series of video clips featuring patients undergoing painful medical treatment. They were asked to either put themselves explicitly in the shoes of the patients (imagine self) or focus on the patients' feelings and affective expressions (imagine other). The behavioral data confirmed that explicitly projecting oneself into an aversive situation leads to higher personal distress, whereas focusing on the emotional and behavioral reactions of another's plight is accompanied by higher empathic concern and lower personal distress. The neuroimaging data are consistent with this finding and provide some insights into the neural correlates of these distinct responses. The self perspective evoked stronger hemodynamic responses in brain regions involved in coding the motivational–affective dimensions of pain, including bilateral insular cortices, anterior midcingulate cortex (aMCC), and the amygdala, as well as subjective reports of anxiety and personal distress. When the participants were imagining what the patient was feeling, decreased activity was detected in the amygdala, with reduced feelings of anxiety and increased reports of sympathy and concern for the patient.

Altogether, the available empirical findings reveal both similarities and differences in the neural systems involved in first- and third-person perspective taking. Perspective-taking strategy may help keep feelings of personal distress at a minimum while boosting empathic concern. This is something that psychiatrists and psychotherapists know well when interacting with their patients or clients.

■ MODULATION OF EMPATHIC RESPONDING

Usually pain does not occur in a social vacuum. Social context matters in how one experiences pain and perceives it in others. For instance, social support can modulate the neural activity in brain areas involved the perception of threat. Coan, Schaefer, and Davidson (2006) scanned female participants when they were threatened with electric shock while either their husbands or an unknown man held their hand. While hand-holding by both the husband and stranger resulted in reduced neural responses in areas associated with physiological arousal due to threat (aMCC), support from the husband also regulated neural responses in regions associated with emotion regulation (right dorsolateral prefrontal cortex and caudate).

In another fMRI study, children (aged between 7 to 11 years) were presented with short video clips depicting painful situations that either occurred accidentally or were intentionally caused by another individual (figure 7.2; Decety, Michalska & Akitsuki, 2008). The first condition was associated with activation in neural regions involved in processing nociceptive information, such as the aMCC, AIC, thalamus, somatosensory cortex, SMA, and periaqueductal gray. When the videos depicted hurtful action intentionally done by another, signal increase was detected in the amygdala, mPFC, and OFC as well as in the nociception-processing network. In addition, both mPFC and OFC increased their effective connectivity with the frontoparietal attention network, which consists of the superior precentral sulcus, superior intraparietal sulcus, and TPJ. This network plays a critical role in reorienting attention to salient stimuli in the environment (Corbetta & Shulman, 2002).

Akitsuki and Decety (2009) used a similar paradigm with adult participants. Regions showing significant effects of pain were consistent with previous fMRI studies of empathy for pain. Most interestingly, empathy for pain was modulated by the social context in which the painful situations occurred. Participants' ratings of pain intensity when observing someone being hurt intentionally by another individual were significantly greater than their ratings of accidentally caused pain. The neural circuits involved in theory of mind and emotion regulation showed a significant main effect of social context, and functional connectivity was modulated by the social context. Stronger connectivity between the left amygdala and the ventromedial prefrontal cortex was found when participants observed painful situations caused by another individual than when pain was accidental.

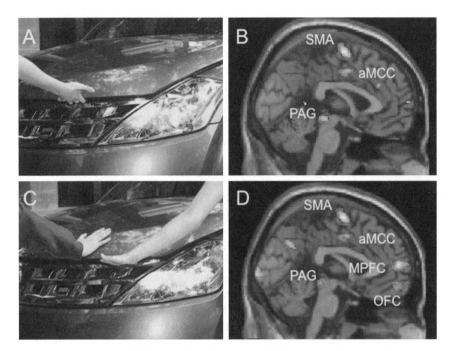

Figure 7.2 Functional MRI Study of Pain Empathy in Children. Seventeen typically developing children with a mean age of 9 years were scanned while presented with short (2.2 seconds) video clips depicting painful and nonpainful situations. The situations involved a person whose pain was caused by accident (as in *A*), a person whose pain was intentionally inflicted by another individual (as in *C*), and one- or two-agent situations without any pain as baselines. Consistent with previous fMRI studies of pain empathy with adults, the perception of other people in pain was associated with increased neurohemodynamic activity in neural circuits involved in processing the firsthand experience of pain, including the insula, somatosensory cortex (not shown), the anterior midcingulate cortex (aMCC), periaqueductal gray (PAG), and supplementary motor area (SMA) (*B*). When children observed an individual harming another, regions of the prefrontal cortex that are consistently involved in representing social interaction and moral behavior, such as the temporoparietal junction (not shown), the medial prefrontal cortex (mPFC), and orbitofrontal cortex (OFC), were additionally recruited (*D*). Interestingly, children indicated in the postscan debriefing that they thought that the situations in which pain was caused by another person were unfair, and asked about the reason that could explain this behavior. (Reproduced with permission from Decety, Michalska & Akitsuki, 2008.)

Although the neuroscience research provides evidence for a universal neurological mechanism underlying empathy, it does not address the effect of a host of social factors that might influence an empathic response, such as attitudes, expertise, group membership, and likability. Understanding how such factors impact the ability to perceive and respond with care to the cognitive, affective, and motivational internal states of another is crucial to understanding the conditions in which empathy will be expressed.

One way to more fully elucidate how a priori attitudes may moderate empathy for pain is to explore the effect of social stigma on the empathic response. Stigmatization occurs when an individual is (1) labeled, (2) negatively stereotyped, (3) discriminated against, and (4) experiences status loss. Stigmatized individuals possess or are believed to possess some attribute or characteristic that conveys a social identity that is devalued in a particular context (Crocker, Major, & Steele, 1998). As a result of such devalued and dehumanized out-group status, it can be predicted that people will experience less empathy for stigmatized individuals. Decety, Echols, and Correll (2009) combined behavioral and fMRI measures to explore whether perception of pain is modulated by the target's stigmatized status and whether or not the target bore responsibility for that stigma. During fMRI scanning, participants were exposed to a series of short video clips featuring age-matched individuals experiencing pain who were similar to the participant (Healthy), stigmatized but not responsible for their stigmatized condition (infected with AIDS as a result of a blood transfusion), or stigmatized and responsible for their stigmatized condition (infected with AIDS as a result of intravenous drug use). Explicit pain and empathy ratings for the targets were obtained outside the MRI environment, along with a variety of implicit and explicit measures of empathy and AIDS bias. Participants were more sensitive to the pain of AIDS Transfusion targets than Healthy and AIDS Drug targets, as evidenced by significantly higher pain and empathy ratings during video evaluation and significantly greater hemodynamic activity in areas associated with pain processing (i.e., AIC, aMCC, and PAG). In contrast, significantly less activity was observed in the aMCC for AIDS Drug targets than for Healthy controls. Behavioral results were moderated by the extent to which participants blamed AIDS Drug individuals for their condition. Controlling for both explicit and implicit AIDS bias, the more participants blamed these targets, the less pain they attributed to them as compared with Healthy controls. The study thus reveals that empathic response is moderated early in information processing by *a priori* attitudes toward the target group.

Empathy in patient–physician communication is associated with improved patient satisfaction and compliance with recommended treatment. However, as Hodges and Biswas-Diener (2007) argue, there are costs to being too empathic. For instance, paying attention to another's suffering in the course of caring for patients experiencing trauma or pain can exhaust the emotional resources of medical practitioners, reducing their capacity for or their interest in bearing the suffering of others. Empathy may thus be viewed as a double-edged sword, facilitating caring and compassion but at the same time leaving the physician vulnerable (Sabo, 2006). It is therefore critical that physicians develop effective emotion appraisal and regulation processes in the context of providing care to their patients. One fMRI study provided the first evidence of the impact of medical expertise on the neural response to witnessing another person experiencing a painful situation (Cheng et al., 2007). Brain hemodynamic responses were compared in a group of physicians and a group of matched control participants when they were exposed to short video clips showing hands and feet being pricked by a needle (painful situations) or being touched by a Q-tip (nonpainful situations). Unlike control participants, physicians showed a significantly reduced neurohemodynamic empathic response in the AIC and ACC and no activation of the PAG (a mediator of the fight-or-flight response) when shown the clips of body parts being pricked by a needle. Instead, cortical regions underpinning executive functions and self-regulation (dorsolateral and medial prefrontal cortex) and executive attention (precentral cortex, superior parietal cortex, and temporoparietal junction) were found to be activated. Connectivity analysis further demonstrated that activation in the medial and dorsolateral prefrontal cortices subserving executive control and self-regulation was inversely correlated with activity in the AIC in the physicians, indicating an executive suppression of the emotional response to the other's pain.

To determine at what stage of information processing this regulation occurs, Decety, Yang, and Cheng (2010) recorded event-related potentials (ERPs) from physicians and matched controls as they were exposed to the same visual stimuli. Control participants showed an early N100 differentiation between pain and no pain over the frontal area as well as a late positive potential around 300–800 ms over the centroparietal regions. No such early and late ERP responses were detected in the physicians. These results indicate that emotion regulation in physicians has very early effects, inhibiting the bottom-up processing of the perception of pain in others. One may suggest that physicians' downregulation of pain empathy dampens their negative arousal in response to the pain of others and thus may have beneficial consequences for being of assistance.

Summing up, current neurophysiological evidence clearly indicates that perceiving or imagining another individual in pain is associated with hemodynamic responses in the neural network that processes the motivational–affective and sensory dimensions of pain in the observer. This network if modulated by perceived agency, social context, and attitudes.

■ CONCLUSION

In recent decades there has been increased interest in the biological mechanisms that underpin the experience of empathy. Much of this new work relies on functional neuroimaging studies, with an emphasis on the perception of pain. The combined results of these studies demonstrate that when individuals perceive others in pain or distress, they partly use the same neural mechanisms as when they are in painful situations themselves. Such a shared neural mechanism offers an interesting foundation for intersubjectivity, because it provides a functional bridge between first-person information and third-person information (Sommerville & Decety, 2006) that offers a possible route to understanding others by allowing us to draw analogies between ourselves and them. Yet a minimal distinction between self and other is essential for social interaction in general and for empathy in particular, and new work in social neuroscience demonstrates that the self and other are distinguished at both the experiential and neural levels. A handful of cognitive neuroscience studies also indicate that the neural response to others in pain can be modulated by various situational and dispositional factors. Taken together, these data support the view that empathy is an adaptive phenomena that operates by way of conscious as well as non-conscious processes, which far from functioning independently contribute to different aspects of a common subjective experience.

An interesting issue yet to be explored is whether there are gender differences in empathy, and if so, whether they are learned or relate to hormonal and innate differences in the way the brain was shaped by evolutionary pressure? More specific differences might be biologically based, as suggested by the results of an fMRI study that investigated neural responses in men and women to infant crying and laughing (Seifritz et al., 2003). Women but not men, independent of parental status, showed neural deactivation in the ACC in response to infants' emotional expressions. In addition, the response pattern in the amygdala and interconnected limbic structures changed fundamentally with parental experience in both men and women. Nonparents showed stronger activation from laughing, whereas parents showed stronger activation for crying. These results seem to demonstrate that the emotion-sharing component may be subject to personal experience and that emotion regulation is differently biologically instantiated in men and women.

Finally, it is often assumed that empathy is a prerequisite for altruism and prosocial behavior and that we are, by nature, moral creatures. Despite this supposed link between empathy and prosocial behavior, neuroscience has yet to identify the mechanism of such a link. Empathy may well be viewed as a neutral capacity whose outcome will result in positive or negative consequences for the target, depending on a complex interplay of situational, motivational and personality factors. One of the challenges for a social neuroscience approach to empathy and prosocial behavior is the difficulty of taking into account situational variables. To provide interpretable data, neuroscience experiments—especially functional neuroimaging studies—require intra-individual comparisons and repeated-measures designs. To be financially feasible, they require small samples. These conditions limit opportunities to study the effects of potentially important situational variables. This is but one example of the perennial challenge objective science faces in the attempt to understand human subjectivity in all its richness and complexity.

■ ACKNOWLEDGMENT

The writing was supported by grant BCS-0718480 from the National Science Foundation.

■ REFERENCES

Allman, J. M., Watson, K. K., Tetreault, N. A., & Hakeem, A. Y. (2005). Intuition and autism: A possible role for von Economo neurons. *Trends in Cognitive Sciences, 9,* 367–373.

Akitsuki, Y., & Decety, J. (2009). Social context and perceived agency modulate brain activity in the neural circuits underpinning empathy for pain: An event-related fMRI study. *NeuroImage, 47,* 722–734.

Ax, A. F. (1964). Goals and methods of psychophysiology. *Psychophysiology, 62,* 8–25.

Barrett, L., Henzi, P., & Dunbar, R. I. M. (2003). Primate cognition: From what now to what if. *Trends in Cognitive Sciences, 7,* 494–497.

Barrett, L. F., Mesquita, B., Ochsner, K. N., & Gross, J. J. (2007). The experience of emotion. *Annual Review of Psychology, 58,* 373–403.

Basch, M. F. (1983). Empathic understanding: A review of the concept and some theoretical considerations. *Journal of the American Psychoanalytic Association, 31,* 101–126.

Batson, C. D. (2009). These things called empathy: Eight related but distinct phenomena. In J. Decety and W. Ickes (Eds.), *The Social Neuroscience of Empathy* (pp. 3–15). Cambridge, MA: MIT Press.

Batson, C. D., Batson, J. G., Singlsby, J. K., Harrell, K. L., Peekna, H. M., & Todd, R. M. (1991). Empathic joy and the empathy-altruism hypothesis. *Journal of Personality and Social Psychology, 61,* 413–426.

Batson, C. D., Fultz, J., & Schoenrade, P. (1987). Distress and empathy: Two qualitatively distinct vicarious emotions with different motivational consequences. *Journal of Personality, 55,* 19–39.

Baumeister, R. F., & Leary, M. R. (1995). The need to belong: Desire for interpersonal attachments as a fundamental human motivation. *Psychological Bulletin, 117,* 497–529.

Bell, S., & Ainsworth, M. (1972). Infant crying and maternal responsiveness. *Child Development, 43,* 1171–1190.

Benuzzi, F., Lui, F., Duzzi, D., Nichelli, P.F., & Porro, C.A. (2008). Does it look painful or disgusting? Ask your parietal and cingulate cortex. *Journal of Neuroscience, 28,* 923–931.

Bjorklund, D. F., & Bering, J. M. (2003). Big brains, slow development and social complexity: The development and evolutionary origins of social cognition. In M. Brune, H. Ribbert, & W. Schiedfenhovel (Eds.), *The social brain: Evolution and pathology* (pp. 113–151). Hoboken, NJ: Wiley.

Botvinick, M., Jha, A. P., Bylsma, L. M., Fabian, S. A., Solomon, P. E., & Prkachin, K. M. (2005). Viewing facial expressions of pain engages cortical areas involved in the direct experience of pain. *NeuroImage, 25,* 312–319.

Brunet-Gouet, E., & Decety, J. (2006). Social brain dysfunctions in schizophrenia: A review of neuroimaging studies. *Psychiatry Research, 148,* 75–92.

Bunge, S. A., Dudukovic, N. M., Thomasson, M. E., Vaidya, C. J., & Gabrieli, J. D. E. (2002). Immature frontal lobe contributions to cognitive control in children: Evidence from fMRI. *Neuron, 33,* 301–311.

Cacioppo, J. T. (2002). Social neuroscience: Understanding the pieces fosters understanding the whole and vice versa. *American Psychologist, 57,* 819–831.

Carr, L., Iacoboni, M., Dubeau, M. C., Mazziotta, J. C., & Lenzi, G. L. (2003). Neural mechanisms of empathy in humans: A relay from neural systems for imitation to limbic areas. *Proceedings of the National Academy of Sciences of the United States of America, 100,* 5497–5502.

Chakrabarti, B., Bullmore, E., & Baron-Cohen, S. (2006). Empathizing with basic emotions: common and discrete neural substrates. *Social Neuroscience, 1*(3-4), 364-384.

Cheng, Y., Lin, C., Liu, H. L., Hsu, Y., Lim, K., Hung, D., & Decety, J. (2007). Expertise modulates the perception of pain in others. *Current Biology, 17,* 1708–1713.

Cheng, Y., Yang, C. Y., Lin, C. P., Lee, P. R., & Decety, J. (2008). The perception of pain in others suppresses somatosensory oscillations: A magnetoencephalography study. *NeuroImage, 40,* 1833–1840.

Coan, J.A., Schaefer, H. S., & Davidson, R. J. (2006). Lending a hand: Social regulation of the neural response to threat. *Psychological Science, 17,* 1032–1039.

Corbetta, M., & Shulman, G. L. (2002). Control of goal-directed and stimulus-driven attention in the brain. *Nature Neuroscience Reviews, 3,* 201–215.

Craig, A. D. (2002). How do you feel? Interoception: The sense of the physiological condition of the body. *Nature Reviews Neuroscience, 3,* 655–666.

Craig, A. D. (2007). Interoception and emotion: A neuroanatomical perspective. In M. Lewis, J. M. Haviland-Jones, & L. F. Barrett (Eds.), *Handbook of emotion* (3rd ed., pp. 272–288). New York, NY: Guilford Press.

Craig, K. D. (2009). The social communication model of pain. *Canadian Psychology, 50,* 22–32.

Crocker, J., Major, B., & Steele, C. (1998). Social stigma. In D. Gilbert, S. T. Fiske, & G. Lindzey (Eds.), *The handbook of social psychology* (4th ed., Vol. 2, pp. 504–553). New York, NY: McGraw-Hill.

D'Argembeau, A., Ruby, P., Collette, F., Degueldre, C., Balteau, E., Luxen, A., et al. (2007). Distinct regions of the medial prefrontal cortex are associated with self-referential processing and perspective taking. *Journal of Cognitive Neuroscience, 19,* 935–944.

Davis, M. H., Conklin, L., Smith, A., & Luce, C. (1996). Effect of perspective taking on the cognitive representation of persons: A merging of self and other. *Journal of Personality and Social Psychology, 70,* 713–726.

Decety, J. (2005). Perspective taking as the royal avenue to empathy. In B. F. Malle & S. D. Hodges (Eds.), *Other minds: How humans bridge the divide between self and other* (pp. 135–149). New York, NY: Guilford Press.

Decety, J. (2010). To what extent is the experience of empathy mediated by shared neural circuits? *Emotion Review, 2,* 204-207.

Decety, J. (2011). Dissecting the neural mechanisms mediating empathy. *Emotion Review, 3,* 92-108.

Decety, J., Echols, S. C., & Correll, J. (2009). The blame game: The effect of responsibility and social stigma on empathy for pain. *Journal of Cognitive Neuroscience, 22,* 985–997.

Decety, J., & Grèzes, J. (2006). The power of simulation: Imagining one's own and other's behavior. *Brain Research, 1079,* 4–14.

Decety, J., & Hodges, S. D. (2006). A social cognitive neuroscience model of human empathy. In P. A. M. van Lange (Ed.), *Bridging social psychology: Benefits of transdisciplinary approaches* (pp. 103–109). Mahwah, NJ: Erlbaum.

Decety, J., & Jackson, P. L. (2004). The functional architecture of human empathy. *Behavioral and Cognitive Neuroscience Reviews, 3,* 71–100.

Decety, J., & Lamm, C. (2007). The role of the right temporoparietal junction in social interaction: How low-level computational processes contribute to meta-cognition. *Neuroscientist, 13,* 580–593.

Decety, J., & Meyer, M. (2008). From emotion resonance to empathic understanding: A social developmental neuroscience account. *Development and Psychopathology, 20,* 1053–1080.

Decety, J., & Michalska, K.J. (2010). Neurodevelopmental changes in the circuits underlying empathy and sympathy from childhood to adulthood. *Developmental Science, 13,* 886-899.

Decety, J., Michalska, K. J., & Akitsuki, Y. (2008). Who caused the pain? A functional MRI investigation of empathy and intentionality in children. *Neuropsychologia, 46,* 2607–2614.

Decety, J., Michalska, K. J., & Kinzler, K. D. (2011). The contribution of emotion and cognition to moral sensitivity: A neurodevelopmental study. *Cerebral Cortex,* in press.

Decety, J., & Sommerville, J. A. (2003). Shared representations between self and others: A social cognitive neuroscience view. *Trends in Cognitive Sciences, 7,* 527–533.

Decety, J., Yang, C. Y., & Cheng, Y. (2010). Physicians down regulate their pain empathy response: An event-related brain potential study. *NeuroImage, 50,* 1676–1682.

De Waal, F. B. M. (1996). *Good natured: The origins of right and wrong in humans and other animals.* Cambridge, MA: Harvard University Press.

De Waal, F. B. M., &, Thompson, E. (2005). Primates, monks and the mind: The case of empathy. *Journal of Consciousness Studies, 12,* 38–54.

de Waal, F. B. M., & van Roosmalen, A. (1979). Reconciliation and consolation among chimpanzees. *Behavioral Ecology and Sociobiology, 5,* 55–66.

Diamond, A. (2002). Normal development of prefrontal cortex from birth to young adulthood: Cognitive functions, anatomy, and biochemistry. In D. T. Stuss and R. T. Knight (eds.), *Principles of frontal lobe function* (pp. 446–503). New York, NY: Oxford University Press.

Dimberg, U., Thunberg, M., & Elmehed, K. (2000). Unconscious facial reactions to emotional facial expressions. *Psychological Science, 11,* 86–89.

Dinstein, H., Hasson, U., Rubin, N., & Heeger, D. J. (2007). Brain areas selective for both observed and executed movements. *Journal of Neurophysiology, 98,* 1415–1427.

Dondi, M., Simion, F., & Caltran, G. (1999). Can newborns discriminate between their own cry and the cry of another newborn infant? *Developmental Psychology, 35,* 418–426.

Eisenberg, N., & Eggum, N. D. (2009). Empathic responding: Sympathy and personal distress. In J. Decety and W. Ickes (Eds.), *The social neuroscience of empathy* (pp. 71–83). Cambridge, MA: MIT Press.

Eisenberg, N., Shea, C. L., Carlo, G., & Knight, G. P. (1991). Empathy-related responding and cognition: A chicken and the egg dilemma. In W. M. Kurtines (Ed.), *Handbook of Moral Behavior and Development,* Vol 2: Research (pp. 63–88). Hillsdale, NJ: Erlbaum.

Fadiga, L., Fogassi, L., Pavesi, G., & Rizzolatti, G. (1995). Motor facilitation during action observation: A magnetic stimulation study. *Journal of Neurophysiology, 73,* 2608–2611.

Fogassi, L., Ferrari, P. F., Gesierich, B., Rozzi, S., Chersi, F., & Rizzolatti, G. (2005). Parietal lobe: From action organization to intention understanding. *Science, 308,* 662–667.

Fossati, P., Hevenor, S. J., Graham, S. J., Grady, C., Keightley, M. L., Craik, F., et al. (2003). In search of the emotional self: An fMRI study using positive and negative emotional words. *American Journal of Psychiatry, 160,* 1938–1945.

Gallese, V., Fadiga, L., Fogassi, L., & Rizzolatti, G. (1996). Action recognition in the premotor cortex. *Brain, 119,* 593–609.

Geary, D. C., & Flinn, M. (2001). Evolution of human parental behavior and the human family. *Parenting: Science and Practice, 1,* 5–61.

Harris, P. L. (2000). Understanding emotion. In M. Lewis & J. M. Haviland-Jones (Eds.), *Handbook of emotions* (pp. 281–292). New York, NY: Guilford Press.

Hatfield, E., Rapson, R. L., & Le, Y. C. (2009). Emotional contagion and empathy. In J. Decety & W. Ickes (Eds.), *The social neuroscience of empathy* (pp. 19–30). Cambridge, MA: MIT Press.

Haviland, J. M., & Lewica, M. (1987). The induced affect response: Ten-week-old infants' responses to three emotion expressions. *Developmental Psychology, 23,* 97–104.

Hickok, G. (2009). Eight problems for the mirror neuron theory of action understanding in monkeys and human. *Journal of Cognitive Neuroscience, 21,* 1229–1243.

Hodges, S. D., & Biswas-Diener, R. (2007). Balancing the empathy expense account: Strategies for regulating empathic response. In T. F. D. Farrow & P. W. R. Woodruff (Eds.), *Empathy in mental illness* (pp. 389–405). Cambridge, England: Cambridge University Press.

Hodges, S. D., & Wegner, D. M. (1997). The mental control of empathic accuracy. In W. Ickes (ed.), *Empathic accuracy* (pp. 311–339). New York, NY: Guilford.

Hornak, J., Bramham, J., Rolls, E. T., Morris, R. J., O'Doherty, J. O., Bullock, P. R., & Polkey, C. E. (2003). Changes in emotion after circumscribed surgical lesions of the orbitofrontal and cingulated cortices. *Brain, 126,* 1691–1712.

Jackson, P. L., Brunet, E., Meltzoff, A. N., & Decety, J. (2006). Empathy examined through the neural mechanisms involved in imagining how I feel versus how you feel pain. *Neuropsychologia, 44,* 752–761.

Jackson, P. L., Meltzoff, A. N., & Decety, J. (2005). How do we perceive the pain of others: A window into the neural processes involved in empathy. *NeuroImage, 24,* 771–779.

Jackson, P. L., Rainville, P., & Decety, J. (2006). From nociception to empathy: The neural mechanism for the representation of pain in self and in others. *Pain, 125,* 5–9.

Johnson, S. C., Baxter, L. C., Wilder, L. S., Pipe, J. G., Heiserman, J. E., & Prigatano, G. P. (2002). Neural correlates of self-reflection. *Brain, 125,* 1808–1814.

Kawashima, R., Sato, K., Itoh, H., Ono, S., Furumoto, S., Gotoh, R., Koyama, M., Yoshioka, S., Takahashi, T., & Takahashi, K. (1996). Functional anatomy of go/no-go discrimination and response selection—a PET study in man. *Brain Research, 728,* 79–89.

Lamm, C., Batson, C. D., & Decety, J. (2007). The neural basis of human empathy: Effects of perspective-taking and cognitive appraisal. *Journal of Cognitive Neuroscience, 19,* 42–58.

Lamm, C., Meltzoff, A. N., & Decety, J. (2010). How do we empathize with someone who is not like us? *Journal of Cognitive Neuroscience, 3,* 362–376.

Lamm, C., Nusbaum, H. C., Meltzoff, A. N., & Decety, J. (2007). What are you feeling? Using functional magnetic resonance imaging to assess the modulation of sensory and affective responses during empathy for pain. *PLoS ONE, 12,* e1292.

Langford, D. J., Tuttleb, A. H., Brown, K., Deschenes, S., Fischer, D. B., Mutso, A., Root, K. C., Sotocinal, S. G., Stern, M. A., Mogil, J. S., & Sternberg, W. F. (2010). Social approach to pain in laboratory mice. *Social Neuroscience, 5,* 163–170.

Leslie, K. R., Johnson-Frey, S. H., & Grafton, S. (2004). Functional imaging of face and hand imitation: Towards a motor theory of empathy. *NeuroImage, 21,* 601–607.

Levenson, R. W., Ekman, P., & Friesen, W. V. (1990). Voluntary facial action generates emotion-specific autonomic nervous system activity. *Psychophysiology, 27,* 363–384.

Lorberbaum, J. P., Newman, J. D., Horwitz, A. R., Dubno, J. R., Lydiard, R. B., & Hammer, M. B. (2002). A potential role for thalamocingulate circuitry in human maternal behavior. *Biological Psychiatry, 51,* 431–445.

MacLean, P. D. (1985). Brain evolution relating to family, play, and the separation call. *Archives of General Psychiatry, 42,* 405–417.

Morrison, I., Lloyd, D., di Pellegrino, G., & Roberts, N. (2004). Vicarious responses to pain in anterior cingulate cortex: Is empathy a multisensory issue? *Cognitive and Affective Behavioral Neuroscience, 4,* 270–278.

Murphy, F. C., Nimmo-Smith, I., & Lawrence, A. D. (2003). Functional neuroanatomy of emotions: A meta-analysis. *Cognitive, Affective, & Behavioral Neuroscience, 3,* 207–233.

Newman, J. D. (2007). Neural circuits underlying crying and cry responding in mammals. *Behavioural Brain Research, 182,* 155–165.

Niedenthal, P. M., Barsalou, L. W., Winkielman, P., Krauth-Gruber, S., & Ric, F. (2005). Embodiment in attitudes, social perception, and emotion. *Personality and Social Psychology Review, 9,* 184–211.

Ostrowsky, K., Magnin, M., Ryvlin, P., Isnard, J., Guenot, M., & Mauguiere, F. (2002). Representation of pain and somatic sensation in the human insula: A study of responses to direct electrical cortical stimulation. *Cerebral Cortex, 12,* 376–385.

Parr, L. A. (2001). Cognitive and physiological markers of emotional awareness in chimpanzees (*Pan troglodytes*). *Animal Cognition, 4,* 223–229.

Parr, L. A., & Waller, B. (2007). The evolution of human emotion. In J. Kaas (Ed.), *Evolution of the nervous system* (Vol. 5, pp. 447–472). New York, NY: Elsevier.

Phan, K. L., Wager, T., Taylor, S. F., & Liberzon, I. (2002). Functional neuroanatomy of emotion: A meta-analysis of emotion activation studies in PET and fMRI. *Neuroimage, 16,* 331–348.

Pineda, J. A. (2005). The functional significance of mu rhythms: Translating seeing and hearing into doing. *Brain Research Review, 50,* 57–68.

Porges, S. W. (2001). The polyvagal theory: Phylogenetic substrates of a social nervous system. *International Journal of Psychophysiology, 42,* 123–146.

Povinelli, D. J. (2001). *Folk physics for apes.* New York, NY: Oxford University Press.

Preston, S. D., & de Waal, F. B. M. (2002). Empathy: Its ultimate and proximate bases. *Behavioral and Brain Sciences, 25,* 1–72.

Rolls, E. T. (1999). *The brain and emotion.* Oxford, England: Oxford University Press.

Ruby, P., & Decety, J. (2001). Effect of subjective perspective taking during simulation of action: A PET investigation of agency. *Nature Neuroscience, 4,* 546–550.

Ruby, P., & Decety, J. (2003). What you believe versus what you think they believe? A neuroimaging study of conceptual perspective taking. *European Journal of Neuroscience, 17,* 2475–2480.

Ruby, P., & Decety, J. (2004). How would you feel versus how do you think she would feel? A neuroimaging study of perspective taking with social emotions. *Journal of Cognitive Neuroscience, 16,* 988–999.

Sabo, B. M. (2006). Compassion fatigue and nursing work: Can we accurately capture the consequences of caring work? *International Journal of Nursing Practice, 12,* 136–142.

Seifritz, E., Esposito, F., Neuhoff, J. G., Lüthi, A., Mustovic, H., & Dammann, G. (2003). Differential sex-independent amygdala response to infant crying and laughing in parents versus nonparents. *Biological Psychiatry, 54,* 1367–1375.

Singer, T., Seymour, B., O'Doherty, J., Kaube, H., Dolan, R. J., & Frith, C. D. (2004). Empathy for pain involves the affective but not the sensory components of pain. *Science, 303,* 1157–1161.

Sommerville, J. A., & Decety, J. (2006). Weaving the fabric of social interaction: Articulating developmental psychology and cognitive neuroscience in the domain of motor cognition. *Psychonomic Bulletin and Review, 13,* 179–200.

Swick, D., Ashley, V., & Turken, A. U. (2008). Left inferior frontal gyrus is critical for response inhibition. *BMC Neuroscience, 9,* 102e.

Symonds, L. L., Gordon, N. S., Bixby, J. C., & Mande, M. M. (2006). Right-lateralized pain processing in the human cortex: An fMRI study. *Journal of Neurophysiology, 95,* 3823–3830.

Tkach, D., Reimer, J., & Hatsopoulos, N. G. (2007). Congruent activity during action and action observation in motor cortex. *Journal of Neuroscience, 27,* 13241–13250.

Toga, A. W., Thompson, P. M., & Sowell, E. R. (2006). Mapping brain maturation. *Trends in Neurosciences, 29,* 148–159.

Turella, L., Pierno, A. C., Tubaldi, F., & Castiello, U. (2009). Mirror neurons in humans: Consisting or confounding evidence? *Brain and Language, 108,* 10–20.

Van der Gaag, C., Minderaa, R. B., & Keysers, C. (2007). Facial expressions: What the mirror neuron system can and cannot tell us. *Social Neuroscience, 2*(3), 179–222.

Warneken, F., & Tomasello, M. (2009). The roots of human altruism. *British Journal of Psychology, 100,* 455–471.

Williams, A. C. (2002). Facial expression of pain: An evolutionary account. *Behavioral and Brain Sciences, 25,* 439–488.

Wilson, E. O. (1988). *On human nature.* Cambridge, MA: Harvard University Press.

Zelazo, P., Carlson, S., & Kesek, A. (2008). The development of executive function in childhood. In C. A. Nelson and M. Luciana (Eds.), *Handbook of developmental cognitive neuroscience* (pp. 553–574). Cambridge, MA: MIT Press.

8 Parental and Romantic Attachment Systems

Neural Circuits, Genes, and Experiential Contributions to Interpersonal Engagement

■ JAMES E. SWAIN

Back in early 2002, I had the incredible good fortune to begin an ongoing and fruitful professional relationship and friendship. I was working as a child psychiatry fellow after finishing basic neuroscience, medical and child psychiatry training, and thinking about getting back into research, in which I hoped to use brain imaging to study complex mental states. So I optimistically sent a letter of career interests to several senior colleagues. The director of research at the Yale Child Study Center, Dr. James Leckman, responded and a few stimulating conversations ensued, after which he, invited me to visit and consider a postdoctoral position there. Jim is a world expert on Tourette syndrome and childhood-onset neuropsychiatric disorders, so I prepared myself accordingly. However, after a first meeting and a lovely dinner with him and his wife, Hannah, he asked me what I might do if I had unlimited resources to establish my research career. Though feeling somewhat unprepared for that, I said that it seemed that too much research was focused on negative emotions and states such as fear and anxiety and that I would "love" to be among the researchers that consider more positive emotions such as joy, happiness, and love that might contribute to mental health resiliency. Fortunately, he and I were already thinking along the same lines.

A month later I had accepted a position, and Jim had informed me of a request for applications to the aptly named Institute for Research on Unlimited Love. We brainstormed a project idea to use brain imaging to study the brain basis of how parents "fall in love" with their infants and make all the important adjustments in the early postpartum period. To make a long story short, we got that grant and the rest, may I say, is history. For the last 9 years, I have been delighted to pursue this research, currently at the University of Michigan, in which I have been privileged to build many other relationships such as those with my colleagues represented in this book.

■ BACKGROUND

Early parenting and romantic love involve a repertoire of social-bonding behaviors that cross species (Winslow & Insel, 2004) and cultures (Jankowiak & Fischer, 1992). They are both discrete stages in life, involving a personal choice, a psychological transition, and a cultural creation, in addition to being necessities for the species and psychobiological transformation. In 1956, the pediatrician and psychoanalyst Donald Winnicott drew attention to the simplifying construct of "primary maternal preoccupations." He described this state as "almost an illness" that a mother must experience to meet the physical and psychological needs of her infant (Winnicott, 1956). Like parental love, romantic love has been described as consisting of intense focused attention on a preferred individual, obsessive thinking, and increased energy (Fisher, Aron, Mashek, Li, & Brown, 2002; Gonzaga, Keltner, Londahl, & Smith, 2001; Hatfield & Sprecher, 1986; Leckman & Mayes, 1999; Shaver, Schwartz, Kirson, & O'Connor, 1987). Intense romantic love is a cross-culturally universal phenomenon, as was observed in a survey of 166 contemporary societies (Jankowiak & Fischer, 1992). Recent advances in our understanding of the genetic, epigenetic (aspects of genetic expression that do not involve code but rather the code's expression), and neurobiological aspects of love-related behaviors in human and model mammalian species have relevance for psychopathological risk and resiliency. A selection of these caring systems are discussed below.

■ NEURAL CIRCUITS OF EARLY PARENTAL LOVE

Although the events in the central nervous system that accompany parental care and romantic social behaviors in humans are largely unknown, it is likely that there is a substantial degree of conservation across mammalian species. Some of the foundational animal model work is described below, along with hints of similar processes in humans.

Lesion and gene-knockout experiments in rodents have identified critical brain regions for parenting behaviors (Leckman & Herman, 2002). Among these evolutionarily ancient brain structures are the limbic/olfactory systems, including the amygdala, the hypothalamus, the ventral part of the bed nucleus of the stria terminalis, and the lateral septum. Genes important for parenting behavior include those that encode for three transcription factors, the enzymes dopamine beta hydroxylase and neuronal nitric oxide synthase, the receptors for prolactin and estrogen, and the neuropeptide oxytocin (Leckman & Herman, 2002).

While information about these systems in humans and other primate species is limited, the available data are consistent with the involvement of at least some of the same circuitry a in rodents. Blood or salivary levels of adrenal glucocorticoids are helpful indirect indices of relationships and emotional states of pair bonding. For example, Fleming, Steiner, and Corter (1997) found that first-time mothers with high levels of circulating cortisol were better able to identify their own infants' odors. In these same primiparous mothers, the level of affectionate infant contact (affectionate burping, stroking, poking, and hugging) by the mother was associated with higher levels of salivary cortisol.

In addition, several systematically evaluated experimental interventions had long-term effects on maternal behaviors in rats (Pryce, Bettschen, & Feldon, 2001). The findings suggested that maternal behavior in the days following birth serves to epigenetically program the subsequent maternal behavior of the adult offspring as well as establishing the pups' level of hypothalamic-pituitary-adrenal responsiveness to stress (Francis, Diorio, Liu, & Meaney, 1999).

These types of animal studies have laid the foundation for work in humans examining similar behaviors and investigating similar brain circuits and hormone regulations in which early life events have long-term consequences.

■ INTEGRATING PSYCHOLOGY AND NEUROBIOLOGY OF PARENTAL AND ROMANTIC LOVE

One of the landmarks of contemporary developmental psychology has been its focus on attachment between infant and parent (Bowlby, 2000). The same conceptual framework can be applied to assess the nature and quality of the romantic attachments formed in adulthood (Hazan & Shaver, 1987), their associated behaviors and thoughts (Leckman & Mayes, 1999), and the brain regions and neurochemicals important for these systems (see table 8.1).

In both parenting and romance, there is an anxious tension between the joyous reveries of being "at one" with each other and intrusive worries that something terrible will happen that places the desired outcome in jeopardy. Other clear thematic parallels include the tendency to be preoccupied with small details of the other's appearance and the tendency to see the lover or the new infant as "perfect." Or as one mother said after her baby was born, "I just can't believe it, here she is and she's so perfect, I can't believe she's really mine , . . it's just like falling in love"(personal communication).

Similarities between the behavioral repertoires of early romantic and early parental love are also striking. In both instances there is a compelling urge to shape behavior to the perceived needs of the other. Frequently, these actions have a "just right" character, in that they exactly fit the needs of the other. The heightened sense of responsibility that usually accompanies both states leads to an increased level of vigilance and steps to ensure the safety of the infant or lover. Beyond the intimacies of the home environment, both states are marked by culturally defined rituals (Feygin, Swain, & Leckman, 2006; Leckman et al., 2004). In couples dating for less than 6 months, stable levels of romantic preoccupations predicted the capacity to successfully negotiate disagreements. (Shulman et al., 2008).

TABLE 8.1 *Brain Areas and Neurochemicals Associated with Early Parental and Romantic Love*

Feature of Parental/Romantic Love	Brain Areas	Neurochemicals
Selective recognition/exclusivity of focus	Face areas, occipitotemporal cortex	Glutamate and GABA
Altered mental state/altered autonomic and behavioral responsivity conditioned by the absence, presence, or mere cues of the other(s)	Midbrain, hypothalamus, frontal cortex	Dopamine, oxytocin, vasopressin
Clear onset of hedonic transformation	Caudate, amygdala, hippocampus	Dopamine
Intrusive thoughts and images (preoccupations): • Longing for reciprocity • Idealization of the other • Heightened awareness of the other • Heightened sense of empathy, responsibility, and worries about the well-being of the other • Separation distress • Upsetting aggressive thoughts focused on the self or the other	Inferior frontal, insula (mirror neurons), basal ganglia	Glutamate and GABA, serotonin, norepinephrine

Many of the behaviors and associated emotional states seen in courtship overlap with the repertoire of the early parent–child relationship. Specific examples include parental behaviors such as comforting embraces, caressing, grooming, kissing, feeding, mutual gaze, and the use of terms of endearment like "baby." Similarly, needy infant-like appeals by gesture or whimper are common elements of lovers' behavioral repertoires.

Among the neural structures that we would expect underlie these states are subcortical regions that mediate reward (Depue & Morrone-Strupinsky, 2005; Robbins & Everitt, 1996; Swain, Mayes, & Leckman, 2005). Indeed, Romantic love can be like cocaine, producing exhilaration, excessive energy, sleeplessness, and loss of appetite (Fisher et al., 2002), and also bear resemblances to addiction-like parenting behaviors in animal models (Insel, 2003). Consistent with animal studies of cocaine addiction (David, Segu, Buhot, Ichaye, & Cazala, 2004), acute cocaine injection has been shown to activate the ventral tegmental area (VTA) in functional magnetic resonance imaging (fMRI) studies of humans (Breiter et al., 1997). In addition, fMRI studies have shown that secondary rewards like money activate the nucleus accumbens/subcallosal region and VTA (Breiter et al., 1997; Delgado, Locke, Stenger, & Fiez, 2003; Knutson, Fong, Adams, Varner, & Hommer, 2001). Furthermore, chocolate, acting as a food reward, activates the VTA and subcallosal region (Small, Zatorre, Dagher, Evans, & Jones-Gotman, 2001). Small et al. (2001) found that these regions decreased their metabolic activity with decreasing desire for more chocolate. Given the overlap of brain function in mediating rewarding and reinforcing aspects of love as well as addiction, effective prevention and treatment of addiction may benefit from adjusting social or living environments and addressing individuals' personal relationships. It may be that studying the degree to which social as well as addictive processes engage the reward system and the way such rewarding experiences are integrated will provide biological risk markers for comorbid depressive symptoms of anhedonia following emotional loss or of susceptibility to addiction itself.

In addition to basic appetitive reward functions of the nucleus accumbens, striatum, and dopamine in the brain, studies of monogamous prairie voles suggest that these factors could regulate complex social bonds. When a female prairie vole mates with a male, she forms a distinct preference for that partner. But a female prairie vole will also come to prefer a male present at the time a dopamine agonist is infused into her nucleus accumbens, even if she has not mated with that male. This indicates the importance of striatal dopamine in mediating affiliative behaviors. Indeed, a striatal output region through the ventral pallidum is critical to mate-preference behaviors in male prairie voles (Lim et al., 2004). Similarly, electrochemical studies in male rats have shown increased dopamine release in the dorsal and ventral striatum in response to the presence of a receptive female rat, more so even than during copulation (Robinson, Heien, & Wightman, 2002). Thus, several lines of evidence from both human fMRI and animal studies support the prediction that multiple reward regions involving dopamine and regulated by neuropeptides including oxytocin (discussed below) are active during feelings of romantic and parental love.

Based on other neural systems research, the anterior caudate nucleus of the brain is likely also important for romantic and parental love. The caudate plays a role in reward detection and expectation, representation of goals, and integration of sensory inputs to prepare for action (Schultz, 2000). The caudate nucleus could represent rewards and goals in a complex behavioral state like romantic love because it has widespread afferents from all of the cortex except primary visual cortex (Goldman-Rakic & Selemon, 1990) and is organized to integrate diverse sensory, motor, and limbic functions that would also be critical parts of parental or romantic behaviors (Haber, 2003).

■ THE NEUROBIOLOGY OF EMPATHY AND PARENTING

Empathy, defined as appropriate perception, experience, and response to another's emotion, is especially relevant to parenting, in which infant's needs are great yet communication is exclusively nonverbal. The growing field of cognitive neuroscience, propelled by modern brain imaging techniques, is revealing networks of brain activity relating to empathy and emotional mirroring (Gallese, Keysers, & Rizzolatti, 2004) that seem to overlap significantly with brain responses seen in parenting that are reviewed in this chapter and relevant to the brain basis of social cognition that is important for romantic love. The cingulate and insular cortices emerge as key brain areas that regulate empathy and parenting in humans.

In an fMRI study focusing on the neuroanatomy of empathy, Singer (Singer et al., 2004) measured brain activity while volunteers experienced a painful stimulus or observed a signal indicating that a loved one present in the same room had received a similar pain stimulus. Singer et al. found that circuits responding to the sensory-discriminative components of pain were separated from circuits involved in the autonomic-affective aspects. Specifically, the posterior insula, the sensorimotor cortex, and the caudal anterior cingulate, brain stem, and cerebellum were active while participants were receiving pain stimuli, while for the emotional aspects of experiencing the pain of a loved one, the rostral anterior cingulate and anterior insula were specifically active. Such decoupled representations, which may even be independent of the sensory inputs of the outside world, have been postulated to be necessary for our empathic abilities to mentalize, that is, to understand the thoughts, beliefs, and intentions of others (Frith & Frith, 2003), as in parental and romantic dyads.

In another relevant study of the cingulate's role in mediating the brain basis of social behavior, Eisenberger, Lieberman, and Williams (2003) used virtual reality to simulate shunning. In this study, subjects were involved in a virtual game of Cyberball that included three players. When the subject player was suddenly excluded from the game, there was a rapid change in the anterior cingulate cortex. Perhaps the cingulate mediates the separation–attachment system, which is critical to parenting and romantic love. Thus, in addition to registering pain, the anterior cingulate may be an important part of the brain circuit that processes a range of emotional signals (own's own pain or social pain such as in witnessing the pain of a loved one; social rejection; or stimuli of one's child or romantic love) in order to shift attention, make decisions, recruit memory, regulate mood, or direct behavior as needed.

The insula has also been proposed as an important center for integrating social emotional information (Carr, Iacoboni, Dubeau, Mazziotta, & Lenzi, 2003), along with its connections to mirror neuron areas in the posterior parietal, inferior frontal, and superior temporal cortices. In one study, subjects were shown pictures of standard emotional faces (happy, sad, angry, surprised, disgusted, and afraid) and fMRI was used to measure responses to mere observation and to observation as well as internal simulation of the emotion observed. As expected, imitation (i.e., observation with internal simulation) produced greater activity in frontotemporal areas in the mirror network, including the premotor face area, the dorsal pars opercularis of the inferior frontal cortex, and the superior temporal sulcus. Imitation also produced greater activity in the right anterior insula and right amygdala. This is particularly intriguing in light of evidence that responses in the anterior insula are associated with pleasant "caress-like touch" (Olausson et al., 2002), orgasm (Ortigue, Grafton, & Bianchi-Demicheli, 2007), and the emotional and interpersonal interactions that may go awry in mental illness such as autism (Dapretto et al., 2006). A further confirmation of the insula's role in emotion recognition comes from the study of patients with strokes. Stroke patients with insular lesions showed a significantly greater deficit in emotion recognition than other stroke patients (Bodini, Iacoboni, & Lenzi, 2004).

We speculate that the cingulate and insula will continue to emerge as key areas that are important during the transformations that are typical in the initial formation of a new family, as neuroimaging studies below are beginning to support. Perhaps future studies of high-risk families, such as these with mothers who suffered previous mental illness episodes or child abuse, will fail to show a typical pattern of activation in these limbic response and cortical regulation regions, while early intervention programs shown to have beneficial long-term effects on child development (Olds et al., 2004) will be associated with changed activation patterns in them.

■ NEUROCHEMICALS OF LOVE

An association has recurrently been found between increased activity in the hypothalamic-pituitary-adrenal (HPA) axis and the subsequent expression of social behaviors and attachments such as those of parental and romantic love. The HPA axis and adrenal steroids are particularly responsive to social and environmental demands. Under stressful conditions, the HPA axis is activated and there may be an increase in sexual, parental, and social behaviors and the formation of social bonds (Kyrou & Tsigos, 2009). Animal studies indicate that adrenal steroid-neuropeptide interactions involving oxytocin and vasopressin as well as other neurotransmitters and hormones regulate the development of social attachments (Carter, 1998; Carter, Grippo, Pournajafi-Nazarloo, Ruscio, & Porges, 2008). Positive social behaviors, perhaps mediated through a central oxytocinergic system, may modulate the activity of the HPA axis and the autonomic nervous system, perhaps even accounting for health benefits that are attributed to positive social interactions and emotions (Uvnas-Moberg, 1998). A selection of human studies highlighting the importance of neurochemicals in parental and romantic love is detailed below.

To investigate the phenomenon of falling in love, Marazzitti and colleagues studied pituitary, adrenal, and gonadal hormones (Marazziti & Canale, 2004). Follicle-stimulating hormone (FSH), luteinizing hormone (LH), estradiol, progesterone, dehydroepiandrosterone sulphate (DHEAS), cortisol, testosterone, and androstenedione were studied in a group of 24 subjects of both sexes who had fallen in love within the previous six months and an equal number of control subjects. Levels of estradiol, progesterone, DHEAS and androstenedione did not differ between the groups and were within the normal ranges. Cortisol levels, however, were significantly higher among subjects who had recently fallen in love than among controls. FSH and testosterone levels were lower in men in love, while women of the same group presented higher testosterone levels. All hormonal differences were gone when the subjects were retested 12–24 months later.

The increased cortisol and low FSH levels are consistent with the stressful and arousing conditions associated with the initiation of a social contact. The changes of testosterone concentrations, which varied in opposite directions in the two sexes, may reflect changes in behavioral or temperamental traits that have yet to be clarified. These results are supported by the finding that men in committed romantic relationships have testosterone levels 21% lower than men not involved in such relationships (Burnham et al., 2003), perhaps pointing to differences between initial romantic love and long-term love. Perhaps evolution favors possible benefits of reduced testosterone in long-term love as in the case of becoming a parent, in which considerable and sustained investment is required for offspring survival. This reduction may lead to decreased risk taking and aggression once men have committed to immediate family–related situations.

In addition to testosterone, other biochemical and environmental factors are emerging in the regulation of affiliation. For example, Emanuele et al. (2006) investigated associations between the early romantic phase of a loving relationship and alterations in circulating levels of neurotrophins Neurotrophins are peptides that affect neuronal growth and function. Plasma levels of the neurotrophins NGF (nerve growth factor), BDNF (brain derived neurotrophic factor), NT-3 (neurotrophic factor) and NT-4 were measured in 58 subjects who had recently fallen in love and two control groups, consisting of subjects who either were single or were already involved in long-lasting relationships. NGF levels were significantly higher in the subjects in love than in either control group. There was also a significant positive correlation between levels of NGF and the intensity of romantic love (as assessed with the Passionate Love Scale (Hatfield & Sprecher, 1986)). No differences in the concentrations of other NTs were detected. When 39 of the original subjects in love returned after 12–24 months, during which they had maintained the same relationships but were no longer in the same romantic state, their plasma NGF levels had decreased and become indistinguishable from those of the control groups. Taken together, these findings suggest that some behavioral or psychological features associated with falling in love could be related to raised NGF levels in the bloodstream.

Kissing, an integral part of romantic and parental behavior, also appears to modulate neurotrophin release. In one study, kissing significantly reduced allergic wheal responses and plasma levels of NGF, BDNF, NT-3, and NT-4 in patients with allergic rhinitis and atopic dermatitis to exposure to house dust mites and the pollen of Japanese cedars (Kimata, 2003). Perhaps kissing, which may confer some reassurance of environmental safety, can assist in down regulating immune responses to non–life-threatening allergens in the environment.

Looking at parallels between the neurochemistry of romantic love and obsessive–compulsive disorder (OCD), Marazziti, Akiskal, Rossi, and Cassano (1999) compared 20 subjects who had fallen in love within the prior 6 months with 20 unmedicated OCD patients and 20 control individuals. They evaluated the serotonin (5-HT) transporter, which has been linked to both neuroticism and sexual behavior. The density of binding sites for serotonin transporter was significantly lower than that in controls both in individuals who had recently fallen in love and in individuals with OCD. Marazziti et al. concluded that the early phases of a romantic relationship may be mediated by the same neurochemical mechanisms at work in OCD. This idea partly fits with some brain imaging findings in humans (discussed below) that suggest the importance of anxiety in affiliative circumstances.

The role of oxytocin and vasopressin in the formation of social bonds has also received considerable attention in several animal species (Insel, 2003). Some of the same processes that require oxytocin described in animals are also present in the regulation of an array of human social behaviors and cognitions (Kirsch et al., 2005), including social reduction of stress (Heinrichs, Baumgartner, Kirschbaum, & Ehlert, 2003) and mechanisms of trust (Kosfeld, Heinrichs, Zak, Fischbacher, & Fehr, 2005; Zak, Kurzban, & Matzner, 2004). Oxytocin released in mothers during breast feeding is also associated with reduced levels of maternal anxiety and attenuated physiological stress responses in humans (Chiodera & Coiro, 1987; Legros, Chiodera, & Geenen, 1988) and with more attuned patterns of maternal behavior across species (Champagne & Meaney, 2001; Uvnas-Moberg, 1998; Uvnas-Moberg & Eriksson, 1996). Perhaps among the many complex aspects of breast feeding, oxytocin in the mother may play a role in transmitting infant cues and encouraging other parenting behaviors. This idea has gained some support in recent human neuroimaging studies, described in the next section, comparing mothers who had delivered vaginally or by cesarean and breast-feeding mothers with formula-feeding mothers.

Recent data suggest that oxytocin might also be one of the key mediators of romantic love in humans. In one study, 45 healthy volunteer subjects were assessed using the Italian version of the Experiences in Close Relationships questionnaire (ECR), a self-report measure of romantic attachment (Marazziti et al., 2006). The results showed that in romantic attachment, preoccupation with the attachment and oxytocin levels are positively linked to a statistically significant degree ($r = 0.30$, $p = 0.04$); that is, the higher the oxytocin levels, the higher the score on the anxiety scale of the ECR. This study's authors argues that oxytocin may link anxious preoccupations of romantic love and its rewards. It would be interesting to test if oxytocin also mediates the link between parental preoccupations and parenting behaviors (resembling obsessions and compulsions respectively), which may be important in relationship formation, as discussed in relation to neuroimaging findings below. Oxytocin also appears to mediate social support (Heinrichs et al., 2003) and trust (Kosfeld et al., 2005; Zak et al., 2004), which are key parts of parental and romantic experiences.

In conclusion, there is increasing evidence that romantic love is associated with an array of changes, some of which seem to be specific to each sex, in neurochemicals including steroid sex and stress hormones; other signaling molecules of the HPA axis including oxytocin and vasopressin; immune-related neurotrophins; and serotonin.

■ NEUROIMAGING OF EARLY PARENTAL AND ROMANTIC LOVE

Studies of human brain responses to emotionally charged infant stimuli are beginning to uncover the neural substrates of normal parenting (Squire & Stein, 2003; Swain, 2008; Swain, Lorberbaum, Kose, & Strathearn, 2007; Swain et al., 2008; Swain et al., 2010). Investigators have begun to use fMRI to measure brain activity while healthy parents experience baby stimuli. This noninvasive approach to parental neurophysiology was begun by Lorberbaum and colleagues (Lorberbaum et al., 1999, 2002) using baby cries as stimuli. Building on the thalamocingulate theory of maternal behavior in animals developed by MacLean (1990), they predicted that baby cries would selectively activate the thalamus as well as the cingulate and related cortical areas a month postpartum. They found responses in these brain areas as well as midbrain, hypothalamus, striatum, septal regions and insula (Lorberbaum et al., 1999, 2002), regions also known to be important for rodent maternal behavior (Leckman & Herman, 2002). These promising human neuroimaging findings have encouraged follow-up studies to address the many methodological considerations they raise, including whether parental neural responses to baby sounds would be different for mothers and fathers, whether parents are first-time or veteran, whether the cries are from their own babies, and how the developing parent–infant bond is supported by different brain structures, selectively reviewed below.

Parents tend to be highly anxious and preoccupied in the immediate postpartum period (Kim, Mayes, Feldman, Leckman, & Swain, 2010; Leckman et al., 1999). Accordingly, Swain et al. (2003) hypothesized that parental responses to baby cries might produce activations in thalamus–cortical–basal ganglia circuits such as those important for human rituals and obsessive–compulsive disorder (Baxter, 2003; Leckman et al., 2004) in addition to emotional alarm centers including amygdala and insula. Using the uniquely compelling sound of the cry of one's own baby compared with another baby's cry, Swain et al. found, in a group of 9 first-time mothers at 2–4 weeks postpartum, regions of relative activation that included midbrain, basal ganglia, cingulate, amygdala and insula. Preliminary analysis of parenting interview data showed that mothers were significantly more preoccupied than fathers, confirming an earlier study (Leckman et al., 1999) and perhaps accounting for a relative lack of activation in fathers in amygdala and basal ganglia in response to their own babies' cries (Swain et al., 2004b). When the group of primiparous mothers was given the same stimuli at 3–4 months postpartum, activations had shifted from amygdala and insula to medial prefrontal cortex and hypothalamus (Swain et al., 2004a), reflecting a regional brain response change as the parent–infant relationship develops. There may, however, be parent brain areas that are stable in the postpartum period over time and sex. Activation in areas of insula and orbitofrontal cortex (OFC) in response to cries of parents' own babies (as compared with those of others' babies) correlated with parental preoccupation in both mothers and fathers at two time points within the first 4 months postpartum (Swain, Leckman, Mayes, Feldman, & Schultz, 2005, Swain et al., 2011).

Consistent with the earlier discussion of the importance of oxytocin in regulating social bonds, recent parent neuroimaging studies link this hormone with parental brain activity in response to infant stimuli. Swain and colleagues have found that mothers who had delivered vaginally showed greater brain activity in response to the cries of their own babies (as compared with others' babies) than mothers who had delivered by cesarean, corresponding to the former's higher oxytocin levels (Swain et al., 2008). Likewise, they found that breast-feeding mothers showed greater activation to their own baby's cries than did formula-feeding mothers, who have lower oxytocin levels (Kim, Feldman, Leckman, Mayes, & Swain, 2010). Along the same lines, Strathearn and colleagues have linked measurements of serum oxytocin in parents in response to a free-play session at 7 months postpartum with attachment security as well as with brain responses on viewing their own infants' faces in reward regions of the striatum (Strathearn, Fonagy, Amico, & Montague, 2009). These observations strengthen the link between parenting, oxytocin and reward neurocircuitry that promises to overlap with the rewards of romantic love.

Several groups with similar interests are using a range of variants of own-versus-other stimuli, such as photographs and brief video clips (Aron et al., 2005; Bartels & Zeki, 2000, 2004; Kim, Leckman, et al., 2010; Leibenluft, Gobbini, Harrison, & Haxby, 2004; Lenzi et al., 2008; Nitschke et al., 2004; Noriuchi, Kikuchi, & Senoo, 2008; Ortigue, Bianchi-Demicheli, Hamilton, & Grafton, 2007; Ranote et al., 2004; Swain et al., 2003, 2004a, 2004b; Swain, Leckman, et al., 2005) to expand our understanding of how parts of parental brain circuits also regulate aspects of romantic love. Among the first to make this link using brain imaging were Bartels and Zeki (2000, 2004), who used photographs of mothers' own, familiar, and unfamiliar infants (9 months to 6 years of age) and of their romantic and nonromantic friends (of more than 2 years' acquaintance) as stimuli. In response to parent's own babies, Bartels and Zeki found activation in anterior cingulate, insula, basal ganglia (striatum), and midbrain (periaqueductal gray)—regions that may mediate the emotionally rewarding aspects of maternal behavior. They also reported decreases in activity in areas important for negative emotions, social assessment, and avoidance, suggesting a push–pull mechanism in some of these circuits for maternal and romantic behavior in which love stimuli activate reward circuits and shut down avoidance circuits.

Studies using similar methods with photographs of romantic partners (Aron et al., 2005; Ortigue, Bianchi-Demicheli, et al., 2007) found that quantified individual self-reports of passionate love correlated with activation in subcortical, dopaminergic reward circuits and with time-dependent activations of the cingulate, insula, and other regulatory cortical regions. The correlation between brain response to romantic partner and duration of relationship over the first 18 months in the cingulate (Aron et al., 2005) agrees with the first prospective study of gray matter density in early parenthood (Kim et al., 2010). In this study, comparison of gray matter volume at 3-4 months to 2-4 weeks postpartum showed increased density in the cingulate. These regional findings then may be related to the processing of abstract representations of self and others, driven by dopamine-related motivation and reward systems, which are in turn regulated by cortical regulation loops for interpreting, predicting, and planning social behaviors. Prominent among these regions are the orbitofrontal cortex and insula, which may be required for emotional responses and habitual behavioral responses. These regions are activated in fMRI studies in a range of normal and abnormal emotion-control states including OCD (Feygin et al., 2006; Leckman & Mayes, 1999; Swain et al., 2007; Swain, 2011), as well as in theory-of-mind tasks (Vollm et al., 2006).

Finally, in an attempt to address the effects of early life events on later parenting, as elaborated in animal models (Kaffman & Meaney, 2007), brain volumetric density as well as functional responses to baby cry in cortical emotion processing regions have been shown to vary according to a measure of perceived maternal quality at 2-4 weeks postpartm (Kim, Leckman, et al., 2010). Romantic love is likely also under the influence of such early life experiences.

In summary, the growing field of imaging brains according to parental or other affiliative-related status indicates that relevant stimuli activate centers for emotional response and control. Combinations of well-controlled and ethologically valid stimuli and sensitive psychometric data collection may clarify the specific importance of these brain circuits to mediating normal parental and romantic behavior. We will then be able to understand abnormalities (potentially treatable) of parental and romantic care circuitry that may be manifest in depression and anxiety in the peri-partum, as well as may relate to relationship problems. These understandings could help to correct mental health problems which have such profound deleterious effects on the quality of parent–infant interactions subsequent long-term health risks and resiliencies of infants.

■ CONCLUSIONS AND FUTURE DIRECTIONS

Forming strong interpersonal bonds involves understanding the needs of the other, providing care and protection, and a preoccupation with the interests and wants of the other. How humans transition to being parents or part of a pair bond involves a set of highly conserved behaviors and mental states, reflecting both genetic endowment and early life experiences. These systems likely include empathy, emotion regulation, and motivation centers that would be reinforced by good parenting in early life, and later by the pleasures of romance and reinforcements of being a parent. We are just beginning to understand some of the biological substrates of these relationships.

While we have focused on parenting and romantic processes, there are many other forms of interpersonal relationship—adoption, foster care, step-parenting, teaching, mentoring, grandparenting—involving similar genetic, neurobiological, and experiential systems. that have the potential to inform clinical practice, particularly early intervention programs for high-risk expectant parents. To paraphrase Winnicott (1960), good enough genes combined with good enough parental thoughts and care ensure positive outcomes in childhood and beyond. Measures of related "primary parental preoccupations" (Leckman, et al., 2004) may be useful in future early intervention programs as an index of change within key domains of functioning. Viewing parenting as an interaction among genes, past parenting, current experience, psychological state, neurobiological systems, and environmental constraints brings many disciplines to the study of parenting. Future multidisciplinary studies should permit the examination of in what ways successful early intervention programs influence brain development, problem-solving abilities, stress response, later parenting ability, and vulnerability to psychopathology. The resulting knowledge will have far-reaching consequences for human mental health.

■ ACKNOWLEDGMENTS

This work was supported in part by grants from the Institute for Research on Unlimited Love (unlimitedloveinstitute.org) #168, the National Alliance for Research on Schizophrenia and Depression (narsad.org) (Young Investigator Awards 2004, 2007), the Yale Center for Risk, Resilience and Recovery, the Michigan Institute for Clinical Health Research (UL1RR024986), the Klingenstein Third Generation Foundation (ktgf.org) (Fellowship, 2010), and a grant from the Univerity of Notre Dame Science of Generosity initiative (http://generosity research.nd.edu/).

■ REFERENCES

Aron, A., Fisher, H., Mashek, D. J., Strong, G., Li, H., & Brown, L. L. (2005). Reward, motivation, and emotion systems associated with early-stage intense romantic love. *Journal of Neurophysiology, 94*, 327–337.

Bartels, A., & Zeki, S. (2000). The neural basis of romantic love. *Neuroreport, 11*, 3829–3834.

Bartels, A., & Zeki, S. (2004). The neural correlates of maternal and romantic love. *Neuroimage, 21*, 1155–1166.

Baxter, L. R., Jr. (2003). Basal ganglia systems in ritualistic social displays: Reptiles and humans; function and illness. *Physiology & Behavior, 79*, 451–460.

Bodini, B., Iacoboni, M., & Lenzi, G. L. (2004). Acute stroke effects on emotions: An interpretation through the mirror system. *Current Opinions in Neurology, 17*, 55–60.

Bowlby, J. (2000). *Attachment* New York, NY: Basic Books.

Breiter, H. C., Gollub, R. L., Weisskoff, R. M., Kennedy, D. N., Makris, N., Berke, J. D., . . . Hyman, S. E (1997). Acute effects of cocaine on human brain activity and emotion. *Neuron, 19*, 591–611.

Burnham, T. C., Chapman, J. F., Gray, P. B., McIntyre, M. H., Lipson, S. F., & Ellison, P. T. (2003). Men in committed, romantic relationships have lower testosterone. *Hormones and Behavior, 44*, 119–122.

Carr, L., Iacoboni, M., Dubeau, M. C., Mazziotta, J. C., & Lenzi, G. L. (2003). Neural mechanisms of empathy in humans: A relay from neural systems for imitation to limbic areas. *Proceedings of the National Academy of Sciences of the United States of America, 100,* 5497–5502.

Carter, C. S. (1998). Neuroendocrine perspectives on social attachment and love. *Psychoneuroendocrinology, 23,* 779–818.

Carter, C. S., Grippo, A. J., Pournajafi-Nazarloo, H., Ruscio, M. G., & Porges, S. W. (2008). Oxytocin, vasopressin, and sociality. *Progress in Brain Research, 170,* 331–336.

Champagne, F., & Meaney, M. J. (2001). Like mother, like daughter: Evidence for nongenomic transmission of parental behavior and stress responsivity. *Progress in Brain Research, 133,* 287–302.

Chiodera, P., & Coiro, V. (1987). Oxytocin reduces metyrapone-induced ACTH secretion in human subjects. *Brain Research, 420,* 178–181.

Dapretto, M., Davies, M. S., Pfeifer, J. H., Scott, A. A., Sigman, M., Bookheimer, S. Y., & Iacoboni, M. (2006). Understanding emotions in others: Mirror neuron dysfunction in children with autism spectrum disorders. *Nature Neuroscience, 9,* 28–30.

David, V., Segu, L., Buhot, M. C., Ichaye, M., & Cazala, P. (2004). Rewarding effects elicited by cocaine microinjections into the ventral tegmental area of C57BL/6 mice: Involvement of dopamine D1 and serotonin1B receptors. *Psychopharmacology (Berlin), 174,* 367–375.

Delgado, M. R., Locke, H. M., Stenger, V. A., & Fiez, J. A. (2003). Dorsal striatum responses to reward and punishment: Effects of valence and magnitude manipulations. *Cognitive, Affective,& Behavioral Neuroscience, 3,* 27–38.

Depue, R. A., & Morrone-Strupinsky, J. V. (2005). A neurobehavioral model of affiliative bonding: Implications for conceptualizing a human trait of affiliation. *Behavioral and Brain Sciences, 28,* 313–350 (discussion, 350–395).

Eisenberger, N. I., Lieberman, M. D., & Williams, K. D. (2003). Does rejection hurt? An fMRI study of social exclusion. *Science, 302,* 290–292.

Emanuele, E., Politi, P., Bianchi, M., Minoretti, P., Bertona, M., & Geroldi, D. (2006). Raised plasma nerve growth factor levels associated with early-stage romantic love. *Psychoneuroendocrinology, 31,* 288–294.

Feygin, D. L., Swain, J. E., & Leckman, J. F. (2006). The normalcy of neurosis: Evolutionary origins of obsessive–compulsive disorder and related behaviors. *Progress in Neuropsychopharmacology and Biological Psychiatry, 30,* 854–864.

Fisher, H. E., Aron, A., Mashek, D., Li, H., & Brown, L. L. (2002). Defining the brain systems of lust, romantic attraction, and attachment. *Archives of Sexual Behavior, 31,* 413–419.

Fleming, A. S., Steiner, M., & Corter, C. (1997). Cortisol, hedonics, and maternal responsiveness in human mothers. *Hormones and Behavior, 32,* 85–98.

Francis, D., Diorio, J., Liu, D., & Meaney, M. J. (1999). Nongenomic transmission across generations of maternal behavior and stress responses in the rat. *Science, 286,* 1155–1158.

Frith, U., & Frith, C. D. (2003). Development and neurophysiology of mentalizing. *Philosophical Transactions of the Royal Society of London B: Biological Sciences, 358,* 459–473.

Gallese, V., Keysers, C., & Rizzolatti, G. (2004). A unifying view of the basis of social cognition. *Trends in Cognitive Sciences, 8,* 396–403.

Goldman-Rakic, P. S., & Selemon, L. D. (1990). New frontiers in basal ganglia research. Introduction. *Trends in Neurosciences, 13,* 241–244.

Gonzaga, G. C., Keltner, D., Londahl, E. A., & Smith, M. D. (2001). Love and the commitment problem in romantic relations and friendship. *Journal of Personality and Social Psychology, 81,* 247–262.

Haber, S. N. (2003). The primate basal ganglia: Parallel and integrative networks. *Journal of Chemical Neuroanatomy, 26,* 317–330.

Hatfield, E., & Sprecher, S. (1986). Measuring passionate love in intimate relationships. *Journal of Adolescence, 9,* 383–410.

Hazan, C., & Shaver, P. (1987). Romantic love conceptualized as an attachment process. *Journal of Personality and Social Psychology, 52,* 511–524.

Heinrichs, M., Baumgartner, T., Kirschbaum, C., & Ehlert, U. (2003). Social support and oxytocin interact to suppress cortisol and subjective responses to psychosocial stress. *Biological Psychiatry, 54,* 1389–1398.

Insel, T. R. (2003). Is social attachment an addictive disorder? *Physiology & Behavior, 79,* 351–357.

Jankowiak, W. R., & Fischer, E. F. (1992). A cross-cultural perspective on romantic love. *Ethnology, 31,* 149–155.

Kaffman, A., & Meaney, M. J. (2007). Neurodevelopmental sequelae of postnatal maternal care in rodents: Clinical and research implications of molecular insights. *Journal of Child Psychology and Psychiatry, 48,* 224–244.

Kim, P., Feldman, R., Leckman, J. F., Mayes, L. C., & Swain, J. E. (2010a). Breastfeeding, brain activation to own infant cry, and maternal sensitivity. *Journal of Child Psychology and Psychiatry, in press.* Epub ahead of print, doi: 10.1111/j.1469-7610.2011.02406.x.

Kim, P., Leckman, J. F., Mayes, L. C., Newman, M.-A., Feldman, R., & Swain, J. E. (2010b). Perceived quality of maternal care in childhood and structure and function of mothers' brain. *Developmental Science, 13(4),* 663–673.

Kim, P., Leckman, J. F, Mayes, L. C., Feldman, R., Wang, X., & Swain, J. E., (2010c).The plasticity of human maternal brain: longitudinal changes in brain anatomy during the early postpartum period. *Behavioral Neuroscience, 124(5),* 695–700.

Kim, P., Mayes, L. C., Feldman, R., Leckman, J. F., & Swain, J. E. (2010d). Primary parental preoccupation and the transition from adulthood to parenthood. *Infant Mental Health Journal.* Manuscript submitted for publication.

Kimata, H. (2003). Kissing reduces allergic skin wheal responses and plasma neurotrophin levels. *Physiology & Behavior, 80,* 395–398.

Kirsch, P., Esslinger, C., Chen, Q., Mier, D., Lis, S., Siddhanti, S., . . . Meyer-Lindenberg, A. (2005). Oxytocin modulates neural circuitry for social cognition and fear in humans. *Journal of Neuroscience, 25,* 11489–11493.

Knutson, B., Fong, G. W., Adams, C. M., Varner, J. L., & Hommer, D. (2001). Dissociation of reward anticipation and outcome with event-related fMRI. *Neuroreport, 12,* 3683–3687.

Kosfeld, M., Heinrichs, M., Zak, P. J., Fischbacher, U., & Fehr, E. (2005). Oxytocin increases trust in humans. *Nature, 435,* 673–676.

Kyrou, I., Tsigos, C. (2009). Stress hormones: physiological stress and regulation of metabolism. *Current Opinion in Pharmacology, 9(6),* 787–793.

Leckman, J. F., Feldman, R., Swain, J. E., Eicher, V., Thompson, N., & Mayes, L. C. (2004). Primary parental preoccupation: Circuits, genes, and the crucial role of the environment. *Journal of Neural Transmission, 111,* 753–771.

Leckman, J. F., & Herman, A. E. (2002). Maternal behavior and developmental psychopathology. *Biological Psychiatry, 51,* 27–43.

Leckman, J. F., & Mayes, L. C. (1999). Preoccupations and behaviors associated with romantic and parental love. Perspectives on the origin of obsessive–compulsive disorder. *Child & Adolescent Psychiatric Clinics of North America, 8,* 635–665.

Leckman, J. F., Mayes, L. C., Feldman, R., Evans, D. W., King, R. A., & Cohen, D. J. (1999). Early parental preoccupations and behaviors and their possible relationship to the symptoms of obsessive–compulsive disorder. *Acta Psychiatrica Scandinavica Supplement, 396*, 1–26.

Legros, J. J., Chiodera, P., & Geenen, V. (1988). Inhibitory action of exogenous oxytocin on plasma cortisol in normal human subjects: Evidence of action at the adrenal level. *Neuroendocrinology, 48*, 204–206.

Leibenluft, E., Gobbini, M. I., Harrison, T., & Haxby, J. V. (2004). Mothers' neural activation in response to pictures of their children and other children. *Biological Psychiatry, 56*, 225–232.

Lenzi, D., Trentini, C., Pantano, P., Macaluso, E., Iacoboni, M., Lenzi, G. L., & Ammaniti, M. (2009). Neural basis of maternal communication and emotional expression processing during infant preverbal stage. *Cerebral Cortex, 19(5), 1124–1133.*

Lim, M. M., Wang, Z., Olazabal, D. E., Ren, X., Terwilliger, E. F., & Young, L. J. (2004). Enhanced partner preference in a promiscuous species by manipulating the expression of a single gene. *Nature, 429*, 754–757.

Lorberbaum, J. P., Newman, J. D., Dubno, J. R., Horwitz, A. R., Nahas, Z., Teneback, C. C., George, M. S. (1999). Feasibility of using fMRI to study mothers responding to infant cries. *Depression and Anxiety, 10*, 99–104.

Lorberbaum, J. P., Newman, J. D., Horwitz, A. R., Dubno, J. R., Lydiard, R. B., Hamner, M. B., George, M. S. (2002). A potential role for thalamocingulate circuitry in human maternal behavior. *Biological Psychiatry, 51*, 431–445.

MacLean, P. D. (1990). *The triune brain in evolution: Role in paleocerebral functions.* New York, NY: Plenum Press.

Marazziti, D., Akiskal, H. S., Rossi, A., & Cassano, G. B. (1999). Alteration of the platelet serotonin transporter in romantic love. *Psychological Medicine, 29*, 741–745.

Marazziti, D., & Canale, D. (2004). Hormonal changes when falling in love. *Psychoneuroendocrinology, 29*, 931–936.

Marazziti, D., Dell'osso, B., Baroni, S., Mungai, F., Catena, M., Rucci, P., . . . Dell'Osso, L (2006). A relationship between oxytocin and anxiety of romantic attachment. *Clinical Practice and Epidemiology in Mental Health, 2*, 28.

Nitschke, J. B., Nelson, E. E., Rusch, B. D., Fox, A. S., Oakes, T. R., & Davidson, R. J. (2004). Orbitofrontal cortex tracks positive mood in mothers viewing pictures of their newborn infants. *Neuroimage, 21*, 583–592.

Noriuchi, M., Kikuchi, Y., & Senoo, A. (2008). The functional neuroanatomy of maternal love: Mother's response to infant's attachment behaviors. *Biological Psychiatry, 63*, 415–423.

Olausson, H., Lamarre, Y., Backlund, H., Morin, C., Wallin, B. G., Starck, G., . . . Bushnell, M. C. (2002). Unmyelinated tactile afferents signal touch and project to insular cortex. *Nature Neuroscience, 5*, 900–904.

Olds, D. L., Kitzman, H., Cole, R., Robinson, J., Sidora, K., Luckey, D. W., . . . Holmberg, J. (2004). Effects of nurse home-visiting on maternal life course and child development: Age 6 follow-up results of a randomized trial. *Pediatrics, 114*, 1550–1559.

Ortigue, S., Bianchi-Demicheli, F., Hamilton, A. F., & Grafton, S. T. (2007). The neural basis of love as a subliminal prime: An event-related functional magnetic resonance imaging study. *Journal of Cognitive Neuroscience, 19*, 1218–1230.

Ortigue, S., Grafton, S. T., & Bianchi-Demicheli, F. (2007). Correlation between insula activation and self-reported quality of orgasm in women. *Neuroimage, 37*, 551–560.

Pryce, C. R., Bettschen, D., & Feldon, J. (2001). Comparison of the effects of early handling and early deprivation on maternal care in the rat. *Developmental Psychobiology, 38*, 239–251.

Ranote, S., Elliott, R., Abel, K. M., Mitchell, R., Deakin, J. F., & Appleby, L. (2004). The neural basis of maternal responsiveness to infants: An fMRI study. *Neuroreport, 15*, 1825–1829.

Robbins, T. W., & Everitt, B. J. (1996). Neurobehavioural mechanisms of reward and motivation. *Current Opinion in Neurobiology, 6*, 228–236.

Robinson, D. L., Heien, M. L., & Wightman, R. M. (2002). Frequency of dopamine concentration transients increases in dorsal and ventral striatum of male rats during introduction of conspecifics. *Journal of Neuroscience, 22*, 10477–10486.

Schultz, W. (2000). Multiple reward signals in the brain. *Nature Reviews Neuroscience, 1*, 199–207.

Shaver, P., Schwartz, J., Kirson, D., & O'Connor, C. (1987). Emotion knowledge: Further exploration of a prototype approach. *Journal of Personality and Social Psychology, 52*, 1061–1086.

Shulman, S., Mayes, L. C.. Cohen, T. H., Swain, J. E., Leckman, J. F. (2008). Romantic attraction and conflict negotiation among late adolescent and early adult romantic couples. *Journal of Adolescence, 31(6)*, 729–745.

Singer, T., Seymour, B., O'Doherty, J., Kaube, H., Dolan, R. J., & Frith, C. D. (2004). Empathy for pain involves the affective but not sensory components of pain. *Science, 303*, 1157–1162.

Small, D. M., Zatorre, R. J., Dagher, A., Evans, A.C., & Jones-Gotman, M. (2001). Changes in brain activity related to eating chocolate: From pleasure to aversion. *Brain, 124*, 1720–1733.

Squire, S., & Stein, A. (2003). Functional MRI and parental responsiveness: A new avenue into parental psychopathology and early parent–child interactions? *British Journal of Psychiatry, 183*, 481–483.

Strathearn, L., Fonagy, P., Amico, J., & Montague, P. R. (2009). Adult attachment predicts maternal brain and oxytocin response to infant cues. *Neuropsychopharmacology, 34*, 2655–2666.

Swain, J. E. (2008). Baby stimuli and the parent brain: Functional neuroimaging of the neural substrates of parent–infant attachment. *Psychiatry (Edgmont), 5*, 28–36.

Swain, J. E. (2011). The Human Parental Brain: In vivo neuroimaging Progress in Neuro-Psychopharmacology and Biological Psychiatry. *35(5)*: 1242–54.

Swain, J. E., Leckman, J. F., Mayes, L. C., Feldman, R., Constable, R. T., & Schultz, R. T. (2003). *The neural circuitry of parent–infant attachment in the early postpartum.* In American College of Neuropsychopharmacology,San Juan. Puerto Rico.

Swain, J. E., Leckman, J. F., Mayes, L. C., Feldman, R., Constable, R. T., & Schultz, R. T. (2004a). Brain circuitry and psychology of human parent–infant attachment in the postpartum. In International Academy of Child and Adolescent Psychiatry and Allied Professions, 16th World Congress(p. 365). Berlin, Germany .

Swain, J. E., Leckman, J. F., Mayes, L. C., Feldman, R., Constable, R. T., & Schultz, R. T. (2004b). Neural substrates and psychology of human parent–infant attachment in the postpartum. *Biological Psychiatry, 55*, 153S.

Swain, J. E., Leckman, J. F., Mayes, L. C., Feldman, R., & Schultz, R. T. (2005). Early human parent- infant bond development: fMRI, thoughts and behaviors. *Biological Psychiatry, 57*, 112S.

Swain, J. E., Leckman, J. F., Mayes, L. C., Feldman, R., Hoyt, E., Kang, K., Kim, P., David, D., Nguyen, S., Constable, R. T., Schultz R. T. (2011). Functional brain activations of parents listening to their own baby-cry change over the early postpartum. *Developmental Psychobiology,* in submission.

Swain, J. E., Lorberbaum, J. P., Kose, S., & Strathearn, L. (2007). Brain basis of early parent–infant interactions: Psychology, physiology, and in vivo functional neuroimaging studies. *Journal of Child Psychology and Psychiatry, 48*, 262–287.

Swain, J. E., Mayes, L. C., & Leckman, J. F. (2005). Endogenous and exogenous opiates modulate the development of parent–infant attachment. *Behavioral and Brain Sciences, 28*, 364–365.

Swain, J. E., Tasgin, E., Mayes, L. C., Feldman, R., Constable, R. T., & Leckman, J. F. (2008). Maternal brain response to own baby-cry is affected by cesarean section delivery. *Journal of Child Psychology and Psychiatry, 49*, 1042–1052.

Uvnas-Moberg, K. (1998). Oxytocin may mediate the benefits of positive social interaction and emotions. *Psychoneuroendocrinology, 23*, 819–835.

Uvnas-Moberg, K., & Eriksson, M. (1996). Breastfeeding: Physiological, endocrine and behavioural adaptations caused by oxytocin and local neurogenic activity in the nipple and mammary gland. *Acta Paediatrica 85*, 525–530.

Vollm, B. A., Taylor, A. N., Richardson, P., Corcoran, R., Stirling, J., McKie, S., . . . Elliott, R. (2006). Neuronal correlates of theory of mind and empathy: A functional magnetic resonance imaging study in a nonverbal task. *Neuroimage, 29*, 90–98.

Winnicott, D. W. (1956) Primary maternal preoccupation. In: Collected papers: through paediatrics to psycho-analysis; 1975. New York: Basic Books. [1956]. p. 300–5.

Winnicott, D. W. (1960). The theory of the parent–infant relationship. *International Journal of Psychoanalysis, 41*, 585–595.

Winslow, J. T., & Insel, T. R. (2004). Neuroendocrine basis of social recognition. *Current Opinion in Neurobiology, 14*, 248–253.

Zak, P. J., Kurzban, R., & Matzner, W. T. (2004). The neurobiology of trust. *Annals of the New York Academy of Sciences, 1032*, 224–227.

PART FOUR

The Psychology of Caregiving Motivation

9 Parental Investment in Caregiving Relationships

■ DAPHNE B. BUGENTAL, DAVID A. BEAULIEU,
AND RANDY CORPUZ

Within this essay, we propose a new way of conceptualizing the provision of care in parent–child relationships. Common wisdom holds that parents are (or should be) reliably motivated to care for their own children. When this does not happen, it is interpreted as a pathological or criminal response. Attention is typically given to violations that involve parental abuse or neglect. However, there are shades of gray in this process, and children may experience problems within caregiving relationships at a more subtle level. Even children in the same family may experience different parenting histories (as siblings often report and parents regularly deny). Although it is relatively easy to account for small differences in parental response to different children, it is difficult to explain more polarized patterns in which one child is subject to neglectful or harsh parenting and another child receives a high level of care.

Some variations in parental care may be thought of in terms of a "Cinderella effect" (i.e., good care of biological children and neglect of stepchildren), a fairy-tale representation of events that are often observed in real life (Anderson, Kaplan, Lam, & Lancaster, 1999; Anderson, Kaplan & Lancaster, 1999). However, there are many circumstances in which differential care is not based on biological relatedness. As one possible resolution, one could explain these differences in terms of child effects, that is, the extent to which children—as a result of their behaviors—influence and regulate the responses of caregivers (as initially proposed by Bell, 1968). Although this account adds to the picture, it fails to account for circumstances in which children manifesting the same behaviors elicit very different responses from different caregivers. One early approach considered the combined effects of parents and children in terms of the fit (or misfit) between children's temperament patterns and caregivers' styles of socialization (Thomas & Chess, 1977).

In this essay, we present and consider evidence for a new way of understanding the complex interactions that occur in parental care. Making use of bioeconomic concepts (drawn from evolutionary psychology), we consider the interactive effects of (1) the child's reproductive value (i.e., the ability to convert parental investment into future reproductive success) and (2) parental resources (i.e., access to resources needed for effective care provision). After considering the implications and history of this approach, we move on to discuss existing support for the model presented here. Finally, we consider how the model can be used as a basis for early interventions that foster increased parental investment in high-risk children (e.g., children at risk of not meeting developmental milestones). Although investment in high-risk children might be thought of as purely altruistic, we will document the ways in which this seemingly risky investment strategy can yield tangible benefits for children, parents, and society.

■ PARENTAL INVESTMENT STRATEGIES

Parental Investment

We conceptualize parental investment strategies from an evolutionary framework, an approach that borrows concepts and terms from economics. As such, our approach bears similarities to the concepts and language employed by social inter-dependence theory (Kelley et al., 2003) in representing interpersonal relationships. However, interdependence theory focuses on mutual relationships in which costs and benefits are negotiated from both sides—a strategy that is appropriate when both individuals have choices in pursuing, retaining, or abandoning the relationship. In contrast, parent–child interactions are asymmetrical. The power to negotiate the terms of such a relationship is unquestionably in favor of the parent. For example, parents decide how much to invest in each offspring, which can range from total abandonment to extraordinarily high levels of caregiving.

From a purely evolutionary framework, parental investment is viewed as a zero-sum allocation of parental resources. Such a viewpoint takes into consideration the fact that any investment in one particular offspring results in a missed opportunity to invest those resources in other offspring (Trivers, 1972, 1974). Given the zero-sum nature of this process, it is in the parent's best reproductive interests to invest in offspring who are more likely to convert those resources into reproductive success. Note here that we are talking about motivational systems that occur automatically rather than through a reflective appraisal processes. For example, mothers are more likely to abandon at birth a child who appears sickly. In our evolutionary past, such children would have been less likely to survive to reproductive age and thus less likely to increase a parent's reproductive success. This form of abandonment occurs even in the most-industrialized societies, where modern medicine allows the survival of such children. This example suggests that we all come equipped with a computational "tool kit" that originally evolved because its computations served to promote individuals' successful reproduction and thus the passing along of their genes (Tooby & Cosmides, 2005).

Parental Resources

The concept of resources has been employed in many different disciplines and has been defined as "(1) something that can be used for support or help, (2) an available supply that can be drawn on when needed, (3) the ability to deal with a difficult or troublesome situation effectively, or (4) a means that can be used to cope with a difficult situation" (Resource, 2009). Parental resources may be (1) material, for example, the availability of finances in industrialized countries or the availability of basic provisions (e.g., food, clothing, and shelter) in subsistence-level settings; (2) social, for example, position in a power hierarchy, availability of interpersonal support, or availability of group support; (3) skill based, for example, problem-solving skills or skills in creating products or outcomes needed by others; (4) temporal, that is, the availability of time (which may overlap with financial resources if funding allows the possibility of hiring others); and (5) attention or emotional, for example, the availability of a parent's attention or emotional engagement. Our particular focus is on *scarce* (limited) resources. Parents, like all care providers, must decide when and for whom they will expend their time, money, influence, skills, or attention. Parents must make decisions about their use of resources to benefit different children, themselves, or others.

Within the field of biology, the term "resource holding potential" (Parker & Rubinstein, 1981) refers to the individuals' capacity (combined across types of resources) to influence their own outcomes or the outcomes of others in desired ways. In our discussion of parental resources, we are referring to any kind of resource—or capacity to generate resources—that would facilitate parents' ability to provide the type and amount of care that would optimize the child's outcomes in ways consistent with the child's reproductive success (e.g., facilitating their health or their acquisition of communally valued skills). Finally, parental resources may involve the *perceived* ability or capacity to provide care for and enhance the outcomes of the young. For example, a mother who shows an insecure attachment pattern with her own parents may perceive herself as unable to influence the outcomes of her own children (Grusec, Adam & Mammone, 1993), and thus her actual effectiveness may be hindered.

Reproductive Value of the Young

The reproductive value of the young is reflected in the presence of markers of the child's probable reproductive success. Just as investors may evaluate a new company based on its "growth opportunities," parents respond, automatically, to the "growth opportunities" shown by children early in life. We will refer to children who show indicators of future health problems as "high risk," because such children would have been risky investments in our evolutionary past. Likewise, children who show indicators of future good health will be considered "low risk," because such children would have had a better chance of achieving reproductive success in our evolutionary past.

Low-birth-weight infants or infants born prematurely are at elevated risk for later health problems (as summarized by Hagen, 1999), as well as cognitive deficits (Beauchamp et al., 2008) and behavior problems (Rose, Feldman, Rose, Wallace, & McCarton, 1992) at older ages. In our evolutionary past, these outcomes would have predicted low reproductive potential. In responding to children at birth, parents are more influenced by appearance cues to the child's health than by medical evidence of their risk for morbidity and mortality. That is, parents appear to respond to cues that would have been predictive in our distant evolutionary past (and that still are predictive within contemporary cultures that function at a subsistence level). For example, Weiss (1998) observed that parents who decided at birth to relinquish a child for adoption did so on the basis of appearance cues rather than conditions identified by medical staff (e.g., a heart problem) as posing a known risk for elevated levels of morbidity or mortality.

The processes involved in parental investment can be represented by use of an economic metaphor. All investors seek (over the long term) to maximize their assets and reduce their losses. An infant's best investment strategy is to gain the attention of the biological parents and to provide signals that generate attention and lead to the provision of care. The mother's best parental investment strategy is to maximize her total reproductive success (across offspring). However, parental investment strategies—as with financial strategies—shift depending on the amount and stability of the resources of the investor. Investors who have substantial or increasing financial resources will optimize their payoffs over time by creating a diverse portfolio that includes high-risk investments (that carry the potential for exceptionally high payoffs) as well as lower-risk investments. In contrast, investors who have a lower, fixed, or declining level of resources will optimize their payoffs by adopting a conservative strategy that involves relatively low risk.

If this metaphor is applied to parental investment, something similar is predicted. Mothers who have low or unstable resources (financial, temporal, social, or emotional) can ill afford to invest in a child who poses a high risk to their reproductive success. For example, investment in one high-risk child (who may not survive to reproduce) will limit their capability to care for other—or future—children (due to the depletion of their scarce resources). However, mothers who have high, stable resources can "afford" to invest in a high-risk child because they can do so without jeopardizing their ability to care for other or future children. Although this process plays out quite directly in nonhumans (or in subsistence-level settings among humans), it is manifested at a more subtle level in more affluent, better-educated contemporary cultures.

■ HISTORY OF PARENTAL INVESTMENT THEORY

Initial Formulation

The initial formulation of parental investment theory began with a proposal regarding sex differences in the provision of parental care to the young (Trivers, 1972). Females are more limited than are males in their parental investment opportunities in that they can give birth to only a limited number of offspring. Thus they bear a high reproductive cost if they mate with partners who fail to share in child care. As a result, females are "choosy" in their efforts to select partners who provide cues to their capability and motivation to provide care for offspring. In contrast, males can potentially father a very large number of offspring and are less discriminating in their mating choices. However, they bear a high reproductive cost if they invest in the provision of care for a child who is biologically unrelated (an investment that provides no payoff in terms of their own reproductive success). As a result, males are particularly vigilant for cues to a partner's sexual fidelity and their relatedness to the partner's child or children.

Formulations in connection with parental investment were subsequently extended to include conflict between the interests of parents and their children (Trivers, 1974). Any investment in one particular offspring results in the missed opportunity to invest those resources in other offspring. Thus parents refrain from investing all their resources in a single offspring, because such one-sided investment strategies would harm other offspring. Children, in turn, maximize their own reproductive success by employing a strategy in which they attempt to gain as much parental investment as possible. Thus the strategies followed by parents and children involve a conflict of (reproductive) interests.

Discriminative Parental Solicitude

Daly and Wilson (1984, 1988) shifted the direction of thought on investment to consider the ways that parents differentially invest (1) in different kinds of children and (2) under different circumstances. They described children as differing in their "reproductive value" based on cues to their probable reproductive success. Parents (in particular, females, who have traditionally been the primary investing parents) are sensitive to offspring characteristics and to context features relevant to caregiving. Daly and Wilson proposed that parents are more likely to invest in children who provide early cues to good health and strength than in children who manifest apparent "defects" (i.e., medical or physical conditions that create reproductive risk). Although they viewed high investment in children with low reproductive value as an exception to normative responses, they also noted that women were sensitive to their probability of having other children. As women approached the end of their childbearing years, they were expected to be more likely to invest in a newborn child without regard for his or her reproductive value.

Daly and Wilson's second proposed key predictor of parental investment was the availability of sufficient resources to provide for child rearing. For example, very young mothers or mothers facing economic challenges, lacking a partner, or lacking social support can be seen as having low access to resources for care provision. Thus they are less likely to show parental investment (and more likely to engage in child mistreatment or infanticide).

A third proposed factor predicting parental investment involves biological relatedness. Among both humans and nonhumans, parental investment in unrelated offspring is rare. Among males, lack of certainty about paternity forms an additional reason for low parental investment.

Contingent Model of Parental Investment

An extension of existing thought on parental investment took place when joint attention was given to the interactive effects of a child's reproductive value and the resources held by the parent (Bugental & Beaulieu, 2003; Davis & Todd, 1999; Mann, 1992). Mann (1992) discussed two possible options that a mother can choose with a high-risk infant: (1) increased investment to meet the child's needs—a costly strategy that nonetheless has the potential to increase the child's reproductive value (and thus the mother's own reproductive success), and (2) relatively low investment, a response pattern that poses little cost to the mother and increases the possibility of providing care for other children. In selecting between options, mothers also respond to the availability of resources. When resources are scarce, mothers serve their own reproductive interests best by investing in low-risk children (those who are most likely to survive and reproduce). Mothers are more likely to invest in high-risk children if resources are more plentiful, due to their perception that the resources are ample enough to allow all children to survive.

Davis and Todd (1999) conducted a computer simulation study in which they tested the reproductive benefits offered by different parental investment strategies among birds. The predictor variables involved the reproductive value of the young (e.g., size) and the availability of food resources to the mother (e.g., foraging possibilities). The net reproductive benefits to mothers were measured as the total size (weight) of a surviving brood of chicks. Consistent with notions of contingent parental investment, optimal strategies depended on both the reproductive value of the young and the availability of resources. When resources were scarce, the most successful strategy was to feed the chick with the greatest reproductive potential first. However, when resources were more plentiful, the most successful strategy was to feed the smallest chick first. Findings support the proposal that parents serve their own reproductive interests best by preferential investment in low-risk offspring when they have low access to resources and preferential investment in high-risk offspring when they have high access to resources. Support for this pattern of investment is also provided by evidence regarding parental investment strategies from observations of birds (Gottlander, 1987) and nonhuman primates (Nakamichi, 1986).

The essence of the contingent model is shown in figure 9.1, which compares the predicted allocation of benefits to children who differ in the level of risk they pose. The model assumes that parental investment represents a zero-sum situation. That is, if a parent invests time or material resources in a particular child, they will have less capability to invest such resources in other endeavors (e.g., investing in other offspring or investing in themselves). The unique prediction in this model is the advantage for high-risk offspring who have mothers with high resources. The rationale for the adaptiveness of this strategy (as presented by Bugental & Beaulieu, 2003) is that mothers with high resources can afford to invest in high-risk offspring

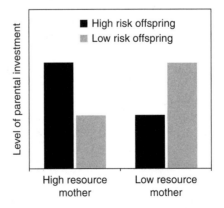

Figure 9.1 Parental Investment Model. Level of investment in high versus low risk children by mothers with high or low resources.

without creating hardship for their lower-risk offspring. If resources are more than adequate, preferential investment in high-risk offspring is unlikely to pose a threat to the welfare of siblings.

Evidence for contingent parental investment has in the past relied primarily on ethnographic research. One of the most dramatic findings involved an observational study of mothers who lived in the shantytowns of Brazil (Scheper-Hughes, 1985). Mothers were operating at a subsistence level and lacked resources necessary to support all their children. As a result, they preferentially provided food to children based on indications of their likelihood of surviving to adulthood. Children who showed markers of vigor (e.g., robust crying patterns in infancy) were more likely to be fed than children who seemed weaker. Although mothers were attached to all their children, their folk belief was that some children were not meant to live. Very different patterns are found in financially advantaged countries. For example, Field (1982) observed that mothers often make extreme efforts to provide for and socially engage their preterm infants. Similar patterns of exceptional solicitude have been found among mothers of children with craniofacial anomalies (Coy, Speltz, & Jones, 2002).

■ EMPIRICAL SUPPORT FOR CONTINGENT MODEL OF INVESTMENT

We have conducted a series of studies that empirically test the contingent investment model. We made use of both experimentally varied levels and naturally occurring differences in maternal resources. In addition, we focused our attention on children who were preterm at birth. In our evolutionary past, preterm children would have experienced a substantially higher level of morbidity and mortality than other children. Despite the reduced level of risk in the present time, preterm children still provide visible markers of risk. Although such features are unreliable cues to a child's viability in advantaged cultures, they are still represented in others' perceptions of the child's attractiveness. Thus infants who are substantially premature are often seen as less attractive due to the fact that their facial features are typically less "babyish" (Maier, Holmes, & Slaymaker, 1984).

In testing the proposed model (shown in figure 9.1), we measured two types of parental resources. The resources measured included (1) mothers' participation in a cognitively based intervention that increased their problem-solving focus and feelings of empowerment (Bugental & Beaulieu, 2003; Bugental,Beaulieu, & Silbert-Geiger 2010 , and (2) mothers' depressive symptoms as an indicator of reduced attention or emotional resources (Beaulieu & Bugental, 2008).

We operationalized parental investment in several different ways. These included assessments of (1) mothers' willingness to exert effort and time to obtain information about the child (Bugental & Beaulieu, 2003), (2) the proportion of time mothers reported spending with the child as opposed to time spent on other members of the family (Bugental, Beaulieu, & Silbert-Geiger, 2010), (3) the proportion of the family budget mothers spent on the child (Bugental et al., 2010), and (4) mothers' preference for obtaining benefits for the child as opposed to themselves (Beaulieu & Bugental, 2008).

Empowerment of Mothers as a Result of an Early Intervention

Two studies tested the outcomes of an intervention that was designed to decrease mistreatment and increase child health and welfare. Families in the first study (Bugental et al., 2002) were randomly assigned to (1) a home visitation intervention that focused on parental support and education (labeled the HV condition), (2) a home visitation program that added a cognitive reappraisal/problem-solving component (labeled HV+), or (3) a control condition in which no services were provided. Families were selected on the basis of family risk (e.g., poverty, lack of support, and family history of abuse). Thirty percent of the children were at medical risk due to preterm status or low Apgar scores. The HV+ condition (in comparison with the HV condition) assisted parents in acquiring cognitive resources—for instance, skills in obtaining information relevant to child development; knowledge about effective ways to manage caregiving challenges; and ways to obtain information and make contact with community agencies that can provide valuable resources. Mothers in the HV+ condition were also found to increase their self-perceived power or control within the caregiving relationship (as measured by the Parent Attribution Test—Bugental & Shennum, 1984).

Six months after the conclusion of the program, we invited parents back to obtain further information on their children's age-related progress (information that had potential value for parents' understanding of their children). Most parents had to drive at least an hour to come to our lab. Thus their participation involved a major expenditure of time and effort. We compared parent willingness to come to our lab to learn important information about their child as an indication of their level of parental investment. Resources were defined as relatively high for those who participated in the HV+ condition and relatively low for those who participated in the HV condition. Child risk was defined in terms of the child's birth status (i.e., preterm versus full term). Consistent with the model, the highest level of investment was shown by mothers in the HV+ condition whose children were born prematurely, and the lowest level of investment was shown by mothers with preterm children in the HV condition.

Families in the second study (Bugental & Schwarz, 2009) were drawn from a similar demographic background but children with medical problems at birth were overselected. Half of the children were preterm, allowing a more complete test of the effects of child risk status at birth on parental investment patterns. Parents were randomly assigned to either the HV+ or the HV condition. Bugental et al. (2010) conducted a follow-up study testing our parental investment model when children reached age 3. Maternal resources were again measured as a function of mother's participation in the HV+ intervention versus the HV condition. Maternal investment patterns were assessed in terms of material goods and time, contingent on the child's birth status. Mothers were asked to indicate their (1) allocation of time to different activities (including provision of care) and (2) allocation of their monthly income to expenditures for the child (some essential costs, e.g., food, and some discretionary, e.g., entertainment). Mothers in the HV+ condition showed peak levels of time investment and discretionary financial investment in high-risk (i.e., preterm) and relatively low investment in low-risk (i.e., full-term) children. In contrast, mothers in the HV condition showed peak levels of time and financial investment in low-risk children. Of particular note, greater amounts of maternal investment predicted better health among at-risk children, consistent with our predictions. This supports the prediction that mothers with high resources are likely to increase the probability that high-risk children will be healthy and survive to adulthood and thus have the capacity to have children of their own. Ultimately, this investment pattern would serve to optimize replication of parents' genes.

Effects of Maternal Depression on Patterns of Parental Intervention

An additional study investigated the presence or absence of maternal postpartum depression (as measured by the Beck Depression Inventory, Beck, Steer, & Garbin, 1988). Differences in maternal depression predict mothers' availability and emotional resources; that is, depressed mothers show lower responsiveness to the attention bids of infants than do nondepressed mothers (e.g., Donovan, Leavitt, & Walsh, 1998; Mettesacker, Bade, Haverkock, & Pauli-Pott, 2004). Child risk was again measured on the basis of the child's birth status. We shifted our measure of parental investment to assess mothers' willingness to provide material benefits to their child as opposed to themselves—the basic competition between investment in caregiving and investment in one's own personal needs (Trivers, 1974).

Mothers were shown pictures of a number of items that we would bring for them on a return visit (as thanks for their participation). Some items were gifts for a child and others were gifts for an adult. They were asked to select their three top choices. Preference for gifts for the child would reflect high maternal investment, and preference for gifts for themselves, lower maternal investment. Supporting the contingent model, depressed mothers preferred gifts for themselves if the child was premature (high risk) but gifts for the child if the child was full term (low risk). Nondepressed mothers showed the reverse pattern. That is, they preferred gifts for themselves if the child was full term but gifts for the child if the child were born preterm.

■ RIVAL EXPLANATIONS

There are competing views of the reasons for differential parental investment in high- versus low- risk children. It might be argued that for parents who have been trained in their own early lives to show concern for others, providing exceptional care for high-risk children likely has a compassionate basis. Such differential responding could also be interpreted as a moral issue, supported by religious precepts. All major religions argue for the importance of giving to those who have less or providing care for those who are most in need or most vulnerable.

Arguing against this cultural explanation, there is evidence showing that non-humans often provide extra care to offspring who are most in need. This includes the earlier-cited research on birds, a class of animals that are not reasonably interpreted as showing compassion. Nonhuman parents, like human parents, have automatic computational processes that reflect the relative costs and benefits of their offspring as well as the accessibility of resources in their environment (for a review, see Maestripieri & Carroll, 1998). Manifestations of similar patterns across species suggest that contingent parental investment represents an adaptation that allows parents to optimize their reproductive success in different ways in the face of changing environmental circumstances. Neither humans nor nonhumans show fixed responses in all settings. Instead, they show "if–then" contingent patterns that optimize their response to shifting environments—a framework shared by evolutionary psychology and behavioral ecology (White, Dill, & Crawford, 2007; Krebs & Davies, 1993).

■ CONCLUSIONS AND IMPLICATIONS

A basic question in caregiving theory and research concerns the reasons **why** individuals should choose to provide valuable resources (time, money, attention, and effort) to others rather than retaining those resources for their own personal benefit. In answering this question with respect to preferential parental provision of care, an evolutionary perspective provides the most complete account. An evolutionary perspective is also useful in explaining why parental investment patterns are sensitive to the availability of resources. Finally, this perspective provides guidelines as to how parental investment in high-risk children can be enhanced, improving the long-term life outcomes of those children.

In the intervention program described here, we were able to demonstrate that parents' acquisition of effective problem-solving skills predicts increased investment of time and effort in costly (preterm) offspring. Higher levels of care, in particular for medically fragile children, have clear implications for reduced levels of morbidity and mortality. The observed changes in at-risk children's health as a function of increased parental investment are consistent with predictions offered by a contingent parental investment model. Mothers with high resources (in contrast with mothers with low resources) ultimately optimize their own reproductive success (gene replication) by strongly investing in high-risk infants.

Public policies can assist economically disadvantaged parents by providing resources, which in turn may allow greater investment in high-risk children. For example, Medicaid provides early assistance with the exceptionally expensive medical care needed by at-risk children. Programs such as WIC (a government-sponsored special supplemental nutrition program for women, infants, and children) allow parents to feed all their children adequately. Still needed, however, is empirical evidence that parents who are provided greater resources actually manifest increased investment in their high-risk children.

Cultures—like individuals—differ in their advocated and enacted child investment policies. As proposed by Cosmides and Tooby (1992), evolved mechanisms ultimately generate culture as well as individual behavioral patterns. Wealthier countries, as a whole, have public policies in support of providing assistance to disadvantaged or high-risk children, such as the McGovern–Dole Food for Education Program, designed to build a global school lunch program for economically needy children, and educational programs directed to special-needs children. Programs that provide assistance to children belonging to financially disadvantaged families (e.g., Head Start) provide a high economic return rate by virtue of their ability to prevent later, very costly problems (Heckman, 2006).

In poorer countries, policies (sometimes unacknowledged publicly) favor abandoning at-risk children at birth. For example, poor mothers in Romania have been encouraged to abandon their potentially costly medically at-risk (e.g., low birth weight) physically or mentally disabled children (UNICEF, 2005). Such children have then been placed in orphanages that do not meet anything close to acceptable standards of care.

It appears that different societies or subcultures—like individuals—promote diametrically opposed points of view with respect to investment in costly children. The differences are based primarily on differences reflecting the availability of resources or different philosophies about ways to deploy resources. For example, some people invoke traditional conservative beliefs suggesting that needy children—like stray animals—should not be fed, the argument being that they will simply grow up to breed and therefore continue a cycle of dependency (Corbin, 2010). It is interesting to note, however, that proponents of either perspective regularly cite the implications of policies for children's survival and reproduction success.

We have focused in this essay on the theoretical advantages of evolutionary theory in understanding variations in parental provision of care to at-risk children. This approach to investment in the young—at either a societal or an individual level—also provides guidelines for designing interventions and policies that optimize benefits for children's later health. Such programs are cost-effective when they make use of early services (construable as investment patterns) to promote child health and welfare—and thus prevent an even greater cost to society at later ages.

■ REFERENCES

Anderson, K. G., Kaplan, H., Lam, D., & Lancaster, J. (1999). Paternal care by genetic fathers and stepfathers II: Reports by Xhosa high school students. *Evolution and Human Behavior, 20,* 433–451.

Anderson, K. G., Kaplan, H., & Lancaster, J. (1999). Paternal care by genetic fathers and stepfathers I: Reports from Albuquerque men. *Evolution and Human Behavior, 20,* 405–431.

Beauchamp, M. H., Thompson, D. K., Howard, K., Doyle, L. W., Egan, G. F., Inder, T. H., & Anderson, P. J. (2008). Preterm hippocampal volumes correlate with later working memory deficits. *Brain, 131,* 2986–2994.

Beaulieu, D. A., & Bugental, D. B. (2006). An evolutionary approach to socialization. In J. E. Grusec & P. D. Hastings (Eds.), *Handbook of socialization: Theory and research* (pp. 71–95). New York, NY: Guilford Press.

Beaulieu, D. A., & Bugental, D. B. (2008). Contingent parental investment: An evolutionary framework for understanding early interaction between mothers and children. *Evolution and Human Behavior, 29,* 249–255.

Beck, A., Steer, R., & Garbin, M. (1988). Psychometric properties of the Beck Depression Inventory: Twenty-five years of evaluation. *Clinical Psychology Review, 8,* 77–100.

Bell, R. Q. (1968). A reinterpretation of the direction of effects in studies of socialization. *Psychological Review, 75*, 81–95.

Bugental, D. B., & Beaulieu, D. A. (2003). A bio-social-cognitive approach to understanding and promoting the outcomes of children with medical and physical disorders. In R. Kail (Ed.), *Advances in child development and behavior* (Vol. 3, 129–164). New York, NY: Academic Press.

Bugental, D. B., Beaulieu, D. A., & Silbert-Geiger, A. (2010). Increases in parental investment and child health as a result of an early intervention. *Journal of Experimental Child Psychology, 106*, 30–40.

Bugental, D. B., Ellerson, P. C., Lin, E. K., Rainey, B., Kokotovic, A., & O'Hara, N. (2002). A cognitive approach to child abuse prevention. *Journal of Family Psychology, 16*, 243–258.

Bugental, D. B., & Schwartz, A. (2009). A cognitive approach to child mistreatment prevention among medically at-risk infants. *Developmental Psychology, 45*, 284–288.

Bugental, D. B., & Shennum, W. A. (1984)."Difficult" children as elicitors and targets of adult communication patterns: An attributional-behavioral transactional analysis. *Monographs of the Society for Research in Child Development, 49*(1, Serial No. 205).

Corbin, C. (2010, January 27). South Carolina Lt. Gov. under fire for comparing welfare users to stray animals. Foxnews.com. Retrieved from http://www.foxnews.com/politics/2010/01/27/south-carolina-andre-bauer-welfare-comments-controversy/

Cosmides, L., & Tooby, J. (1992). The psychological foundations of culture. In J. H. Barkow, L. Cosmides, & J. Tooby (Eds.), *The adapted mind: Evolutionary psychology and the generation of culture* (pp. 19–136). New York, NY: Oxford University Press.

Coy, K., Speltz, M. L., & Jones, K. (2002). Facial appearance and attachment in infants with orofacial clefts: A replication. *Cleft-Palate-Craniofacial Journal, 39*, 66–72.

Daly, M., & Wilson, M. (1984). A sociobiological analysis of human infanticide. In G. Hausfater & S. B. Hrdy (Eds.), *Infanticide: Comparative and evolutionary perspectives* (pp. 487–502). New York, NY: Aldine de Gruyter.

Daly, M., & Wilson, M. (1988). *Homicide*. New York, NY: Aldine de Gruyter.

Davis, J. N., & Todd, P. M. (1999). Parental investment by simple decision rules. In G. Gigerenzer & P. M. Todd (Eds.), *Simple heuristics that make us smart* (pp. 309–326). New York, NY: Oxford University Press.

Donovan, W., Leavitt, L., & Walsh, R. (1998). Conflict and depression predict maternal sensitivity to infant cries. *Infant Behavior and Development, 21*, 505–517.

Field, T. M. (1982). Interaction coaching for high-risk infants and their parents. *Prevention in Human Services, 1*, 5–24.

Gottlander, K. (1987). Parental feeding behavior and sibling competition in the pied flycatcher, *Ficedula. Ornis Scandinavica, 18*, 269–276.

Grusec, J. E., Adam, E., & Mammone, N. (1993, April). *Mental representations of relationships, parent belief systems, and parenting behavior.* Paper presented at the biennial meeting of the Society for Research in Child Development, New Orleans, LA.

Hagen, E. H. (1999). The functions of postpartum depression. *Evolution and Human Behavior. 20*, 325–359.

Heckman, J. J. (2006). Skill formation and the economics of investing in disadvantaged children. *Science, 312*, 1900–1902.

Kelley, H. H., Holmes, J. G., Kerr, N. L., Reis, H. T., Rusbult, C. E., & Van Lange, P. A. M. (2003). *An atlas of interpersonal situations.* New York, NY: Cambridge University Press.

Krebs, J. R., & Davies, N. B. (1993). *An introduction to behavioral ecology.* Oxford, England: Wiley-Blackwell.

Maestripieri, D., & Carroll, K. A. (1998). Child abuse and neglect: Usefulness of animal data. *Psychological Bulletin, 123*, 211–223.

Maier, R. A., Holmes, D. L., & Slaymaker, F. L. (1984). The perceived attractiveness of pre-term Infants. *Infant Behavior and Development, 7*, 403–414.

Mann, J. (1992). Nurturance or negligence: Maternal psychology and behavioral preference among preterm twins. In J. H. Barkow, L. Cosmides, & J. Tooby (Eds.), *The adapted mind* (pp. 367–390). New York, NY: Oxford University Press.

Mettesacker, B., Bade, U., Haverkock, A., & Pauli-Pott, U. (2004). Predicting maternal reactivity and sensitivity: The role of infant emotionality, maternal depression/anxiety, and social support. *Infant Mental Health Journal, 25*, 47–61.

Nakamichi, M. (1986). Behavior of infant Japanese monkeys (*Macaca fuscata*) with congenital limb malformations during the first three months. *Developmental Psychobiology, 19*, 334–335.

Parker, G. A., & Rubinstein, D. I. (1981). Role assessment, strategy, and acquisition of information in asymmetric animal conflicts. *Animal Behaviour, 29*, 221–240.

Resource. (2009). In *American Heritage dictionary of the english language* (4th ed.). Boston: Houghton Mifflin.

Rose, S. A., Feldman, J. F., Rose, S. L., Wallace, I. F., & McCarton, C. (1992). Behavior problems at 3 and 6 years: Prevalence and continuity in full-terms and preterms. *Development and Psychopathology, 4*, 361–374.

Schepher-Hughes, N. (1985). Culture, scarcity, and maternal thinking: Maternal detachment and infant survival in a Brazilian shantytown. *Ethos, 13*, 291–317.

Thomas, A., & Chess, S. (1977). *Temperament and development*. Oxford, England: Brunner/Mazel.

Tooby, J., & Cosmides, L. (2005). Conceptual foundations of evolutionary psychology. In D. M. Buss (Ed.), *The handbook of evolutionary psychology* (pp. 5–67). Hoboken, NJ: Wiley.

Trivers, R. (1972). Parental investment and sexual selection. In B. Campbell (Ed.), *Sexual selection and the descent of man* (pp. 136–179). Chicago: Aldine.

Trivers, R. (1974). Parent–offspring conflict. *American Zoologist, 14*, 249–264.

UNICEF (2005, January 20). Babies still abandoned in Romanian hospitals: Pattern unchanged for 30 years, says UNICEF [Press Release]. Retrieved from http://www.unicef.org/media/media_24892.html

Weiss, M. (1998). Parents' rejection of their appearance-impaired newborns: Some critical observations regarding the social myth of bonding. *Marriage and Family Review, 27*, 191–209.

White, D. W., Dill, L. M., & Crawford, C. B. (2007). A common, conceptual framework for behavioral ecology and evolutionary psychology. *Evolutionary Psychology, 5*, 275–288.

10 The Role of Empathic Emotions in Caregiving

Caring for Pediatric Cancer Patients

■ LOUIS A. PENNER, FELICITY W. K. HARPER,

AND TERRANCE L. ALBRECHT

This essay focuses on a particular kind of caregiving—parents[1] caring for children who have pediatric cancer. Whereas a cancer diagnosis was once essentially a death sentence for a child, today the treatment of pediatric cancer is one of medicine's true success stories. Due to treatment advances, nearly 80% of children diagnosed with a pediatric cancer will live 5 years and 75% will live for 10 years (Centers for Disease Control and Prevention, 2004, National Cancer Institute, 2008). Further, today a substantial portion of children diagnosed with this disease do not simply survive; many are cured. In contrast, in the 1960s the survival rates for most pediatric cancers were less than 30% (Pizzo & Poplack, 2001).

But these remarkable results are not without substantial costs and challenges for the patients/survivors and their caregivers (most commonly their mothers). One of these is dealing with the difficult and invasive treatments the children must receive. As part of our research on how pediatric cancer patients and their families cope with cancer, we video-record children and their caregivers while the children are receiving treatments for their cancer. The description of one such treatment episode below comes from these video recordings:

"Sam," a 6-year-old cancer patient, and his mother have been waiting in a clinic room for almost two hours. He is scheduled to receive an intramuscular injection in his leg. Sam asks to be put "asleep" for the injection, but his mother explains (several times) that they won't give him general anesthetic for this procedure. Sam, who was playing and chatting with his mother up until now, becomes defiant and says he will not take the injection. Two nurses enter the room and one informs him that he has to take the injection now. He again refuses and tells them and his mother that "I'm not playing; you ain't giving me no shots."

One nurse firmly repeats that Sam has to have the injection and tells him he will receive it in sixty seconds. She begins a count, starting at 1. Sam first retreats to a corner and cowers, then begins to simultaneously threaten and plead with his mother and the nurses. When the countdown reaches 30, he is screaming and crying and hits his mother several times. At about 40, his mother picks him up, roughly pushes him down on the examination table, and begins to unbutton his pants. The count continues. At 50, he is struggling with his mother and one nurse approaches him with the syringe and what appears to be a very long needle. The countdown ends, and while the mother forces Sam back and restrains his arms, the second nurse places her body across his lower torso to keep him immobile. As the needle is quickly inserted, he screams and calls the nurses "fucking bitches." The mother yells at him to "watch his mouth" and the screaming continues for about 30 seconds after the injections. He refuses to speak to his mother. The episode is over, but Sam will receive another treatment within a week or two and this may continue for a year or longer. Although Sam's reaction to the treatment is somewhat stronger than what we usually see, it is not atypical.

As this narrative illustrates, cancer treatments are stressful not only for the child but the caregiver as well. Indeed, parents report that medical procedures (e.g., lumbar punctures, bone marrow aspirations, and port starts) create a significant physical and psychological burden (e.g., Barbi et al., 2005). Further, this burden is not substantially reduced by using general anesthesia to put children to sleep during treatment procedures (Busoni, 2004; Kain et al., 2003); nor does the frequent repetition of procedures desensitize the parents to the challenges of treatment (Liossi, 1999).

The experience of being a parent of a pediatric cancer patient also takes a substantial longer-term psychological and physical toll on the caregiver. Stuber (1996) found that almost 40% of mothers and 33% of fathers of pediatric leukemia survivors reported symptoms consistent with severe posttraumatic stress (cf. Barakat et al., 1997; Phipps, Dunavant, Lensing, & Rai, 2005). Miller, Cohen, and Ritchey(2002) compared parents of children with cancer to a matched control group of parents of medically healthy children. Parents of children with cancer scored significantly higher than control parents on measures of perceived stress, negative affect, and depressive symptoms. There was also evidence that the chronic stress of pediatric cancer impaired the immune system's ability to respond to anti-inflammatory signals. Specifically, parents of pediatric cancer patients showed less suppression of the pro-inflammatory cytokine interleukin-6 with the administration of a synthetic glucocorticoid than did control parents.

Thus parental caregiving for pediatric cancer patients seems to be an instance of what Brown and Brown (2006) call a *costly long-term investment* (CLI). That is, a caregiver must invest considerable personal resources in maintaining the well-being of another person over an extended period of time. Indeed, Brown and Brown include "expending considerable time and energy to raise offspring" (p. 1) as an example of CLI.

If we consider parental caregiving for children with cancer as an example of CLI, then we can ask questions about the parents that may inform our understanding of the nature of caregiving. In this essay, we address four such questions. First, what is the nature of the emotions parents experience when they need to help their children cope with cancer-related treatments and procedures? Second, do different kinds of parental emotions have different consequences for their children? Third, what sort of caregiving behaviors are associated with different kinds of emotions? And fourth, are enduring characteristics of the children associated with differences in the kinds of emotions parents display? Once we have presented data addressing these questions, we discuss their relevance to evolutionary theories of the nature of caregiving.

■ EMPATHIC EMOTIONS IN RESPONSE TO OTHERS' DISTRESS

The theoretical foundation for our study of parents' emotions during cancer treatment comes from the large social psychology literature on direct helping in dyads (Dovidio, Piliavin, Schroeder, & Penner, 2006; Penner, Dovidio, Piliavin & Schroeder, 2005). More specifically, we are guided by theoretical models of how the affective reactions of potential helpers affect their motivation to help. It is generally agreed that the sight of another person in pain produces empathic emotional responses in the observer (Goubert et al., 2005. Theories of interpersonal helping, especially Daniel Batson's (1991) empathy-altruism hypothesis, suggest the sight of another person in distress can elicit two distinct kinds of empathic responses. Batson labeled the first *personal distress*, described as an unpleasant and aversive affective state brought on by observing another person's distress. This response is characterized by emotions such as anxiety, nervousness, and distress. According to Piliavin, Dovidio, Gaertner, and Clark (1981), empathic distress occurs because people find distress in others personally unpleasant and upsetting. Although empathic distress motivates helping, the primary goal of that helping is to reduce one's own distress; helping the person in need is only instrumental to this outcome. Thus empathic personal distress is typically believed to result in an "egoistic" motivation for helping (Penner et al., 2005).

Batson labeled the second kind of empathic response *empathic concern*, which he defined as "an other-oriented emotional response congruent with the welfare of another person" (Batson & Oleson, 1991, p. 63). Empathic concern is characterized by positively toned emotions such as warmth, tenderness, and softheartedness directed at the person in distress. Helping motivated by this kind of empathic response is intended solely to increase or improve the well-being of the person in need; any rewards to the helper are incidental to the act of offering help. Thus empathic concern results in helping motivated by an altruistic concern for the welfare of the person in distress (Batson, 1991). Batson assumes, more or less as a given, that other-oriented emotions are elicited when people see family members or loved ones in distress; however, there is a dearth of research investigating such motives (or personal distress) among intimates.

As already noted, our work builds on this prior theory and research on helping, but it also differs in some substantial ways. The major difference is the outcome under study. We use the traditional "bystander intervention" helping paradigm to examine how the potential helpers' emotions affect the frequency or amount of helping. However, in the vast majority of interactions we study, parents *must* provide help to their children when the children receive treatment. So the primary question we ask about the parents' empathic responses to their children is not whether the emotions lead to helping, but rather what is their impact on the child's reactions to treatment, specifically their distress?

We are not, of course, the first researchers to propose that parents have emotional responses to their child's distress or to study their impact on their children's reactions to medical treatments. There is a large literature on this topic. However, most pediatric cancer researchers have either implicitly or explicitly assumed that clinic visits, in which children receive a painful or invasive procedure, will elicit only negative empathic affect in their parents. Accordingly, these researchers have almost exclusively measured parental emotions such as distress and anxiety and examined how these emotions affect children's reactions to medical procedures. (e.g., McMurtry, McGrath, & Chambers, 2006; Srivastava, Betts, Rosenberg, & Kramer, 2001). The prosocial-behavior literature would suggest, however, that parents simultaneously experience personal distress and empathic concern as their children confront cancer treatments. Thus we extended the existing research by investigating both kinds of empathic responses in parents of children receiving cancer treatments.

■ **RESEARCH OVERVIEW**

There were three data-collection sessions in our study of children with cancer and their families. In the first session, after parents were consented (and children assented), parents completed questionnaires assessing their own personality (and other dispositional variables) and their children's personality and temperament. A date was scheduled for the second session, in which parents and children would be video-recorded during a cancer treatment–related procedure (i.e., intramuscular injections, port access, lumbar puncture, or bone marrow aspiration).

In the second session (four to six weeks later), parents completed measures of their emotional responses while waiting for procedures to begin. These measures included assessments of both empathic concern and personal distress as well as other positive and negative emotions. We used Batson's (1991) measure to assess empathic concern and Spielberger's (1977) measure of state anxiety to assess personal distress. During the procedure, remote-controlled cameras video-recorded the episode from the time the parent and child entered the procedure room until the procedure was completed. Immediately after the procedure was completed, parents, attending nurses, and children were asked to rate the amount of pain or distress the child had experienced during the procedure. At a later time, independent judges (who were blind to the earlier ratings) observed the video recordings and rated the children's distress during the procedure episode. In a third session four to eight weeks after the recorded treatment episode, parents provided information about the child's quality of life and social and behavioral problems. These three assessment sessions provided the data we use to answer the set of questions posed earlier.

■ **PARENTS' EMOTIONS AND CAREGIVING**

The first question of interest concerns the kinds of emotional empathic responses parents reported while waiting for the treatments to begin. Because our measures of empathic concern and personal distress have different psychometric properties and there are no normative data on the former measure, it is not possible to state which kind of emotion was stronger among the parents. However, parents' responses to the measures of both kinds of emotions covered the full range of possible scores and were normally distributed. Consistent with previous research on personal distress and empathic concern, the two kinds of empathic responses were uncorrelated. That is, it was possible for parents to simultaneously experience high levels of personal distress and high levels of empathic concern.

■ PARENTS' EMOTIONAL RESPONSES AND CHILDREN'S REACTIONS TO TREATMENTS

This leads to the second question of how parental personal distress and parental empathic concern are related to children's pain or distress during treatment. Because personal distress is assumed to motivate self-oriented helping that is intended to reduce the helper's discomfort, parents high in personal distress might be hypersensitive to the stressful aspects of the treatments and their children's reactions to them. This might make them relatively ineffective helpers. Thus we (Penner et al., 2008) predicted that the greater the parent's personal distress, the greater the child's pain or distress would be. In contrast, empathic concern is assumed to prompt other-oriented helping in which the primary focus is on improving the well-being of the recipient. Thus parents with high levels of empathic concern should focus their attention on improving their child's well-being rather than on other aspects of the situation. Such a focus might make them relatively effective helpers. Thus we predicted that the greater the parental empathic concern, the less the children's pain or distress would be during treatment.

We examined these relationships in two related ways. First, we correlated personal distress and empathic concern with each rating of the child's pain or distress provided by parents, nurses, and children immediately after the procedure and with the observers' later ratings of the children's distress in the video-recorded treatment episodes.[2] The results provided only modest support for the personal-distress hypothesis. Parents' self-reports of personal distress correlated significantly and positively with their own reports of their children's pain (i.e., the higher the state anxiety, the greater the pain rating of children during the procedure) but not with any of the pain or distress ratings by the other raters. The results for empathic concern were much stronger. All the empathic-concern correlations were negative (i.e., the higher the empathic concern, the lower the pain or distress ratings of children during the procedure), significantly so with four of the six ratings of pain or distress. In the second, related analysis, we examined whether *differences* between levels of parental empathic concern and personal distress predicted children's reactions. Since the two scores were uncorrelated, we subtracted personal distress from empathic concern and correlated this difference score with each of the six ratings. The correlations were all negative and significant. Thus, the higher the parental empathic concern—either in an absolute sense or relative to personal distress—the less pain and distress experienced by their children.

■ PARENTAL EMOTIONAL RESPONSES AND PARENTAL CAREGIVING BEHAVIORS

Now we consider the parents' behaviors during treatments. Our colleague Rebecca Cline (Cline et al., 2006) developed a typology of the ways parents communicated with their children. The typology contains four distinct communication patterns: normalizing (trying to "normalize" the situation by engaging the child in everyday activities, such as coloring or playing games), distancing (physically and or psychologically disengaging from the child), and the two patterns that were of the greatest interest to us—supportive and invalidating.

According to Cline and colleagues (2006), a pattern of supportive communication is one in which "the parent engages in empathic, supportive, and/or comforting responses . . . the parent is (a) partner, protector, and/or comforter" (p. 890). This is best illustrated by the following narrative from one of the video-recorded parent–child interactions:

The child is receiving a lumbar puncture (a spinal tap) and has been placed on the bed where the procedure will be performed. While waiting for the procedure to begin, the father sits in a chair next to the bed. The child is awake on the table. The father leans toward his son, while he rubs the boy's back, speaks softly to him, and touches his face. As the nurses prepare the child for the procedure, the father remains physically close to his son, keeping constant eye contact with him, and smiling at his son. The father moves to the foot of the bed while the nurses perform the spinal tap, but keeps constant visual contact with the child. After the procedure is done, he returns to the child's side and continues to provide a lot of physical contact. He holds the child so that his band-aid can be applied. He kisses his son, assists with moving tubes, and covers the child with a blanket. Finally, at the child's request, the father lies down on the bed with his son as he recovers from the procedure.

In contrast to supportive communication, a pattern of invalidating communication is one in which the parent, "denies, invalidates, and/or challenges the validity (merit, worth, or accuracy) of the child's experience" (Cline et al., p. 890). Invalidating parents may show anger and frustration; minimize or deny their children's pain or distress responses; and engage in name-calling, ridicule, or criticism of their children. Consider this example of invalidation taken from another video-recorded interaction:

An 11-year-old boy is in bed waiting for his spinal tap procedure to begin. He reaches out to touch his mother, who is seated in a chair next to him. The mother initially ignores the child's touch and eventually slaps his arm and moves her chair out of his reach to the foot of the bed. Later in the same interaction, the mother begins commenting on the child's appearance (in front of the child):
Mother: "He gained like 30 pounds in like half a year."
(The patient stretches out his arm towards his mother; she touches his upper arm.)
Mother: "Look at his arm. Look at how big his stretch marks are . . . like pregnant women."

Fortunately, only about 20% of the patients we have observed thus far display an invalidating communication pattern; most parents display supportive and positive communication patterns. However, one might very reasonably expect that children of supportive and of invalidating parents will react very differently to the treatment procedures—and in fact, they did. Relative to supportive parents, the children of invalidating parents were rated as experiencing significantly higher pain or distress by five of the six judges, including the independent observers (Cline et al., 2006).

This brings us to the third question in this essay: What is the relationship between parental empathic responses and parental caregiving behaviors? Using the empathic-response difference score described above, Penner et al. (2008) found that supportive parents displayed significantly more empathic concern than invalidating parents. In another study, Peterson et al. (2007) coded the parents' nonverbal behaviors during the treatment procedures. These behaviors included how much parents touched their children and the distance parents stood from their children during the procedure. Using their data, we found that preprocedure empathic responses predicted how far parents placed themselves from and how frequently they touched the child during the actual procedure. The pattern of touching and distance is in accord with the other findings just presented (i.e., more empathic concern yields more effective behaviors).

All of these findings are correlational, but they are consistent with the notion that parents' empathic responses (i.e., relative levels of empathic concern and personal distress) may cause different patterns of communication (e.g., supportive versus invalidating), which in turn affect children's levels of pain or distress.

■ CHILDREN'S ATTRIBUTES AND PARENTS' EMPATHIC RESPONSES

The final question asked in this essay is whether the children's attributes were related to their parents' emotional responses before treatment episodes. As we have previously noted, there was a fair amount of variability in the parents' personal distress and empathic concern just before the treatments began. We considered whether some of this variability might be related to the children's enduring attributes.

There are different models of how children's enduring attributes might be related to their parents' empathic affective responses. One is a compensatory-type model, which proposes that children who are less able to cope with stressors or have psychosocial problems will elicit more empathic concern (and less personal distress) from their parents. In short, greater need in an intimate elicits more positively valenced empathic responses from a helper. The other possible model, based on social-psychological and evolutionary theories of helping (cf. Dovidio et al., 2006), proposes essentially the opposite. The more able children are to cope with stressors, the more positively valenced the empathic response in their parents.

To explore the validity of the two models, we correlated children's general ability to cope with stressors in their life with their parents' empathic responses just before treatment. Specifically, the developmental psychology literature suggests that some of the attributes associated with effective coping among children are resilience (i.e., the ability to bounce back in response to difficulties), attention shifting in response to stressful stimuli, and adaptability (e.g., Eisenberg et al., 2004; Rothbart & Bates, 2006). We used validated measures of these three constructs and correlated them with parents' empathic responses just before treatments.

The data supported the second, noncompensatory model. There were significant positive associations between the parents' positive empathic emotions and

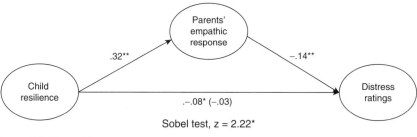

Figure 10.1 Mediated Relationship Among Children's Resilience, Parents' Empathic Responses, and Children's Distress as Rated by Observers. Estimates of path coefficient were made using a bootstrap procedure (Preacher & Hayes, 2008).

resilience, attention shifting, and adaptability. Negative emotions were unrelated to these child attributes.

We also found that child resilience was significantly and negatively associated with several of the ratings of the children's pain or distress; the strongest relationship was with the observers' ratings of distress. That is, the higher the child resilience, the lower the observers' ratings of their distress during treatments. These findings prompted us to conduct a mediational analysis of the relationship between children's resilience, parents' empathic responses, and the observers' ratings of children's distress. This analysis (see figure 10.1) showed that the direct relationship between children's resilience and ratings of child distress is almost totally mediated by parents' empathic responses. In other words, children's resilience affects parents' empathic responses, which in turn affect children's distress.

■ AN EVOLUTIONARY PERSPECTIVE ON PARENTAL CAREGIVING

Although the primary purpose of the research we have reported is much more practical than theoretical, we believe that our data may tell us some important things about the nature of parental caregiving. To address this issue, we consider these data from the perspective of Brown and Brown's (2006) Selective Investment Theory (SIT) of caregiving. As the theory is discussed in detail elsewhere in this volume, we provide only a cursory overview of the portions of the theory of most relevance here.

SIT attempts to explain why people are willing to provide sustained care to individuals in need and proposes that an essential problem for humans is how to minimize "self versus other motivational conflicts associated with altruistic decision making" (Brown & Brown, 2006, p. 1). Brown and Brown argue that altruistic behaviors are directly motivated by "social bonds," which they describe as "overarching, emotion regulating mechanisms designed to promote reliable, high-cost altruism among individuals who depend on one another for survival and reproduction (e.g., offspring, mates, coalition members)" (p. 1). Social bonds between caregivers and recipients lead caregivers to resolve the conflict between their self-ish, egocentric motives and their altruistic motives in favor of the latter, resulting in the provision of care.

We would propose that empathic concern is one of the emotion-regulating states that is coordinated by social bonds. That is, positive emotions among care-givers (such as love, compassion, warmth, and the like) might cultivate empathic concern and constitute proximal causes of other-oriented or altruistic actions. From the vantage point of SIT, such emotions may serve to resolve the conflict between selfish and altruistic motives in favor of the latter.

Our findings also suggest a potential mechanism through which people's altru-istic actions may confer survival advantages on caregivers and their kin or inti-mates. As previously discussed, we found that (1) the more parents were motivated by empathic concern, the less was their children's pain or distress; (2) high-empathic concern parents were much more likely to engage in warm, caring, and supportive communication with their children than they were to engage in what we have called invalidating communication; and (3) children of supportive par-ents experienced significantly less pain or distress than children of invalidating parents.

Thus it does not seem unreasonable to argue that parents who experience high levels of empathic concern (relative to personal distress) may not only be more likely to help but also be more effective caregivers. If we extrapolate from the stress-ful situations we study to other situations in which children face threatening or even dangerous circumstances and require help from a caregiver, our findings raise the possibility that because high-empathic concern parents are better helpers, their children may be more likely to survive these situations. If so, models that use inclu-sive fitness to explain the origins of human altruism like SIT would argue this should increase the likelihood that the genetic characteristics associated with such altruistic behaviors will be present among the descendants of such caregivers.

Like almost all evolutionary explanations, it is not easy to create a paradigm that provides a strong test of this argument. A small percentage of the children we study have died, but it would be patently illogical to attribute their deaths to the parents' reactions to their treatments. Thus we must look for more subtle relation-ships between the parents' emotional responses and how well the children in our study were doing with regard to their cancer. We currently have some data that may speak to this. We will acknowledge at the outset that all of the findings are correlational and certainly subject to alternative interpretations, but in the spirit of this volume we think they are worth considering.

We can examine some possible longer-term benefits of higher levels of parental empathic concern and other positive emotions at the time of treatment. As already noted, about three months after the video-recorded treatment episodes, we inde-pendently assessed the children's cancer-related quality of life; for this we used an instrument specifically developed to assess cancer-related problems in children (Varni, Seid, & Kurtin, 2001). The children of caregivers with more positive empathic responses at the time of treatment had fewer posttreatment difficulties with factors such as nausea, fatigue, cognitive functioning, and emotional responses to cancer. These relationships remain significant even when we control for the children's attributes associated with coping with stressors. Obviously, this does not prove that positive empathic responses among helpers have long-term benefits for the recipients of help, but it is consistent with such an argument.

Our data may also seem consistent with kin selection theories of the evolution of helping and caregiving. These theories posit that humans are, overall, more likely to help kin than unrelated strangers, but they are also more likely to help kin who seem robust and healthy than kin who do not. In ancestral environments, helping healthy genetic relatives, who, with this help, are likely to survive and reproduce,, would, in turn, have increased the helper's inclusive fitness. In contrast, helping relatives who are unhealthy and/or unlikely to reproduce confers no genetic benefits on the helper (see Burnstein, Crandall, & Kitayama, 1994).

In this context, recall the answer to the fourth question we posed. We found that the more resilient and adaptive children elicited more positive empathic responses from their parents at the time of treatment. These findings suggest a kin selection process in which the characteristics of the child affect the affective responses of the caregiver such that the most adaptive children are most likely to elicit the most positive emotions from their caregivers. The prosocial behavior literature suggests that this would increase the likelihood that the caregivers give help (Penner et al., 2005), and our data suggest that it may also result in their providing more effective help. In other words, empathic concern may be the proximal meditational mechanism that elicits helping that favors certain kin over others.

There are, of course, many remaining unanswered questions about parents' emotions and motives and the provision of care to children in a pediatric cancer context. We have suggested that parents' altruistically motivated or other-oriented helping may yield substantial long-term benefits for the child, but in fact thus far we have only examined relatively short-term benefits. Future research needs to examine the more enduring benefits of this kind of helping (for both children and parents) and more precisely identify the parental behaviors that mediate this relationship. We also need to better understand other social, dispositional, and situational variables responsible for variations in parental emotions and motives when their children experience invasive medical procedures and other stressful events. Further, it would be valuable to tie this research to the kinds of neuroimaging and neurophysiological research described elsewhere in this volume. That is, we assume that certain neurophysiological events are the immediate cause of the motives and behaviors we have observed, but the relations between neurophysiological events and parental caregiving are largely not yet known. It remains for neurophysiological and other kinds of research discussed in this volume to further inform our understanding of the causes and consequences of long-term costly parental caregiving. This may serve the interests of both basic research on the nature of caregiving and practical applications of this research to problems such as better coping with treatments for pediatric cancer.

■ **ACKNOWLEDGEMENTS**

The research reported in this essay and the writing of the essay were partially supported by the following grants: Penner (NCI 1 R01 CA138981-01), Harper

(NCI 1R03CA141992-01), Albrecht (NCI 5-R01-CA-100027-01). We wish to thank Rebecca Cline and Amy Peterson for their contributions to this research.

■ NOTES

1. Throughout this essay we will use the word *parent* to describe an adult caregiver who has primary long-term responsibility for a child's well-being. Although potentially important, we will not distinguish between biological parents and unrelated adult caregivers.

2. The parents and nurses rated both pain and distress; the children just rated pain; and the observers only rated distress. The was substantial convergent validity among the raters (Penner et al., 2008).

■ REFERENCES

Barakat, L. P., Kazak, A. E., Meadows, A. T., Casey, R., Meeske, K., & Stuber, M. L. (1997). Families surviving childhood cancer: A comparison of posttraumatic stress symptoms with families of healthy children. *Journal of Pediatric Psychology, 22,* 843–859.

Barbi, E., Badina, L., Marchetti, F., Vecchi, R., Giuseppin, I., Bruno, I., et al. (2005). Attitudes of children with leukemia toward repeated deep sedations with propofol. *Journal of Pediatric Hematology and Oncology, 27,* 639–643.

Batson, C. D. (1991). *The altruism question: Toward a social-psychological answer.* Hillsdale, NJ: Erlbaum.

Batson, C. D., & Oleson, K. C. (1991). Current status of the empathy-altruism hypothesis. In M. S. Clark (Ed.), *Review of personality and social psychology* (Vol. 2, pp. 62–85). Newbury Park, CA: Sage.

Brown, S. L. & Brown, R. M. (2006). Selective Investment Theory: Recasting the functional significance of close relationships. *Psychological Inquiry, 17,* 1–29.

Burnstein, E., Crandall, C., & Kitayama, S. (1994). Some neo-Darwinian decision rules for altruism: Weighing cues for inclusive fitness as a function of the biological importance of the decision. *Journal of Personality and Social Psychology, 67,* 773–789.

Centers for Disease Control and Prevention. (2004). Cancer survivorship—United States, 1971–2001. *Morbidity and Mortality Weekly Report, 53*(24), 526–529.

Cline, R. J. W., Harper, F. W. K., Penner, L. A., Peterson, A. M., Taub, J. W., & Albrecht, T. L. (2006). Parent communication and child pain and distress during painful pediatric cancer treatments. *Social Science and Medicine, 63,* 883–898.

Dovidio, J., Piliavin, J., Schroeder, D., & Penner, L. (2006). *The social psychology of prosocial behavior.* Mahwah, NJ: Lawrence Erlbaum.

Eisenberg, N., Spinrad, T. L., Fabes, R. A., Reiser, M., Cumberland, A., Shepard, S. A., . . . Thompson, M.. (2004). The relations of effortful control and impulsivity to children's resiliency and adjustment. *Child Development, 75,* 25–46.

Goubert, L., Craig, K. D., Vervoort, T., Morley, S., Sullivan, M. J. L., Williams, A., . . . Crombez, G. (2005). Facing others in pain: The effects of empathy. *Pain, 118,* 285–288.

Kain, Z. N., Caldwell-Andrews, A. A., Mayes, L. C., Wang, S. M., Krivutza, D. M., & LoDolce, M. E. (2003). Parental presence during induction of anesthesia: Physiological effects on parents. *Anesthesiology, 98,* 58–64.

Liossi, C. (1999). Management of paediatric procedure–related cancer pain. *Pain Reviews, 6,* 279–302.

McMurtry, C., McGrath, P. & Chambers, C. (2006). Reassurance can hurt: Parental behavior and painful medical procedures. *Journal of Pediatrics, 148,* 560–561.

Miller, G. E., Cohen, S., & Ritchey, A. K. (2002). Chronic psychological stress and the regulation of pro-inflammatory cytokines: A glucocorticoid resistance model. *Health Psychology, 21,* 531–541.

National Cancer Institute (2008). *A snapshot of pediatric cancers.* Retrieved May 20, 2010, from http://planning.cancer.gov/disease/Pediatric-Snapshot.pdf

Penner, L. A., Cline, R. J., Albrecht, T. L., Harper F. W. K., Peterson, A. M., Ruckdeschel, J. C. (2008). Parents' empathic responses and pain and distress in pediatric patients. *Basic and Applied Social Psychology, 30,* 102–113.

Penner, L. A., Dovidio, J. F., Piliavin, J. A., & Schroeder, D. A. (2005). Prosocial behavior: Multilevel perspectives. *Annual Review of Psychology, 56,* 365–392.

Peterson, A. M., Cline, R. J. W., Foster, T. S., Penner, L. A., Parrott, R., Keller, C. M., . . . Albrecht, T. L. (2007). Parents' interpersonal distance and touch behavior and child pain and distress during painful pediatric oncology procedures. *Journal of Nonverbal Behavior, 31,* 79–97.

Phipps, S., Dunavant, M., Lensing, S., & Rai, S. N. (2005). Psychosocial predictors of distress in parents of children undergoing stem cell or bone marrow transplantation. *Journal of Pediatric Psychology, 30,* 139–153.

Piliavin, J. A., Dovidio, J. F., Gaertner, S., & Clark, R. D. (1981). *Emergency intervention.* New York, NY: Academic Press.

Pizzo, P. A., & Poplack, D. A (Eds.). (2001). *Principles and practice of pediatric oncology* (4th ed.). Philadelphia, PA: Williams & Wilkens.

Preacher, K. J., & Hayes, A. F. (2008). Asymptotic and resampling strategies for assessing and comparing indirect effects in multiple mediator models. *Behavior Research Methods, 40,* 879–891.

Rothbart, M. K., & Bates, J. E. (2006). Temperament. In N. Eisenberg, W. Damon, & R. M. Lerner (Eds.), *Temperament handbook of child psychology, Vol. 3: Social, emotional, and personality development* (6th ed., pp. 99–166). Hoboken, NJ: Wiley.

Spielberger, C. D. (1977). *State-Trait Anxiety Inventory for Adults.* Redwood, CA: Mind Garden Inc.

Srivastava, T., Betts, G., Rosenberg, A. R., & Kainer, G. (2001). Perception of fear, distress and pain by parents of children undergoing a micturating cystourethrogram: A prospective study. *Journal of Paediatrics & Child Health, 37,* 271–273.

Stuber, M. L. (1996). Psychiatric sequelae in seriously ill children and their families. *Psychiatric Clinics of North America, 19,* 481–493.

Varni, J. W., Seid, M., & Kurtin, P. S. (2001). PedsQL 4.0: Reliability and validity of the Pediatric Quality of Life Inventory version 4.0 generic core scales in healthy and patient populations. *Medical Care, 39,* 800–812.

11 The Costs and Benefits of Informal Caregiving

RICHARD SCHULZ AND JOAN K. MONIN

Former U.S. First Lady Rosalynn Carter is often quoted as pointing out that you either are, were, or will be a caregiver. The provision of support or assistance by one family member to another is a normative and pervasive aspect of human interaction. Providing help to a family member with a chronic illness or disability is often not very different from the tasks and activities that characterize interactions among families without the presence of illness or disability. For example, when a wife provides care to her husband with Alzheimer's disease by preparing his meals or keeping the house free of clutter, she is engaging in activities she might normally do for her husband. However, assistance with personal care needs, such as bathing or dressing, is viewed as extraordinary and defines what is typically thought of as informal or family caregiving. Although specific definitions of caregiving vary widely from one context to another, they all include the idea that support or assistance is provided because of limited or diminished abilities of the care recipient, typically resulting from acute or chronic illness or disability.

Caregiving addresses critical individual needs and therefore is a great benefit to recipients and to society as a whole, but it often comes at a considerable cost to the caregiver in terms of their health and well-being. Our goal in this chapter is to explore both the costs and benefits of caregiving at the individual level and to identify factors associated with these divergent outcomes. Much of the caregiving literature focuses on the psychological and physical health effects of caregiving; we therefore begin by examining the detrimental or negative health effects of caregiving. An emerging literature suggests that caregivers may also benefit both physically and psychologically from providing help. We next examine that literature. Because health and well-being are inextricably intertwined with economic status, we also address issues of work and caregiving. In the conclusion of our essay we reconcile these divergent literatures and show how caregiving can both help and harm the caregiver depending on the intensity of care demands, the magnitude of care-recipient suffering, and the amount of control over care-recipient outcomes.

■ DETRIMENTAL HEALTH EFFECTS OF CAREGIVING

Clinical observation and early empirical research on family caregiving strongly suggested that assuming a caregiving role is stressful and burdensome to family members. Researchers and clinicians were quick to note that caregiving has all the features of a chronic stress experience: Providing care generates physical and psychological strain over extended periods of time, is accompanied by high levels of unpredictability and uncontrollability, has the capacity to generate secondary stress in multiple life domains, and frequently requires high levels of vigilance on the part of the caregiver. Indeed, caregiving fits the recipe for chronic stress so well that it came to be viewed as an ideal platform for studying the health effects of chronic stress exposure (Vitaliano, Zhang, & Scanlan, 2003).

It should come as no surprise that the dominant conceptual model for caregiving assumes that the onset and progression of chronic illness and physical disability is stressful for both care recipient and caregiver and, as such, can be studied within the framework of traditional stress-coping models. Within this framework, objective stressors for caregivers include care recipients' physical disability, cognitive impairment, and problem behaviors, as well as the type and intensity of care provided. These objective stressors in turn generate psychological stress, impair health behaviors, and perturb physiological systems within the body in ways that can cause illness and death (Vitaliano et al., 2003).

Magnitude of Physical and Mental Health Effects

Several recent reviews document the link between caregiving and health (Gouin, Hantsoo, & Kiecolt-Glaser, 2008; Pinquart & Sörensen, 2003b; Vitaliano et al., 2003). For example, Vitaliano et al. (2003) reviewed 23 studies to compare the physical health of dementia caregivers with demographically similar non-caregivers, and across 11 health categories caregivers exhibited a slightly greater risk of health problems than did non-caregivers. We briefly summarize in tables 11.1 and 11.2, respectively, the wide range of physical and psychological outcome variables represented in the literature. All of these variables have been linked to stressors such as the duration and type of care provided and the functional and cognitive disabilities of the care recipient, as well as secondary stressors such as finances and family conflict. As a result of these stressors, providing care has been linked to psychological distress, worsening of health habits, detrimental physiological responses, psychiatric and physical illness, and increased mortality (Christakis & Allison, 2006; Haley, Roth, Howard, & Safford, 2010; Pinquart & Sörensen, 2003a, 2003b, 2007; Schulz & Beach, 1999; Schulz, O'Brien, Bookwala, & Fleissner, 1995; Schulz, Visintainer, & Williamson, 1990; Vitaliano et al., 2003).

Measures of psychological well-being such as depression, stress, and burden have been most frequently studied in the caregiving literature and yield consistent and relatively large health effects (Marks, Lambert, & Choi, 2002; Pinquart & Sörensen, 2003b; Schulz et al., 1995, 1997; Teri, Logsdon, Uomoto, & McCurry, 1997). These effects are moderated by age, socioeconomic status (SES), and the availability of informal support. Specifically, older caregivers, low-SES caregivers, and caregivers with limited support networks report lower levels of health than caregivers who are younger and have more economic and interpersonal resources (Vitaliano et al., 2003).

Detrimental physical health effects of caregiving are generally smaller than psychological health effects, regardless of whether they are measured by global self-report instruments or physiological measures such as stress hormones (Vitaliano et al., 2003). Although relatively few studies have focused on the association between caregiving and self-care behaviors, there is evidence to suggest

TABLE 11.1 *Physical Health Measures*

Type of Measure	Specific Indicators	Comment
Global Health Measures		
	Self-reported health (current health, health compared with others, changes in health status)	Overall, effects are small. Self-report measures are most common and show largest effects. One prospective study (Schulz & Beach, 1999) reports increased mortality for strained caregivers when compared to non-caregivers; another (SL Brown, Smith, Schulz et al., 2009) reports reduced mortality among caregivers, possibly because caregivers were not stressed. Higher age, lower SES, and lower levels of informal support are related to poorer health. Greater negative effects are found for dementia vs. nondementia caregivers and spouses vs. nonspouses.
	Chronic conditions (chronic illness checklists)	
	Physical symptoms (Cornell Medical Index, Abramson, Terepolsky, Brook, & Kark, 1965)	
	Medications (number and types)	
	Health service utilization (clinic visits, days in hospital, physician visits)	
	Mortality	
Physiological Measures		
	Antibodies and functional immune measures (immunoglobulin, Epstein–Barr virus, T-cell proliferation, responses to mitogens, response to cytokine stimulation, lymphocyte counts)	Effect sizes for all indicators are generally small. Stronger relationships are found for stress hormones and antibodies than other indicators. Evidence linking caregiving to metabolic and cardiovascular measures is weak. Men exhibit greater negative effects on most physiological indicators.
	Stress hormones and neurotransmitters (Adrenocorticotropic hormone, epinephrine, norepinephrine, cortisol, prolactin)	
	Cardiovascular measures (blood pressure, heart rate)	
	Metabolic measures (body mass, weight, cholesterol, insulin, glucose, transferrin)	
	Speed of wound healing	
Health Habits		
	Sleep, diet, exercise	A few studies report impaired health behaviors among stressed caregivers.
	Self-care, medical compliance	

TABLE 11.2 *Psychological Health Measures*

Type of Measure	Specific Indicators	Comment
Depression	Clinical diagnosis, symptom checklists, antidepressant medication use	Measures are the most frequently studied caregiver outcomes with largest effects. Greater negative effects are found for dementia than for non-dementia caregivers. Higher age, lower SES, and lower levels of informal support are related to poorer mental health. Positive mental health effects and benefit are reported in a few studies among caregivers in early stages of caregiving career.
Anxiety	Clinical diagnosis, symptom checklists, anxiolytic medication use	
Stress	Burden	
Subjective Well-Being	Global self-ratings; global quality-of-life ratings	
Positive aspects of caregiving	Self-ratings of benefit finding	
Self efficacy	Self-ratings	

that individuals engaged in heavy-duty caregiving manifest impaired self-care (Lee, Colditz, Berkman, & Kawachi, 2003; Schulz et al., 1997). Several recent large-population studies further support the relationship between caregiving and physical health. Fredman and colleagues (2008) found that among healthy, community-dwelling elderly adults, caregivers had modestly elevated rates of mortality and incident mobility limitations when compared to non-caregivers. In another study they found that older women who were long-term caregivers (4 years or more) or who cared for a person with dementia—considered to be a highly stressful type of caregiving—declined more in walking speed, a risk factor for mortality, than did short-term or non-caregivers (Fredman, Doros, Cauley, Hillier, & Hochberg, 2010). Haley and colleagues (2010) similarly showed that caregiving strain in spousal caregivers was significantly associated with higher estimated stroke risk.

The prevalence of depressive symptoms, clinical depression, and reduced quality of life among caregivers make caregiving an important public health issue in the United States, particularly given the fact that depression is the second leading cause of disability worldwide. Moreover, even if the detrimental effects of caregiving on physical health are relatively small, the large number of people affected means that the overall impact is significant. Recognition of these facts, coupled with the knowledge that caregivers represent a major national health resource, has resulted in national policy aimed at supporting caregivers.

Methodological Issues

Although the literature on caregiving is vast, much of it is based on cross-sectional analyses of relatively small ($N < 100$), nonprobability opportunity samples.

Confounding effects are often not controlled through study design or statistical analysis. Thus caution is advised before concluding unequivocally that caregiving leads to adverse health effects. Even large, longitudinal, or case control studies are subject to a number of biases. Differences in illness rates between caregivers and non-caregivers are not necessarily the result of caregiving experience and may instead reflect differences that existed prior to taking on the caregiving role. For example, individuals of low SES are more likely to take on the caregiving role than persons of high SES, and low SES is also a risk factor for poor health status. Higher rates of illness in spousal caregivers also may be the result of assortative mating (people tend to choose others who are similar to them) and so may reflect shared health habits (e.g., diet and exercise) and life circumstances (e.g., access to medical care and job stress). As a result, older spouses tend to develop illness and disability conjointly; when one individual develops health problems requiring a caregiver, chances are the partner also has health problems, although they may be less severe.

Prospective studies (Schulz & Beach, 1999; Shaw et al., 1997) that link caregiver health declines to increasing care demands provide more compelling evidence of the health effects of caregiving. Since family caregiving cannot be experimentally manipulated, the best alternative study design is one in which individuals are followed longitudinally and their health is assessed as they move into and out of a caregiving role. A handful of studies have assessed caregiver outcomes such as depression and physical health status before and after individuals take on the caregiving role (Burton, Zdaniuk, Schulz, Jackson, & Hirsch, 2003; Hirst, 2005; Lawton, Moss, Hoffman, & Perkinson, 2000; Seltzer & Li, 2000). Burton et al. (2003) and more recently Hirst (2005) provide compelling evidence that moving into a demanding caregiving role, defined as providing assistance with basic activities of daily living for 20 hours or more of care per week, results in increased depression and psychological distress, impaired self-care, and lower self-reported health. Transitioning from no care to providing low to moderate amounts of care has little impact on the health of the caregiver, suggesting that a threshold of care demands has to be reached before negative health effects are observed. Hours of care provided is associated with several other factors, including the level of illness and disability and the amount of suffering experienced by the care recipients, as well as restrictions in freedom of the caregiver, all of which may contribute to the negative health effects among caregivers.

Findings on the effects of transitioning out of the caregiving role because of patient improvement, institutionalization, or death help to complete the picture on the association between caregiving and health. Improved care-recipient functioning is associated with reductions in caregiver distress (Nieboer, Schulz, Scheier, & Matthews, 1998), and the death of the care recipient has been found to reduce caregiver depression, enabling them to return to normal levels of functioning within a year of the care recipient's death (Schulz et al., 2003). In the short term, the effects of the transition to nursing homes are less positive, as caregivers continue to exhibit high levels of psychiatric morbidity after placement (Schulz et al., 2004). While institutionalization typically reduces the amount of hands-on care provided by the caregiver, it does not necessarily reduce the perceived suffering of the care recipient, and can introduce new stressors such as feelings of guilt about institutionalizing a loved one.

A related shortcoming of the existing literature is that while researchers have been able to link caregiving stressors to caregiver responses, they have rarely shown the sequential progression of illness effects. For example, while many studies show that caregiving causes psychological distress, virtually none have shown within persons over time that stress results in physiological dysregulation such as increased cortisol secretion or changes in immune function. Similarly, researchers interested in the effects of caregiving on health behaviors or physiological responses have not yet demonstrated within persons that these effects are directly linked to illness outcomes. To be sure, demonstrating sequential causal relationships among variables thought to be critical in the path from caregiver stress to illness is challenging, but such efforts should receive high priority. Large-sample longitudinal studies that include a rich array of biological, psychosocial, and behavioral measures would be required to achieve this goal.

■ BENEFICIAL HEALTH EFFECTS OF CAREGIVING

Caregiving is not always a negative experience. In studies of caregiving that use large population based samples, a significant proportion of caregivers report neither strain nor negative health effects (Schulz et al., 1997). This is particularly true for caregivers in the early stages of a caregiving career (Burton et al., 2003; Hirst, 2005). Even when caregiving demands become more intense and are associated with high levels of distress and depression, caregivers acknowledge positive aspects of the caregiving experience. They report that it makes them feel good about themselves, makes them feel useful and needed, gives meaning to their lives, enables them to learn new skills, and strengthens relationships with others. Because studies on the positive aspects of caregiving are typically given short shrift in the review literature on caregiving, we focus in detail here on recent studies suggesting that caregiving can have beneficial effects on the health of the caregiver. We begin with studies suggesting that caregiving may decrease the risk of mortality.

Caregiving and Decreased Risk of Mortality

There is an emerging literature showing that caregiving is associated with a lower risk of mortality (S. L. Brown, Nesse, Vinokur, & Smith, 2003; S. L. Brown et al., 2009; O'Reilly, Connolly, Rosato, & Patterson, 2008). These effects remain even after controlling for caregivers' baseline health status, decreasing the possibility of a "healthy caregiver" effect—"that those in a caring role may be self-selected because of their current 'healthiness' and thus present with lower mortality risks" (O'Reilly et al., 2008, p. 1284). Instead, the positive effects of caregiving found in these studies are generally attributed to the benefits of helping (S. L. Brown et al., 2003).

These beneficial effects of caregiving are contradictory to those from other studies that show increased risk of mortality among caregivers (Christakis & Allison, 2006; Schulz & Beach, 1999). What might account for this inconsistency?

One explanation may be that researchers have found negative effects more consistently with strained caregivers (Schulz & Beach, 1999), whereas positive effects have been found with relatively less burdened caregivers. For example, O'Reilly and colleagues (2008) found that caregivers from the 2001 Northern Ireland Census had lower risk of mortality than non-caregivers, but risk increased with the time spent caregiving. Beneficial mortality effects were larger among those who spent 1–19 hours a week providing care than those providing care more than 20 hours a week. Those providing 1–19 hours of care were also more affluent, suggesting that they had more resources to deal with the burden of providing care. In contrast to the O'Reilly et al. study, S. L. Brown and colleagues (2009) found that high numbers of caregiving hours (more than 14 hours per week) were associated with decreased mortality risk compared with non-caregivers, whereas low numbers of caregiving hours (1–14 hours per week) were not associated with mortality risk, even after controlling for spousal impairments, age, employment status, and caregiver health at baseline.

Another important difference between studies demonstrating positive and negative health effects concerns the conceptualization and measurement of caregiving. Studies showing positive effects tend to define caregiving more broadly, whereas studies showing negative effects focus on the provision of care to a particular close relationship partner. For example, the O'Reilly study (2008) assessed caregiving with the census question "Do you look after, or give any help or support to family members, friends, neighbors or others because of: long term physical or mental ill-health or disability; problems related to old age?" This question makes it unclear who exactly is receiving support or what the nature of the relationship between caregiver and recipient is. S. L. Brown, Nesse, Vinokur, and Smith (2003) measured instrumental support given to others (friends, relatives, and neighbors), excluding relationship partners. It is possible that those who are able to give support to others are least involved in caring for a close relationship partner. Being responsible for the care of a close relationship partner is presumably a very different experience from providing support to others in one's social network.

O'Reilly and colleagues (2008) did try to assess whether caregiving relationships were between spouses by examining marital status, but one cannot be certain that those who were married were necessarily taking care of their spouses. Also, S. L. Brown and colleagues (2003) examined emotional support given to spouses; however, they measured emotional support with a scale that typically assesses relationship quality, the Dyadic Adjustment Scale (Spanier, 1976), and two items asking participants whether they made their spouses feel loved and cared for and whether they were willing to listen if their spouses needed to talk. This emphasis on relationship quality and emotional as opposed to instrumental support is different from what is used in most other studies examining the association between caregiving and mortality. Finally, S. L. Brown and colleagues' (2009) study showing decreased mortality among spousal caregivers assessed caregiving based on the spouse's report of help received rather than the caregiver's report of help provided. It is unclear if the same results would have emerged if the caregiver's perspective was measured instead.

Studies Linking Caregiving with Positive Physical and Psychological Health Outcomes

Although the majority of studies show that caregiving is associated with poor health and impaired psychological functioning (Dunlop et al., 2005; Ory, Yee, Tennstedt, & Schulz, 2000; Schulz et al., 1997), some studies show positive health correlates (Beach, Schulz, Yee, & Jackson, 2000; W. M. Brown, Consedine, & Magai, 2005; Jenkins, Kabeto, & Langa, 2009; Taylor, Ford, & Dunbar, 1995). Like the mortality studies, most of these studies control for sociodemographic factors and baseline health status, decreasing the probability of a healthy-caregiver effect.

As with the mortality studies, inconsistencies may stem from differences in caregiver strain. For example, Beach, Schulz, Yee, and Jackson (2000) found that helping in the context of caregiving is associated with better health outcomes (decreased anxiety and depression); however, caregivers who experience more strain and who have highly impaired partners suffer from poorer health outcomes.

Sociodemographic characteristics may also serve as a proxy for caregiver strain. Jenkins, Kabeto, and Langa (2009) found that once age, education, and net worth were controlled for, the negative association between caregiving and health (Activities of Daily Living/ Instrumental Activities of Daily Living functioning and self-rated health) disappeared. Those who were older, less educated, and had a lower net worth were more likely to suffer the negative consequences of being a caregiver. Conversely, younger caregivers with low levels of strain may experience better health outcomes than non-caregivers. For example, Taylor and colleagues (1995) found a tendency for caregivers to report better health and functioning than non-caregivers over a 3-year period, however, the median number of caregiving hours per week was 7, caregivers were on average 55 years old, and many of the caregivers discontinued providing care over the 3-year period of their study.

In sum, the combination of feeling strained in the caregiving role and other vulnerabilities such as advanced age and low SES consistently yield negative health effects. At this time, a definitive single, well-designed study that shows how variations in SES, age, caregiving hours, and strain produce different health effects is lacking. Such a study would presumably show positive health effects for relatively high-SES, younger, less strained caregivers who spend relatively few hours providing care, and negative health effects for relatively low-SES, older, more strained caregivers who spend a large number of hours providing care.

Why Might Caregiving be Beneficial to Health?

The positive health effects of caregiving have been attributed mainly to the benefits of helping (Brown et al., 2003). This is based on empirical evidence that helping is associated with reduced stress (Cialdini, Darby, & Vincent, 1973; Midlarsky, 1991) and improved health (Schwartz & Sendor, 2000) and that older adults who volunteer have a reduced risk of morbidity and mortality (W. M. Brown et al., 2005; Krause, Herzog, & Baker, 1992; Musik, Herzog, & House, 1999; Oman, Thoresen, & McMahon, 1999). S. L. Brown and colleagues (2009) hypothesize that helping can serve as a stress buffer, citing prior findings that increased instrumental support given to other people accelerated recovery from depressive symptoms (S. L. Brown, House, Brown, & Smith, 2008). Suggested mechanisms for the stress-buffering effect include increased positive emotion (e.g., Cialdini & Kenrick, 1976), which can speed cardiovascular recovery from the effects of negative emotion (Fredrickson, Mancuso, Branigan, & Tugade, 2000), and increased levels of hormones such as oxytocin, which decreases activity in the hypothalamic-pituitary-adrenal axis and contributes to cellular repair and storage of nutrients (Heaphy & Dutton, 2008).

S. L. Brown and colleagues (2003) also provide an evolutionary explanation for the association between helping and longevity. They refer to kin selection theory (Hamilton, 1964a, 1964b) and reciprocal altruism theory (Trivers, 1971), which suggest that human reproductive success was contingent on the ability to give resources to relationship partners. Giving to others triggers a desire for self-preservation on the part of the giver and enables prolonged investment in kin (De Catanzaro, 1986) and reciprocal altruism.

Other researchers have emphasized the role of caregiving in enhancing relationships and providing personal strength and meaning to caregivers. For example, Motenko (1989) noted that "caregiving is expression of bonds which tie people to their loved ones" (p. 166) and is an important way of expressing intimacy, love, and basic emotions to another person. Motenko suggested that this expression is necessary to maintain personal continuity in values, self-respect, and identity, and this may be especially true for women, who often define their identity based on caring and nurturing others (Baker-Miller, 1976; Chodorow, 1978; Gilligan, 1982). Consistent with this, O'Reilly and colleagues (2008) found that the decrease in mortality associated with caregiving was larger for women.

Caring for a loved one can also provide meaning to the lives of caregivers. Farran, Keane-Hagerty, Salloway, Kupferer, and Wilken (1991) emphasized that the caregiving experience can provide opportunities for creative expression, as seen when caregivers develop innovative approaches to solving day-to-day challenges. Also, caregivers often feel a sense of fulfillment knowing that they are taking care of someone they love. Finding personal strength and fulfilling a duty to a loved one may promote caregivers' health, psychological well-being, and life satisfaction. Similarly, researchers have found that a sense of usefulness in old age is associated with better self-rated health and decreased mortality (Okamoto & Tanaka, 2004).

To capture the positive aspects of caregiving, researchers have developed scales such as the Caregiving Satisfaction Scale (Lawton, Kleban, Moss, Rovine, & Glickman, 1989), which includes items such as "You really enjoy being with (care recipient)?" and "Helping has made you feel closer to (care recipient)?" and the Positive Aspects of Caregiving measure (Tarlow et al., 2004) which includes two factors: Self Affirmation (e.g., "Providing help to (care recipient) has made me feel useful") and Outlook on Life (e.g., "Providing help to (care recipient) has enabled me to develop a more positive attitude toward life"). Using these scales as well as more specific questions, studies have shown that many caregivers experience satisfaction (Lawton et al., 1989), pleasure and rewards (Donelan et al., 2002; Wolff, Dy, Frick, & Kasper, 2007), enjoyment (Cohen, Gold, Shulman, & Zucchero, 1994), and uplifts and daily events that evoke joy (Pruchno, Michaels, & Potashnik, 1990) when caring for their family members (see Kramer, 1997, and Tarlow et al., 2004, for reviews). Measures assessing positive aspects of caregiving have been linked with enhanced well-being and health for caregivers (Cohen, Colantonio, & Vernich, 2002; Motenko, 1989; Pinquart & Sörenson, 2003b; see Kramer, 1997, for a review). For example, in a national sample of caregivers derived from the Canadian Study of Health and Aging, positive feelings about caring, such as companionship and a sense of fulfillment, were associated with fewer depressive symptoms, a reduced sense of burden, and better self-rated health (Cohen et al., 2002). In a meta-analysis, Pinquart and Sörensen (2003a) found that perceived uplifts of caregiving, such as feeling useful or experiencing increased closeness to the care recipient, were associated with lower levels of caregiver burden and depression. They also found that perceived uplifts were largely independent of objective caregiving stressors. Motenko (1989) found that among women caring at home for a husband with dementia, gratification was associated with greater well-being, and wives who perceived continuity in marital closeness since their partner's illness had greater gratification than those who perceived change. Thus there is reason to believe that caregiving is not only a source of stress but also has the potential to provide benefits to caregivers and enhance relationships. This may be especially true for caregivers who are in the early stages of caregiving careers, are less strained, and provide care to family members who are less impaired.

■ ECONOMIC COSTS OF CARE

Informal caregivers have been characterized as the backbone of our long-term-care system, providing the majority of long-term care in the US. While this is a great benefit to society, it comes at a considerable cost to some caregivers in terms of their health and well-being, as noted previously in this chapter. In addition, caregiving can also have direct economic consequences because it may conflict with the ability to engage in paid employment. Middle-aged women at the peak of their earning power provide the majority of care to older disabled relatives (National Alliance for Caregiving and American Association of Retired Persons, 2009). The increasing labor force participation of women, along with the increasing demand for care, raise important questions about how effectively and at what cost the roles of caregiver and worker can be combined.

Although there are many issues one might address on the relationship between work and caregiving, we focus here on two central questions. The first question concerns the causal relationship between caregiving and employment. Does employment affect caregiving or does caregiving affect employment? The decision to provide care for an ill or disabled relative may hinge on the potential caregiver's employment status, magnitude of caregiving demands, and job flexibility. Employed people with little flexibility in their jobs who are faced with extensive caregiving demands may be less likely to assume the caregiving role. Indeed, the fact that men are a minority among caregivers may be due in part to their higher labor force participation rates. And for those already employed, increased caregiving may necessitate reducing work hours or stopping work completely. Thus causal processes may operate in both directions: Being employed reduces the likelihood of becoming a caregiver, and becoming a caregiver reduces the likelihood of maintaining employment.

A second question concerns the possible moderating role of employment on the relation between caregiving and the psychosocial well-being of the caregiver. Although employment is generally beneficial to women's health (Ross & Mirowsky, 1995), is this true in the context of caregiving, where care demands may compete with work demands?

Does Employment Affect Caregiving?

Numerous studies have explored the effects of caregiving on employment, but relatively few have asked whether employment affects caregiving. Several studies suggest that social structural factors like employment status explain at least in part gender differences in caregiving. It is well established that adult daughters spend more time giving assistance to their parents than do sons, and researchers have been interested in assessing the extent to which this gap is explained by structural variation in employment rates and the kinds of positions that women and men tend to hold. Using data from the National Survey of Families and Households, Sarkisian and Gerstel (2004) found that both employment status and job characteristics (e.g., wages and self-employment) are important factors in explaining the gender gap in help given to parents. Similar results are reported by Gerstel and Gallagher (1994), who show that the differential helping rates of wives vs. husbands are in part explained by different rates of employment. Employed wives give more help than employed husbands, but less than homemaker wives. Wives employed in jobs similar to those of men give care in ways similar to men.

The 1996 General Social Survey of Canada addressed this question by comparing whether paid employment reduces the provision or intensity of specific types of help offered by women to older parents and parents-in-law. Rosenthal, Hayward, Martin-Matthews, & Denton (2004) focused on a subsample of women aged 40–64 who had at least one living parent or parent-in-law. The results showed that employment status was not significantly related to the total amount of time spent helping parents or parents-in-law, although there was some variability in the type of help provided as a function of employment status. Overall, being employed did not reduce women's provision of help. Using British data, Henz (2006) also found that whether a person worked part time or full time did not affect caregiving, nor did most aspects of job flexibility. There is some evidence that among dual-earner couples, husbands and wives strategically allocate caregiving responsibilities to accommodate their respective work roles, although women still carry the heavier caregiving load (Chesley & Moen, 2006).

Does Caregiving Affect Employment?

The majority of research on caregiving and work has focused on the effects of caregiving on women's employment. The primary hypothesis tested in these studies is that informal care provision reduces labor force participation. Because caregiving tends to occur during peak employment years (ages 35–64), it has the potential to profoundly alter the economic well-being of women.

Early findings in this line of research were equivocal, with some studies showing reductions in labor force participation while others showed no effect. For example, McLanahan and Monson (1990) found that being a caregiver reduced married women's chances of being employed and lowered the number of hours they worked. Doty, Jackson, and Crown (1998) found that employed female caregivers rearranged work to manage challenges associated with both being employed and serving as a caregiver. Ettner (1995a, 1995b) found that caregiving reduced women's hours worked for pay, and that impact on employment status was related to the magnitude of caregiving demands. On the other hand, Wolf and Soldo (1994) found no effect of caregiving to parents on married daughters' hours worked for pay, and Moen, Robinson, and Fields (1994) found that caregiving did not interrupt women's labor force participation. Multiple factors contribute to this mixed bag of findings, including the fact that many of the early studies were cross-sectional, making it difficult to infer causality; variability in the type of help being provided (e.g., ADL vs. IADL assistance); and varying definitions of caregiving (e.g., some studies define caregiving as coresidence with elderly household members).

Recent longitudinal studies have helped clarify this issue. Pavalko and Artis (1997) used data from the National Longitudinal Survey of Mature Women to examine the causal relationship between employment and caring for an ill or disabled friend or relative over a three-year period. They found that employment status does not affect whether or not women start caregiving, but that women who do start are more likely to reduce employment hours or stop work. For their sample of women in late midlife, the causal relationship between employment and caregiving was largely unidirectional, with women reducing hours to meet caregiving demands. Similar findings were reported by Spiess and Schneider (2002) in an analysis of midlife caregiving employment in Europe, by Kneipp, Castleman, and Gailor (2004) and Henz (2006) in analyses of low-income caregivers, by Latif (2006) in a study of the relations between caregiving and labor market behavior among Canadian adults, and by Johnson and LoSasso (2006). These results show that time spent helping parents strongly reduces female labor supply at midlife and that this effect is stronger among individuals of lower social class.

Wakabayashi and Donato (2005) used two waves of data (1987 and 1992) from the National Survey of Families and Households to examine whether and how caregiving transitions affect women's labor force participation, and the implications of those transitions for their earnings. They found that the initiation of parental caregiving led to a substantial reduction in caregivers' weekly hours worked and annual earnings. However, the effects were different across various subgroups. Younger women (aged 19–25) and older women (46 years and older) experienced large declines in their hours worked and corresponding reductions in average income of $750 and $3064, respectively. Women with less than a high school education also showed large declines in hours worked. These findings were extended in a subsequent study focusing on the long-term consequences of eldercare by asking how caring for elderly parents affects women's subsequent risk of living in poverty (Wakabayashi & Donato, 2006). Using the Health and Retirement Study longitudinal panel data, they showed that being a caregiver in 1991 increased women's risks of living in households with incomes below the poverty threshold, receiving public assistance, and being covered by Medicaid in 1999. Caregivers who spent 20 hours a week assisting their parents with personal care were 25% more likely than non-caregivers to live in poverty, 27% more likely to be recipients of public assistance, and 46% more likely to receive Medicaid eight years later, controlling for race, education, marital status, household income, and health.

Overall, recent findings indicate that elder caregiving has both short- and long-term economic impacts on female caregivers. Employed caregivers can absorb low levels of caregiving demand (e.g., 14 hours or less per week) with little impact on their labor force participation. However, heavy-duty caregiving demands (e.g., 20 hours or more per week) are associated with significant work adjustment involving either reduced hours or stopping work altogether, and with associated declines in annual incomes. Women with less than a high school education are most vulnerable to these negative effects. These short-term effects increase the probability of long-term negative impacts in the form of lower economic and health status of the caregiver. The long-term impacts may be attributable in part to the difficulty of re-entering the labor force once caregivers stop working (Pavalko & Artis, 1997; Spiess & Schneider, 2002; Wakabyashi & Donato, 2005).

Does Employment Affect the Burden or Stress of Care Provision?

The vast majority of caregiving literature has focused on the nature of caregiving demands and their impact on caregiver burden and physical and mental health. This literature has documented significant psychiatric and physical morbidity among caregivers exposed to high levels of chronic caregiving stress. A subset of this literature has focused on the role of work as a moderator of the relation between caregiving demands and caregiver well-being. Two opposing models have been proposed to explain the effects of multiple roles on well-being. One perspective (e.g., the scarcity hypothesis, depletion perspective, or role conflict theory) argues that multiple roles deplete women's limited energy and resources, resulting in adverse health outcomes. The second perspective (e.g., the expansion hypothesis, role enrichment hypothesis, or positive spillover effects) asserts that benefits accrue to people who operate in multiple roles or domains because they increase opportunities for prestige, recognition, and financial reward, which in turn can bolster women's self-concept and well-being (Bainbridge, Cregan, & Kulik, 2006; Cannuscio et al., 2004; Neal & Hammer, 2007).

Support for both perspectives can be found when they are applied to caregiving and work. For example, several early studies showed that caregivers who combine family care with work responsibilities report higher levels of physical and emotional stress (Brody, 1985; Enright & Friss, 1987; Meisenheimer, 1990; Neal, Chapman, Ingersoll-Dayton, & Emlen, 1993; Steuve & O'Donnell, 1989). In contrast, Martire, Stephens, and Atienza (1997) found protective effects of full-time employment for women involved in parent care. Skaff and Pearlin (1992) also found that caregivers who were involved in an outside work role experienced significantly less stress than caregivers who were not. The former reported greater self-worth, more personal satisfaction, and greater ability to combat fears of inadequacy. In their review of this literature, Martire and Stephens (2003) conclude that while parent care and employment often conflict, occupying both roles can be beneficial for the health of adult daughters. The positive effects of work on caregiver well-being may be due to the greater amount of time away from caregiving (work may provide respite or distraction from caregiving); the fact that full-time workers enjoy higher pay and benefits, enabling them to outsource some tasks; and the fact that the workplace may be an important source of social support for caregivers. Finally, a number of studies report that employment status does not confer additional mental health risk or benefit to informal caregivers (Cannuscio et al., 2004).

The resolution of these disparate literatures likely rests with complex interactions involving the nature of the caregiving experience and the characteristics of the work role. Bainbridge et al. (2006) suggest that type of disability (mental vs. nonmental) may interact with hours of work to determine caregiver stress outcomes. They found that spending more time in a work role generally had no effect on caregiver stress outcomes. However, caregivers who were caring for a person with a mental disability experienced significantly fewer stress outcomes as they spent more hours engaged in outside work. Chesley and Moen (2006), Neal and Hammer (2007), and Fredriksen and Scharlach (1997) emphasize the importance of workplace characteristics to caregiving outcomes. Factors such as job classification (e.g., salaried vs. hourly workers), work demand, work control, workplace support, and flexibility have the potential of contributing to or alleviating caregiver stress. Unraveling causal relationships between work, caregiving, and caregiver distress will require ambitious studies that not only examine the association among these factors but also follow adults into and out of caregiving and work roles.

■ CONCLUSION

Family caregiving is a dynamic process that at any point can be characterized by multiple factors. Although its onset may be insidious, it has a time dimension typically measured in months or years and an endpoint marked by the death of the care recipient, sometimes preceded by placement in a long-term care facility. It also has an intensity dimension, measured in hours of care provided or the amount and type of care provided. Duration and intensity tend to covary; inasmuch as illness and disability in late life typically increase over time, the intensity of care provided increases as well, as the caregiver moves through the middle and late stages of a caregiving episode. Finally, because caregiving is an intensely interpersonal experience, it has a strong emotional component. The attitudes, behaviors, and emotions of both caregiver and care recipient undoubtedly play a key role in defining the caregiving experience.

Our own recent work draws attention to the effects of the care recipient's suffering—which also tends to increase with time and intensity of care provided—and the role it plays in shaping the caregiver's response to caregiving (Monin & Schulz, 2009; Schulz et al., 2007, 2008, 2009). We differentiate three types of suffering—physical, psychological, and existential/spiritual—and in several studies show that each independently contributes to caregiver psychological and physical morbidity. Expressions of suffering provide important signals of the need for help, which activate responses in humans through mechanisms such as cognitive empathy, mimicry, and conditioned learning. From an evolutionary perspective, it is critical that mammals have well-developed systems for signaling and responding to distress. Young children need to be able to communicate when they are suffering, and their parents need to respond to signs of suffering for the survival and optimal development of their offspring. Signaling systems such as the expression of pain are clearly innate, although they are likely to become more elaborated and nuanced through experience and learning. Some components of the response system, such as mimicry, may also be innate but are likely further developed through experience and learning. By middle and late adulthood both systems are highly entrenched and serve as part of the motivational system that underlies caregiving. What makes caregiving in late life uniquely challenging is that the ability to effectively respond to suffering may be compromised, particularly in the late stages of a caregiving career when there is little that anyone can do to alleviate the suffering of the care recipient.

In general, we would expect the negative effects of caregiving to be greatest when all three factors—duration of caregiving, intensity of caregiving, and the magnitude of care-recipient suffering—are at their peak. This combination is most likely to lead to chronic stress experiences characterized by high demand but low control and mismatch between effort and reward (Dimsdale, 2008). Caregivers faced with prolonged and daunting care demands with little reward in terms of reducing care-recipient suffering should be at highest risk for negative outcomes. Our views here diverge somewhat from the perspective of S. L. Brown et al. (2003) and W. M. Brown et al. (2005), who argue that helping is fulfilling in its own right; our perspective is that caregivers perceive helping that fails to reduce care-recipient suffering as futile and derive little benefit from it. Conversely, the benefits of helping should be maximized when they effectively relieve the suffering of another individual. A more detailed description of these ideas can be found in our recent theoretical discussion of suffering in the context of caregiving (Monin & Schulz, 2009).

We have seen that caregiving is associated with both positive and negative outcomes for the caregiver. It can elevate or depress mood, increase or decrease health and well-being, and contribute to a sense of meaning to life or to despair. For some individuals the caregiving role competes with the work role and the latter can serve as a source of additional stress. Research on the effects of work on caregiving and, conversely, on the effects of caregiving on work suggests causal effects in both directions: Employment status affects who takes on the caregiving role, and the onset of caregiving affects hours worked and whether one stays in the workforce. Because labor force participation for both men and women continues to change, with more women entering the labor force and both men and women increasingly working after retirement, it will be important to continue to monitor the relation between caregiving and work.

The predominantly negative effects on caregivers observed in the literature are likely due to the fact that most caregiving studies selectively focus on the middle to late stages of a caregiving episode, when both care demands and care recipient suffering are high, and caregivers have little control over recipient outcomes and little reward for the time and effort expended. Conversely, studies that show positive effects of caregiving likely reflect caregiving experiences that afford high levels of control over care-recipient outcomes such as suffering and favorable effort–reward ratios. Identifying how and when caregivers transition from a positive to a negative caregiving experience is an important unresolved question that should receive high priority in future research. Finding an answer to these questions will require fine-grained longitudinal studies of caregiving that look at caregivers' behavior and emotion regulation strategies as well as care recipients' response.

■ REFERENCES

Abramson, J. H.,Terespolsky, L., Brook, J. G., & Kark, S. L. (1965). Cornell Medical Index as a health measure in epidemiological studies. *British Journal of Preventive and Social Medicine, 19,* 103–110.

Bainbridge, H. T. J., Cregan, C., & Kulik, C. T. (2006). The effect of multiple roles on caregiver stress outcomes. *Journal of Applied Psychology, 91*(2), 490–497.

Baker-Miller, J. (1976). *Towards a new psychology of women.* New York, NY: Penguin.

Beach, S. R., Schulz, R., Yee, J. L., & Jackson, S. (2000). Negative and positive health effects of caring for a disabled spouse: Longitudinal findings from the Caregiver Health Effects Study. *Psychology and Aging, 15,* 259–271.

Brody, E. M. (1985). Parent care as a normative family stress. *The Gerontologist, 25,* 19–29.

Brown, S. L., House, J. S., Brown, R. M., & Smith, D. M. (2008). Coping with spousal loss: The buffering effects of helping behavior. *Personality and Social Psychology Bulletin, 34,* 849–861.

Brown, S. L., Nesse, R. M., Vinokur, A., & Smith, D. M. (2003). Providing social support may be more beneficial than receiving it: Results from a prospective study of mortality. *Psychological Science, 14,* 320–327.

Brown, S. L., Smith, D. M., Schulz, R., Kabeto, M. U., Ubel, P. A., Poulin, M., . . . Langa, K. M. (2009). Caregiving behavior is associated with decreased mortality risk. *Psychological Science, 20*(4), 488–494.

Brown, W. M., Consedine, N. S., & Magai, C. (2005). Altruism relates to health in an ethnically diverse sample of older adults. *Journal of Gerontology: Social Sciences, 60B*(3), 143–152.

Burton, L. C., Zdaniuk, B., Schulz, R., Jackson, S., & Hirsch, C. (2003). Transitions in spousal caregiving. *The Gerontologist, 43,* 230–241.

Cannuscio, C. C., Colditz, G. A., Rimm, E. B., Berkman, L. F., Jones, C. P., & Kawachi, I. (2004). Employment status, social ties, and caregivers' mental health. *Social Science & Medicine, 58*(7), 1247–1256.

Chesley, N., & Moen, P. (2006). When workers care—dual-earner couples' caregiving strategies, benefit use, and psychological well-being. *American Behavioral Scientist, 49*(9), 1248–1269.

Chodorow, N. (1978). *The reproduction of mothering.* Berkeley and Los Angeles, California: University of California Press.

Christakis, N., & Allison, P. D. (2006). Mortality after the hospitalization of a spouse. *New England Journal of Medicine, 354,* 719–730.

Cialdini, R. B., Darby, B. K., & Vincent, J. E. (1973). Transgression and altruism: A case for hedonism. *Journal of Experimental Social Psychology, 9,* 502–516.

Cialdini, R. B., & Kenrick, D. T. (1976). Altruism as hedonism: A social development perspective on the relationship of negative mood state and helping. *Journal of Personality and Social Psychology, 34,* 907–914.

Cohen, C. A., Colantonio, A., & Vernich, L. (2002). Positive aspects of caregiving: Rounding out the caregiving experience. *International Journal of Geriatric Psychiatry, 17*(2), 184–188.

Cohen, C. A., Gold, D. P., Shulman, K. I., & Zucchero, C. A. (1994). Positive aspects in caregiving: An overlooked variable in research. *Canadian Journal on Aging, 13,* 378–391.

De Cantanzaro, D. (1986). A mathematical model of evolutionary pressures regulating self-preservation and self-destruction. *Suicide and Life-Threatening Behavior, 16,* 166–181.

Dimsdale, J. E. (2008). Psychological stress and cardiovascular disease. *Journal of the American College of Cardiology, 51*(13), 1237–1246.

Donelan, K., Hill, C. A., Hoffman, C., Scoles, K., Hollander Feldman, P., Levine, C., & Gould, D. (2002). Challenged to care: Informal caregivers in a changing health system. *Health Affairs, 21*(4), 222–231.

Doty, P., Jackson, M. E., & Crown, W. (1998). The impact of female caregivers' employment status on patterns of formal and informal eldercare. *The Gerontologist, 38*(3), 331–341.

Dunlop, D. D., Semaink, P., Song, J., Manheim, L. M., Shih, V., & Chang, R. W. (2005). Risk factors for functional decline in older adults with arthritis. *Arthritis & Rheumatism, 52*(4), 1274–1282.

Enright, R. B. & Friss, L. (1987). *Employed caregivers of brain-impaired adults.* San Francisco, CA: Family Survival Project.

Ettner, S. L. (1995a). The impact of "parent care" on female labor supply decisions. *Demography, 32*(1), 63–80.

Ettner, S. L. (1995b). The opportunity costs of elder care. *Journal of Human Resources, 31*(1), 189–205.

Farran, C. J., Keane-Hagerty, E., Salloway, S., Kupferer, S., & Wilken, C. S. (1991). Finding meaning: An alternative paradigm for Alzheimer's disease family caregivers. *The Gerontologist, 31*(4), 483–489.

Frederickson, B., Mancuso, R., Branigan, C., & Tugade, M. (2000). The undoing effect of positive emotions. *Motivation and Emotion, 24,* 237–258.

Fredman, L., Cauley, J. A., Satterfield, S., Simonsick, E., Spencer, S. M., Ayonayon, H. N., & Harris, T. B. (2008). Caregiving, mortality, and mobility decline. *Archives of Internal Medicine, 168*(19), 2154–2162.

Fredman, L., Doros, G., Cauley, J. A., Hillier, T. A., & Hochberg, M. C. (2010). Caregiving, metabolic syndrome indicators, and 1-year decline in walking speed: Results of caregiver-SOF. *Journal of Gerontology: Medical Sciences, 65A*(5), 565–572.

Fredriksen, K. I., & Scharlach, A. E. (1997). Caregiving and employment: The impact of workplace characteristics on role strain. *Journal of Gerontological Social Work, 28*(4), 3–22.

Gerstel, N., & Gallagher, S. (1994). Caring for kith and kin—gender, employment, and the privatization of care. *Social Problems, 41*(4), 519–539.

Gilligan, C. (1982). *In a different voice.* Cambridge, MA: Harvard University Press.

Gouin, J. P., Hantsoo, L., & Kiecolt-Glaser, J. K. (2008). Immune dysregulation and chronic stress among older adults: A review. *Neuroimmunomodulation, 15,* 251–259.

Haley, W. E., Roth, D. L., Howard, G., & Safford, M. M. (2010). Caregiving strain and estimated risk for stroke and coronary heart disease among spouse caregivers. *Stroke, 41*(2), 331–336.

Hamilton, W. D. (1964a). The genetic evolution of social behavior: I. *Journal of Theoretical Biology, 7,* 1–16.

Hamilton, W. D. (1964b). The genetic evolution of social behavior: II. *Journal of Theoretical Biology, 7,* 17–52.

Heaphy, E. D. & Dutton, J. E. (2008). Positive social interactions and the human body at work. Linking organizations and physiology. *Academy of Management Review, 33,* 137–162.

Henz, U. (2006). Informal caregiving at working age: Effects of job characteristics and family configuration. *Journal of Marriage and Family, 68,* 411–429.

Hirst, M. (2005). Career distress: A prospective, population-based study. *Social Science & Medicine, 61,* 697–708.

Jenkins, K. R., Kabeto, M. U., & Langa, K. M. (2009). Does caring for your spouse harm one's health? Evidence from a United States nationally-representative sample of older adults. *Ageing & Society, 29,* 277–293.

Johnson, R. W., & LoSasso, A. T. (2006). The impact of elder care on women's labor supply. *Inquiry, 43*(3), 195–210.

Kneipp, S. M., Castleman, J. B., & Gailor, N. (2004). Informal caregiving burden: An overlooked aspect of the lives and health of women transitioning from welfare to employment? *Public Health Nursing, 21*(1), 24–31.

Kramer, B. J. (1997). Gain in the caregiving experience: Where are we? What next? *The Gerontologist, 37*(2), 218–232.

Krause, N., Herzog, A. R., & Baker, E. (1992). Providing support to others and well-being in later life. *Journal of Gerontology: Social Sciences, 47*(5), 300–311.

Latif, E. (2006). Labour supply effects of informal caregiving in Canada. *Canadian Public Policy—Analysis de Politiques, 32*(4), 413–429.

Lawton, M. P., Kleban, M. H., Moss, M., Rovine, M., & Glickman, A. (1989). Measuring caregiving appraisal. *Journal of Gerontology: Social Sciences, 44,* 61–71.

Lawton, M. P., Moss, M., Hoffman, C., & Perkinson, M. (2000). Two transitions in daughters' caregiving careers. *The Gerontologist, 40,* 437–448.

Lee, S. L., Colditz, G. A., Berkman, L. F., & Kawachi, I. (2003). Caregiving and risk of coronary heart disease in U.S. women: A prospective study. *American Journal of Preventive Medicine, 24*(2), 113–119.

Marks, N., Lambert, J. D. & Choi, H. (2002). Transitions to caregiving, gender, and psychological well-being: A prospective U.S. national study. *Journal of Marriage and Family, 64,* 657–667.

Martire, L. M., & Stephens, M. A. P. (2003). Juggling parent care and employment responsibilities: The dilemmas of adult daughter caregivers in the workforce. *Sex Roles, 48*(3–4), 167–173.

Martire, L. M., Stephens, M. A. P., & Atienza, A. A. (1997). The interplay of work and caregiving: Relationships between role satisfaction, role involvement, and caregivers' well-being. *Journal of Gerontology: Social Sciences, 52*(5), S279-S289.

McLanahan, S. S., & Monson, R. A. (1990). *Care for the elderly: Prevalence and consequences.* (NSFH Working Paper Number 18). Madison: Center for Demography and Ecology, University of Wisconsin.

Meisenheimer, J. (1990). Employee absences in 1989: A new look at data from the CPS. *Monthly Labor Review, 113*(8), 28–33.

Midlarsky, E. (1991). Helping as coping. In M. S. Clark (Ed.), *Prosocial behavior* (pp. 238–264). Thousand Oaks, CA: Sage.

Moen, P., Robinson, J., & Fields, V. (1994). Women's work and caregiving roles: A life course approach. *Journal of Gerontology: Social Sciences, 49,* S176-S186.

Monin, J. K., & Schulz, R. (2009). Interpersonal effects of suffering in older adult caregiving relationships. *Psychology and Aging, 24*(3), 681–695.

Motenko, A. K. (1989). The frustrations, gratifications, and well-being of dementia caregivers. *The Gerontologist, 29*, 166–172.

Musik, M. Herzog, A. R., & House, J. S. (1999). Volunteering and mortality among older adults: Findings from a national sample. *Journal of Gerontology: Social Sciences, 54B*, S137-S180.

National Alliance for Caregiving and American Association of Retired Persons. (2009). *Caregiving in the U.S.* Washington, DC.

Neal, M. B., Chapman, N. J., Ingersoll-Dayton, B., & Emlen, A. (1993). *Balancing work and caregiving.* Newbury Park, CA: Sage.

Neal, M. B. & Hammer, L. B. (2007). Working couples caring for children and aging parents: Effects on work and well-being. Mahwah, NJ: Lawrence Erlbaum.

Nieboer, A., Schulz, R., Scheier, M., & Matthews, K. (1998). Spousal caregivers' activity restriction and depression: A model for changes over time. *Social Science & Medicine, 47*, 1361–1371.

Okamoto, K., & Tanaka, Y. (2004). Subjective usefulness and 6-year mortality risks among elderly persons in Japan. *Journal of Gerontology: Social Sciences, 59B*(5), 246–249.

Oman, D., Thoresen, C., & McMahon, K. (1999). Volunteerism and mortality among the community dwelling elderly. *Journal of Health Psychology, 4*, 301–316.

O'Reilly, D., Connolly, S., Rosato, M., & Patterson, C. (2008). Is caring associated with an increased risk of mortality? A longitudinal study. *Social Science & Medicine, 67*, 1282–1290.

Ory, M. G., Yee, J. L., Tennstedt, S. L., & Schulz, R. (2000). The extent and impact of dementia care: Unique challenges experienced by family caregivers. In R. Schulz (Ed.), *Handbook of dementia caregiving: Evidence-based interventions for family caregivers* (pp. 1–32). New York, NY: Springer.

Pavalko, E. K., & Artis, J. E. (1997). Women's caregiving and paid work: Causal relationships in late midlife. *Journal of Gerontology: Social Sciences, 52B*(4), S170–S179.

Pinquart, M., & Sörensen, S. (2003a). Associations of stressors and uplifts of caregiving with caregiver burden and depressive mood: a meta-analysis. *Journal of Gerontology: Social Sciences, 58*, P112–P128.

Pinquart, M., & Sörensen, S. (2003b). Differences between caregivers and noncaregivers in psychological health and physical health: A meta-analysis. *Psychology and Aging, 18*(2), 250–267.

Pinquart, M., & Sörensen, S. (2007). Correlates of physical health of informal caregivers: A meta-analysis. *Journal of Gerontology: Social Sciences, 62*, P126–P137.

Pruchno, R. A., Michaels, J. E., & Potashnik, S. L. (1990). Predictors of institutionalization among Alzheimer's disease victims with caregiving spouses. *Journal of Gerontology: Social Sciences, 45*, 259–266.

Rosenthal, C. J., Hayward, L., Martin-Matthews, A., & Denton, M. (2004). Help to older parents and parents-in-law: Does paid employment constrain women's helping behaviour? *Canadian Journal on Aging (Supplement)*, S97–S112.

Ross, C. E., & Mirowsky, J. (1995). Does employment affect health? *Journal of Health and Social Behavior, 36*(3), 230–243.

Sarkisian, N., & Gerstel, N. (2004). Explaining the gender gap in help to parents: The importance of employment. *Journal of Marriage and the Family, 66*(2), 431–451.

Schulz, R., & Beach, S. (1999). Caregiving as a risk factor for mortality: The Caregiver Health Effects Study. *Journal of the American Medical Association, 282*, 2215–2219.

Schulz, R., Beach S. R., Hebert, R., Martire, L. M., Monin, J. K, Tompkins, C.A. , & Albert, S.M. (2009). Spousal suffering and partner's depression and cardiovascular disease: The Cardiovascular Health Study. *American Journal of Geriatric Psychiatry, 17*(3), 246–254.

Schulz, R., Belle, S. H., Czaja, S. J., McGinnis, K. A., Stevens, A., & Zhang, S. (2004). Long-term care placement of dementia patients and caregiver health and well-being. *Journal of the American Medical Association, 292*, 961–967.

Schulz, R., Hebert, R. S., Dew, M. A., Brown, S. L., Scheier, M. F., Beach, S. R., . . . Nichols, L. (2007). Patient suffering and caregiver compassion: New opportunities for research, practice, and policy. *The Gerontologist, 47*(1), 4–13.

Schulz, R., McGinnis, K. A., Zhang, S., Martire, L. M., Hebert, R. S., Beach, S. R., . . . Belle, S. H. (2008). Dementia patient suffering and caregiver depression. *Alzheimer Disease & Associated Disorders, 22*(2), 170–176.

Schulz, R., Mendelsohn, A. B., Haley, W. E., Mahoney, D., Allen, R. S., Zhang, S., . . . Belle, S. H. (2003). End of life care and the effects of bereavement on family caregivers of persons with dementia. *New England Journal of Medicine, 349*, 1936–1942.

Schulz, R., Newsom, J., Mittelmark, M., Burton, L., Hirsch, C., & Jackson, S. (1997). Health effects of caregiving: The Caregiver Health Effects Study: An ancillary study of the Cardiovascular Health Study. *Annals of Behavioral Medicine, 19*, 110–116.

Schulz, R., O'Brien, A. T., Bookwala, J., & Fleissner, K. (1995). Psychiatric and physical morbidity effects of Alzheimer's disease caregiving: Prevalence, correlates, and causes. *The Gerontologist, 35*, 771–791.

Schulz, R., Visintainer, P., & Williamson, G. M. (1990). Psychiatric and physical morbidity effect of caregiving. *Journal of Gerontology: Social Sciences, 45*, P181–P191.

Schwartz, C., & Sendor, M. (2000). Helping others helps oneself: Response shift effects in peer support. In K. Schmaling (Ed.), *Adaptation to changing health: Response shift in quality-of-life research* (pp. 43–70). Washington, DC: American Psychological Association.

Seltzer, M. M., & Li, L. W. (2000). The dynamics of caregiving: Transitions during a three-year prospective study. *The Gerontologist, 40*, 165–178.

Shaw, W. S., Patterson, T. L., Semple, S. J., Ho, S., Irwin, M. R., Hauger, R. L., & Grant, I. (1997). Longitudinal analysis of multiple indicators of health decline among spousal caregivers. *Annals of Behavioral Medicine, 19*, 101–109.

Skaff, M. M., & Pearlin, L. I. (1992). Caregiving: Role engulfment and the loss of self. *The Gerontologist, 32*, 656–664.

Spanier, G. B. (1976). Measuring dyadic adjustment: New scales for assessing the quality of marriage and similar dyads. *Journal of Marriage and the Family, 38*, 15–28.

Spiess, C. K., & Schneider, U. (2002). *Midlife caregiving & employment: An analysis of adjustments in work hours and informal care for female employees in Europe* (Working Paper No. 9, pp. 1–36). European Network of Economic Policy Research Institutes. Available at: *http://www.enepri.org*

Steuve, A., & O'Donnell, L. (1989). Interactions between women and their elderly parents: Constraints of daughters' employment. *Research on Aging, 11*(3), 331–353.

Tarlow, B. J., Wisniewski, S., Belle, S., Rubert, M., Ory, M. G., & Gallagher-Thompson, D. (2004). Positive aspects of caregiving: Contributions of the REACH project to the development of new measures for Alzheimer's caregiving. *Research on Aging, 26*(4), 429–453.

Taylor, R., Ford, G., & Dunbar, M. (1995). The effects of caring on health: A community-based longitudinal study. *Social Science & Medicine, 40*(10), 1407–1415.

Teri, L., Logsdon, R., Uomoto, J., & McCurry, S. M. (1997). Behavioral treatment of depression in dementia patients: A controlled clinical trial. *Journal of Gerontology: Social Sciences, 52*, 159–166.

Trivers, R. L. (1971). The evolution of reciprocal altruism. *Quarterly Review of Biology, 46*, 35–57.

Vitaliano, P. P., Zhang, J., & Scanlan, J. M. (2003). Is caregiving hazardous to one's physical health? A meta-analysis. *Psychological Bulletin, 129,* 946–972.

Wakabayashi, C., & Donato, K. M. (2005). The consequences of caregiving: Effects on women's employment and earnings. *Population Research and Policy Review, 24,* 467–488.

Wakabayashi, C., & Donato, K. M. (2006). Does caregiving increase poverty among women in later life? Evidence from the Health and Retirement Survey. *Journal of Health and Social Behavior, 47,* 258–274.

Wolf, D. A., & Soldo B. J. (1994). Married women's allocation of time to employment and care of elderly parents. *The Journal of Human Resources, 29*(4), 1259–1276.

Wolff, J. L., Dy, S. M., Frick, K. D., & Kasper, J. D. (2007). End-of-life care: Findings from a national survey of informal caregivers. *Archives of Internal Medicine, 167,* 40–46.

12 Too Close for Comfort?

Lessons from Excesses and Deficits of Compassion in Psychopathology

■ JUNE GRUBER AND DACHER KELTNER

Compassion is a central focus of many spiritual and ethical traditions, from Buddhism and Confucianism to Christianity. It is a state and disposition people seek to cultivate on the assumption it will make for more morally coherent lives and more cooperative communities. The empirical evidence bears this assumption out: Elevated levels of compassion promote greater altruism, relationship-enhancing behaviors, and cooperation (for a review see Goetz, Keltner, & Simon-Thomas, 2010).

In the present chapter, we raise an intriguing question not considered explicitly in the literature on compassion: Are there pathological levels of compassion? One approach to begin to address this question is to examine individuals who exhibit notable absences or extremes in compassion. Intuitively, it would seem that people who experience little compassion would encounter several kinds of problems in social adjustment—troubles attending to others in need, a lack of empathy, an absence of strong social connections. It is less intuitive, however, to consider the scenario of how and for whom experiencing too much compassion—an overly attentive concern for the welfare of others—might yield maladaptive social and emotional outcomes.

The aim of our essay is to give an overview of emergent findings related to the experience and expression of compassion in psychopathology. We focus on three "themes" for considering the empirical relationship between psychopathology and disturbed compassion. A first theme is that certain psychopathologies involve an *excess* of compassion-related behaviors. A second theme is that psychopathologies are often noteworthy because compassion is absent. Our final theme is that some psychopathologies may permit preservations of compassion despite difficulties in other domains of functioning.

■ DEFINING COMPASSION

We define compassion as a feeling that (a) results from witnessing another's suffering and (b) motivates a subsequent desire to help (e.g., Lazarus, 1991; Nussbaum, 1996, 2001). Our characterization contrasts with the view of compassion as an attitude (e.g., Sprecher & Fehr, 2005), or as a general benevolent response to others regardless of blame (Post, 2002) or suffering. Compassion is distinct from empathy or the vicarious experience of another's emotions (Lazarus, 1991) as well as perspective taking, which is an effortful process in which one imagines how another feels (Eisenberg & Miller, 1987). "Sympathy" is often used to define a similar state to what we are describing as compassion (e.g., Darwin, 2004; Eisenberg et al., 2007; Feather, 2006; Post, 2002). Our definition of compassion overlaps considerably with researchers' descriptions of empathic concern (Davis, Hall, & Meyer, 2003), empathy (Batson, Ahmad, Lishner, & Tsang, 2002), and pity (Nussbaum, 1996; Weiner, Perry, & Magnusson, 1988), although pity most typically refers to a feeling of concern for someone inferior to the self (Fiske, Cuddy, Glick, & Xu, 2002).

■ EVOLUTIONARY FUNCTIONS OF COMPASSION

Sympathy will have been increased through natural selection; for those communities, which included the greatest number of the most sympathetic members, would flourish best, and rear the greatest number of offspring. (Darwin, 2004, p. 130)

In the quote above, Darwin describes what appears to be a core function of compassion: ensuring the welfare of vulnerable others and offspring. In more specific terms, compassion is thought to have emerged as the affective element of a caregiving system, designed to help raise vulnerable offspring to the age of viability (thus ensuring that genes are more likely to be replicated). Human offspring are born more dependent on their caregivers than those of any other mammal, requiring evolutionarily unprecedented care to reach the age of independence and reproductive engagement (Bowlby, 1969; Hrdy, 2000; Mikulincer & Shaver, 2003). As Darwin reasoned, this tendency to reliably experience state-like feelings of compassion for vulnerable young offspring in moments of need or suffering would have directly increased the chances of offspring surviving and ultimately reaching the age of reproductive viability.

Across radically different cultures, caregiving observed in kin and nonkin alike involves similar behaviors, including soothing touch, skin-to-skin contact, and specific vocalizations, some of which resemble the displays of compassion we will detail in a later section. The nonhuman primates most closely related to humans—chimpanzees and bonobos—have been observed to show caregiving oriented toward vulnerable and wounded conspecifics, suggesting that caregiving is a primate adaptation. Within this vulnerable-offspring perspective, compassion is the brief affective state associated with caregiving toward those who suffer or are in need.

There are other adaptive advantages associated with compassion. Some evidence suggests that the tendency to feel compassion is a desirable emotion or attribute in mate selection processes (Buss et al., 1990). Likewise, the trait-like tendency to experience compassion is an important criterion in the formation of cooperative relations with nonkin (Goetz, Keltner, & Simon-Thomas, 2010; Trivers, 1971). These lines of reasoning suggest that compassion is an evolved emotion and disposition and should likewise be subject to significant and meaningful individual variation. In sum, the work discussed above represents an important opportunity for the study of individual differences in compassion, to which we now turn.

■ PSYCHOPATHOLOGY AS A WINDOW INTO COMPASSION

Prosocial emotions such as compassion can compel individuals to form long-term interpersonal relationships (Gonzaga, Turner, Keltner, Campos, & Altemus, 2006; Keltner & Haidt, 2003); they also broaden and build social resources vital to healthy adaptation (Fredrickson, 1998). Little is understood, however, about whether feeling too much or too little compassion can bring about poor psychological outcomes. In this essay, we posit that abnormalities in compassion—deficits as well as extremes—play an important role in characterizing several different psychopathologies. In this vein, the study of subgroups of people with deficits (e.g., narcissism, autism, or sociopathy), potential extremes (e.g., mania), and apparent preservations in compassion despite more widespread emotional impairment (e.g., depression) presents two conceptual opportunities. A first is to characterize the specific social and emotional dysfunctions of various clinical disorders. By pinpointing how compassion is altered in people diagnosed with narcissism or autism, for example, insights are gained with respect to likely maintenance factors, social effects, and potential pharmacological interventions related to these two disorders. The second opportunity is to further understand the nature of compassion more generally by studying its upper and lower boundaries. Research on individual variation in compassion offers the promise of documenting potential core appraisal processes, physiological mechanisms, and socio-contextual factors critical for the successful experience and display of compassion.

■ LESSON 1: FAR FROM COMFORTING: NOTABLE ABSENCES OF COMPASSION

As Darwin (2004) long ago observed, the relative absence of emotion can be unsettling and ultimately dysfunctional. He relied on observations of patients in the mental hospitals of his era to speculate about the nature and function of emotion. Since his time, an emerging body of empirical research has begun to systematically examine emotion-related symptoms and impairments in a variety of psychopathologies (e.g., Keltner & Kring, 1998). With respect to compassion, relative deficits can be observed across several disorders, ranging from impairments in understanding complex emotions, in autism, to an absence of experiencing compassion in contexts in which it is normative, in both narcissistic personality disorder and sociopathy.

Absence of Compassion Understanding in Autism

Autism is a developmental disorder characterized by impairments in communication and social interaction and by repetitive behavior (American Psychiatric Association, 2000). One of the central social disturbances associated with autism is difficulty with theory of mind (ToM). ToM involves an appreciation of social norms and the awareness of others' evaluations (Tager-Flusberg, 1999). Studies suggest that individuals with high-functioning autism, while acquiring language in typical fashion, are significantly delayed in understanding others' mental states (e.g., Baron-Cohen, Leslie, & Frith, 1985). This delay in ToM has been found to have significant influences upon emotion understanding, in particular on understanding more social emotions. For example, Capps, Yirmiya, & Sigman (1992) found that when children with autism were asked to provide narratives of self-conscious emotions, they had difficulties giving clear and specific examples of those experiences, and instead described general, factual knowledge of the emotions. Capps et al. concluded that self-conscious emotions are problematic for children with autism due to their decreased ability to engage in social referencing and perspective taking. This autism-related deficit in self-conscious emotions also extends to impaired emotion recognition. When asked to judge emotions depicted in photos of human facial expressions, high-functioning autistic children were specifically impaired in recognizing self-conscious emotional expressions, such as embarrassment, while they performed comparably to controls on the identification of non-self-conscious emotions, such as anger or fear (Heerey, Keltner, & Capps, 2003). This is important because the recognition of self-conscious emotion involves understanding violations of social norms and negative social evaluations, both important aspects of ToM.

Like the self-conscious emotions, compassion requires an explicit understanding of the mental states of others, as well as inferences about individuals' intentions and capacity to respond to suffering (Goetz et al., 2010). These appraisal processes depend heavily upon ToM. One might therefore expect deficits in ToM to disrupt knowledge, recognition, and even experience of compassion in autistic children.

Recently, researchers have begun to postulate that trouble experiencing emotions like compassion in autism involves a failure or distortion in the development of the mirror neuron system. Mirror neurons are thought to underlie ToM by enabling the generation of an executive plan to perform an action like the one being watched, thereby enabling the observer to get into the mental shoes of the other person (Williams, Whiten, Suddendorft, & Perret, 2001). Indeed, neuroimaging work by Dapretto and colleagues (2006) indicates that children with autism have significantly less mirror neuron activity than controls.

In sum, these findings suggest that autism may be related to deficits in compassion. High-functioning autistic individuals may be expected to less readily identify the suffering of others, and to feel and express less compassion, than neurologically normal individuals These assertions, however, await further empirical attention.

Aggressive Tendencies and Sociopathic Disorder

One of the most compelling lines of possible inquiry in the study of individual differences in compassion is to relate deficits in compassion to extreme forms of aggressive behavior. In studies of individuals in highly violent situations, for example, during war, the experience of compassion has been documented to inhibit aggressive behavior (Keltner, 2009). A relationship between aggression and lack of compassion is also reflected in compassion-related responses of children prone to aggression, referred to as externalizers (Achenbach & Ebdelbrock, 1986). Externalizing children are known for their high levels of aggression, bullying, vandalism, and acting out. These children show deficits in social emotions like embarrassment (Keltner, Moffitt, & Stouthamer-Loeber, 1995). It follows that if presented with images of suffering, these children might show diminished compassion-related experience, expression, physiology, and action.

One way to test this possibility would be to extend the work of Eisenberg and colleagues, who study prosocial behavior in children. Their studies demonstrate, for example, that when presented with videos depicting the need and suffering of other children (e.g., children who have been in a car accident), highly prosocial children show greater compassion-related experience, more pronounced facial displays of compassion (oblique eyebrows), and greater parasympathetic response than those with lower levels of prosociality (Eisenberg et al., 1989). It would be interesting to determine whether children high in externalizing behavior show diminished compassion responses using similar methodologies.

Links between compassion and aggressive tendencies may also be revealed in sociopathy, a form of antisocial personality disorder involving a pervasive pattern of disregard for the welfare of others (American Psychiatric Association, 2000). Of interest to the present essay, sociopathy is characterized by a callous unconcern for the feelings of others or a lack of compassion specifically. Moreover, it has been posited that the emotional core of sociopathy lies in the simultaneous superficial veneer of prosociality and interpersonal charm with an underlying absence of "social emotions" including compassion as well as love, shame, guilt, and remorse (Mealey, 1995). Although sociopaths are cognitively aware of the disturbing nature of their behavior, including problematic social consequences, they fail to experience an emotional response to any such behaviors.

In early work with adult sociopathy, Robert Hare postulated that individuals engage in violent behaviors due in part to a lack of concern for the suffering of others (i.e., compassion-related deficits). The recognition of suffering in others acts as a powerful constraint upon the escalation of aggressive behavior. Hare (1978) documented that sociopaths showed reduced skin conductance responses when presented with the suffering of others. This work implies deficits in compassion may be associated with extreme violence in adults, as compassion constrains the escalation of violent behaviors.

Further work has confirmed the notion that sociopathy is associated with deficits in self-conscious emotions like compassion. For example, work on acquired sociopathy following frontal-lobe injury has revealed that injured individuals have intact social knowledge about how one should behave yet fail to behave in ways that take social norms into account. Additional work by Mendez, Chen, Shapira, and Miller (2005) on acquired sociopathy in neurodegenerative disorders such as frontotemporal dementia includes documentation of aggressive behaviors that appear to represent an absence of compassion, including unsolicited sexual behaviors, physical assault of others, and traffic violations. Those authors conclude that an important component of sociopathy includes diminished emotional concern for the consequences of actions and their affective impact on others.

Absence of Compassion in Narcissism

Narcissistic personality disorder is a chronic personality disorder characterized by a pervasive pattern of grandiosity, self-focus, drive for power, and seeking attainment of admiration from others as part of a hubristic pride (American Psychiatric Association: Task Force on DSM-IV, 2000; Tracy & Robins, 2004). From a clinical perspective, narcissists are depicted as manipulative and interpersonally exploitative, often wholly nonempathic, and unwilling to reciprocate prosocial behaviors towards others. A tendency to seek out others who can provide positive feedback and elevate their self-esteem is common. Morf & Rhodewalt (2001) describe this as the "narcissistic paradox" in which narcissists' attempts to seek out self-affirmation from others ultimately sabotage the social relationships upon which they depend.

It is no surprise that narcissism is associated with deficits in self-conscious emotions like compassion. Prevailing theories of narcissism centrally emphasize emotion-related impairments, including absences of emotions including shame and compassion or empathy (Livesley & Schroeder, 1991; Wright, O'Leary, & Balkin, 1989). Consistent with these intuitions, researchers have found that higher scores on the Narcissistic Personality Inventory are negatively correlated with self-reported empathy or compassion and need for social intimacy (Watson & Morris, 1991). Work examining narcissism in ongoing romantic relationships found that narcissism was negatively correlated with relationship commitment (Campbell, Foster, & Finkel, 2002). Interestingly, narcissistic traits have been associated with a tendency to perform poorly in tasks of social judgment, such as inferring the emotions of others using the Interpersonal Perception Task (Ames & Kammrath, 2004). Ames and Kammrath (2004) argue that narcissism may be characterized by a lack of compassion that gives rise to more general interpersonal insensitivity. Future work using standardized compassion-eliciting stimuli and naturalistic observations of how compassion unfolds in the course of social interaction is warranted. Such work has the potential to reveal fundamental insights about narcissism as a "selfish" disorder insofar as it involves excessive attention to the self with accompanying deficits in orienting toward the welfare of others.

■ LESSON 2: TOO CLOSE FOR COMFORT? POTENTIAL EXTREMES IN COMPASSION IN MANIA

Extreme manifestations of compassion can be indexed in several ways. They may be evident in the maximum intensity, or magnitude of self-reported compassion experience. Or extremes of compassion may be evident in compassion-related behaviors, including maximal contractions of emotion-relevant facial actions (e.g., Eisenberg et al., 1989) or heightened physical touch (Hertenstein, Keltner, App, Bulleit, & Jaskolka, 2006). Extremes can be evident in the duration of the emotion or its frequency across some epoch of time. Within a social functional approach to emotion, emotional extremes are likely to be highly dysfunctional within relationships and may even be a marker of different psychopathologies.

A prime candidate for potentially elevated levels of compassion is bipolar disorder, also referred to as manic-depressive illness. The core diagnostic criterion for bipolar disorder involves a single lifetime episode of mania, involving an abnormally expansive and persistently elevated mood (American Psychiatric Association: Task Force on DSM-IV, 2000). Mania also includes symptoms of grandiosity, heightened motor activity, pressured speech, decreased need for sleep, and engagement in risky and often impulsive behaviors. Recent empirical studies corroborate these diagnostic assertions by demonstrating that individuals at risk for or diagnosed with bipolar disorder exhibit elevated positive emotional responses across a variety of contexts relative to healthy controls (e.g., Gruber, in press; Gruber, Johnson, Oveis, & Keltner, 2008). Specifically, research suggests that individuals with bipolar disorder exhibit greater positive emotional reactivity than healthy controls, independent of current symptom levels (Johnson, 2005; Gruberr, in press). Several studies suggest that people with bipolar disorder generally report higher global positive affect in their everyday lives than do those without the disorder (Hofmann & Meyer, 2006; Lovejoy & Steuerwald, 1995).

We originally hypothesized that mania, due to its extreme presentations of positive emotions more generally, would be a ripe example of extreme manifestations of compassion. This was based on clinical features of mania involving overly intimate social encounters, such as initiating conversations with strangers or sexually promiscuous behaviors (American Psychiatric Association, 2000). Our hypothesis was based as well on the assumption that mania is associated with the misperception that others are communicating overly prosocial intentions, which in turn leads an individual with bipolar disorder to behave in ways that are "too close for comfort."

Only recently have researchers compared compassion in mania with other discrete positive emotions that differ in their function, design, and response profile (e.g., Shiota, Keltner, & John, 2006). Initial work did not support our speculation that mania is an excess of compassion. Self-report data on a variety of discrete positive emotions including compassion suggest that bipolar disorder (i.e., mania) is associated with elevations in positive emotion that are specific to reward and achievement-oriented emotions as opposed to prosocial emotions like compassion. Specifically, people at risk for mania reported greater levels of reward- and achievement-oriented emotions (e.g., joy and pride, respectively) relative to compassion in response to emotional film clips (Gruber et al., 2008). Such individuals also report higher trait levels of self-reported reward and pride relative to trait compassion (Gruber & Johnson, 2009). These preliminary findings do not suggest elevations in compassion associated with mania, but rather increased levels of positive emotions focused on reward and pursuit of goals.

However, a major limitation of this incipient line of research has been its constrained ecological validity, the methods used to elicit compassion, and the measures relied upon to capture compassion-related behavior. Simply put, compassion is an emotion embedded within rich social contexts; one experiences compassion in interacting with others and trying to soothe others in distress or pain. Thus, it is absolutely crucial for researchers to examine links between mania and compassion in more social contexts. Emerging evidence from our laboratory suggests that this line of inquiry is promising. In a recent study participants at risk for mania were brought into the laboratory and asked to try to communicate a variety of positive and negative emotions to a person with whom they were unacquainted by simply touching the stranger on the forearm; the stranger would try to communicate emotion to them in the way. Individuals at risk for mania tended to attribute increased prosociality (e.g., love) across a variety of touches received from an unknown partner (Piff, Purcell, Gruber, Hertenstein, & Keltner, 2011). This suggests that mania may be associated with a bias toward perceiving the emotions of others as overly prosocial and compassionate.

In sum, work to date has yet to reveal a clear answer as to whether mania is associated with an excess of compassion. While individuals with or at risk for mania do not self-report experiencing more dispositional compassion or more compassion in response to films of others suffering, they overestimate the compassion of others in dyadic interactions. Future work is warranted to disentangle the differential emotion profile for compassion in mania.

■ LESSON 3: JUST RIGHT? PRESERVED COMPASSION IN THE FACE OF DEPRESSION

Studies of emotion and psychopathology do not typically examine the ways in which emotions are preserved in the face of emotional distress. The ability to maintain a preserved sense of compassion for others despite more general emotion dysregulation may highlight potential areas of resilience or protection against relapse or exacerbation of a disorder.

Preserved Compassion in Depression?

A core symptom of depression, anhedonia, involves deficits in the ability to experience positive emotion (American Psychiatric Association, 2000). Disturbances in positive emotion play a central role in current theories of depression. Deficits in positive emotion also assist in uniquely locating depression in affective space by differentiating depression from other forms of psychopathology, including anxiety (e.g., Kring & Bachorowski, 1999; Watson, Clark, & Carey, 1988).

Several lines of evidence converge to suggest diminished positive emotion at both trait and state levels of measurement in depression. Past studies indicate that depression is characterized by low levels of trait positive emotion (Lovejoy & Steuerwald, 1995; Watson et al., 1988). A recent meta-analysis that included 19 laboratory studies comparing emotion reactivity of individuals with major depression with that of healthy controls indicates that depression is associated with reduced reactivity to positive stimuli (Bylsma, Morris, & Rottenberg, 2008). Recent work in this area has taken a more nuanced approach by examining the experience of compassion relative to other positive emotions. Specifically, Gruber, Oveis, Keltner, and Johnson (2011) examined self-reported compassion compared with pride, happiness and amusement across two studies at trait levels and at state levels in response to emotionally evocative films. Indeed, individuals experiencing depression were just as likely to respond to another's distress and suffering by experiencing feelings of wanting to help as those who were not depressed. These findings are especially important given that a cardinal symptom of depression is experiencing flattened positive feelings about the self and often reporting less pleasure in daily activities.

In sum, despite a generally disrupted positive emotional system in depression, there is a relative preservation of the ability to experience prosocial emotions, like compassion, that are other-oriented.

■ CONCLUSIONS AND FUTURE DIRECTIONS

Students of emotion have long been interested in the intersection of emotion and psychopathology. Empirical research on this intersection offers the promise of several conceptual gains in the two fields (e.g., Keltner & Kring, 1998; Kring & Sloan, 2009). For affective scientists, the study of the relations between emotions and psychopathology remains one of the clearest routes to understanding the functions of particular emotions. For clinical scientists, the kind of research we have detailed in this chapter offers similar promise for understanding the social expression and underpinnings of different disorders. More generally, individual differences in emotional behavior early in life may help to explain individuals' life courses, the problems they systematically encounter, and relational difficulties (e.g., Malatesta, 1990). This framework, which treats emotional behaviors as one mediator between person and environment, could readily be extended to the study of specific psychopathologies.

In our essay, we have detailed several promising lines of research on compassion and emotional disorders. Specifically, we concentrated on three conceptual themes that illustrate the relationship between aberrant forms of compassion and psychopathology. We first reviewed populations characterized by unusual deficits in compassion-related behaviors, focusing on autism, aggression, sociopathy, and narcissism. Next we reviewed as an exploratory possibility that mania is associated with excesses in compassion. We concluded by focusing on disorders with a resilient and intact preservation of compassion despite widespread emotional disruption, homing in on depression. Just as important, this work points to likely etiologies and treatments of different disorders. And in the broader sense, this research promises answers to an abiding question concerning the boundary conditions of how compassion operates as a moral and prosocial emotion.

■ REFERENCES

Achenbach, T. M. & Ebdelbrock, C. S. (1986). *Manual for the Teacher's Report Form and teacher version of the Child Behavior Profile.* Burlington: Department of Psychiatry, University of Vermont.

American Psychiatric Association: Task Force on DSM-IV. (2000). *Diagnostic and statistical manual of mental disorders* (4th ed., text rev.). Washington, DC: American Psychiatric Association.

Ames, D. R., & Kammrath, L. K. (2004). Mind-reading and metacognition: Narcissism, not actual competence, predicts self-estimated ability. *Journal of Non-Verbal Behavior, 28,* 187–210.

Baron-Cohen, S., Leslie, A. M., & Frith, U. (1985). Does the autistic child have a "theory of mind'? *Cognition, 21*, 37–46.

Batson, C. D., Ahmad, N., Lishner, D. A., & Tsang, J. (2002). Empathy and altruism. In C. R. Snyder & S. L. Lopez (Eds.), *Handbook of positive psychology* (pp. 485–498). New York, NY: Oxford University Press.

Buss, D. M., Abbott, M., Angleitner, A., Biaggio, A., Blanco-Villasenor, A., Bruchon Schweitzer, M., Hai-Yuan, C., Czapinksi, J., et al. (1990). International preferences in selecting mates: A study of 37 societies. *Journal of Cross Cultural Psychology, 21*, 5–47.

Bylsma, L. M., Morris, B. H., & Rottenberg, J. (2008). A meta-analysis of emotional reactivity in major depressive disorder. *Clinical Psychology Review, 28*, 676–691.

Campell, W. K., Foster, C. A., & Finkel, E. J. (2002). Does self-love lead to love for others? A story of narcissistic game playing. *Journal of Personality and Social Psychology, 83*(2), 340–354.

Capps, L., Yirmiya, N., & Sigman, M. (1992). Understanding of simple and complex emotions in non-retarded children with autism. *Journal of Child Psychology and Psychiatry, 33*, 1169–1182.

Dapretto, M., Davies, M. S., Pfeifer, J. H., Scott, A. A., Sigman, M., Bookheimer, S. Y., & Iacobini, M. (2006). Understanding emotions in others: Mirror neuron dysfunction in children with autism spectrum disorders. *Nature Neuroscience, 9*(1), 28–30.

Davis, M. H., Hall, J. A., & Meyer, M. (2003). The first year: Influences on the satisfaction, involvement, and persistence of new community volunteers. *Personality and Social Psychology Bulletin, 29*, 248–260.

Darwin, C. (2004). *The descent of man, and selection in relation to sex*. London, England: Penguin Books. (Original work published 1871)

Eisenberg, N., Fabes, R. A., Miller, P. A., Fultz, J., Shell, R., Mathy, R. M., & Reno, R. R., (1989). Relation of sympathy and personal distress to prosocial behavior: A multimethod study. *Journal of Personality and Social Psychology, 57*, 55–66.

Eisenberg, N., Michalik, N., Spinrad, T. L., Hofer, C., Kupfer, A., Valiente, C., et al. (2007). The relations of effortful control and impulsivity to children's sympathy: A longitudinal study. *Cognitive Development, 22*, 544–567.

Eisenberg, N., & Miller, P. A. (1987). The relation of empathy to prosocial and related behaviors. *Psychological Bulletin, 101*, 91–119.

Feather, N. T. (2006). Deservingness and emotions: Applying the structural model of deservingness to the analysis of affective reactions to outcomes. *European Review of Social Psychology, 17*, 38–73.

Fiske, S. T., Cuddy, A. J., Glick, P., & Xu, J. (2002). A model of (often mixed) stereotype content: Competence and warmth respectively follow from perceived status and competition. *Journal of Personality and Social Psychology, 82*, 878–902.

Fredrickson, B. L. (1998). What good are positive emotions? *Review of General Psychology, 2*, 300–319.

Goetz, J. L., Keltner, D., & Simon-Thomas, E. (2010). Compassion: An evolutionary analysis and empirical review. *Psychological Bulletin, 136*, 351–374.

Gonzaga, G. C., Turner, R. A., Keltner, D., Campos, B., & Altemus, M. (2006). Romantic love and sexual desire in close bonds. *Emotion, 6*, 163–179.

Gruber, J. (in press). A review and synthesis of positive emotion disturbance in bipolar disorder. *Clinical Psychology and Psychotherapy*.

Gruber, J. & Johnson, S. L. (2009). Positive emotional traits and ambitious goals among people at risk for mania: The need for specificity. *International Journal of Cognitive Therapy, 2*(2), 179–190.

Gruber, J., Johnson, S. L., Oveis, C., & Keltner, D. (2008). Risk for mania and positive emotional responding: Too much of a good thing? *Emotion, 8*(1), 23–33.

Gruber, J., Oveis, C., Johnson, S. L., & Keltner, D. (2011). A discrete emotions approach to positive emotion disturbance in depression. *Cognition and Emotion, 25*(1), 40–52.

Hare, R.D. (1978). Electrodermal and cardiovascular correlates of psychopathy. In R. D. Hare and D. Schalling (Eds,), *Psychopathic behaviour: approaches to research* (pp. 107–144). London, England: Wiley.

Heerey, E. A., Keltner, D., & Capps, L. M. (2003). Making sense of self-conscious emotion: Linking theory of mind and emotion in children with autism. *Emotion, 3*, 394–400.

Hertenstein, M. J., Keltner, D., App, B., Bulleit, B. A., & Jaskolka, A. R. (2006). Touch communicates distinct emotions. *Emotion, 6*, 528–533.

Hofmann, B. U., & Meyer, T. D. (2006). Mood fluctuations in people putatively at risk for bipolar disorders. *British Journal of Clinical Psychology, 45*, 105–110.

Hrdy, S. B. (2000). *Mother nature: Maternal instincts and how they shape the human species.* New York, NY: Ballantine Books.

Johnson, S. L. (2005). Mania and dysregulation in goal pursuit. *Clinical Psychology Review, 25*, 241–262.

Keltner, D. (2009). *Born to be good: The science of a meaningful life.* New York: W. W. Norton & Company.

Keltner, D., & Haidt, J. (2003). Approaching awe, a moral, aesthetic, and spiritual emotion. *Cognition and Emotion, 17*, 297–314.

Keltner, D., & Kring, A. M. (1998). Emotion, social function, and psychopathology. *Review of General Psychology, 2*, 320–342.

Keltner, D., Moffitt, T. E., & Stouthamer-Loeber, M. (1995). Facial expressions of emotion and psychopathology in adolescent boys. *Journal of Abnormal Psychology, 104*, 644–652.

Kring, A. M., & Bachorowski, J. A. (1999). Emotions and psychopathology. *Cognition & Emotion, 13*(5), 575–599.

Kring, A. M., & Sloan, D. S. (2009). *Emotion regulation and psychopathology.* New York, NY: Guilford Press.

Lazarus, R. S. (1991). *Emotion and adaptation.* Oxford, England: Oxford University Press.

Livesley, W. J., & Schroeder, M. L. (1991). Dimensions of personality disorder: The DSM-III-R Cluster B diagnoses. *Journal of Nervous and Mental Disease, 179*, 320–328.

Lovejoy, M. C., & Steuerwald, B. L. (1995). Subsyndromal unipolar and bipolar disorders: Comparisons on positive and negative affect. *Journal of Abnormal Psychology, 104*, 381–384.

Malatesta, C. Z. (1990). The role of emotions in the development and organization of personality. *Nebraska Symposium on Motivation, 36*, 1–56

Mealey, L. (1995). The sociobiology of sociopathy: An integrated evolutionary model. *Behavioral and Brain Sciences, 18*, 523–599.

Mendez, M. F., Chen, A. K., Shapira, J. S., & Miller, B. L. (2005). Acquired sociopathy and frontotemporal dementia. *Dementia and Geriatric Cognitive Disorders, 20*, 99–104.

Mikulincer, M., & Shaver, P. R. (2003). The attachment behavioral system in adulthood: Activation, psychodynamics, and interpersonal processes. In M.P. Zanna (Ed.), *Advances in experimental social psychology* (Vol. 35, pp. 53–152). San Diego, CA: Academic Press.

Morf, C. C. & Rhodewalt, F. (2001). Unraveling the paradoxes of narcissism: A dynamic self-regulatory processing model. *Psychological Inquiry, 12*(4), 177–196.

Nussbaum, M. C. (1996). Compassion: The basic social emotion. *Social Philosophy and Policy, 13*, 27–58.

Nussbaum, M. C. (2001). *Upheavals of thought: The intelligence of emotions*. New York, NY: Cambridge University Press.

Piff, P. K., Purcell, A., Gruber, J., Hertenstein, M., & Keltner, D. (2010). *Mania and touch*. Manuscript in preparation.

Post, S. G. (2002). The tradition of agape. In S. G. Post, L. G. Underwood, J. P. Schloss, & W. B. Hurlbut (Eds.), *Altruism and altruistic love: Science, philosophy, & religion in dialogue* (pp. 51–64). New York, NY: Oxford University Press.

Shiota, M. N., Keltner, D., & John, O. P. (2006). Positive emotion dispositions differentially associated with big five personality and attachment style. *Journal of Positive Psychology, 1*(2), 61–71.

Sprecher, S., & Fehr, B. (2005). Compassionate love for close others and humanity. *Journal of Social and Personal Relationships, 22,* 629–651.

Tager-Flusberg, H. (1999). A psychological approach to understanding the social and language impairments in autism. *International Review of Psychiatry, 11,* 325–334.

Tracy, J. L., & Robins, R. W. (2007). Show your pride: Evidence for a discrete emotion expression. *Psychological Science, 15,* 194–197.

Trivers, R. L. (1971). The evolution of reciprocal altruism. *Quarterly Review of Biology, 46,* 35–57.

Watson, D., Clark, L. A., & Carey, G. (1988). Positive and negative affectivity and their relation to anxiety and depressive disorders. *Journal of Abnormal Psychology, 97,* 346–353.

Watson, D. & Morris, R. J. (1991). Narcissim, empathy, ad social desirability. *Perosnality and individual Differences, 12*(6), 575–579.

Weiner, B., Perry, R. P., & Magnusson, J. (1988). An attributional analysis of reactions to stigmas. *Journal of Personality and Social Psychology, 55,* 738–748.

Williams, J. H. G., Whiten, A., Suddendorft, T., & Perret, D. I. (2001). Imitation, mirror neurons, and autism. *Neuroscience and Biobehavioral Reviews, 25,* 287–295.

Wright, F., O'Leary, J., & Balkin, J. (1989). Shame, guilt, narcissism, and depression: Correlates and sex differences. *Psychoanalytic Psychology, 6,* 217–230.

13 Egosystem and Ecosystem

Motivational Perspectives on Caregiving

■ JENNIFER CROCKER AND AMY CANEVELLO

As self researchers, we became interested in motivation based on evidence that people are motivated to maintain, enhance, and protect their self-esteem (Baumeister, 1998). Although psychologists widely assume that people need self-esteem, they have seldom explored the consequences of pursuing it. Our research suggested that the pursuit of self-esteem has both short-term and long-term costs, interfering with satisfaction of fundamental human needs for relatedness, competence, and autonomy, and that it leads to poor self-regulation and mental health issues such as anxiety and depression (Crocker & Park, 2004; Knee, Canevello, Bush, & Cook, 2008; Park & Crocker, 2005). We therefore began to explore alternative sources of motivation that might create similar enthusiasm without the costs. Eventually, our research led us to conclude that when people are motivated by caring about the well-being of others, instead of what others think about the self, they are more likely to satisfy their own as well as others' fundamental human needs (Canevello & Crocker, 2010; Crocker & Canevello, 2008; Crocker, Canevello, Breines, & Flynn, 2010).

Our insights into human motivation were shaped by our experiences in workshops at Learning as Leadership, a company devoted to helping people achieve their personal, professional, and business goals. We each experienced profound changes in both our personal and professional lives as a result of the workshops and witnessed the impact on other workshop participants, ranging from high school students to business leaders, academics, and even a former astronaut. We felt that their work captured an essential truth that was not clearly represented in the social-psychological research literature—that people driven by their egos often inadvertently create what they do not want, and by shifting to an alternative motivational framework they are more likely to create what they do want. We resolved to explore the consequences of this shift in motivational perspectives in our own research. In this essay, we describe some of the results of that work.

■ A TWO-SYSTEM VIEW OF MOTIVATION

Social scientists typically assume that humans are ultimately motivated by self-interest (Miller, 1999). To be sure, people sometimes give care and support for egoistic reasons. People often help others, including strangers, to reduce their own negative emotional state resulting from awareness of others' distress (Cialdini, Darby, & Vincent, 1973) or because others are viewed as part of the self (Cialdini et al., 1997). People sometimes provide care to loved ones to reduce their own anxiety, feel in control, look good to others, keep their partners in the relationship, or boost their self-esteem (Feeney & Collins, 2003; Helgeson, 1994). Game theory, social exchange theory, and interdependence theory all suggest that altruism, generosity, and giving ultimately benefit the giver (Axelrod, 1984; Axelrod & Dion, 1988; Rusbult & Van Lange, 2003; Thibaut & Kelley, 1959). Norms of reciprocity, backed up with punishment for defection, encourage people to respond to cooperation with cooperation and to competition with competition.

Giving to others has such clear benefits for the self that researchers have debated for decades whether giving is ever truly altruistic or self-sacrificing (Batson, 1987; Cialdini et al., 1997; Neuberg et al., 1997). This debate has been difficult to resolve, in part because of two assumptions that underlie it. First, researchers often assume that the only alternative to selfishness is self-sacrifice. This assumption reflects a zero-sum view of caregiving, in which giving support to others must come at the expense of the self. We suggest that at times, giving care and support to others has considerable benefits for the self—it is good for both others and the self. A second assumption we question is the idea that if giving has benefits, then giving must be motivated by the desire to obtain those benefits. We agree with Batson (1987) that the intentions people have for caregiving can be distinguished from the benefits that follow. The motivational question is not whether giving benefits the self, but whether those benefits constitute the primary reason why people give care and support to others. We suggest that people sometimes give support because they care about others, without regard to benefits they might obtain as a result. The benefits that follow make such giving sustainable over time. Paradoxically, we suggest that caregiving to benefit the self actually undermines the benefits people receive from others.

■ EGOSYSTEM AND ECOSYSTEM MOTIVATION

In this essay, we consider the motivations people have for caregiving and the consequences of these motivations for the self and others. We argue that there are at least two fundamentally different views, or motivational perspectives, that people can have about caregiving. Caregiving in the *egosystem* is viewed as a means for people to satisfy their own needs and desires; although their behavior may appear selfless or self-sacrificing, they provide care because of what they will obtain or what it means about them. In contrast, caregiving in the *ecosystem* results from genuine concern for the well-being of others; although such caregiving often has benefits for the self, those benefits are not the primary reasons why people provide care.

We argue that these two motivational perspectives on caregiving have paradoxical effects. Caregiving in the egosystem, which aims to obtain benefits for the self, actually undermines the support the caregiver receives from others, undermines relationship quality, decreases the caregiver's self-esteem and mental health, and even decreases the regard the care recipient has for the caregiver. Because caregivers often are unaware of these paradoxical effects, when they feel that their needs are not being met, they can persist with giving care in the egosystem, creating just the opposite of what they really want. In contrast, caregiving in the ecosystem actually does benefit the self, in the form of increased support received from others, increased self-esteem and mental health in the caregiver, and increased regard by the recipient for the caregiver.

The motivation to contribute to others' well-being and the egoistic motivation to benefit the self involve distinct constellations of mutually reinforcing goals, cognitions, and feelings. When people genuinely care about the well-being of others, they have compassionate goals; construe the relation between self and others as an ecosystem; feel peaceful, clear, and loving; and have empathic concern when others are in distress. When people primarily want to benefit the self, they construe the relation between self and others as an egosystem; have self-image goals; and feel conflicted, confused, and fearful. These constellations of attributes shape the relational and emotional experiences of the self and other people's experiences and goals.

■ COGNITIONS, GOALS, AND FEELINGS IN THE EGOSYSTEM

People with an egosystem perspective typically do not believe that they will be able to meet their needs in collaboration with their social environments. They view satisfaction of needs as a zero-sum proposition, so satisfaction of one person's needs and desires detracts from satisfaction of another's. One person's success, for example, necessarily comes at the expense of others' success in this framework. In this view, taking care of others has costs to the self (Crocker & Canevello, 2008). Consequently, in the egosystem people prioritize their own needs and desires over the needs and desires of others. Although they may give support and care to others, they do so to prove something or obtain something for themselves. Thus, in egosystem motivation people search for a course of action that will benefit themselves, even at the expense of others.

People with egosystem perspectives have self-image goals: They want others to see the self as having desired qualities as a means to get others to satisfy, or at least not thwart, their needs and desires. For example, a job applicant with an egosystem perspective may want to *appear* competent, caring, or creative to get an employer to offer a job. The applicant might describe accomplishments, but not difficulties, in a previous position, or rehearse answers so weaknesses are not apparent in an interview. The applicant is likely to focus on beating the competition for the job. These goals are normal and very typical in this context, and it may be difficult to imagine any other type of goal one could have in this situation. Self-image goals may sometimes have the intended result of impressing a prospective employer. However, self-image goals create anxiety, which can paradoxically create a negative impression on others.

Emotionally, when people have self-image goals they feel competitive with others, even close others; these competitive feelings, in turn, lead them to feel conflicted, confused, and fearful (Crocker & Canevello, 2008; Crocker, Liu, & Canevello, 2008; Moeller, Crocker, & Canevello, 2008). In this framework, positive outcomes for the self come at the expense of others. People may feel conflicted about the costs for close others, or they may fear that others will want to retaliate somehow. The aroused negative, self-conscious feelings that accompany self-image goals are directly linked to these zero-sum views of relationships between self and others—the view that benefits to the self come at a cost to others and vice versa.

◼ COGNITIONS, GOALS, AND FEELINGS IN THE ECOSYSTEM

In biology, an ecosystem is an ecological community of species together with its physical environment considered as a unit. In a healthy ecosystem, the species fulfill each others' biological needs for nutriments, oxygen, carbon dioxide, light and shade, and so on, creating an often delicate balance of mutually interdependent life. Harm to one element of the ecosystem can negatively affect other species in the ecosystem. Although species may compete for resources, the health of one species depends on the health of others.

We draw on the biological notion of an ecosystem as a metaphor for a motivational framework in which people see themselves as part of a larger whole, a system of individuals whose actions have consequences for others, with repercussions for the entire system that ultimately affect the well-being of all. In the ecosystem, people believe that people should take care of one another, so they feel cooperative. They view desired outcomes of the self and others as non–zero sum, so one person's success does not detract from others' success (Crocker & Canevello, 2008). They believe that taking care of others is not inherently costly to the self and that if they take into account the needs of others, they will be able to meet their own needs in a way that is sustainable for the self and others.

People with an ecosystem perspective have compassionate goals; they want to be constructive and supportive and not harm others (Crocker, 2008; Crocker, Olivier, & Nuer, 2009). For example, a job applicant with an ecosystem perspective might focus on contributing to an organization or its clients, customers, or stakeholders. The applicant might ask questions about the needs of the organization and help the prospective employer realistically evaluate how effectively the applicant could address those needs. The applicant is likely to focus on the opportunity to make a contribution and want the employer to hire the person who can best contribute. The applicant may have clear goals and be realistic about the contribution he or she could make. Thus, in ecosystem motivation the self is part of a larger system and can contribute to others.

Emotionally, when people have compassionate goals, they feel peaceful, clear, and loving (Crocker & Canevello, 2008; Crocker et al., 2008; Moeller et al., 2008). As we describe later, the calm, positive, other-directed feelings experienced by people who have compassionate goals are directly linked to their non–zero-sum view of relationships between self and others—their belief that benefits to an individual can also benefit others.

◼ THE INTERACTION OF EGOSYSTEM AND ECOSYSTEM MOTIVATION

Egosystem and ecosystem motivations are not opposite ends of a continuum or negatively correlated motivational states. People often have both egosystem and ecosystem perspectives, and both self-image and compassionate goals. For example, a politician responding to a crisis might have the compassionate goal to improve the lives of constituents and also have the self-image goal of being seen in ways that would increase the chances of being reelected.

Furthermore, egosystem and ecosystem motivation fluctuates moment by moment. Although people differ in how often they have compassionate and self-image goals, virtually everyone has the capacity for both types of motivation. People typically alternate between these two motivational frameworks repeatedly, perhaps many times a day, in response to internal and external cues about whether their own needs will be met. Research on compassionate and self-image goals shows that they have qualities of traits and states; that is, compassionate and self-image goals fluctuate from day to day or week to week around people's average or typical levels (Canevello & Crocker, 2010; Crocker & Canevello, 2008).

■ IMPLICATIONS FOR CAREGIVING

People can have either ecosystem or egosystem motivational perspectives and they can have compassionate or self-image goals, or both, when providing care and support to others. When people have compassionate goals, they give support because they care about the other's well-being; when people have self-image goals, they give support because of what it means about the self, how others see the self, and what they will obtain as a result (e.g., a boost to self-esteem, other's gratitude or admiration, or feeling important).

Compassionate and self-image goals predict changes in both support and responsiveness. Although related, support and responsiveness represent distinguishable aspects of caregiving. When people are responsive, they tune in to and react to others' states (i.e., their feelings, desires, and needs) and try to make others feel validated and understood. When people are supportive, they may provide help, information, and assistance but do not necessarily attend to others' emotional and psychological needs or try to make others feel good about themselves. Both types of caregiving are important; both responsiveness and support can provide reassurance that one's needs are likely to be met.

We investigated associations between compassionate and self-image goals and caring for others in a longitudinal study of first-semester freshman roommate dyads. Because first-year roommates are randomly assigned (within gender), these relationships provide an opportunity to examine caregiving motivations and behaviors in relationships unbiased by self-selection or relationship history. In the Roommate Goals Study, 65 roommate pairs completed pretest and posttest measures and 21 daily diary reports of their goals, support they gave and received, their own and their roommates' responsiveness, and the quality of their roommate relationship.

Giving and Receiving Support

When students have compassionate goals (averaged over 21 days), they give increased support to their roommates; self-image goals predict giving decreased support to roommates, although not significantly (Crocker & Canevello, 2008, Study 2). Roommates of students with compassionate goals report receiving increased support, although only when the giver is low in self-image goals. Apparently, students' self-image goals undermine their roommates' feelings of being supported, perhaps because support providers' self-image goals signal that they care more about obtaining something for the self than about the well-being of the recipient. Consequently, when support providers have compassionate goals and give support but are also high in self-image goals, recipients may not experience their support as caring and supportive. Because recipients do not feel supported, they should be less likely to care for and respond to the support provider's needs.

Consistent with this reasoning, students' chronic compassionate goals also predict increases in how much support their roommate gives back to them, and again, students' self-image goals undermine the support their roommates give back. Path models indicated that participants' goals interacted to predict increases in the support their roommates reported receiving, which in turn predicted increases in the support their roommates reported giving back, which in turn predicted increases in the support participants reported receiving from their roommates. In other words, people with high compassionate goals and low self-image goals create a supportive interpersonal environment for others *and* themselves. As a result, people with chronic compassionate goals increase in trust, developing confidence that they can depend on others (Crocker & Canevello, 2008, Study 1).

Responsiveness

Compassionate goals also predicted responsiveness to roommates in the Roommate Goals Study (Canevello & Crocker, 2010). Specifically, students' compassionate goals for their roommate relationship on one day predicted increased responsiveness toward their roommates the following day; self-image goals predicted decreased responsiveness the following day. Changes in responsiveness strongly predicted parallel changes in students' perceptions of their roommates' responsiveness over the same time period, reflecting intrapersonal and interpersonal processes. First, in a process of projection, students who become more or less responsive perceive similar changes in their roommates' responsiveness, independent of the roommates' actual behavior. Second, when students' responsiveness changes from one day to the next, their roommates perceive those changes and reciprocate by becoming more or less responsive themselves. Over time, compassionate goals can create an upward spiral of reciprocal responsiveness within students and between roommates; self-image goals can create a downward spiral (Canevello & Crocker, 2010).

Consequences for Relationship Quality

These upward and downward spirals of responsiveness in roommate dyads predict changes in the quality of the roommate relationship for students and for their roommates over three weeks (Canevello & Crocker, 2010). Specifically, when students with compassionate goals became more responsive over the course of the study, they perceived their roommates as more responsive and consequently felt closer to their roommates, more satisfied with their roommate relationships, and more committed to their roommates. Furthermore, their roommates noticed this increased responsiveness, so the roommates also felt closer, more satisfied with the relationship, and more committed. Thus, compassionate goals led to an upward spiral of responsiveness, which contributed to students' and their roommates' increased relationship quality. Self-image goals predicted a downward spiral of decreased responsiveness, which contributed to decreased relationship quality for both people.

Consequences for Psychological Distress

Compassionate and self-image goals also predict changes in anxiety and symptoms of depression over the first semester of college (Crocker et al., 2010). In two longitudinal studies, we examined the associations between self-image and compassionate goals and anxiety and depression (i.e., distress). In the Goals and Adjustment to College Study, 199 college freshmen completed 12 surveys over 12 weeks. Compassionate goals predicted decreased anxiety and depression from pretest to posttest, and self-image goals predicted increased anxiety and depression. In the Roommate Mental Health Study, 115 first-semester roommate pairs completed 12 surveys over 12 weeks. Compassionate goals on one week predicted lower distress (anxiety and depression) the same week and decreases in distress the following week; chronic compassionate goals averaged across the weekly reports predicted decreased distress over the semester.

We also examined whether changes in support given to or received from roommates accounted for the effects of compassionate and self-image goals on change in distress over a semester. When change in support given and received were entered together into regression analyses predicting change in distress, increased support given to roommates fully accounted for the effects of compassionate goals on decreased distress; increased support received from roommates was unrelated to change in distress.

These results reinforce previous research demonstrating the benefits of giving support (e.g., Brown, Brown, House, & Smith, 2008; Deci, La Guardia, Moller, Scheiner, & Ryan, 2006) and have potentially important implications for the support literature, which emphasizes the support people receive as a predictor of well-being. Giving support motivated by compassionate goals directly benefits others because they feel supported and indirectly benefits the self because others tend to reciprocate support. The reduction in distress that follows, however, is due to giving rather than receiving more support. The idea that giving support improves well-being more effectively than receiving support, and that increases in support received are a side effect of giving support in the first place, suggests that support interventions might focus on giving rather than receiving support. Of course, the present studies involve healthy college students; giving support might not be as beneficial for everyone. Yet, Brown and her colleagues showed that caregiving in older couples attenuates depression and even predicts decreased mortality, indicating that giving support might benefit many people (Brown et al., 2009; Brown, Nesse, Vinokur, & Smith, 2003).

■ CHANGING GOALS

The research described thus far suggests that compassionate goals prompt caregiving, which benefits the self, whereas self-image goals interfere with caregiving, with costs to the self. But what leads to changes in compassionate and self-image goals? We hypothesize that people have compassionate goals when they trust that their needs will be met in collaboration with others or their social environment; this trust allows people to focus on others' needs. In contrast, people have self-image goals when they lose trust that their needs will be met; this loss of trust prompts people to focus on taking care of themselves and attempting to manipulate others into meeting their needs, activating their egosystem motivation.

Both unresponsiveness in relationship partners and psychological distress may signal to people that their needs are not being met or might not be met, prompting a shift in goals. Unresponsiveness in relationship partners suggests that others are not attending to one's needs and desires or are incapable of addressing or unmotivated to address them. Consequently, perceived unresponsiveness in relationship partners may signal that others cannot be relied on and that therefore people either need to take care of themselves or act in ways that get others to see them as people who deserve to have their needs and desires met. Thus, unresponsiveness may serve as a cue to become less concerned with supporting others and more concerned with constructing desired images of the self. Results of the Roommate Goals Study support this conjecture. Specifically, when students rate their roommates as less responsive over three weeks, their compassionate goals decrease and their self-image goals increase over the same time interval (Canevello & Crocker, 2010).

Anxiety and depression may also serve as a cue that one's needs are not being met or might not be met in the future. Evolutionary explanations for anxiety and depression suggest that negative mood may signal difficulties with current goals and foster shifts to more attainable, self-protective, or less risky goals (Keller & Nesse, 2006; Nesse, 1991; Nesse & Ellsworth, 2009; Wrosch & Miller, 2009). Specifically, anxiety or depression may signal that one's needs or desires are not currently being met or not likely to be met collaboratively with others as an ecosystem perspective suggests. Therefore, psychological distress may prompt a shift away from compassionate goals that prioritize others' well-being and toward self-image goals that prioritize getting others to meet one's needs and desires through construction of desired self-images. Findings from the Roommate Mental Health Study support this conjecture. Specifically, when students feel distressed their compassionate goals decline and their self-image goals increase, consistent with the idea that distress signals problems with one's current goals. This shift in goals does not appear to be adaptive, however; self-image goals predict increased distress, and compassionate goals predict both increased support and decreased distress, suggesting that people who are anxious and depressed are caught in a downward spiral in which distress fosters goals that lead to more distress.

■ LINKS TO EVOLVED MOTIVATIONAL SYSTEMS

Accumulating evidence suggests that self-image goals and compassionate goals may involve distinct physiological processes, reflecting two evolved motivational systems. Specifically, egosystem perspectives and self-image goals may be associated with the self-preservation, or fight-or-flight, system, whereas ecosystem perspectives and compassionate goals may be associated with the species-preservation, or tend-and-befriend, system (Henry & Wang, 1998; Taylor et al., 2000).

Self-Image Goals and the Self-Preservation System

Losing trust that one's needs will be met may activate both self-image goals and the self-preservation fight-or-flight stress response regulated by stress hormones such as cortisol (Henry & Wang, 1998), creating an association between self-image goals and cortisol. The fight-or-flight response involves evolutionarily old parts of the brain and is found in many species, including reptiles. Short-term activation of the fight-or-flight response mobilizes individual resources and facilitates adaptive responses to immediate survival threats. Because responses to life-or-death threats must be fast, this system does not foster thoughtful, analytical, planful, or empathic responses, which require time that could cost lives. Activation of this system benefits individual survival in the short term; prolonged activation is costly for physical and mental health (Sapolsky, 1998).

Psychological threats can activate the self-preservation system (see Dickerson & Kemeny, 2004, for a review). Specifically, self-image threats elicit cortisol responses in laboratory experiments. This response does not appear to be adaptive; research shows that self-image threats of various sorts diminish people's capacity for rational thought (Baumeister, Twenge, & Nuss, 2002; Steele, Spencer, & Aronson, 2002), reduce their ability to self-regulate (Twenge, Catanese, & Baumeister, 2002), decrease prosocial behavior (Twenge, Baumeister, DeWall, Ciarocco, & Bartels, 2007), and can instigate aggression (Bushman & Baumeister, 1998; Twenge, Baumeister, Tice, & Stucke, 2001).

Compassionate Goals and the Species-Preservation System

Compassionate goals may involve the species-preservation, tend-and-befriend system, which increases others' chances of survival by fostering protective and care-giving behaviors (Brown & Brown, 2006). This system is regulated by reproductive hormones such as oxytocin, vasopressin, and progesterone (Brown & Brown, 2006; Henry & Wang, 1998; Taylor et al., 2000). The species-preservation motivational system downregulates cortisol and the fight-or-flight response, enabling people to attend to others' needs in stressful circumstances (Henry & Wang, 1998).

The species-preservation motivational system evolved more recently than the self-preservation system; it is found in all mammals, for whom reproduction requires not only giving birth but also caring for young (Henry & Wang, 1998). Activation of the species-preservation system motivates giving (Brown & Brown, 2006). Oxytocin, in particular, increases trust and generosity toward strangers

(Zak, Kurzban, & Matzner, 2004, 2005), and is associated with positive, other-directed emotions such as love (Gonzaga, Turner, Keltner, Campos, & Altemus, 2006). Activation of this system benefits long-term survival of individuals, their offspring, and their social groups by fostering learning, supportive relationships, and self-regulation (Brown et al., 2009).

■ CONCLUSION

Although in its infancy, research on egosystem and ecosystem motivational perspectives may contribute to understanding caregiving in several ways. First, research suggests that these two motivational perspectives reflect fundamentally different views on how the self relates to others and involve constellations of cognitions (e.g., zero-sum or non–zero-sum beliefs), goals (self-image or compassionate goals), and feelings (e.g., conflicted, confused, and fearful or peaceful, clear, and loving). Second, research suggests that giving motivated by compassionate goals benefits the self and others, by creating supportive and responsive relationships, enhancing relationship quality, and reducing distress; giving in the ecosystem is, indeed, non–zero sum in its effects. Self-image goals, reflecting an egosystem motivational perspective, undermine the benefits of giving in the ecosystem for the self and others. Even when they have compassionate goals, people with self-image goals do not make others feel more supported; consequently others do not give more support in return. People with self-image goals become increasingly distressed over time. These findings ironically suggest that when people give without regard for what they will receive in return they reap tremendous benefits. However, when people give to obtain those benefits, the benefits diminish.

At the outset of this essay, we argued that people sometimes provide care out of genuine concern for the well-being of others and that caregiving that stems from this motivational perspective has unintended benefits for the self, leading to satisfaction of fundamental human needs for mutually supportive relationships. We also suggested that people are more likely to have this ecosystem motivational perspective when their own needs are satisfied or they trust that their own needs will ultimately be met. Lack of responsiveness in relationship partners may serve as a cue that one needs to protect oneself. Activation of the self-preservation system may interfere with caregiving driven by the species-preservation system. One might argue, then, that caregiving in the ecosystem is really motivated by self-interest.

We do not agree with this interpretation. Although perceived self-image threats, anxiety, or concern about one's own needs' being met may often, even typically, lead to a shift from compassionate goals to self-image goals, most of the time this shift is neither inevitable nor helpful. It results from confusing ego threats with survival threats, and as we have seen is costly to both the self and others. In our experience, when confronted with self-image threats, people can choose to shift from self-image goals to compassionate goals. Two things seem to abet this shift. First, awareness of the costs of self-image goals, that they often create the opposite of what people really want, can motivate them to monitor and clarify their goals, so they have a better chance to create what they do want. People can anchor their behavior in what Learning as Leadership calls a "never again"—in clarity about what they do not want to create for themselves and others. Second, clarity about what is really important in the situation can serve as a compass that provides a direction forward, a sense of what they want to create for themselves and others even if it damages their ego, or others have negative images of them. With these two guides, people who recognize that their self-image goals are taking over can choose to shift to a more compassionate, ecosystem perspective. The paradoxical aspect of compassionate goals is that they have benefits for the self only if people do not adopt them primarily to obtain benefits for the self. That is, the costs and benefits of egosystem and ecosystem perspectives for caregiving depend on the intentions underlying caregiving rather than the behavior itself.

This emphasis on intentions or motivational perspectives that guide behavior increases the difficulty of studying the effects of compassionate and self-image goals. Research linking these two motivational perspectives with distinct physiological systems may provide converging evidence regarding the intentions underlying caregiving. A second obstacle to research is the cynicism of many researchers. Social psychologists, and particularly those who study the self, sometimes seem invested in a view of people as self-serving, self-protective, self-enhancing, and defensive. This skepticism creates a resistance to the possibility that people ever could genuinely care about the well-being of others or risk their own egos to benefit others. Again, evidence that compassionate goals are linked with a distinct physiological system that motivates caregiving may help to wear down this resistance.

■ ACKNOWLEDGMENTS

Preparation of this manuscript was supported by National Institute of Mental Health grant R01 MH58869. We are indebted to Lara and Noah Nuer, Marc-Andre Olivier, Carole Levy, Filaree Radich, and other facilitators and coaches at Learning as Leadership for their generosity, encouragement, and guidance, which led us to our current research program.

■ REFERENCES

Axelrod, R. (1984). *The evolution of cooperation*. New York, NY: Basic Books.
Axelrod, R., & Dion, D. (1988). The further evolution of cooperation. *Science, 242*, 1385–1390.
Batson, C. D. (1987). Prosocial motivation: Is it ever truly altruistic? In L. Berkowitz (Ed.), *Advances in experimental social psychology* (Vol. 20, pp. 65–122). San Diego, CA: Academic Press.
Baumeister, R. F. (1998). The self. In D. T. Gilbert, S. T. Fiske, & G. Lindzey (Eds.), *The handbook of social psychology* (4 ed., Vol. 2, pp. 680–740). New York, NY: McGraw-Hill.
Baumeister, R. F., Twenge, J. M., & Nuss, C. K. (2002). Effects of social exclusion on cognitive processes: Anticipated aloneness reduces intelligent thought. *Journal of Personality and Social Psychology, 83*, 817–827.
Brown, S. L., & Brown, R. M. (2006). Selective Investment Theory: Recasting the functional significance of close relationships. *Psychological Inquiry, 17*, 1–29.
Brown, S. L., Brown, R. M., House, J. S., & Smith, D. M. (2008). Coping with spousal loss: Potential buffering effects of self-reported helping behavior. *Personality and Social Psychology Bulletin, 34*, 849–861.

Brown, S. L., Fredrickson, B. L., Wirth, M. M., Poulin, M. J., Meier, E. A., Heaphy, E. D. Schultheiss, O. C. (2009). Social closeness increases salivary progesterone in humans. *Hormones and Behavior, 56*, 108–111.

Brown, S. L., Nesse, R. M., Vinokur, A. D., & Smith, D. M. (2003). Providing social support may be better than receiving it: Results from a prospective study. *Psychological Science, 14*, 320–327.

Bushman, B. J., & Baumeister, R. F. (1998). Threatened egotism, narcissism, self-esteem, and direct and displaced aggression: Does self-love or self-hate lead to violence? *Journal of Personality and Social Psychology, 75*, 219–229.

Canevello, A., & Crocker, J. (2010). Creating good relationships: Responsiveness, relationship quality, and interpersonal goals. *Journal of Personality and Social Psychology, 99*, 78–106.

Cialdini, R. B., Brown, S. L., Lewis, B. P., Luce, C., & Neuberg, S. L. (1997). Reinterpreting the empathy–altruism relationship: When one into one equals oneness. *Journal of Personality and Social Psychology, 73*, 481–494.

Cialdini, R. B., Darby, B. L., & Vincent, J. E. (1973). Transgression and altruism: A case for hedonism. *Journal of Experimental Social Psychology, 9*, 502–516.

Crocker, J. (2008). From egosystem to ecosystem: Implications for learning, relationships, and well-being. In H. A. Wayment & J. J. Brauer (Eds.), *Transcending self-interest: Psychological explorations of the quiet ego* (pp. 63–72). Washington, DC: American Psychological Association.

Crocker, J., & Canevello, A. (2008). Creating and undermining social support in communal relationships: The role of compassionate and self-image goals. *Journal of Personality and Social Psychology, 95*, 555–575.

Crocker, J., Canevello, A., Breines, J. G., & Flynn, H. (2010). Interpersonal goals and change in anxiety and dysphoria in first-semester college students. *Journal of Personality and Social Psychology, 98*, 1009–1024.

Crocker, J., Liu, M. Y., & Canevello, A. (2008). *Interpersonal goals, zero-sum relationship views, and relationship affect.* Unpublished manuscript.

Crocker, J., Olivier, M.-A., & Nuer, N. (2009). Self-image goals and compassionate goals: Costs and benefits. *Self and Identity, 8*, 251–269.

Crocker, J., & Park, L. E. (2004). The costly pursuit of self-esteem. *Psychological Bulletin, 130*, 392–414.

Deci, E. L., La Guardia, J. G., Moller, A. C., Scheiner, M. J., & Ryan, R. M. (2006). On the benefits of giving as well as receiving autonomy support: Mutuality in close friendships. *Personality and Social Psychology Bulletin, 32*, 313–327.

Dickerson, S. S., & Kemeny, M. E. (2004). Acute stressors and cortisol responses: A theoretical integration and synthesis of laboratory research. *Psychological Bulletin, 130*, 355–391.

Feeney, B. C., & Collins, N. L. (2003). Motivations for caregiving in adult intimate relationships: Influences on caregiving behavior and relationship functioning. *Personality and Social Psychology Bulletin, 29*, 950–968.

Gonzaga, G. C., Turner, R. A., Keltner, D., Campos, B., & Altemus, M. (2006). Romantic love and sexual desire in close relationships. *Emotion, 6*, 163–179.

Helgeson, V. S. (1994). Relation of agency and communion to well-being: Evidence and potential explanations. *Psychological Bulletin, 116*, 412–428.

Henry, J. P., & Wang, S. (1998). Effects of early stress on adult affiliative behavior. *Psychoneuroendocrinology, 23*, 863–875.

Keller, M. C., & Nesse, R. M. (2006). The evolutionary significance of depressive symptoms: Different adverse situations lead to different depressive symptom patterns. *Journal of Personality and Social Psychology, 91*, 316–330.

Knee, C. R., Canevello, A., Bush, A. L., & Cook, A. (2008). Relationship-contingent self-esteem and the ups and downs of romantic relationships. *Journal of Personality and Social Psychology, 95*, 608–627.

Miller, D. T. (1999). The norm of self-interest. *American Psychologist, 54*, 1053–1060.

Moeller, S. J., Crocker, J., & Canevello, A. (2008). *Feeling clear and connected: How other-directed motivation benefits self-regulation.* Unpublished manuscript, University of Michigan, Ann Arbor.

Nesse, R. M. (1991). What good is feeling bad? The evolutionary benefits of psychic pain. *The Sciences, 31*, 30–37.

Nesse, R. M., & Ellsworth, P. C. (2009). Evolution, emotions, and emotional disorders. *American Psychologist, 64*, 129–139.

Neuberg, S. L., Cialdini, R. B., Brown, S. L., Luce, C., Sagarin, B. J., & Lewis, B. P. (1997). Does empathy lead to anything more than superficial helping? Comment on Batson et al. (1997). *Journal of Personality and Social Psychology, 73*, 510–516.

Park, L. E., & Crocker, J. (2005). Interpersonal consequences of seeking self-esteem. *Personality and Social Psychology Bulletin, 31*, 1587–1598.

Rusbult, C. E., & Van Lange, P. A. M. (2003). Interdependence, interaction and relationships. *Annual Review of Psychology, 54*, 351–375.

Sapolsky, R. M. (1998). *Why zebras don't get ulcers: An updated guide to stress, stress-related diseases, and coping.* New York, NY: Freeman.

Steele, C. M., Spencer, S. J., & Aronson, J. (2002). Contending with group image: The psychology of stereotype and social identity threat. In M. P. Zanna (Ed.), *Advances in experimental social psychology* (Vol. 34, pp. 379–440). San Diego, CA: Academic Press.

Taylor, S. E., Klein, L. C., Lewis, B. P., Gruenewald, T. L., Gurung, R. A. R., & Updegraff, J. A. (2000). Biobehavioral responses to stress in females: Tend-and-befriend, not fight-or-flight. *Psychological Review, 197*, 411–429.

Thibaut, J. W., & Kelley, H. H. (1959). *The social psychology of groups.* New York, NY: Wiley.

Twenge, J. M., Baumeister, R. F., DeWall, C. N., Ciarocco, N. J., & Bartels, J. M. (2007). Social exclusion decreases prosocial behavior. *Journal of Personality and Social Psychology, 92*, 56–66.

Twenge, J. M., Baumeister, R. F., Tice, D. M., & Stucke, T. S. (2001). If you can't join them, beat them: Effects of social exclusion on aggressive behavior. *Journal of Personality and Social Psychology, 81*, 1058–1069.

Twenge, J. M., Catanese, K. R., & Baumeister, R. F. (2002). Social exclusion causes self-defeating behavior. *Journal of Personality and Social Psychology, 83*, 606–615.

Wrosch, C., & Miller, G. E. (2009). Depressive symptoms can be useful: Self-regulatory and emotional benefits of dysphoric mood in adolescence. *Journal of Personality and Social Psychology, 96*, 1181–1190.

Zak, P. J., Kurzban, R., & Matzner, W. T. (2004). The neurobiology of trust. In R. Yahuda & B. McEwen (Eds.), *Biobehavioral stress response: Protective and damaging effects.* (pp. 224–227). New York, NY: New York Academy of Sciences.

Zak, P. J., Kurzban, R., & Matzner, W. T. (2005). Oxytocin is associated with human trustworthiness. *Hormones and Behavior, 48*, 522–527

14 Caregiving in Adult Close Relationships

■ ELLEN BERSCHEID

Most human behavior takes place in the context of ongoing relationships with others (Reis, Collins, & Berscheid, 2000). Caregiving is no exception. Moreover, it is likely that the lion's share of caregiving acts take place within ongoing relationships that are close—that is, relationships in which the partners are highly interdependent (Kelley et al., 2002). Because interdependence takes time to develop, these tend to be relatively long-term relationships as opposed to the brief, single-interaction episodes between strangers that have been the focus of much caregiving theory and research conducted under the rubrics of "social support" and "prosocial behavior." Moreover, within an ongoing close relationship, unlike caregiving between strangers, the distress experienced by the partner for which care is needed may have been caused by the other partner, who also may be the only available source of effective care.

Understanding and predicting caregiving behavior within an ongoing relationship requires that the relationship context be taken into consideration, specifically: (a) each partner's characteristics and their interaction; (b) characteristics of the relationship, including its history relevant to caregiving; (c) characteristics of the social and physical environments in which the relationship is embedded; and (d) any interactions among the foregoing factors. The size and complexity of this constellation is reflected in the results of a diary study of caregiving in ongoing relationships (Iida, Seidman, Shrout, & Fujita, 2008). Couples' daily reports of giving and receiving care revealed that whether the partner gave care when care was needed, and how such care was received, was a function of many factors, including the characteristics of the care provider, characteristics of the recipient, and characteristics of their relationship. In sum, understanding and predicting caregiving in an ongoing relationship will be a far more difficult task than understanding and predicting caregiving between strangers in brief interaction episodes (not an easy task in itself, as the voluminous social-support and prosocial-behavior literatures attest).

■ CAREGIVING IN CLOSE RELATIONSHIPS AS A VARIETY OF LOVE

Acts of caregiving, particularly in the context of a close relationship, have been viewed as a type of love for thousands of years. Indeed, both Bowlby (e.g., 1973) and Harlow (e.g., 1958), who in the mid-20th century introduced love into the scientific arena with theory and research on maternal caregiving, viewed caregiving as a form of love. Caregiving in adult–child relationships has continued to be of interest to developmental psychologists, who have focused most of their efforts on identifying the effects of the child's receipt of different patterns of caregiving from the adult caregiver, as opposed to identifying the causal antecedents of the caregiving behavior of the adult (Berscheid & Collins, 2000).

At the same time that Bowlby and Harlow were conducting their pioneer work on maternal caregiving, social psychologists began their efforts to unravel the mysteries of love in adult relationships. These began, as do so many efforts to investigate psychological phenomena (e.g., emotion and personality), with itemizing and labeling the phenomena of interest. Each taxonomic scheme, listing the varieties of love that seem to appear within adult relationships, differed from the next (see Rubin, 1988), resulting in a welter of putative forms of love, unaccompanied by an explication of each type of love posited and theory detailing the presumed causal conditions, behavioral manifestations, and temporal course of that type of love.

Romantic love appears in virtually all taxonomies, and because it has been of special interest to love scholars and laypersons alike, "romantic relationships" subsequently became the focus of love scholars, who subsequently turned to psychometric techniques to identify the dimensions underlying the responses of partners describing their experiences in such relationships (usually the dating relationships of young adults). The dimensions that have emerged from these psychometric analyses have been viewed as representing forms of love, and they too have been given numerous labels, which also have rarely been accompanied by explications of each putative variety of love or formal theory specifying the causal conditions associated with it.

Alongside efforts to understand love phenomena in so-called romantic relationships, and mostly independent of them, psychologists have attempted to identify the factors that contribute to the satisfaction and stability of adult relationships, with the marital relationship, the nucleus of the family, being of special interest. The two literatures—the love literature and the marital-satisfaction and stability literature—have made contact primarily at the point of initiation of the marital relationship. Romantic love, in this country and now throughout much of the world, is regarded as the sine qua non of marriage; most people report that they would not marry another unless they were "in love" with that person, and many report that they would dissolve their marriage if they no longer loved their spouse (e.g., Simpson, Campbell, & Berscheid, 1986).

Despite the role of romantic love in the marital relationship, the causal conditions associated with it and its temporal course in a relationship, although of perennial interest to many, are not known, because longitudinal studies are lacking to determine the fate of romantic love or any other variety of love—including caregiving love—in close adult relationships. This is true even though one of the most consistent findings of marital research is that satisfaction with the marital relationship diminishes over time, not infrequently to the extent that the partners dissolve the relationship. To understand marital relationship satisfaction and stability, marital researchers have focused almost exclusively on the role of conflict and the negative sentiments toward partners that accompany it.

The need to put the partners' love for each other into the satisfaction-and-stability equation has become apparent as results have become available from some longitudinal studies of marital satisfaction and stability, which have grown in number (see Karney & Bradbury, 1995). From the results of their own longitudinal study, for example, marital researchers Caughlin and Huston (2006) conclude that "enduringly happy relationships involve more than just the absence of antagonism and strife—affectionate and supportive behaviors are also important" (p. 132). They also observe that "there are shockingly few studies that have assessed constructs such as affectionate behavior and love over time in a marriage" (p. 139). There are, in fact, shockingly few studies that have examined the fate of any kind of love in any type of close relationship.

To track the course of love over time, it is first necessary to identify, from the bewildering varieties of love that have been posited over the years, those kinds of love that are important to track. A similar problem confronted personality researchers, who needed to identify a limited range of types of personality traits from the multitude that had been posited and who managed to boil the extensive array down to five major personality traits, often referred to as the "Big Five." According to Costa and McCrae (1992), the five-factor model evolved from (a) consideration of the pervasiveness of certain terms in lay vocabularies of personality, (b) their frequency of appearance in theories of personality, (c) consideration of their similarity in substance if not in name, and (d) their emergence in factor analytic studies of responses to various personality scales. Although Costa and McCrae acknowledge that the five factors cannot account for the full range of personality traits, they argue that the model helps specify the range of traits that any comprehensive personality instrument should measure.

Four types of love—romantic love, companionate love, caregiving love, and attachment love—meet the criteria that were used to develop the Big Five model and should be included in any comprehensive instrument measuring qualitative and quantitative changes in love in a relationship over time, as well as in a much needed temporal model of love (Berscheid, 2010). Such a model would provide adequate conceptualization of each of the four types of love, describe the causal conditions believed to give rise to each type, detail each type's behavioral manifestations, and, from theory incorporating all four and their relationships to each other, derive hypotheses about the fate of each type of love over time in the relationship, especially the relative vulnerability of each to negative sentiment arising in the relationship. It should be noted that adult attachment love is unlikely to be independent of caregiving love, for this type of love is assumed to be the result of the sustained receipt of caregiving love from the relationship partner—although this remains an empirical question that can be answered only by longitudinal studies guided by hypotheses derived from a temporal model of love.

■ THE NEED TO CONCEPTUALIZE THE CAREGIVING-LOVE CONSTRUCT

Like most forms of love, caregiving love has been given many names over the years. The several names given to this type of love, and the differing nuances associated with each, suggest that conceptualization of the caregiving-love construct will not be easily accomplished.

The oldest name for caregiving love is *agape*. The word agape in the Christian Bible, originally written in Greek, is sometimes simply translated as "love" and other times as "charity." Charity is defined by one modern dictionary as "generosity and helpfulness toward the needy or suffering" or "aid given to those in need" (Merriam-Webster, 1993, p. 193). In other words, "charity" is not an accurate descriptor of acts of "generosity and helpfulness" toward a relationship partner who is not in need of such acts (but who may welcome them for a number of reasons, including their symbolic significance, e.g., indicating that the giver is favorably disposed toward the recipient and wishes to please him or her). This view of caregiving love, it should be noted, includes "aid given to those in need" that requires *no personal cost* to the provider and aid that is given in *expectation of future benefits*.

The phrases *sacrificial love* and *altruistic love*, often used to describe caregiving acts in a relationship, refer to caregiving acts that do exact personal cost from the provider, sometimes a high cost. A related term is *selfless love*, which refers both to caregiving acts that are costly to the caregiver to perform and to acts that exact no cost but are given without the expectation of future benefit.

It seems clear that the first fork in the road in conceptualizing caregiving love involves deciding whether the term should refer to any act of care that is simply a response to the perception of another's need for that care (perception of need being an implied necessary but not sufficient condition for caregiving love in all definitions) or whether other restrictions should apply. One possible restriction, as the above indicates, is that the act of caregiving must be costly for the caregiver to perform. If so, how costly becomes a question; that is, there is a need to specify some threshold of cost above which the act will qualify as costly, for presumably any caregiving act will entail some cost, if only the time it takes to perform. Moreover, the question arises of whether it is necessary that the caregiver know of the cost *before* performing the act rather than only after the act is performed and its cost has become apparent.

Independent of whether the act of care is or is not costly for the giver to perform, another possible restriction is that the caregiving act must be performed without conscious or unconscious expectation of future benefit, either from the recipient or from others. Again, how much benefit becomes an issue. Moreover, in calculating benefit it is necessary to identify not only the positive benefits from the partner and others that may accrue from the caregiving act but also the magnitude of negative sanctions and punishments that are avoided by giving the needed care (e.g., some acts of care are compelled by law). The problem of calculating cost–benefit ratios will be especially difficult in close relationships, where each partner's welfare is dependent on the other's welfare and thus if one partner responds to the other's need with care, the caregiver is likely protecting and enhancing his or her own welfare as well.

Caregiving love is associated with several other labels, each of which appears to have caregiving at its core. *Pure love*, for example, refers to caregiving acts untainted by incentives for personal gain or the avoidance of punishment. Pure love is often regarded as *true love,* and it also is viewed as *unconditional love,* which refers to acts of giving care to people who need it even under conditions in which they do not deserve such care (e.g., people who have in the past threatened or damaged the welfare of the caregiver and can be expected to do so again in the future or people who clearly brought their plights on themselves by careless or irresponsible behavior). *Maternal love,* the caregiving that people believe mothers provide their children, is viewed as an exemplar of pure love, its unconditional feature being reflected in the phrase "a person whom only a mother could love." Maternal love, in fact, has emerged as the prototype, or best example, of what love is (Fehr & Russell, 1991). Unfortunately, maternal love is not necessarily a feature of the mother–child relationship, as the need for societal laws against child neglect and child endangerment, and the legal penalties they prescribe, reflect.

Which fork in the road toward conceptualizing the caregiving construct is taken—conceptualizing a caregiving act simply as one that is performed in response to perception of another's need or whether additional restrictions should apply—may depend on whether one looks at caregiving from the perspective of the recipient or of the provider of care. From the point of view of the individual in distress and in need of care, what matters is that care is received. To a child in need of care, for example, it matters little that its mother is giving care only because she wishes to be regarded as a "good mother" by outside observers or is aware of the legal penalties for child neglect.

Restricting a definition of caregiving love to provisions of care that exact cost or are of no benefit to the caregiver requires a decision about what is important about caregiving and exactly what it is that is to be understood and predicted. With respect to this last consideration, it is necessary to specify when and why the motivation of the caregiver must be identified. The caregiver's motivations for performing any one caregiving act are likely to be several in number, some conscious and some unconscious. If verbal self-report is the method by which motivation is to be discerned, as it usually is, problems instantly arise, for the conscious motivations that are reported are vulnerable to self-esteem and social-approval distortions and the unconscious motivations are inaccessible for self-report.

■ THE "CAREGIVING SYSTEM" HYPOTHETICAL CONSTRUCT

The need to adequately conceptualize the caregiving construct may have been obscured by the indiscriminate use of the term *caregiving system,* introduced by Bowlby (1969). Particularly unfortunate is the popular assumption that all acts of caregiving are the result of "activation" of a caregiving system, an assumption that embodies a number of others. First and foremost, for example, it assumes that the components of such a system have been identified and the dynamics of their interaction are known. It also assumes that the integrity of this system, believed to be innately given, survives intact throughout the lifespan, not impaired or greatly modified by experiential factors deriving from a variety of social and cultural influences. This view of the caregiving system also assumes that it operates similarly across persons embedded in different social and physical environments. This last assumption is necessary because, as Bowlby (1960) observed, "behavioural systems are designed to fit particular environments" and "how the behaviour to which a system gives rise may be unable to occur unless the environment provides the 'right' stimulation" (p. 89). Not only does the environment provide the "triggering," or "activating," stimuli for the hypothesized system to operation, the environment also provides the stimuli that inhibit activation of the system when it otherwise would have been activated as well as the termination stimuli for the system.

Another factor that often appears to be overlooked when the phrase "caregiving system" is used is particularly relevant to caregiving within close relationships. Bowlby (1969) took pains to emphasize that it is "by no means uncommon for more than one system to be active at once" and that the kind of behavior that results when two or more systems are active simultaneously "varies greatly" (p. 97). Within close relationships, it is the emotional system (which has at least been described in broad outline by psychologists) that is most likely to be simultaneously activated when the partner is perceived to be in distress and in need of aid. If the potential caregiver's emotion (e.g., fear or anger) upon awareness of their partner's distress is sufficiently intense (e.g., the potential caregiver experiences flooding autonomic nervous system arousal), the caregiving behavior may be so disrupted that their partner receives no help at all. In interdependent relationships, it is to be expected that one partner's distress will likely distress the other partner, who is the potential caregiver; sometimes the latter will experience even more distress than the former. (Hence sometimes people hide their distress from their partners, anticipating that their partner's knowledge of the distress "would only make matters worse.")

In sum, because the existence of a caregiving system and its nature is not known, its frequent use as an explanatory hypothetical construct may impede the explication of other constructs that may be more useful in advancing an understanding of caregiving in adult relationships. Identifying such a caregiving system in the human adult may be extremely difficult, most certainly more difficult than identifying such a system in rodents confined within uniform environments.

■ RECENT INTEREST IN CAREGIVING IN ONGOING ADULT RELATIONSHIPS

Interest in caregiving in ongoing adult relationships has grown in the past several years (e.g., see Pasch & Bradbury, 1998), in part because, as previously noted, its role in relationship satisfaction and stability is becoming recognized. Relationship scholars' interest in caregiving has resulted in even more names for a caregiving type of love. Some, for example, prefer the phrase *compassionate love*. The word "compassion" carries its own nuances. For example, one dictionary definition of compassion is "sympathetic consciousness of others' distress together with a desire to alleviate it" (Merriam-Webster, 1993, p. 234). Once again, perception of another's distress is said to constitute a necessary condition for an act of compassionate love, but that perception must be accompanied by sympathy for the person in distress and a desire to alleviate the other's distress. That desire, it should be noted, may or may not result in an actual attempt to provide care.

Sprecher and Fehr (2005) recently constructed a Compassionate Love Scale based on their definition of compassionate love as "an attitude toward other(s) . . . containing feelings, cognitions, and behaviors that are focused on caring, concern, tenderness, and an orientation toward supporting, helping, and understanding the other(s), particularly when the other(s) is (are) perceived to be suffering or in need" (p. 630). This definition collects a very large, perhaps too large, number of behaviors under the "compassion" tent. One anticipates that like the construct of "social support," the caregiving construct eventually will be viewed as a "meta-construct" (see Vaux, 1988), too large and unwieldy in itself and in need of unpacking into subsidiary constructs.

Other relationship scholars prefer the term *communal responsiveness*, which was coined by Clark and her associates (e.g, Clark & Monin, 2006). This phrase reflects growing interest in the interactional dynamics of caregiving in ongoing adult relationships (e.g., Cutrona, 1996; Feeney & Collins, 2004). As opposed to relationships in which rewards and benefits are given to another on a quid pro quo basis, mutually "communal responsive" relationships are defined as those in which individuals attend to their partners' needs and welfare and are confident that their partners will do the same if and when their own needs arise. This view emphasizes that an individual's acts of mutual communal responsiveness must be *noncontingent*: They must be given without demanding or expecting immediate benefits in direct return for the caregiving act.

In addition, Clark and Monin emphasize that for a mutually communally responsive relationship to develop, the partner must be willing to receive aid. Not all partners are, which is perhaps why Bolger, Zuckerman, and Kessler (2000) found that "invisible support" is often more effective in reducing a partner's distress than are more obvious forms of caregiving. Clark and Monin theorize that communally responsive acts, given over time in a relationship, contribute to a sense of security and of being loved in all types of human relationships.

Reis, Clark, and Holmes (2004) hypothesize that what partners will view as "responsive" to their needs depends on the type of relationship and its place in a triangularly shaped hierarchy of communal relationships—spouses and children at the peak, followed in descending order by parents, close friends, casual friends, acquaintances, and strangers at the base. (As noted, it is caregiving within this broad base of strangers that has been the focus of most social-support studies, and within this body of theory and research the emphasis has been on delineating the effects of such acts on the recipient.) Sprecher and Fehr (2005) found that people's scores on their Compassionate Love Scale were lowest for strangers, higher for close friend relationships, and highest for dating and marital relationships, which lends empirical evidence to the existence of a relationship caregiving hierarchy. They also found a gender effect, with women typically scoring higher on the scale than men do, as is often found in the social-support literature.

Some current research on caregiving in ongoing adult relationships has been stimulated by the interest in the formation of attachment bonds between the partners in such relationships (e.g., see Hazan & Zeifman, 1999; Kunce & Shaver, 1994). Most normative attachment research (as opposed to research on individual differences in adult attachment "styles," or differing orientations toward close relationships) has been stimulated by Ainsworth's (e.g., 1985) hypothesis that a few of the affectional bonds people form after childhood may possess some of the components that distinguish attachments from other types of affectional bonds. Of particular interest has been her speculation that over the course of a long-term sexual relationship, the partners may develop an attachment to each other as a result of each alternately giving and receiving care from another. Ainsworth cautioned, however, that the caregiving and attachment components may not be symmetrical and reciprocal in all relationships (i.e., only one, or none, of the partners may form an attachment to the other). Because the receipt of care and the resulting reduction of distress are the processes by which attachments are theorized to form, knowledge of caregiving in adult relationships—when, who, for how long, and in what pattern (e.g., continuous or distributed)—is essential. At this time, little is known of the process by which people develop attachments in adulthood, which is not surprising because little is known about caregiving in these relationships.

■ SUMMARY

The need to understand caregiving in ongoing relationships is great. Caregiving in adult–child relationships has received some attention but hardly sufficient to the need. The plight of many children in this country and throughout the world suggests that not all adults give their children caregiving love even when factors suspected to inhibit such care are absent. Even less is known about caregiving in ongoing adult relationships.

Adequate conceptualization of the caregiving construct (or constructs) is needed, for conceptualization of a construct necessarily accompanies the development of theories of causation from which testable hypotheses are derived and that guide the investigation of those hypotheses. The variety of meanings associated with the various phrases that have been used to refer to acts of caregiving within an ongoing relationship suggests that explication of this construct will require considerable effort.

The attention caregiving is currently receiving from adult-relationship scholars is long overdue for those who wish to understand and predict the fate of all close relationships, especially the marital relationship. The presence of caregiving love in a relationship is likely to be essential to the relationship's endurance, but the current emphasis on young relationships and young partners is not optimal for calculating the role that caregiving love plays in sustaining a close relationship. Although caregiving love is of some importance even in young relationships (e.g., it was the first factor extracted in the psychometric study of young adults in romantic relationships; Hendrick & Hendrick, 1986), young people in young relationships may continue for some time without either partner experiencing anything but minor episodes of distress for which the other partner can easily provide care. As the relationship and the partners age, however, many people will need costly and sustained care from their partners. It is at this point that the assumption that their relationship partners possess caregiving love for them is put to the test. If the partner is capable of providing the needed care but fails to do so, one suspects the relationship may be irreparably damaged (the specific criteria people use to arrive at the conclusion that a partner lacks caregiving love constitute yet another realm of questions yet to be answered). One suspects that relationships may survive the fading of romantic love or a diminution of companionate love but few adult close relationships survive destruction of the assumption that one's partner possesses caregiving love for oneself, for it is the provision of care that is the raison d'être of most close relationships (Berscheid, 2002).

Convincing empirical evidence of the crucial role that caregiving love plays in sustaining a close relationship will not be obtained until the four major types of love are measured *independently* of each other within longitudinal studies of several types of close relationships (Berscheid, 2010). Romantic love and companionate love involve a favorable attitude toward the partner, whether in the form of affection, admiration, respect, or positive regard for the partner's characteristics; these no doubt render caregiving more probable, not the least because of the many personal benefits we derive from protecting and enhancing a loved partner's well-being. However, if the bedrock of the caregiving-love construct is taken to be recognition of another's distress and an attempt to alleviate it, then it is possible to exhibit caregiving love not only for people we love in many other ways but also for people we love *in no other way*. It is, of course, the provision of care to people we love in no other way that the world's religions emphasize, including the provision of care to people whom we despise but who are in need—where *Schadenfreude*, the German word for enjoyment derived from the distress of others, is more likely to be felt than caregiving love.

Although it may be easier to provide care for people one loves rather than hates and people whose well-being is vital to our own, the situation changes when the source of their distress is our own behavior rather than agents and circumstances outside of the relationship. As much interpersonal-equity research demonstrates, when we ourselves are the cause of our partner's distress, we are more likely to deny or minimize that distress or to view it as deserved (e.g., Walster, Walster, & Berscheid, 1978). It is in long-term close relationships, including marital relationships, that we are most likely to be both the cause of another's distress and the potential caregiver. These also are the situations in which caregiving love is most crucial to the endurance of the relationship and to the well-being of both partners, and thus these may be the very situations for which it is most important to understand adult caregiving love.

■ REFERENCES

Ainsworth, M. D. S. (1985). Attachments across the life span. *Bulletin of the New York Academy of Medicine, 61*, 792–812.

Berscheid, E. (2002). Relationships with others: The human's greatest strength. In L. G. Aspinwall & U. M. Staudinger (Eds.), *A psychology of human strengths: Perspectives on an emerging field*. Washington, DC: American Psychological Association.

Berscheid, E. (2010). Love in the fourth dimension. *Annual Review of Psychology, 61*, 1–26.

Berscheid, E., & Collins, W. A. (2000). Who cares? For whom and when, how, and why? *Psychological Inquiry, 11*, 107–109.

Bolger, N., Zuckerman, A., & Kessler, R. C. (2000). Invisible support and adjustment to stress. *Journal of Personality and Social Psychology, 69*, 890–902.

Bowlby, J. (1969). *Attachment and loss: Vol. 1. Attachment.* New York, NY: Basic Books.

Caughlin, J. P., & Huston, T. L. (2006). The affective structure of marriage. In D. Perlman & A. Vangelisti (Eds.), *The Cambridge handbook of personal relationships* (pp. 131–155). New York, NY: Cambridge University Press.

Clark, M. S., & Monin, J. K. (2006). Giving and receiving communal responsiveness as love. In R. J. Sternberg & K. Weis (Eds.), *The new psychology of love* (pp. 200–221). New Haven, CT: Yale University Press.

Costa, P. T., & McCrae, R. R. (1992). Four ways five factors are basic. *Personality and Individual Differences, 13*, 653–665.

Cutrona, C. E. (1996). *Social support in couples.* Thousand Oaks, CA: Sage.

Feeney, B. C., & Collins, N. L. (2004). Interpersonal safe haven and secure base caregiving processes in adulthood. In W. S. Rholes & J. A. Simpson (Eds.), *Adult attachment: Theory, research, and clinical interventions* (pp. 300–338). New York, NY: Guilford.

Fehr, B., & Russell, J. A. (1991). The concept of love viewed from a prototype perspective. *Journal of Personality and Social Psychology, 60*, 424–438.

Harlow, H. F. (1958). The nature of love. *American Psychologist, 13*, 673–685.

Hazan, C., & Zeifman, E. (1999). Pair bonds as attachments: Evaluating the evidence. In J. Cassidy & P. R. Shaver (Eds.), *Handbook of attachment: Theory, research, and clinical applications* (pp. 336–354). New York, NY: Guilford.

Hendrick, C., & Hendrick, S. S. (1986). A theory and method of love. *Journal of Personality and Social Psychology, 50*, 392–402.

Iida, M., Seidman, G., Shrout, P. E., & Fujita, K. (2008). Modeling support provision in intimate relationships. *Journal of Personality and Social Psychology, 94*, 460–478.

Karney, B. R., & Bradbury, T. N. (1995). The longitudinal course of marital quality and stability: A review of theory, method, and research. *Psychological Bulletin, 118*, 3–34.

Kelley, H. H., Berscheid, E., Christensen, A., Harvey, J. H., Huston, T. L., Levinger, G., . . . Peterson, D. R. (2002). *Close relationships.* Clinton Corners, NY: Percheron (Original work published 1983).

Kunce, L.J. & Shaver, P. R. (1994). An attachment-theoretical approach to caregiving in romantic relationships. In K. Bartholomew & D. Perlman (Eds.), *Attachment processes in adulthood. Advances in personal relationships* [Vol. 5] (pp. 205–237). London, England: Jessica Kingsley.

Merriam-Webster. (1993). *Merriam Webster's collegiate dictionary* (10th ed.). Springfield, MA: Author.

Pasch, L. A., & Bradbury, T. N. (1998). Social support, conflict, and the development of marital dysfunction. *Journal of Consulting and Clinical Psychology, 66*, 219–230.

Reis, H. T., Clark, M. S., & Holmes, J. G. (2004). Perceived partner responsiveness as an organizing construct in the study of intimacy and closeness. In D. J. Mashek & A. Aron (Eds.), *Handbook of Closeness and Intimacy* (pp. 201–225). Mahwah, NJ: Erlbaum.

Reis, H. T., Collins, W. A., & Berscheid, E. (2000). The relationship context of human behavior and development. *Psychololological Bulletin, 126*, 844–872.

Rubin, Z. (1988). Preface. In R. J. Sternberg & M. L. Barnes, *The psychology of love* (pp. vii–xii). New Haven, CT: Yale University Press.

Simpson, J. A., Campbell, B., & Berscheid, E. (1986). The association between romantic love and marriage: Kephart (1967) twice revisited. *Personality and Social Psychology Bulletin, 12*, 363–372.

Sprecher. S., & Fehr, B. (2005). Compassionate love for close others and humanity. *Journal of Social and Personal Relationships, 22,* 629–651.

Vaux, A. (1988). *Social support: Theory, research, and intervention.* New York, NY: Praeger.

Walster [Hatfield], E., Walster, G. W., & Berscheid, E. (1978). *Equity: Theory and research.* Boston,MA: Allyn & Bacon.

PART FIVE

Implications for Economics, Political Science, and Social Policy

15 A New View of Utility

Maximizing "Optimal Investment"

■ DYLAN M. SMITH, STEPHANIE L. BROWN,
AND MARY L. RIGDON

The only assumption essential to a descriptive and predictive science of human behavior is egoism. (Mueller, 1986)

Mainstream economic models used to inform social policy are currently uninformed by the idea that humans have been designed by evolution to care for others, not just for themselves, and that activation of this other-directed motivational system—the caregiving system—can have significant positive effects on health and well-being. This state of affairs exists despite sound evolutionary arguments to show that helping others is as fundamental to human nature as helping oneself (S. L. Brown & Brown, 2006; Hamilton, 1964; Sober & Wilson, 1998); mounting empirical support for the existence of neurobiological systems that motivate helping (Brown, Brown, & Preston, this volume; Numan, this volume); considerable evidence that helping is associated with decreased mortality (S. L. Brown, Nesse, Vinokur, A, & Smith, 2003; Brown et al., 2009; Oman, 2007), reduced morbidity (W. M. Brown, Consedine, & Magai, 2005), faster recovery from depressive symptoms related to spousal loss (S. L. Brown, Brown, House, & Smith, 2008), and increased positive emotion (Poulin et al., 2010; Yinon & Landau, 1987); and related findings showing that helping partially mediates beneficial effects of religiosity (Koenig, 2007) as well as positive effects of mutual support, social support, self-affirmation, and meditation (e.g., Crocker, Niiya, & Mischkowski, 2008; Rodin & Langer, 1977).

In this essay, we argue that what we know about other-directed motivation and its effects can be used to inform current debates in economics, which highlight a tension between appetitive, consumption motives and those that are dedicated to cultivating a sense of meaning and deeper relationships. For example, consider the conundrum confronting proponents of using the gross domestic product (GDP) to measure utility. GDP has risen sharply in recent decades, yet average levels of well-being in the population have not followed suit. On the contrary, along with the rise in GDP, depression rates have increased. To address this disparity, the current consensus is that beyond the low level of income required for a very basic safety net, additional increases in wealth add little or nothing to emotional well-being (Argyle, 1999; Haring, Stock, & Okun, 1984; Myers, 2000) and may even "impair people's ability to savor everyday positive emotions and experiences" (Quoidbach, Dunn, Petrides, & Mikolajczak, 2010). Yet gaining wealth remains a potent motivator; to make more money, people make great sacrifices, including in the area of personal relationships.

In the remainder of this essay we consider implications of assuming that humans are other-directed—not just self-interested—for developing policy that maximizes utility and for evaluating economic models of human choice. We conclude with the suggestion that policies that incentivize optimal investment in others may go further toward creating more enduring and robust economies than those designed to incentivize profit.

■ ECONOMIC POLICY: WHAT SHOULD WE SEEK TO MAXIMIZE?

What should be the ultimate goals of economic and social policies? Economists judge the benefits of economic policies in terms of maximizing the output of goods and services, as measured by the level and rate of growth of the country's GDP, which is a measure of total economic output, including all goods and services produced. Indeed, GDP (or real GDP) has been the single most influential economic indicator of overall utility—satisfaction or well-being—since its creation during the Great Depression. However, there are many criticisms of the measure, including the way economic output is defined. A person who decides to commute many miles to work increases GDP—by buying cars, wearing them out quickly, and consuming large quantities of gasoline. But the lifestyle required to support commuting carries substantial costs not captured by GDP, such as environmental damage—not to mention the personal costs. At the very least, a person who commutes long hours may have to give up an active role in parenting after school or miss family dinners in favor of spending time driving to and from work.

As another example of inherent trade-offs in policy efforts to maximize GDP, consider the impact of expensive treatments for chronic illnesses on the health care system. Although the cost of health care is detrimental to patients and their families, and now threatens the entire health care system, the cost of health care fuels GDP. Moreover, as rates of chronic illness increase, driving increased demand for treatments, the effect on GDP will be positive. Thus a less healthy population could look better, in terms of GDP, than a healthier one. These issues of measuring well-being using the GDP calculation have been the subject of several recent international conferences (Organization for Economic Co-operation and Development World Forum, 2007; Stiglitz, Sen, & Fitoussi, 2008) and have caused some economists to argue that utility should be defined more broadly, incorporating measures of health and of emotional and social well-being (Boarini, Johansson, & d'Ercole, 2006; Di Tella, MacCulloch, & Oswald, 2004; Frey & Stutzer, 2002a, 2005b; Layard, 2005; Oswald, 1997).

Advocates of this new approach to utility have suggested that measures of well-being should be based on mood rather than GDP (Dolan, 2008; Kahneman, Krueger, Schkade, Schwarz, & Stone, 2004b; Kahneman, Wakker, and Sarin, 1997). Such measures assess the quantity of time people spend engaged in various activities (a measure of "time use") and assess mood quality—hedonic well-being— during those activities. By averaging indicators of time use across a representative sample, one could get a general sense of how a nation's population spends its time. By linking those data with mood quality, one could begin to formulate policy prescriptions that would maximize the time individuals spend engaged in the most hedonically positive activities and minimize time spent in activities that are associated with a negative mood.

But this approach equates mood quality with utility, a controversial notion. It has been noted, for example, that many pursuits are engaged in not for their hedonic value, but rather out of a sense of duty or of meaning and purpose (Smith, Brown, & Ubel, 2008). And as argued elsewhere in this volume, caring for others is not a process that always—or perhaps even usually—results in maximizing pleasure and minimizing pain. Indeed, data collected on mood and time use suggest that caring for children, to take one example, is not accompanied by gleeful moods, and instead has an average hedonic value close to that of doing household chores (Kahneman Krueger, Schkade, Schwarz, & Stone, 2004a).

Would policies that maximize activities that produce the most positive moods end up minimizing time spent caring for and helping others as more pleasurable activities such as watching TV, video-game playing, or eating supplant those that require work and, at best, delay of gratification (e.g., raising children or caring for a spouse or parent)? If so, an inadvertent consequence of pursuing policies that maximize mood may be to lose the benefits associated with caring for others enumerated at the beginning of this essay (e.g., better health outcomes) along with a sense of meaning and purpose that may be derived from investing in the well-being of another person or group. Ironically, economic models of well-being may be more effective at promoting self-interest if they encourage "other-interest"—that is, behaviors aimed at helping others.

▪ FREEDOM OF CHOICE VS. THE TYRANNY OF CHOICE

An important assumption in economics has been that if given freedom of choice, people will generally act rationally to promote their own self-interest. This creates a general prescription for selecting among policy options: Favor policies that increase freedom of choice. If people are provided with more options, then their rational choices will, on average, increase utility. A corollary of this general principle is that we should select policies that are designed to reduce barriers and constraints that make it difficult for people to enact decisions they would otherwise like to make. This approach would favor policies that, for example, make it easier for people to change jobs and to migrate to locations where their skills are most needed.

But the idea that more choices are a good thing has been questioned. The field of behavioral economics is in part a response to the recognition that decisions are not always rational (Ariely, 2009; Camerer, 1999, 2006; Kahneman & Tversky, 2000; Rabin, 1998). In addition, recent empirical work has challenged the idea that providing people with more choices leads to greater utility (Schwartz, 2004a, 2004b). For example, Barry Schwartz and others have argued that in many cases emotional well-being declines with increases in the number of possible options (Schwartz, 2004b). Schwartz suggests that whatever our final choice, we tend to feel more regret and disappointment as options increase. In addition, the assumption that thoughtful, deliberative decision making leads to the most rational, best decision has been questioned. Some research suggests that in many instances, initial, "gut" choices are superior to choices that have been subjected to deliberate scrutiny (Wilson & Schooler, 1991). Schwartz argues that thoughtful deliberation increases expectations, and hence, disappointment.

How does the caregiving system fit into this debate? In contrast to rational-self-interest explanations, models of the caregiving system (e.g., Brown et al., this volume; Mikulincer & Shaver, this volume) do not rely on deliberative choice. Rather, these models are socioemotional, involving emotions such as empathic concern, empathic distress, sympathy, gratitude, joy, and love. Given what we know about the relation between limbic system structures and emotion, it follows that choices affecting the caregiving system are more likely to be mediated by regions in the midbrain than by higher centers associated with abstract reasoning and cognitive control (Greene, Nystrom, Engell, Darley, & Cohen, 2004).

The concept of rational self-interest implies that policy decisions should be based on deliberative, abstract types of information processing, as opposed to processing that may be emotionally charged and potentially "irrational" from an objective standpoint. An unintended consequence of discouraging the use of emotional information, however, may be that in emphasizing cognitive, rational, or deliberative choices, other-directed motivation that promotes happiness, health, and well-being will be left out of the calculus.

Deliberative strategies may be appropriate for choosing among self-interested alternatives that are concrete and have imminent, easily imagined consequences for survival. But such strategies may be ill suited to deciding between concrete alternatives (e.g., more money) and other-directed options that (a) are based on emotional sensitivity to another's needs and (b) have consequences for self and other that are distant and perhaps not well specified. Consider someone who has been offered a higher-paying job but must move across the country to accept it, leaving friends and family behind. Because the incremental increase in wealth is not likely to substantially increase happiness (Argyle, 1999; Haring, et al, 1984; Myers, 2000; Quoidbach et al., 2010), surely the person in this hypothetical—but very common—scenario should be reluctant to accept the new job.

But in making a deliberate and ostensibly rational decision like this, do we have the ability to properly weigh the two very different options? Can we rationally consider the projected costs, stress, hardship, and loneliness that come with a move and with opting not to remain in close proximity to friends and family? Perhaps not. It is probable that activation of the caregiving system does not feel rewarding to us in the same way that concrete reinforcers (e.g., money, candy, or drugs) do. We may not be consciously aware of its activation at all, or of its stress-regulatory properties (Brown et al., this volume). So when we undertake the deliberation, we don't think of the loneliness; we think of the money and its effects, easily imagined.

To take it a step further, it may be difficult, for example, to make informed choices about whether commuting, cellphones, and texting—clearly important tools for enhancing mobility and social communication—will (perhaps paradoxically) undermine the health benefits that social contact can provide (see Crocker & Canevello, this volume). We know that social isolation is a risk factor for morbidity and mortality (House, Landis, & Umberson, 1988), but do we know at what point our bodies perceive technological representations of the "other" as social isolation?

We may not always make choices that maximize our health and well-being because the environment that our bodies were adapted to thrive in is not the industrial, technological environment that we have created for ourselves. Rather, we have produced an artificial landscape that, among other things, dissociates reward from its natural biological context. An example is addiction (as to drugs, alcohol, or sex), which according to some constitutes, as Hyman (2005) puts it, "a pathological usurpation of the neural mechanisms . . . that under normal circumstances serve to shape survival behaviors related to the pursuit of rewards and the cues that predict them" (p. 1414). In part, individuals become addicted because they have choices their evolutionary ancestors did not have, some of which result in a "hijacking of neural systems related to the pursuit of rewards."

■ BOUNDED RATIONALITY AND BOUNDED SELF-INTEREST

As we begin to appreciate that humans are not always rational, do not always prosper with increasing numbers of options, and often act in the interest of others, it makes sense to question assumptions inherent in economic models designed to inform social policy. The recognition that our rationality is bounded has been important (e.g., Kahneman & Tversky, 2000), but the potential existence of a caregiving motivational system seriously questions the primacy of self-interested motives. The assumption of other-directed motivation implies the existence of cost–benefit analyses focused on the well-being of others and suggests that we may sometimes be willing to sacrifice for others without any expectation of future reward (Crocker & Canevello, this volume). Obviously, and as discussed elsewhere, the caregiving system can explain behavior that is difficult to understand from the rational-self-interest perspective. The existence of a caregiving motivational system should make us suspicious of economic models that tether human choice tightly and completely to self-interest. Of course, acknowledging that people are motivated to care for and help others does not imply that they are not self-interested or motivated to maximize pleasure. Rather it suggests that as humans we are pluralistic (Sober & Wilson, 1998), navigating between our own interests and the interests of others.

■ IMPLICATIONS OF A CAREGIVING SYSTEM APPROACH: OPTIMIZING INVESTMENT

So what are the implications of a caregiving system for thinking about utility? What should we seek to maximize? Ultimately, answers to these questions hinge on critical research that examines how we navigate trade-offs between self and other. But based on our current understanding, we can begin to suggest some possibilities. At the very least, the fact that humans can be driven by concern for the welfare of others (and it appears that this concern may benefit health and well-being) suggests that we should do all we can to avoid conditions that limit access to the caregiving system. For example, economic and social policies that promote social isolation and interfere with a sense of safety and security should be eschewed. As several researchers from diverse backgrounds have noted, isolation from others and threats to felt security can interfere with self-regulation of emotional states; negatively impact the development of compassion for others, make caring for others difficult or impossible; and compromise health and well-being (Brown et al.; Crocker & Canevello; Mikulincer & Shaver; Porges & Carter—all this volume).

Other factors that may undermine access to the caregiving system include strong incentives to maximize pleasure or hedonic rewards for the self. Such incentives may interfere with caregiving goals as discussed above, motivating us to sacrifice our close relationships in pursuit of financial and material gain. Specifically, policies that incentivize work and financial success at the expense of proximity to family, loved ones, and close friends undermine important other-directed strategies that can enhance physical and psychological well-being.

We should also consider the effects of the media on our caregiving system goals. Our brains evolved in an environment where the salience of threat corresponded to inherent danger in the environment. But the current media environment supplies near-constant exposure to threatening stimuli (e.g., Dorfman, 2001), promoting unrealistic perceptions of danger and risk and targeting unjustifiably certain beliefs, political philosophies, groups, situations, and locales as threats to personal safety. To the extent that we perceive these threats as signaling constant danger, however unrealistic that perception may be, we invite consequences of prolonged activation of the stress response, development and expression of fear and aggression, immobilization, and other inhibitors of caregiving motivation and behavior (Numan, this volume; Porges & Carter, this volume).

It is possible that the neurobiological system(s) that underlies caring for others is recruited to direct other forms of investment—including creative productions that satisfy both self and others. As reviewed by Numan (2006) and noted in the essay by Brown et al. (this volume), hypothalamic processes have been shown to be critical for other forms of instrumental behavior beyond caregiving. Conceivably, goal-directed motivation and behavior with no phenotypic similarity to caregiving—for example, making a piece of furniture by hand—nevertheless involve the same hypothalamic and motor regions that downregulate stress. If this is true, then we may discover that incentives to encourage people to create with their hands, write, compose music, or make art will prove to be as valuable for well-being as incentives that enable people to care for and stay close to their loved ones.

We may also discover that goal-directed behavior involving investment in the self (e.g., eating healthily, exercising, and avoiding drugs) bolsters the effectiveness of the caregiving system, by causing individuals to feel that they have more resource-providing potential. In this way, investment in the self may also be viewed as investment in others, as opposed to a means of gratifying reward-seeking drives. If this is true, health-promotion and disease-prevention programs may be more effective if they are framed as a means to help individuals meet their own caregiving goals.

Of course, scientific attention to "the caregiving side of the equation" is in its infancy (Berscheid & Collins, 2000). We don't know whether the caregiving system also has a dark side, perhaps promoting undesirable, even violent actions in the interest of benefiting or protecting those we love. Because of this, caution must be used in formulating policies designed to augment caregiving system motives.

Ultimately, a better understanding of the caregiving system may help us to thoughtfully consider the kind of world we would like to leave for subsequent generations. As a society, we may never agree upon an answer to whether caregiving system goals can be reduced to economic concepts of self-interest. However, we can probably all agree that the caregiving system and its underlying biological mechanisms are currently underemphasized in economics. By turning our attention to this neglected area, we may not only inform economic debate; we may discover better ways to maximize utility.

■ **REFERENCES**

Argyle, M. (1999). Causes and correlates of happiness. In D. Kahneman, E. Diener, & N. Schwarz (Eds.), *Well-being: The foundations of hedonic psychology* (pp. 213–229). New York, NY: Russell Sage Foundation.

Ariely, D. (2009). *Predictably irrational: The hidden forces that shape our decisions.* New York, NY: Harper Collins.

Berscheid, E., & Collins, W. A. (2000). Who cares? For whom and when, how, and why? *Psychological Inquiry, 11,* 107–109.

Boarini, R., Johansson, A., & d'Ercole, M. (2006). Alternative measures of well-being (OECD Social, Employment and Migration Working Papers). Paris, France: Organisation for Economic Co-operation and Development. Available at: http://www.oecd.org/data oecd/13/38/36165332.pdf

Brown, S. L., & Brown, M. (2006). Selective Investment Theory: Recasting the functional significance of close relationships. *Psychological Inquiry, 17,* 30–59.

Brown, S. L., Brown, R. M., House, J. S., & Smith, D. M. (2008). Coping with spousal loss: The potential buffering effects of self-reported helping behavior. *Personality and Social Psychology Bulletin, 34,* 849–861.

Brown, S. L., Nesse, R., Vinokur, A. D., & Smith, D. M. (2003). Providing support may be more beneficial than receiving it: Results from a prospective study of mortality. *Psychological Science, 14,* 320–327.

Brown, S. L. Smith, D. M., Schulz, R. Kabeto, M., Ubel, P., Yee, J., . . . Langa, K. (2009). Caregiving and decreased mortality in a national sample of older adults, *Psychological Science, 20,* 488–494.

Brown, W. M., Consedine, N. S., & Magai, C. (2005). Altruism relates to health in an ethnically diverse sample of older adults. *Journal of Gerontology, Series B: Psychological Sciences & Social Sciences, 60B,* 143–152.

Crocker, J., Niiya, Y., & Mischkowski, D. (2008). Why does writing about important values reduce defensiveness? Self-affirmation and the role of positive other-directed feelings. *Psychological Science, 19,* 740–747.

Camerer, C. F. (1999). Behavioral economics: Reunifying psychology and economics, *Proceedings of the National Academy of Sciences of the United States of America, 96*(19), 10575–10577.

Camerer, C. (2006). Behavioral economics. In R. Blundell, W. K. Newey, & T, Persson (Eds.), *Advances in economics and econometrics: Theory and applications, Ninth World Congress,* (Vol. 2, pp. 181–214). Cambridge, England: Cambridge University Press.

Di Tella, R., MacCulloch, R. J., & Oswald , A. J. (2004). The macroeconomics of happiness. *Review of Economics and Statistics, 85,* 809–827.

Dolan, P. (2008). Developing methods that really do value the "Q" in the QALY. *Health Economics, Policy and Law, 3,* 69–77.

Dorfman. L. (2001). *Off balance: Youth, race & crime in the news.* Washington, DC: Youth Law Center.

Frey, B. S., & Stutzer, A. (2002a). *Happiness and economics: How the economy and institutions affect well-being.* Princeton, NJ: Princeton University Press.

Frey, B. S., & Stutzer, A. (2002b). What can economists learn from happiness research? *Journal of Economic Literature, 40*(2), 402–435.

Greene, J., Nystrom, L., Engell, A., Darley, J., & Cohen, J. (2004). The neural bases of cognitive conflict and control in moral judgement. *Neuron, 44,* 389–400.

Hamilton, W. D. (1964). The genetic evolution of social behavior: I and II. *Journal of Theoretical Biology, 7,* 1–52.

Haring, M. J., Stock, W. A., & Okun, M. A. (1984). A research synthesis of gender and social class as correlates of subjective well-being. *Human Relations, 37,* 645–657.

House, J., Landis, K., & Umberson, D. (1988). Social relationships and health. *Science, 241,* 540–545.

Hyman, S. E. (2005). Addiction: A disease of learning and memory. *American Journal of Psychiatry, 162,* 1414–1422.

Kahneman, D,, Krueger, A., Schkade, D. A., Schwarz, N., & Stone, A. A. (2004a). A survey method for characterizing daily life experience: The day reconstruction method. *Science, 306*(5702), 1776–1780.

Kahneman, D., Krueger, A. B., Schkade, D. A., Schwarz, N. & Stone, A. A. (2004b). Toward national well-being accounts. *American Economic Review, 94*(2), 429–434.

Kahneman, D., & Tversky, A. (2000). *Choices, values, and frames.* Cambridge, England: Cambridge University Press.

Kahneman, D., Wakker, P., & Sarin, R. (1997). Back to Bentham? Explorations of experienced utility. *Quarterly Journal of Economics, 112,* 375–405.

Koenig, H. G. (2007). Altruistic love and physical health? In S. G. Post (Ed.), *Altruism and health* (pp. 15–32). New York, NY: Oxford University Press.

Layard, R. (2005). *Happiness: Lessons from a new science.* New York, NY: Penguin.

Mueller, D. (1986). Rational egoism versus adaptive egoism as fundamental postulate for a descriptive theory of human behavior. *Public Choice, 51,* 3–23.

Myers, D. G. (2000). The funds, friends, and faith of happy people. *American Psychologist, 55,* 56–67.

Numan, M. (2006). Hypothalamic neural circuits regulating maternal responsiveness toward infants. *Behavioral and Cognitive Neuroscience Reviews, 5,* 163–190.

Oman D. (2007). Does volunteering foster physical health and longevity? In S. G. Post (Ed.), *Altruism and health* (pp. 15–32). New York, NY: Oxford University Press.

Organization for Economic Co-operation and Development World Forum, Measuring the Progress of Societies (2007, June). Istanbul, Turkey,

Oswald, A. J. (1997). Happiness and economic performance. *Economic Journal, 107*(445), 1815–31.

Poulin, M., Brown, S. L., Smith, D. M., Ubel, P., Jankovik, S., & Langa, K. (2010). Does a helping hand mean a heavy heart? Helping behavior and well-being among spouse caregivers. *Psychology and Aging, 25,* 108–117 .

Quoidbach, J., Dunn, E. W., Petrides, K. V., & Mikolajczak, M. (2010). Money giveth, money taketh away: The dual effect of wealth on happiness. *Psychological Science, 21,* 759–763.

Rabin, M. (1998). Psychology and economics. *Journal of Economic Literature, 36*(1), 11–46.

Rodin, J., & Langer, E. (1977). Long-term effects of a control-relevant intervention with the institutionalized aged. *Journal of Personality and Social Psychology, 35*, 897–902.

Schwartz, B. (2004a). *The paradox of choice: Why less is more.* New York, NY: Harper Collins.

Schwartz, B. (2004b, April). The tyranny of choice. *Scientific American*, 71–75.

Smith, D. M., Brown, S. L., & Ubel, P. A. (2008). Are subjective well-being measures any better than decision utility measures? *Health Economics, Policy and Law, 3*(1), 85–92.

Sober, E., & Wilson, D. S. (1998). *Unto others: The evolution and psychology of unselfish behavior.* Cambridge, MA: Harvard University Press.

Stiglitz, J., Sen, A. & Fitoussi, J.-P. (2008). *Report by the Commission on the Measurement of Economic Performance and Social Progress.* Retrieved from http://www.stiglitz-sen-fitoussi.fr

Wilson, T. D., & Schooler, J. W. (1991). Thinking too much: Introspection can reduce the quality of preferences and decisions. *Journal of Personality and Social Psychology, 60*, 181–192.

Yinon, Y,, & Landau, M. O. (1987). On the reinforcing value of helping behavior in a positive mood. *Motivation and Emotion, 11*, 83–93.

16 Bringing Neuroscience into Political Science

The Caregiving System and Human Sociopolitical Evolution

■ JUDITH S. KULLBERG AND J. DAVID SINGER[†]

> Know thyself—Inscription over the entrance to the temple of Athena at Delphi.

> When we have unified enough certain knowledge, we will understand who we are and why we are here.
> (E. O. Wilson, 1998)

The advances in neuroscience of the last few decades have dramatically expanded our understanding of the human brain and the connection between brain function and behavior. Tools such as functional magnetic resonance imaging (fMRI) and positron emission tomography (PET) have allowed scientists to identify the brain systems underlying emotions, cognitive processes, and choice. Incorporation of human neurophysiology into theories of micro- and macro-level social and political phenomena should allow us to unravel the complex interconnections between nature (biology) and nurture (culture and learning) and build a comprehensive theory of human behavior. For the first time in history, the self-knowledge prescribed by the oracle at Delphi to the ancient Athenians appears to be within the reach of humankind.

Although the implications for the social sciences are enormous, there are still relatively few social scientists attempting to include the findings from neurological research into their explanations of social and political phenomena. The attempt to consider the interconnection between brain function and social processes has been led for the most part by biologists and neuroscientists, who are increasingly interested in phenomena once squarely within the domain of the social sciences, such as social stratification, power, morality, and religion. If the social sciences fail to incorporate knowledge of the brain into theories of social and political processes and phenomena, they may quickly cease to be relevant or become absorbed by an expanded discipline of human biology. Social scientists are getting a late start and have much work to do to bridge the deep chasm separating their models of human behavior and the neuroscience of human cognition and emotion.

[†]In memory of J. David Singer (1925–2009), who saw science as the path to peace and showed us the way.

In an effort toward such integration, this essay considers several major implications of the neuroscience of caregiving and altruism for the discipline of political science. It describes in general, broad-brush terms the nonbiological explanations for human behavior widely used in political science and assesses the validity of those explanations given new knowledge of the neurophysiological foundations of human behavior. It then considers the significance of the caregiving system for political science by applying what we know about caregiving to several enduring questions in political science: the origins of the political community, the basis of group and national identity, and the causes of war.

■ BIOLOGY AND THE SCIENCE OF POLITICS

The belief that models of political behavior should be based on human biology and psychology is not new. Throughout the 20th century, leading scholars periodically called for the integration of the behavioral and social sciences (American Political Science Association, 1951; Corning, 1980; Masters, 1990; Singer, 1965), and a few research programs attempting such integration finally emerged in the 1960s and early 1970s (Caldwell, 1964; Davies, 1963; Somit, 1972). These led to the creation of a "biopolitics" group within the International Political Science Association in 1973 and the formation of the Association for Politics and Life Sciences (APLS) in 1980.[1]

Despite a stirring of interest in human biology within political science in the 20th century, by the end of the century little progress had been made toward building theoretical connections between the two (Somit & Peterson, 1998). As a result, 21st-century studies of political behavior, with few exceptions, are uninformed by the science of human brain function. It is no exaggeration to contend that almost all political scientists are unaware of the substantial and rapidly growing knowledge of the neurobiological basis of individual behavior. This situation can be partially attributed to the lingering legacy of the discipline's behavioral revolution of the 1950s and 1960s. Behavioralists emphasized empirical observation of behavior over theory and tended to dismiss or set aside as unknowable phenomena they could not directly observe and measure, such as individual psychology and the functioning of human brains (Easton, 1953; Farr, 1995).

Whatever the cause, there can be little doubt that human biology remains outside the institutionalized boundaries of the discipline: In a cursory review of current graduate curricula at the top seven Ph.D. programs in political science, we were unable to find a single course devoted entirely to the biology or psychology of human behavior, and only a few on political learning or socialization. Although a small number of political psychology graduate programs have been established within political science departments over the last two decades,[2] research on the psychological dimension of politics is still more frequently conducted by psychologists than it is by political scientists. Given the complete inattention to biology in graduate training and the small niche that political psychology occupies in the discipline, it is hardly surprising that the neuroscientific revolution has had little impact on the larger theoretical debates and paradigmatic development within political science.

If contemporary studies of politics are not based on or informed by neuroscience and biological psychology, how do political scientists conceptualize the determinants of human behavior? Since the late 1950s, political scientists, like their peers in sociology and anthropology, have tended to see behavior, whether of individuals or groups, as largely the product of macro-level factors: of social systems, structures, governmental decision-making processes, or culture transmitted to individuals and across generations through learning or socialization. The human mind, when directly considered or discussed at all, has often been assumed to be a blank slate on which basic beliefs, norms, rules of the game, and behavioral patterns are stamped or imprinted (Somit & Peterson, 2003). This general approach to explaining behavior has been referred to as the Standard Social Science Model (SSSM) by evolutionary psychologists and those calling for synthesis or "consilience" between the natural and social sciences (Tooby & Cosmides, 1995; E. O. Wilson, 1998). These scholars have criticized the SSSM for its very limited attention to human cognition and psychology, its general neglect of micro-level or individual factors, and its circular explanations for individual and group behavior, i.e., the tendency to explain behavior as the product of other behavior, such as beliefs and norms.

The knowledge of brain function and behavior that has accumulated within the field of neuroscience directly challenges the SSSM. The human brain/mind is not a blank slate entirely shaped by culture or learning. Rather, it is the location of behavioral systems, including the caregiving system, that are the products of millions of years of mammalian and human evolution. Although they do not mechanistically produce identical behaviors in all individuals, they constitute a bedrock of behavioral tendencies, a discrete, albeit wide behavioral repertoire with a considerable degree of predictability. Even though our understanding of these systems is rudimentary and expanding, their discovery demolishes the assumption that human behavior is entirely the result of learning and culture. Indeed, the primary causal arrow points from genes to culture, since the evolution of the modern human brain preceded the creation of human cultures. The position that human behavior is neurologically based does not deny the importance of culture; rather, it would appear likely, as will be discussed later in this essay, that culture is interconnected with specific brain systems, generated by them but also feeding back and acting on them in a cybernetic loop. In sum, to the extent that the SSSM has neglected human nature (i.e., those facets of behavior rooted in the genetic structure of human beings) it has generated distorted and incomplete explanations of political life.

Long before the SSSM drew criticism from outside the social sciences, the neglect of individual choice and action and the determinism of the SSSM had prompted some political scientists in the 1960s and 1970s to search for an alternate paradigm. In economics, they discovered and happily embraced rational choice theory. The rational choice model provided a ready-made theoretical and analytical framework or "tool kit" that was quickly applied to a wide range of political phenomena, including elections, public policy, and interest groups (Buchanan & Tullock, 1962; Downs, 1957; Olson, 1965). From a rather shaky start in the midst of the behavioral revolution, the rational choice approach developed a broad following. It now pervades theory and research in all fields of political science.

At the center of rational choice explanations are individual actors. These actors can be individual human beings or abstract individuals such as a groups, organizations, corporations, or even states. Actors are assumed to be self-interested and purposive, that is, to seek to maximize their gains and minimize their losses. They also able to rank their interests or preferred outcomes in terms of their degree of desirability or utility. Since actors are rational, they will always seek to obtain their most preferred outcome before outcomes lower in the hierarchy, or ranking, of preferences.

While economic rational choice models almost always measure outcomes in monetary units, with wealth or profit as the primary goal of economic behavior, outcomes in political science models may be measured not only in monetary units but in other goods that individuals are assumed to pursue in political and social settings, such as power, status, elected office, or particular policy outcomes.

Rational choice or "formal" models are highly stylized and simplified representations of political phenomena. This simplicity is seen as a strength by the models' adherents, who value the "parsimonious" explanations of politics such models offer, but as a weakness by their detractors. The latter fault the models for not incorporating context, culture, values, morality, social relationships, individual psychology, and many other factors that contribute to political processes and outcomes or, at the very least, are intertwined with politics (Friedman, 1996; Green & Shapiro, 1994).

Many of the findings from the expanding study of the linkage between brain and behavior are generating further doubts about the validity and utility of the rational choice approach. The hypothesis that human behavior is purposive and rational, proceeding from a careful calculation of costs and benefits and the weighing of alternative courses of action, does not jibe with what is known about how the brain functions. First, the rational choice model omits emotion, and it is now understood that human cognition is inextricably interconnected with affective or emotional processes. Recent studies suggest that even cognitions of abstract political concepts, such as "representation," "the public good," or "international conflict," are loaded with affect (Morris, Squires, Taber, & Lodge, 2003). Second, the rational choice model emphasizes free will and purposiveness, but emotions that often influence choice or behavior are generated spontaneously in the limbic system outside the conscious control of the individual. This is true not only of emotions connected to behaviors necessary for individual and species survival, like eating and sex, but also of responses to many social stimuli, such as human faces and facial expressions (Winkelman & Berridge, 2003; University of Michigan, 2007). In sum, rather than being the product of rational cost–benefit analysis, much behavior, including evaluations of political objects, appears to be either produced or influenced by the limbic system.

Another weakness of the rational choice model of human behavior is that it is inconsistent with the accumulating arguments for and evidence of a genetically based human capacity for altruism—actions taken to help or advance the well-being of others at some cost to the actor. The evolution of altruism (Brown, Brown, & Preston, this volume; Krebs, this volume) has been partially explained by the theory of inclusive fitness, which asserts that help to genetically related others (kin) improves the likelihood of the transmission of genes that, if not identical to those of the altruist, are very similar (W. D. Hamilton, 1964). Another explanation for altruism, referred to as "reciprocal altruism," asserts that help to others can actually advance altruists' reproductive fitness if it is sufficiently widespread in a population. According to this theory, altruists ultimately benefit over the long run from their altruistic behavior, because there is a high probability that others will reciprocate when they are in need (Trivers, 1971). Other theorists have even argued for the existence of strong altruism—consistent and predictable displays of altruism toward others, even unrelated others, that may lead to an absolute, rather than relative, *decline* in the reproductive fitness of the donor in situations where she risks her life to protect the life of an unrelated individual (D. S. Wilson & Dugatkin, 1992). An important piece of evidence that altruism is a genetically based tendency in humans is the consistent finding that most individuals prefer altruists over nonaltruists as friends, partners, or mates, and tend to avoid or even punish nonaltruists (Andreoni, 1995; Fehr & Gachter, 1998; Fehr, Gachter, & Kirchsteiger, 1997; Henrich et al., 2005). Thus, although they may differ about the specific evolutionary logic that produced and sustains altruism, neuroscientists and evolutionary biologists tend to agree that altruism is a genetically based behavior that has contributed to the reproductive fitness of humans.

The extensive research on altruism is persuasive and points toward a behavioral template in humans that is distinctly different from that advanced by rational choice theorists. Indeed, if human beings had acted only as depicted in rational choice theory, selfishly calculating and then acting to maximize their narrow, individual gains in competition with and at the expense of others, it is quite likely that *Homo sapiens* would not have survived as a species. Given the human life cycle (particularly the small numbers of offspring and very long periods of infant dependency) and the considerable vulnerability of humans to predators and environmental extremes (we lack sharp teeth or claws, have no fur, and have very large brains housed in fragile skulls perched precariously on thin necks and spinal columns prone to injury), altruism was probably a necessary adaptation for the survival of *Homo sapiens*.

In sum, the evidence of a genetic basis for human behavior requires considerable adjustment of the models employed in contemporary political science. As our knowledge of the character and operation of particular neurophysiological systems expands and our understanding of how they affect both individual and group behavior in various contexts increases, it may be possible to use that knowledge to construct new models of political behavior capable of generating probabilistic estimates of particular outcomes (Gintis, 2007). Over time, the accumulation and combination of models that have been subjected to and refined by empirical tests could result in a multilevel, integrated theory of human social and political behavior (Cacioppo & Bernstson, 1992; Cacioppo & Visser, 2003).

■ THE CAREGIVING SYSTEM AND SOCIAL ORGANIZATION

One way to begin the process of integrating neuroscience and social science is to consider the extent to which a specific neurophysiological system is involved in, or can at least partially account for, specific social and political phenomena. If, as the editors of this volume argue, much of prosocial behavior is motivated and shaped by the caregiving system, we should be able to find abundant evidence of its role in the development and maintenance of social and political institutions. If we find such evidence and can thus be confident that the theory of the caregiving has significant explanatory power, we can begin to use knowledge of the neuro-physiology of caregiving to "inform, refine, and constrain" existing theories of politics, thereby strengthening our understanding of social and political processes (Cacioppo & Visser, 2003; E. OWilson, 1998).

We embark on this path fully aware of the many difficulties that will lie along the way. The first of these is that macro-level phenomena such as the establish-ment of political communities, the formation of group identities, and warfare are rarely caused directly by single factors; rather they are the product of multiple causal factors operating at different levels, from the individual to the global. We may strengthen our explanations by adding molecules, genes, cells, and brains to our equations, but we will certainly not simplify them! Indeed, we are multiplying the complexity of our explanations by a large factor, because it is certain that mul-tiple human neurophysiological behavioral systems, not just the caregiving system, are involved in social and political phenomena.

A second, related difficulty is that behavior is the result of interactions between neurophysiological behavioral systems and the environment, both natural and social. To illustrate the interaction between the social dimension of environment and brain physiology, Cacioppo and Visser (2003) recount the tale of a study that failed to show statistically significant effects of amphetamines on chimp behavior because the researchers had not controlled for variation of individual chimp posi-tion in the social hierarchy. It turned out that amphetamines act differently on individuals with different social status, intensifying dominance behavior in higher-ranking individuals and submissive behavior in low-ranking individuals. Similarly, the level of testosterone in male primates has been shown to correlate positively with the likelihood of sexual behavior, but testosterone level itself varies according to the availability of receptive females in the environment. In sum, because of the complexity of the interrelationships between biology and the social environment, the hypotheses about social and political behavior that we have derived from the theory of caregiving system and discuss below are undoubtedly incomplete and, even if ultimately supported in general by available evidence, still in need of much refinement.

We begin with a simplified model of the caregiving system and some prelimi-nary ideas about how it might help us to understand politics. Following Brown and Brown (2006) and the essay by Brown, Brown, and Preston in this volume, we will assume that prosocial (helping or altruistic) behavior is generated by the caregiving system. This system evolved for the purpose of regulating mamma-lian maternal behavior, but is present in both male and females and is involved not only in parenting but in care of related others as well as close allies. This system functions in a very predictable way: Cues of distress or signals of need from others activate structures within the amygdala and hypothalamus in the brain's limbic system, triggering the release of neural transmitters such as oxyto-cin. The neurotransmitters activate other brain structures located in the ventral bed of the stria terminalis—the ventral tegmental area, nucleus accumbens, and ventral pallidum—which organize and motivate the motor responses that comprise caring and helping behavior. In addition, the caregiving system appears to be capable of deactivating emotions, such as fear or desire for food and mates, that would interfere with providing for and helping dependents or others in need. The caregiving system also includes a mechanism for the detection of exploitation, which allows the caregiver to discriminate between kin and non-kin and between allies and strangers or non-allies. This mechanism is centered in a part of the brain, the orbital frontal cortex, that is involved in sensory integration, social memories, and social judgments.

As is true of all biological systems, the caregiving system evolved because it increased the probability of offspring survival, thus enhancing the reproductive fitness of individuals. By extending caregiving to other relatives, it also serves to enhance inclusive fitness.

There is considerable cause for understanding the caregiving system as central to the survival of the human species. It overlaps with neurological structures and processes associated with sex and social attachment (Bowlby, 1969). It predisposes individuals to care for and nurture kin. The prosocial behavior generated by the caregiving system elicits social rewards from others and provides physiological health benefits to the caregiver (Brown et al., 2009). People who behave altruistically are judged to be more attractive by others, experience greater subjective well-being, and appear to function more effectively in daily life than those who do not consistently help or act altruistically toward others (Harvard University, 2010; Phillips, 2008). Even individuals burdened with the care of seriously ill or disabled dependents experience more positive and fewer negative emotions than those not providing such care (Poulin et al., 2010). Caregiving and helping, along with such emotional capacities as empathy and the need for the company of others, can thus be understood as intrinsic human social propensities, "social instincts" that contribute to the collective survival and well-being of humans and sustain social interactions (Cacioppo & Patrick, 2008; de Waal, 2008; Ridley, 1997).

Insofar as it shapes and sustains human relationships, the caregiving system is more than a property of individuals; it is a feature of social groups. We assume that the prosocial behavior generated by the caregiving system is a major source of the social cohesion that has been holding groups of *Homo sapiens* together since the species appeared approximately 200,000 years ago. In addition, it generates a set of predictable responses of individuals to others and to the social environment. These responses vary across individuals and situations, so they should be understood only metaphorically as "instincts" and more precisely as probabilistic tendencies. Another way of conceptualizing the caregiving system is that it generates "epigenetic rules" for how humans should interact with one another. As defined by E. O. Wilson, epigenetic rules are "rules of thumb that allow organisms to find rapid solutions to problems encountered in the environment" and predispose "individuals . . . to make certain choices as opposed to others" (1997, p. 193). The caregiving system provides the genetic rules for how humans should interact with one another.

■ CAREGIVING AND THE ORIGINS OF SOCIETIES AND STATES

If we are correct in our assumptions that the caregiving system is a primary component of social cohesion and that it provides epigenetic rules for social interaction, it should help us to explain many social phenomena, from micro-level interactions between just a few individuals to the properties of entire social systems and the interactions between societies. We can begin to assess the explanatory leverage of the theory of the caregiving system by using it to address a question that has intrigued philosophers, historians, and political scientists for centuries: How and why did humans come to live in societies and to form political communities?

A brief survey of the answers given to this question since antiquity is useful for charting the transformation of human understanding of both humanity and society from ancient times to the present. Aristotle, expressing the common view of educated Greeks of his day, saw the political community as natural and prior to the individual, not in a temporal sense, but in terms of the ultimate *telos*, or end, of humankind. Because humans alone among the creatures have *logos*, or "reasoned speech," Aristotle concluded that the human being is "a political animal," designed for life in a political community. Christian philosophers from late antiquity to the early modern period, including Augustine, Aquinas, and Luther, saw societies as part of God's creation and government as divinely sanctioned, though inevitably imperfect. In contrast to the ancient and religious understanding of society as part of a natural or cosmic order, liberal theorists argued that state and society were products of an explicit contract among equal human beings. Hobbes asserted that humans created "civil society" by transferring all their rights to a "sovereign" who would rule over them and establish order, thus escaping the brutal competition for survival, a "war of all against all" that prevailed in the state of nature (Hobbes, 2009). While they disagreed with Hobbes that humans are naturally aggressive and that only the complete transfer of rights to a monarch could guarantee social order, the liberal philosophers John Locke, Jean-Jacques Rousseau, and Immanuel Kant also depicted "civil society" as the product of an explicit social contract among equal individuals possessing basic human rights (Kant, 2006; Locke, 1966; Rousseau, 1990). Although already several centuries old, the liberal understanding of the origins of society continues to pervade the contemporary world and can be found in preambles of constitutions and in the content of civics courses around the globe, particularly in Western Europe and North America. Liberalism has also had a profound effect on contemporary political science models of representative democracy and theories of society, and it is not difficult to see the close similarity between the tenets of liberalism and the assumptions of the rational choice model.

However appealing or in accord with the ideologies of ideology and specific societies, philosophical explanations for the emergence of society and the state are based on conjecture. To achieve consilience between the social and natural sciences, it is necessary to start with an explanation for the origin of societies and the state that is based on empirical knowledge of the intrinsic characteristics of humans, the factors shaping social relations, and the course of human social evolution.

Knowledge of the caregiving system suggests that humans are disposed by "nature" to live in groups of related individuals nurturing and helping one another, and not, as Hobbes supposed, alone and aggressively competing with others. We expect the "natural" human group to be small, since the caregiving system directs care and help to offspring, close kin, and close allies who mutually enhance one another's reproductive fitness. The prosocial behavior of the caregiving system is primarily activated by cues of need or distress from kin and close allies; it is not typically or as strongly triggered by similar cues from non-kin, strangers, and those who have proven themselves to be untrustworthy. The caregiving system thus exerts both centripetal and centrifugal force. It binds kin and allies closely together in a group, but excludes outsiders and may occasionally lead to aggression against those perceived as a threat to group members. Indeed, as this essay was being written, researchers at the University of Amsterdam reported that in a competitive context, oxytocin—a main neurotransmitter of the caregiving system—is involved in both self-sacrificial behavior toward in-group members and defensive aggression toward out-groups (De Dreu et al., 2010). By strengthening ties and trust within the group and motivating group members to work together to defend the group against competition from other groups, the caregiving system contributes to maintenance of the group.

These propositions about the "natural" form of human social interaction generated by the caregiving system are consistent with archeological and anthropological evidence of how humans lived prior to the emergence of large-scale society. The basic social unit of almost all hominids, and most definitely of humans, is the small hunter-gatherer band composed of approximately 25 related individuals (Johnson & Earle, 2000, p. 41). Humans and their ancestors, who diverged from the progenitors of contemporary great apes around 7 million years ago, lived exclusively in hunter-gatherer bands for more than 6 million years until about 11,000 years ago, when modern humans began to form larger social groups—first tribes, then larger chiefdoms, and finally early states. Even today, small, isolated populations of hunter-gatherer cultures persist in a few remote pockets of desert and Arctic regions (Diamond, 1992).

In addition to the pervasiveness and persistence of the hunter-gatherer band, the internal structure of hunter-gatherer societies supports the hypothesis that the caregiving system is capable of generating and maintaining small social groups. Anthropological studies of hunter-gatherer bands around the globe and in different historical periods have found them to be remarkably similar to one another. They are always composed of extended family groups, which may contain subgroups or encampments of primary family units, that is, mates and children with perhaps a sibling or two. Members of hunter-gatherer bands eat and work alongside one another, cooperate on complex tasks, and share food and other resources (Johnson & Earle, p. 43). The economy of the hunter-gatherer band is based entirely on social relationships rather than formal rules of exchange. Members tend to give food to one another and help others freely with no expectation of direct reward or immediate reciprocation. This "generalized reciprocity" is particularly likely in relations between the closest kin, especially parents and children (Sahlins, 1972). Relations among adult peers in the group, particularly those who are not closely related, tend to be sustained more by "balanced reciprocity," in which the prosocial act of one individual creates obligations for those benefiting from it to reciprocate at some point in the future. Under balanced reciprocity, help is given to others in trust, in the expectation that they would do the same under similar circumstances. In such a pattern of interaction, failure to reciprocate over time jeopardizes relationships (Johnson & Earle, p. 48).

The close correspondence between the hunter-gatherer band and the type of social unit we predicted from our simplified model of the caregiving system is striking. Not only does the evidence support the hypothesis, it additionally suggests that the caregiving system provides the foundation for a primitive communal economy. Moreover, the overall pattern of social interaction within hunter-gatherer bands conforms to both the inclusive fitness and reciprocal altruism theories of prosocial behavior.

Research on hunter-gathers also confirms our expectation that the caregiving system would tend to limit the size of the group. Hunter-gatherers help and share food with members of their own group, but rarely with those outside of the group. Indeed, it appears that the boundaries between hunter-gatherer bands are fairly rigid. The reverse of prosocial behavior, a kind of "negative reciprocity," characterizes interactions between strangers or members of neighboring unrelated groups: They may try to steal from, cheat, or take advantage of each other (Sahlins, 1972). Despite these tensions between individuals from different groups, Johnson and Earle's (2000) review of the ethnological research on hunter-gatherers finds little evidence of sustained or large-scale warfare; they attribute the lack of warfare to the nonterritoriality and egalitarianism of hunter-gatherers. Other scholars, however, argue that many if not all hunter-gatherer bands engaged in occasional raids on one another for food and women and that these raids often resulted in injury and death (Gat, 2006).

In sum, the picture drawn from research on hunter-gatherer groups suggests that human social life prior to the appearance of larger social groups and states was characterized by cooperation, helping, and mutual trust within groups. Although mistrust, competition, and occasional violence probably prevailed *between* groups, social life *within* groups in the "state of nature" was relatively harmonious (Diamond, 1992).

The fact that our ancestors existed in hunter-gatherer bands for millions of years and that modern humans everywhere lived exclusively in such bands until 11,000 years ago constitutes prima facie evidence of a biological template for this social form: No factor except a common genome could imaginably produce such behavioral uniformity. The concordance between the characteristics of hunter-gatherer groups and our predictions about the features of the basic human group that would be generated and sustained by the caregiving system suggests a powerful connection between this specific brain system and social interaction.

How did humans move from the small, family-level societies to the large, complex societies in which we live today? Generalizing from the data amassed by archeologists, anthropologists, and historians, Johnson and Earle (2000) argue that the evolution of human society from the hunter-gatherer band has been driven by three interconnected processes—subsistence intensification, political integration, and social stratification. These have led to the same sequence of change around the globe: "Foragers diversify and adopt agriculture; villages form and integrate into regional polities; leaders come to dominate and transform social relations" (Johnson & Earle, 2000, p. 2). This pattern of change is almost certainly the result not of genetic evolution, but rather of cultural evolution—of culture interacting with genes to produce novel forms of human society, including our own.

Social evolution from the hunter-gatherer band began approximately 11,000 to 13,000 years ago, when the human population increased substantially. Population growth was probably both a cause and an effect of more intensive forms of food production, including the domestication of animals and horticulture (Gat, 2006, pp. 158–159). At the same time, hunter-gatherer bands began to be integrated into or replaced by larger groups. The precise causes for the development of larger social groups will never be completely known, because it preceded written language, but it is likely that integration was a response to a combination of factors, including increased intergroup competition over resources, more permanent or regular settlement, the emergence of territoriality, and environmental change (Diamond, 1997, pp. 268–269; Johnson & Earle, 2000, p. 33).

The first social group to supersede the hunter-gatherer band was the "local group," or "tribe," five to ten times larger than hunter-gatherer bands, with 125 to 250 members. Local groups were more sedentary, with either long-term encampments or permanent settlements. They were also more centralized than hunter-gatherer bands, led either by a single leader ("Big Man") or a council of prominent males. Security concerns were an important dimension of daily life in local groups, as evidenced by fortifications found in archeological sites from this period. These primarily provided protection from raids by other groups for resources. Large-scale warfare was not common in tribal societies, although intergroup violence was frequent (Gat, 2006; Keeley, 1996).

After local groups, various forms of centralized states, which Johnson and Earle (2000) refer to as "regional polities," developed. These include chiefdoms, early states, and finally nation-states, the primary political unit of the contemporary world. Although regional polities vary considerably in size, level of technology, cultural specifics, and institutional complexity, they share central features. All are urbanized to some degree with large centers of permanent population, including a capital, from which the polity is administered. They also have political institutions and bureaucracies, political and economic elites, varying levels of social stratification, religions, markets, and complex economic institutions. Perhaps the quintessential feature of regional states is the military, which allows for organized, large-scale warfare between states.

We will not address the question here of why states emerged and acquired these characteristics, or why they became larger and more complex over time, since there is already an extensive literature on the topic and because many aspects of state development are not directly related to the caregiving system. However, understanding the caregiving system may provide some clues as to how it was possible for the basic form of human society—the kin-based hunter-gatherer band—to be supplanted so quickly by much larger and complex societies. If we are correct that the caregiving system produced and sustained hunter-gatherer bands of modern humans for hundreds of thousands of years, and the ancestors of *Homo sapiens* for millions more, what suddenly changed to cause larger societies to appear? It is conceivable that a genetic change in some component of the caregiving system could have suddenly allowed for the extension of generalized altruism to non-kin, thus allowing for the maintenance of much larger social groups. However, the likelihood that such a genetic change took place and rapidly spread around the globe to produce larger societies appears small, particularly because hunter-gatherer bands continued to exist alongside tribes and regional polities and disappeared in most of the world only very recently, within the last 500 years, and even then only because they were shattered by the imperial expansion of European nations.

Anthropologists have attributed the rise of larger and more complex human groups to the development of mechanisms of integration (Service, 1962). Social and political stratification, bureaucracies, coercion, and state provision of collective goods have all been identified as possible causes for integration. The problem with such explanations is that they rely on a *post hoc, ergo propter hoc* logic: Integration is assumed to be caused by phenomena that may have appeared only after larger societies emerged. For example, bureaucracies certainly contribute to the maintenance of large polities by linking various units together and allowing for the administration of regions and peoples living far from the political center or capital, but this does not mean that bureaucracies created larger societies, that they were the original integrating mechanism. Analysis of the features of larger societies and polities may help us to understand the internal dynamics and social cohesion of those societies, but they provide us with little assistance in determining how expansion occurred.

Given our preceding argument that the hunter-gatherer band was sustained by the neurological template of the caregiving system and is thus the "natural" social unit of *Homo sapiens*, the most obvious means of creating larger social groups would be through agglomeration of bands. In such a process of social evolution, larger societies would be the result of the merging of two or more groups and the subsequent expansion from the merged groups. In an agglomerative explanation for the creation of larger societies, the caregiving system is not replaced by other forms of integration; it is somehow extended to distant kin and even unrelated strangers.

The anthropological, archeological, and historical record provides abundant evidence that larger social groups developed in exactly this way. Most tribes studied by anthropologists have been organized around kinship groups or clans, which were likely the remnants of the original hunter-gatherer bands that had united at some earlier period (Diamond, 1997, p. 271). Indeed, in many tribes, clans preserved some of the characteristics of the original bands: European explorers and later anthropologists documented some tribes in which the clans had managed to maintain their own languages or dialects for perhaps thousands of years. Even in the early forms of regional polities—chiefdoms and early states—clans and kinship groups played important roles in the political or religious life of the society, particularly in the selection of political leaders (Johnson & Earle, 2000, p. 34). Over time, political and social power gradually detached from kinship as various types of institutions, including bureaucracies, provided new types of social integration (Gat, 2006; Johnson & Earle, 2000). However, even today, traces of the original family-level human group—in the form of hereditary monarchies or family-based political cliques—can still be found in the structures of political authority of many contemporary states.

Archeological and anthropological research suggests that the impetus for agglomeration was external to hunter-gatherer bands. The well-documented population growth in the late Pleistocene and early Mesolithic eras appears to have contributed to intergroup competition, much of which was undoubtedly violent, over resources. The advent of horticulture also contributed to territoriality by making it necessary for groups to defend land to protect their food supply. The first groups that were able to combine with one another gained a decided advantage in such competition—strength in numbers—allowing them to dominate their neighbors. Hunter-gatherer bands in close proximity to new, larger groups had the choice of moving into remote or less productive lands or of similarly merging with their neighbors and fighting to protect their own resources.

However great the utility of agglomeration for group and individual survival, it posed the problem of how to maintain unity within groups composed of distinct subunits. One mechanism for integrating and unifying tribes that has long been of interest to anthropologists and ethnographers is mythology and folklore (Levi-Strauss, 1966; Malinowski, 1948). Anthropologists have found that almost all tribes have myths or tales about the origins and character of the group. These "founding myths" depict a single "people" created by a god or gods, sharing common parents or ancestors, or otherwise related to one another through ties of soil or blood, melding the people into a single family (Bierhorst, 2002; Courlander, 1975; Wolfram, 1988). The ubiquity of such myths across societies suggests that they have played an important role in sustaining larger human communities. As Malinowski concluded from his observations of the role of myth among Trobriand islanders, myths provide human societies with an aura of "rightness" or legitimacy:

> The sacred tradition, the myths, enters into their pursuits and strongly controls their moral and social behavior. In other words . . . an intimate connection exists between the world, the mythos, the sacred tales of a tribe, on the one hand, and their ritual acts, their moral deeds, their social organization, and even their practical activities on the other. (1948, p. 96)

By emphasizing kinship and a common identity, such myths could have overridden or deactivated the exploitation detection mechanism of the caregiving system, thus allowing for a dramatic expansion in the number of individuals to whom trust could be extended and help or care rendered. Once such an extension of reciprocal altruism occurred, cohesion could be continually reinforced by norms, ceremonies, institutions, and the history of shared experience to create and sustain large, complex societies, and ultimately early states.

It may seem that by emphasizing the power of myth to shape the human mind and the operation of the caregiving system, we are reverting to the old Standard Social Science model, putting all the emphasis on culture and ignoring biology and brain function. However, a growing literature suggests that the mere imagination of tales, even those known to be false, can change people's memories of past events, or even create new (and false!) "memories" (Garry & Polaschek, 2000;

Mazzoni & Memon, 2003). These findings about the creation of memories through tales are consistent with Malinowski's assertion that myth is "not merely a story told but a reality lived." (1948, p. 100).

The first tribes, chiefdoms, and states of the Pleistocene era were created before written language and thus left no documentary evidence to test our supposition that myths and stories allowed for the extension of the caregiving system to unrelated individuals, thereby contributing to the formation of larger social groups. However, if we move forward to the first known political democracy—the *polis*, or city-state, of ancient Athens—there is an extensive written record to analyze. Athenian philosophers and historians devoted much effort to consideration of the question of the origins and nature of their political community. We can examine their writings, as well as those of Greek poets and dramatists, to consider how the Athenians and their culture used the emotional and behavioral repertoire of the caregiving system to build and sustain the first known democracy.

■ BUILDING A DEMOCRATIC CITY-STATE: MYTHS, ALTRUISM, AND EMPATHY IN ANCIENT ATHENS

The site of constant settlement from approximately 9000 BCE, Athens rose as a regional economic and military power in the 6th to 5th centuries BCE during the same period that it developed institutions of direct democracy. At its zenith, Athens produced a rich intellectual, artistic, and political culture, which has profoundly shaped Western civilization. It is arguable that the achievements of Athens were due in large part to the Athenians' success in overcoming internal divisions and achieving internal unity. Time and again, citizens demonstrated their willingness to sacrifice themselves for the sake of their city, and this proclivity to care for the affairs of the city, perhaps more than any other factor, contributed to its military prowess and victories.

As noted earlier in the chapter, Aristotle argued for the naturalness of the political community. Yet he and other Greek thinkers were fully aware that it was created through human action and was therefore to a certain extent artificial; the truly "natural" and original components within the *polis* were the family and tribe (Greenidge, 1920, pp. 12–13). The ancient Athenians considerred *oikos* (family or household) and *ousia* (one's own) or property to be core components of the *polis*. Families were responsible for many religious ceremonies, maintained connections with the ancestors, and provided the citizens (only males were accorded citizenship) and resources that were essential for governance and defense (Herman, 2006, p. 49). All families were linked to the state through four large clans or tribes, which were supposed by the Athenians to be the remnants of the ancient tribes that had founded the city (Finer, 1999).

Perhaps because of the keen awareness of the dependence of the *polis* on families and tribes, a central theme in much of Greek philosophy and literature was the dividing line and tensions between private life, the sphere of family, and public affairs (Saxonhouse, 1992, pp. 234–235). Families and household life were seen by the Greek philosophers as essential for the city's existence but also in competition with it for the loyalty of citizens, pulling them away from the political community.

It was feared that if these tendencies went unchecked, loyalty to families could weaken or fragment the political community. Indeed, some of the most serious internal conflicts in Athenian history emerged around familial and tribal divisions.

Partially counterbalancing the threat to the unity of the city posed by such divisions were myths regarding the founding of the city. Some were myths of autochthony, tales of the warrior-founders of the city springing up directly from the soil of Athens. Myths of autochthony glossed over or denied the role of women in the birth of warriors and rulers, and depicted the city not as something artificial but as a natural product of the earth. Myths of autochthony "helped to give expression to the unified vision of the city" as the realm of a brotherhood of male warriors (Saxonhouse, 1992, pp. 51–52). Such myths also distinguished Athens from other cities and differentiated citizens of one city from citizens of others, creating a line of demarcation between them.

A second myth, probably not as ancient, concerned the initial act of agglomeration that had created Athens. It told of a hero king, Theseus, who supposedly joined together many small rural communities across Attica to found the Athenian *polis*. In the classical period of Athenian democracy, this merging of communities was celebrated in a festival called the Synoecia (Herman, 2006, p. 45). A goddess, Synoecia ("union of houses"), was created specifically to honor the mythological merger (Kitto, 2007, p. 99).

Such myths of origins probably contributed to the generation of a common identity among Athenians, but they did not prevent internal divisions and conflicts. Following a period of domestic political strife that resulted in the rise of tyrant to power and the brief interruption of democracy, the leader Cleisthenes reformed the tribe system in 508–507 BCE, replacing the four old tribes with ten new ones. His goal in doing so was to weaken the influence of the older tribes, and of the families attached to them (Saxonhouse, 1992, pp. 94–95). He also created many new, smaller community bodies, or *demes* (similar to precincts or wards), and reassigned citizens to the new *demes*. Furthermore, he abolished the use by citizens of their fathers' names as a last name, and required that they use instead the name of their *deme* (Aristotle, 1935). *Demes* were named for heroes and kings from myths, legends, and history, creating a conceptual bond between living citizens and the progenitors of the *polis*. The combined effect of all these reforms was to create "a common national spirit" (Greenridge, 1920, pp. 157–158).

In addition to the founding myths and tribal/*deme* reorganization, the Athenians made use of drama to create a sense of equality and common identity. Plays written at the height of Athenian democracy in the 5th century BCE, particularly the tragedies, worked to create a strong sense of community by activating emotions, particularly the emotions of pity and empathy. The common element of Greek tragedies was human suffering, usually arising through no fault of the heroes and heroines, but brought upon them by the whims of the gods or cruel fate. Tales of great suffering and loss evoked pity in the spectators and, more centrally, empathy, a sense of shared suffering with the heroes. Aristotle, in his work *Poetics*, argued that the tragedies combined these emotions in such a way as to produce *katharsis*, or a purification of the emotions (Aristotle, 1951, p. 296). At a time when human life was short and suffering common, empathy and *katharsis* had great appeal: Up to 30,0000 Athenians and guests from other cities attended performances of the tragedies (E. Hamilton, 1930, p. 171).

In a fascinating analysis of the content, meaning, and political effect of Greek tragedy, Alford (1993) argues that by allowing Athenians to share collectively in one another's pain and to feel sorrow for human fate, the tragedians contributed to the development of democratic values and instilled a sense of civic duty or obligation. The ability to put oneself in the shoes of others, to feel pity and compassion for them, was elevated to the level of civic virtue. It also bound the citizen to the political community, as the Athenian leader Pericles explained during the Peloponnesian War between Athens and Sparta: "Since the *polis* supports individuals in their suffering, but no one person by himself can bear the load that rests upon *polis*, is it not right for us all to rally to her defense?" (Thucydides, 1954, p. 60).

The willingness of Athenians to sacrifice their comfort, security, and lives in the defense of their city was remarkable, and played a large role in the rise of Athens as a great power in the ancient world (Herman, 2006). All able-bodied citizens, from youth until well into middle age, were eligible for military service. The prosperous provided their own armor and weapons, and the very wealthy even paid for the construction of battleships (triremes), outfitted them for war, and covered the cost of training and feeding the crews. In the time of Pericles, during the Peloponnesian war with Sparta, the citizen army was huge, consisting of approximately 29,000 warriors and 250 ships (Finer, 1999, p. 351; Thucydides, 1954, p. 202). It fought often: Between 480 and 338 BCE, Athens was almost continually at war with one or more states. Warfare contributed significantly to the solidarity of the Athenians, even though the city's military organization was unstructured, almost informal, and the warriors spent little time training. Indeed, the core of the Athenian infantry, the hoplites, returned to their fields between wars (Hanson, 1999).

■ CONCLUSION

Although specific to ancient Athens, the foregoing inquiry suggests a great deal about the biological, neurological, and emotional foundations of states. The Athenian case provides supporting evidence for our supposition that large-scale societies are built from and draw upon the emotional and behavioral template of the caregiving system. Indeed, in the analysis of the factors that contributed to the Athenian community, we can see a basic pattern, a formula, for the creation and operation of large societies. Founding myths, narratives, civic rituals, and dramatic presentations instilled a common identity and created a unity of purpose among the many family, kinship, and regional groups that comprised Athenian society. The historian Gabriel Herman argues that the brilliance and accomplishments of ancient Athens can be attributed to the way in which the interests of individual citizens were defined by and inextricably connected with the collective interests of the *polis* (Herman, 2006, p. 393). The creation of a single national identity resulted in a high level of cooperation and mutual assistance among the members of the community and a willingness of citizens to sacrifice themselves for the abstract entity of the *polis*.

In addition to expanding our understanding of the factors that sustain large-scale societies, the model of the caregiving system also has implications for our explanations of interstate conflict and war. The same common identity, unity of purpose, and willingness to sacrifice that are based in the caregiving system and serve to sustain large-scale societies also allow those societies to fight wars. Military organizations appear to draw from the emotions of the caregiving system; in so doing, they significantly contribute to the integration of large-scale societies. As we see in the Athenian case, the creation of a warrior group and the shared experience of warfare itself can reinforce the shared identity and common sense of purpose of the political community.

The great wealth and power of Athens was in large part a function of the city's ability to dominate and control surrounding peoples through the use of military force. The lauded unity of the Athenians allowed them to subjugate surrounding territories a process that resulted in the complete destruction and near genocide of at least one other society. In 416 BCE, the Athenians launched a campaign against the island of Melos, a colony of Sparta. Before attacking, the Athenians sent representatives to the Melians to negotiate a surrender. The Athenians offered to spare the Melians if they would relinquish their independence and submit to the rule of Athens. If they did not surrender before the fighting, they would be killed. In reply, the Melians appealed to universal principles of fair dealing and their right to exist as free people. The Athenians dismissed the existence of any such universal standard of right and responded with the principle of "might makes right": "The strong do what they have the power to do and the weak accept what they have to accept." The Melians rejected this notion and refused the offer of surrender. War commenced, and after a prolonged siege, Athens was victorious. Although the Melians then surrendered, the Athenians, showing no mercy, "put to death all the men of military age" and "sold the women and children as slaves." They occupied the island of Melos and later colonized it with settlers from Athens (Thucydides, 1954, pp. 400–408).

The destruction of the Melians reminds us that across history large-scale societies and states have generated military forces and frequently engaged in interstate conflict and aggression. We would propose that militaries and interstate aggression are also connected to or draw upon the properties and internal dynamics of the caregiving system. States extend the size of the group in which the nurturing, helping, and self-sacrificing behavior generated by the caregiving system prevails, but they also create boundaries. Outside of those boundaries, altruism does not prevail. Just as the caregiving system exerts both a centrifugal and centripetal force on familial or hunter-gatherer societies, it similarly affects the limits of states. Indeed, the caregiving system, with its mechanism for the detection of threats and potential exploitation from strangers and members of out-groups, is involved in the creation of negative reciprocity toward other groups and nations. Military organizations would seem to be the most intense social manifestation or product of the caregiving system, in that they are characterized at the micro-level by a strong bond among comrades and a willingness to sacrifice security and self for comrades, as well as for the state or nation (Stern, 1995). They also generate a fierce antagonism and aggression toward individuals or groups perceived as threats to comrades, the community, or the nation. The consistency with which we see this pattern across nations and over recorded history is a good indication that military organizations are an extension of a neurological process, such as the threat and exploitation detection elements of the caregiving system.

If we are correct that the basic template for dominant organizational features and patterns of interaction within human societies can be found in the neural networks and brain structures of the caregiving system, then knowledge of this system may provide a path away from the continual warfare that has plagued human history and, given the development and proliferation of weapons of mass destruction, now constitutes a genuine threat to the survival of *Homo sapiens* as a species. If the creation of a strong common identity allows the caregiving system to be extended almost indefinitely to non-kin and strangers, the most effective means of reducing international conflict would be to replace the old narratives and founding myths, which emphasize the uniqueness and superiority of specific peoples or nations, with a global or cosmopolitan identity asserting the equality of all humans and strengthening the concept of humanity as a single family (Monroe, 2003).

States themselves can contribute to this process. Several decades ago, the American sociologist Robert Angell (1973) devised a scheme by which to rank states on a dimension that he called "world-mindedness," which included participation in international organizations, level of treaty participation, and tendency to cooperate with other nations. A shift toward world-mindedness can be seen in the contemporary foreign policies of many states, most notably the Scandinavian countries. States can also do much to develop world-mindedness, at least at the international level, by drafting, implementing, and assiduously adhering to international human rights and humanitarian conventions and thus working together to gradually eliminate violence against civilians in wartime, torture, rape, brutal incarceration, displacement, forced labor, and so on. From those far-from-fulfilled goals, the next step could be stronger mechanisms and procedures for resolution of menacing violent conflict between and within states to include early warning and preventive international intervention and, of course, more muscular codification and enforcement of international laws regarding war.

Many states, of course, are skeptical of international institutions and there is good reason to believe that most states will never completely embrace cosmopolitanism, for to do so would risk their internal fragmentation and demise. Another path, perhaps more promising than state-led movement toward a global identity, can be seen in the Culture of Peace movement launched by the Hague Appeal for Peace Conference and UNESCO in 1999–2000. This effort involves direct education of citizens around the globe with a curriculum that emphasizes tolerance, understanding of multiple global cultures, intercultural communication, and human rights. The Culture of Peace movement is quite ambivalent about states, seeing them as bastions of chauvinist sentiments and military interests, and focuses instead on local communities, seeking to build from the ground up a transnational culture of peace that transcends state and cultural boundaries (Adams, 2010; Hague Appeal for Peace Organizing and Coordinating Committee, 1999). "Think globally, act locally" has been a slogan of social movement activists for decades; it may be the path of future human social evolution.

■ IN MEMORY OF J. DAVID SINGER . . .

Professor J. David Singer of the University of Michigan died December 2009 as the result of injuries sustained in a car accident. Although David did not actually write any part of this chapter, he is truly one of its authors, for, as I attempt to explain here, without his vision and encouragement it would not have been written. In terms of its aims, approach, and spirit, it bears his imprint.

First and foremost, David Singer was a scientist. He believed deeply in the power of knowledge to transform society. In 1964 he launched the famous "Correlates of War" (COW) project, which sought to identify the causes of war, with the goal of reducing the frequency of war if not eliminating it altogether. With this project, David became a leading figure in the "behavioral revolution" in political science and trained generations of graduate students in the scientific approach to the study of international relations. He remained committed to the scientific method to the end, insisting on the importance of well-designed research, good measures, and the quantification of data long after positivism had ceased to be considered cutting-edge in the study of international relations.

Although orthodox in his scholarship, David Singer was quite different in several respects from most political scientists of his generation, and it is these differences, I think, that explain the considerable impact that he had as a scholar and as a teacher. First, he rejected the disciplinary norm that political scientists should be completely objective, which in practice meant that they should only study politics and not be actively involved in the political life of their community. David rejected this norm, correctly observing that silence and failure to take a stand on critical issues is tantamount to supporting the powerful, a tendency that he felt was widespread in academe and particularly pronounced in political science. Openly flouting the norm of objectivity, he taught that war and the use of military force were almost always unnecessary evils. He consistently opposed U.S. wars and spoke out about the causes and consequences of militarism. Active his entire adult life in the peace movement, David helped to organize the first "teach-in" on the Vietnam War at the University of Michigan. In the decades after Vietnam, during the Central American wars and the two Iraq wars, he regularly participated in and spoke at peace rallies and conferences in Ann Arbor.

David was a genuine democrat with a little "d". He never forgot his working-class origins or his days as a traveling salesman and relished interacting with people from all walks of life. He always had time for a good conversation and enjoyed questioning and conversing with undergraduate students and janitors as much as with his colleagues. He made every person he spoke with feel that they could think deep thoughts too, and was never too proud to assume that he had nothing to learn from others who were not his academic equals. The high point of his week was the COW seminar, which was open to everyone and at which he presided over wide-ranging discussions and often heated debates. Because of his love of both people and ideas, he was able to forge a strong and vibrant community of scholars around COW that extends today across the great research institutions, state universities, and liberal arts colleges of the United States.

A final characteristic that distinguished David from his peers was his great breadth of knowledge and intellectual interests. He assumed that not only was unification of the sciences achievable, but that political science should be based on knowledge of human biology and psychology. This catholic perspective on science was reflected in his long association with the Mental Health Research Institute at the University of Michigan, where he collaborated with psychologists and medical researchers. It was through his connections to psychology that he met Stephanie Brown. After conversations with her over lunch about human nature, neuroscience, and war, she invited him to participate in the "Self Interest and Beyond" project. David in turn recruited me, insisting that I had to be involved because of an ongoing discussion we had started a decade earlier on the biological and genetic basis for human aggression and cooperation while I was a visiting assistant professor at Michigan.

Although David would undoubtedly have made major corrections to this chapter, and it would have been much better as a result, he was enthusiastic about the effort to conceptualize the implications of the caregiving system for models of political behavior. In part this was because of his vision of science: To his mind, synthesis of separate bodies of scientific knowledge about human behavior could only have positive consequences. But the core reason for his commitment to the project was that he fully accepted Stephanie Brown's assertion that the human capacity to care for others is at the core of what it means to be human. He saw the neuroscience of caregiving as knowledge that could provide a solution to the problems of human aggression and war.

David Singer's life was an excellent illustration of the human capacity for caring and of the positive consequences that flow to others and to society when that capacity is actualized. This chapter was written because of him and is dedicated to him.

■ **NOTES**

1. For a time between 1981 and 1986, the APLS was an official section of the American Political Science Association, but it subsequently opted for autonomy from APSA in order to develop its interdisciplinary character (Dryzek & Schlosberg, 1995).

2. According the web site of the University of California at Irvine [http://aris.ss.uci.edu/polpsych/] which does offer a Ph.D. in political psychology, there was not a single political psychology graduate program in the United States before 1985 and only 20 American universities now offer political psychology graduate programs.

■ REFERENCES

Adams, D. (2010). *World peace through the town hall: A strategy for the global movement for a culture of peace*. Retrieved May 29, 2010, from http://www.culture-of-peace.info/books/worldpeace/introduction.html

Alford, C. F. (1993). Greek tragedy and civilization: The cultivation of pity. *Political Research Quarterly, 46,* 259–280.

American Political Science Association. (1951). *Goals for political science: Report.* New York, NY: Sloane.

Andreoni, J. (1995). "Warm-glow versus cold-prickle: The effects of positive and negative framing on cooperation in experiments. *Quarterly Journal of Economics, 110,* 1–21.

Angell, R. C. (1973). National support for world order. *Journal of Conflict Resolution, 17,* 429–454.

Aristotle. (1935). *The Athenian constitution.* New York, NY: Loeb.

Aristotle. (1951). *Poetics.* New York, NY: The Odyssey Press.

Bierhorst, J. (2002). *The mythology of Mexico and Central America.* New York, NY: Oxford University Press.

Bowlby, J. (1969). *Attachment and loss: Vol. I. Attachment.* London, England: Hogarth.

Brown, S. L., & Brown, R.M. (2006). Selective Investment Theory: Recasting the functional significance of close relationships. *Psychological Inquiry, 17,* 1–29.

Brown, S. L., Smith, D. M., Schulz, R., Kabeto, M. U., Ubel, P. A., Poulin, M., . . . Langa, K. M. (2009). Caregiving behavior is associated with decreased mortality risk. *Psychological Science, 20*(4), 488–494.

Buchanan, J. M., & Tullock, G. (1962). *The calculus of consent.* Ann Arbor: University of Michigan Press.

Cacioppo, J. T., & Patrick, W. (2008). *Loneliness: Human nature and the need for social connection.* New York, NY: W. W. Norton.

Cacioppo, J. T., & Berntson, G. G. (1992). Social psychological contributions to the decade of the brain: Doctrine of multilevel analysis. *American Psychologist, 47,* 1019–1028.

Cacioppo, J. T., & Visser, P. S. (2003). Political psychology and social neuroscience: Strange bedfellows or comrades in arms? *Political Psychology, 24*(4), 647–656.

Caldwell, L. (1964). Biopolitics. *Yale Review, 56,* 1–16.

Corning, P. A. (1983). *The synergism hypothesis: A theory of progressive evolution.* New York, NY: McGraw-Hill.

Courlander, H. (1975). *A treasury of African folklore.* New York, NY: Crown.

Davies, J. C. (1963). *Human nature in politics: The dynamics of political behavior.* New York, NY: John Wiley.

De Dreu, C. K. W., Greer, L. L., Handgraaf, M. J. J., Shalvi, S., Van Kleef, G. A., Baas, M. . . . Feith, S. W. W. (2010). The neuropeptide oxytocin regulates parochial altruism in intergroup conflict among humans. *Science, 328,* 1408–1411.

De Waal, F. (2008). Putting altruism back into altruism: The evolution of empathy. *Annual Review of Psychology, 59,* 279–300.

Depue, R. A., & Morrone-Strupinsky, J. V. (2005). A neurobehavioral model of affiliative bonding: Implications for conceptualizing a human trait of affiliation. *Behavioral and Brain Sciences, 28,* 313–395.

Diamond, J. (1992). *The third chimpanzee: The evolution and future of the human animal.* New York, NY: Harper Collins.

Diamond, J. (1997). *Guns, germs, and steel.* New York, NY: W. W. Norton.

Downs, A. (1957). *An economic theory of democracy.* New York, NY: Harper and Row.

Dryzek, J. S., & Schlosberg, D. (1995). Disciplining Darwin: Biology in the history of political science. In J. Farr, J. S. Dryzek, & S. L. Leonard (Eds.), *Political science in history.* New York, NY: Cambridge University Press.

Easton, D. (1965). *A systems analysis of political life.* New York, NY: John Wiley & Sons.

Elman R. Service. (1962). *Primitive social organization; an evolutionary perspective.* New York: Random House.

Durkheim, E. (1933). *The division of labor in society* (G. Simpson, Trans.). New York, NY: The Free Press.

Farr, J. (1995). Remembering the revolution: Behavioralism in American political science. In J. Farr, J. S. Dryzek, & S. T. Leonard (Eds.), *Political science in history*, 198–224. Cambridge, England: Cambridge University Press.

Fehr, E., & Gachter, S. (1998). Reciprocity and economics: The economic implications of *Homo reciprocans. European Economic Review, 42*, 845–860.

Fehr, E., Gachter, S., & Kirchsteiger, G. (1997). Reciprocity as a contract enforcement device: Experimental evidence. *Econometrica, 65*, 833–860.

Finer, S. E. (1999). *The history of government from the earliest time, Vol. 1: Ancient monarchies and empires.* New York, NY: Oxford University Press.

Friedman, J. (Ed.) (1996). *The rational choice controversy.* New Haven, CT: Yale University Press.

Garry, M., & Polaschek, D. L. L. (2000). Imagination and memory. *Current Directions in Psychological Science, 9*, 6–10.

Gat, A. (2006). *War in human civilization.* New York, NY: Oxford University Press.

Gintis, H. (2007). A framework for the unification of the behavioral sciences. *Behavioral and Brain Sciences, 30*, 1–61.

Green, D. P., & Shapiro, I. (1994). *Pathologies of rational choice theory.* New Haven, CT: Yale University Press.

Greenidge, A. H. J. (1920). *A handbook of Greek constitutional history.* London, England: Macmillan.

Hague Appeal for Peace Organizing and Coordinating Committee. (1999). *The Hague agenda for peace and justice.* Retrieved June 15, 2010, from http://www.haguepeace.org/

Hamilton, E. (1930). *The Greek way.* New York, NY: W. W. Norton.

Hamilton, W. D. (1964). The genetical evolution of social behavior. *Journal of Theoretical Biology, 7*, 1–52.

Hanson, V. D. (1999). *The other Greeks: The family farm and the agrarian roots of Western civilization.* Berkeley: University of California Press.

Harvard University. (2010, April 21). Being naughty or nice may boost willpower, physical endurance. *Science Daily.* Retrieved June 30, 2010, from http://www.sciencedaily.com/releases/2010/04/100419151114.htm

Henrich, J., Boyd, R., Bowles, S., et al. (2005). Models of decision-making and the coevolution of social preferences. *Behavioral and Brain Sciences, 28*, 838–856.

Herman, G. (2006). *Morality and behavior in democratic Athens: A social history.* New York, NY: Cambridge University Press.

Hirschman, A. O. (1977). *The passions and the interests: Political arguments for capitalism before its triumph.* Princeton, NJ: Princeton University Press.

Hobbes, T. (2009). *Leviathan.* New York, NY: Oxford University Press.

Johnson, A. W., & Earle, T. (2000). *The evolution of human societies: From foraging group to agrarian state.* Stanford, CA: Stanford University Press.

Kant, I. (2006). *Toward perpetual peace and other writings on politics, peace and history.* New Haven, CT: Yale University Press.

Keeley, L. (1996). *War before civilization: The myth of the peaceful savage* New York, NY: Oxford University Press.

Kitto, H. D. F. (2007). *The Greeks*. Rutgers, NJ: Transaction Press.

Levi-Strauss, C. (1966). *The savage mind*. Chicago, IL: University of Chicago Press.

Locke, J. (1966). *The second treatise of government*. Oxford, England: Blackwell.

Malinowski, B. (1948). *Magic, science and religion*. Glencoe, IL: The Free Press.

Malthur, V. A., Harada, T., Lipke, T., & Chiao, J. Y. (2010). Neural basis of extraordinary empathy and altruistic motivation. *NeuroImage, 51*, 1468–1475.

Masters, R. (1990). Evolutionary biology and political theory. *American Political Science Review, 84*, 195–210.

Mazzoni, G., & Memon, A. (2003). Imagination can create false autobiographical memories. *Psychological Science, 14*, 186–188.

Monroe, K. R. (1996). *The heart of altruism*. Princeton, NJ: Princeton University Press.

Monroe, K. (2003). How identity and perspective constrain moral choice. *International Political Science Review, 24*(4), 405–425.

Morris, J. P., Squires, N., Taber, C., & Lodge, M. (2003). Activation of political attitudes: A psychophysiological examination of the hot cognition hypothesis. *Political Psychology, 24*(4), 727–745.

Olson, M., Jr. (1965). *The logic of collective action*. Cambridge, MA: Harvard University Press.

Phillips, T., Barnard, C., Ferguson, E. & Reader, T. (2008). Do humans prefer altruistic mates? Testing a link between sexual selection and altruism towards non-relatives. *British Journal of Psychology, 99*, 555–573.

Poulin, M. J., Brown, S. L., Ubel, P. A., Smith, D. M., Jankovic, A. & Langa, K. M. (2010). Does a helping hand mean a heavy heart? Helping behavior and well-being among spouse caregivers. *Psychology and Aging, 25*, 108–117.

Rousseau, J.-J. (1990). *Collected writings of Rousseau*. Hanover, NH: Dartmouth College Press.

Sahlins, M. (1972). *Stone age economics*. Chicago, IL: Aldine.

Saxonhouse, A. (1992). *Fear of diversity: The birth of political science in ancient Greek political thought*. Chicago, IL: University of Chicago Press.

Singer, J. D. (Ed.) (1965). *Human behavior and international politics: Contributions from the social-psychological sciences*. Chicago, IL: Rand-McNally.

Somit, A. (1972). Biopolitics. *British Journal of Political Science, 2*, 209–238.

Somit, A. & Peterson, S. (1998). Biopolitics after three decades—a balance sheet. *British Journal of Political Science, 28*, 559–571.

Somit, A., & Peterson, S. (2003). *Human nature and public policy: An evolutionary approach*. New York, NY: Palgrave Macmillan.

Stern, P. (1995). Why do people sacrifice for their nations? *Political Psychology, 16*, 217–235.

Thucydides (1954). *History of the Peloponnesian war*. New York, NY: Penguin.

Tooby J., & Cosmides, L. (1995). Mapping the evolved functional organization of mind and brain. In M. Gazzaniga (Ed.), *The cognitive neurosciences*. Cambridge, MA: MIT Press.

Trivers, R. (1971). The evolution of reciprocal altruism. *Quarterly Review of Biology, 46*, 35–57.

University Of Michigan. (2007, May 12). High-testosterone people feel rewarded by others' anger, new study finds. *ScienceDaily*. Retrieved June 23, 2010, from http://www.science daily.com/releases/2007/05/070511095337.htm

Wilson, D. S., & Dugatkin, L. S. (1992). Altruism: Contemporary debates. In E. F. Keller & E. A. Lloyd (Eds.), *Keywords in Evolutionary Biology*. Cambridge, MA: Harvard University Press.

Wilson, E. O. (1998). *Consilience: The unity of knowledge*. New York, NY: Knopf.

Winkielman, P., & Berridge, K. (2003). Irrational wanting and subrational liking: how rudimentary motivational and affective processes shape preferences and choices. *Political Psychology, 24*, 657–680.

Wolfram, H. (1988). *The history of the Goths*. Berkeley: University of California Press.

17 Motivation and the Delivery of Social Services

■ JULIAN LE GRAND

Much of my professional career has been concerned with developing ways of improving how societies provide so-called "social" services, such as health care, social care, and education. Every country accepts that these services are of crucial importance to the well-being of its citizens, yet in most places they are an endless source of public controversy and political debate. There is little consensus, both within and between countries, as to whether these services should be financed privately, publicly, or by some mixture of the two. And there is perhaps even less agreement on how they should be delivered—by independent professionals, by government bureaucracies using political fiat, or by employing market mechanisms.

Earlier in this decade, I realized that the controversies over mechanisms for the delivery of social services arose in large part because policy-makers and others involved have different perceptions as to what exactly motivates the professionals and others who deliver the services: physicians, nurses, teachers, social workers, and managers, as well as ancillary workers. In 2003 I published a book on this subject: *Motivation, Agency and Public Policy* (Le Grand, 2003/2006). Almost immediately after the book was published, I was invited to become a senior policy adviser to the then British Prime Minister, Tony Blair, a position I held for two years. The debates over education and health care in which I was involved during that period reinforced my views concerning the importance of policy-makers' perceptions of motivation in affecting the nature and structure of policy. Those views resulted in another book, *The Other Invisible Hand* (Le Grand, 2007).

These books were a long way from being the end of the story. So this essay takes some of the books' arguments a little further. It does so in two ways. First, it sets out four models of social service delivery (originally developed in *The Other Invisible Hand*) and outlines the relatively simplistic theories concerning individual motivation and behavior that are implicit within them. Second, it considers more sophisticated theories of motivation, including some of those discussed in the book *The Other Invisible Hand* and in *Motivation, Agency and Public Policy*, and offers some ideas as to what models of service delivery based on these theories might look like. Inevitably, this second section is somewhat speculative, but it is hoped that it offers at least a direction for further work.

■ MODELS OF SOCIAL SERVICE DELIVERY

The Other Invisible Hand set out four models for delivering social services, termed trust, mistrust, voice, and choice. Here I describe each briefly, illustrating the discussion by brief references to the experiences of the Blair government in the United Kingdom from 1997 to 2007. I do not examine all the relative merits of each model; these are discussed in some detail in the book. Instead I focus on the theories of motivation implicit in the models, that is, on the set of assumptions that policy-makers hold—either explicitly or, more commonly, implicitly—concerning the factors that motivate the professionals and others who work in the agencies that deliver social services.

The Trust Model

Under the trust model, providers of a service are trusted to deliver it. The providers are usually professionals of one kind or another—doctors, nurses, teachers, head teachers, social workers, service managers—and in providing the service, these professionals are trusted to do so, in a word, professionally. Thus, in systems of social service delivery that rely largely upon both government funding and government provision, such as public schooling in the United States and, until relatively recently, health care in Britain under the National Health Service (NHS), the relevant social service agencies (schools or hospitals) are given a global budget by the relevant funding agency, with broad freedoms to spend the money as they will. In systems more reliant upon private provision, such as fee-for-service medical care in the United States (at least before the advent of managed care), professionals are trusted to provide the appropriate service to users and to levy the "correct" charge for the service to the relevant funding agency (which, in the case of US health care, may be the government, insurance companies, or the patients themselves).

Under the trust model, professionals are not subject to high-level central directives. They are not told what to do, or what not to do, by the government or any other employer or agency. Nor are they subject to market or quasi-market pressures. Indeed, they are not subject to outside control of any kind; they are autonomous professionals with discretion to make resource-allocation decisions as they will. Further, the model assumes that there are no conflicts of interest between professionals or between the institutions in which they work. Rather, it is assumed that professionals work, or should work, in collaboration with one another, either informally or through more formal networks. Hence the trust model is sometimes known as a "network" or collaborative model (Mayer, Davis, & Schoorman, 1995; Tomkins, 2001).

Belief in the desirability of the trust model as a form of service delivery is widespread. It is prevalent in many European welfare states, especially (and unsurprisingly) among professionals themselves and their associations. Historically it has been very influential in determining the growth and structure of those states (Le Grand, 2003/2006, Ch. 1). It also fuels some of the political controversies over education and health care in the United States. As Alain Enthoven (2007) has noted with respect to the debates over school education in the U.S., liberal Democrats, especially those opposed to school choice, prefer to rely upon trust. "The teachers unions' are large supporters of the Democratic Party and teachers, understandably, strongly support the trust model" (p. 171). With reference to health care, he points out that "Medicare was based on the trust model, but with a fee-for-service system that includes strong incentives for doctors to do more when less would produce the same outcome" (p. 171).

So what theory of motivation underlies this model? It is simple: that professionals and others who work in social services have strong altruistic or caregiving motivations, and when they make their decisions about the provision of services to users, those motivations predominate; the decisions are in no way influenced by self-interest. Doctors' principal concern is with the health of their patients, teachers', with the educational skills of their pupils, social workers', with the welfare of their clients. Egoistical motivations—concerns about pay, working conditions, status, job stimulation, peer reputation—play an insignificant part in professionals' decision making with respect to their clients; if self-interest at any point conflicts with altruism, it is the latter that dominates.

The trust model formed the basis of early policies towards social services, especially the National Health Service, during the early years of the Blair administration. It also figured in much of the government's rhetoric about education, although there the more market-oriented policies of the previous administration were not rolled back to the same extent as in health. However, disillusion with the performance of both the NHS and the education system rapidly led to an almost complete reversal of policy—a move toward what can be termed a mistrust model, perhaps more familiarly known as command and control. (For reasons to become apparent, in *The Other Invisible Hand*, I labeled the mistrust model the "targets" model. I now think that mistrust is more accurate and of more universal application.)

The Mistrust Model: Command and Control

Mistrust or command-and-control models of service delivery can take various forms, but all versions of them have a fundamental similarity. There is a managerial hierarchy for service provision, and direction from the top of that hierarchy to the service providers. This direction is coupled with external rewards or penalties for those complying or failing to comply with the central directives, since, in the mistrust model, social service staff cannot be trusted to do their jobs properly without outside intervention; they have to be incentivised to do it. The rewards and penalties include direct appeals to self-interest, such as financial gain, promotion, demotion, or job loss.

There can be also more subtle forms of self-interested incentives. One is offering greater autonomy for the organization in the event of success—and the withdrawal of that autonomy in the event of failure. Another is "naming and shaming": the publicizing of poor performance to peers or to the general public, with the intention of humiliating the staff of the organization and hence encouraging them—in their own self-interest—to do better.

The Blair government tried a version of this in England from 2000 onward in health care, education and other social services. In health care, it was not called command and control but instead "targets and performance management" or, more informally, as "targets and terror." For instance, a target was set that 98% of those who attended a hospital accident and emergency department have to be seen, treated, discharged, or admitted into a hospital ward within four hours. Seventy-five percent of ambulances called out on life-threatening emergencies have to reach the point whence the call emanated within 8 minutes. No patient for elective surgery should wait longer than a given period, currently 18 weeks from the date of referral by a general practitioner.

The "terror"—or, put less evocatively, the performance management—element of the model was implemented by direct personal contact between the central authority and the institutions concerned. Phone calls, e-mail, and, if necessary, face-to-face meetings—all were employed to deliver and reinforce the message that the institution concerned had to meet the target or heads would roll.

As several independent studies have shown, the mistrust model, at least in its targets-and-terror form, worked—especially in the English NHS. In particular, waiting times fell dramatically across the service—and did so within the time frames specified by the performance management regime. Moreover, the model appeared to work rather better than the trust model, a version of which was being implemented in the health service in other parts of the United Kingdom, such as Wales and Scotland. There, waiting times and other indicators of health care quality stagnated or, in some cases, actually got worse (Bevan & Hamblin, 2008; Bevan & Hood, 2006a, 2006b; Propper, Sutton, Whitnall, & Windmeijer, 2008).

As with the trust model, the implicit beliefs concerning the motivational structures of professionals and others inherent in this model are clear, albeit rather different in kind. Indeed, the theory of motivation incorporated in the model is diametrically opposed to that of the trust model. Instead of assuming that all social service professionals are principled altruists, the assumption here is that they are all primarily egoists. Thus the incentive structures built into this model all appeal to either personal self-interest or, on occasion, institutional self-interest—which can also be viewed as personal self-interest, since that self-interest will depend at least in part on what happens at institutional level.

This viewpoint could be challenged. It might be argued (and indeed was argued by some supporters of the model within the Blair government) that altruism or caregiving motivations were not being challenged by this regime; merely, "reinforcement" was being applied to ensure that professionals moved even further in the desired direction than they were planning to do anyway. However, this argument raises further questions as to whether the impact of this reinforcement would leave the original motivational structure intact. Does treating service professionals as though they were egoists in fact make them so? In the language of the motivational literature, does the emphasis on extrinsic motivational factors crowd out intrinsic, more altruistic, motivations? Are the rewards and penalties really perceived as reinforcing? If so, they are indeed likely to "crowd in" altruistic motivation. Or are they actually perceived as controlling—in which case they crowd out altruistic motivations, thus converting altruists into egoists and, perhaps, leading to an overall reduction in both the quality and quantity of the service supplied?

Despite the mistrust model's successes, in the later years of the Blair administration the government began to move away from it as the principal weapon in its armory for raising the quality of public education and health care. Politicians and civil servants felt that there were too many costs to the policies involved, including distortions of priorities toward areas that were targeted and away from perhaps equally important areas of care that were not; inefficiencies in resource allocation; gaming behavior by the institutions concerned; and the demoralization and demotivation of staff, who did indeed appear to perceive the system as more controlling than reinforcing.

Partly in response to these concerns, there was a growth in interest in models of social service delivery that did not rely upon direction from the top to improve quality, but on pressure from the bottom—that is, from service users themselves. Two such models can be identified: voice and choice.

The Voice Model

The voice model, derived from the work of Albert Hirschman, is one where service users make attempts "to change, rather than to escape from, an objectionable state of affairs, whether through individual or collective petition to the management directly in charge, through appeal to a higher authority with the intention of forcing a change in management, or through the various types of actions and protests, including those that are meant to mobilize public opinion" (Hirschman, 1970, p. 30).

Put another way, "voice" is shorthand for all the ways in which users can express their dissatisfaction with a service by some form of direct communication with the providers of the service. This could be through informally talking to them face to face—parents talking to teachers about the education of their children, patients chatting to their doctors. It could be more indirect—talking to parent governors of a school, even becoming a parent governor; speaking at a patient or public consultative forum; joining the board of a hospital. Or it could be more formal—invoking a complaints procedure or complaining to elected representatives.

What are the assumptions concerning motivation implicit in the voice model? If voice mechanisms on their own are to deliver improvements in the quality of a social service, the presumption has to be that providers will listen to the voices of their users and then act upon them in a way that meets users' concerns. But this will work only if the providers are altruists. If they are wholly or even partly self-interested, then there is no necessary reason for them to respond positively or helpfully to the voices expressed—unless there is an overlap between their self-interest and the users' self-interest. Of course, if the voice model is coupled with the mistrust or command-and-control model–so that the providers know that they will get into trouble from their superiors in the hierarchy if they do not respond to the voice of users—then there is likely to be a response. But then the voice model has simply been transformed into the mistrust model.

There is a further point here. Even if the providers are altruists, they have to be a particular kind of altruist: one that considers the views of users as a proper assessment of quality. If the providers are in fact more paternalistic—that is, if the doctors, teachers, or social workers consider that they know what is best for the service user—then the voices of users will not be listened to or acted upon unless they happen to coincide with the providers' own views.

The Blair government somewhat halfheartedly flirted with voice models in both education and health, introducing a variety of forums and institutions that gave patients a voice in the running of hospitals and parents a voice in the running of schools. However, perhaps somewhat surprisingly given its political base in a party of the center left, the government put more effort into developing the alternative bottom-up model through which users can express their dissatisfaction: that based on user choice and provider competition, or what Hirschman called "exit."

The Choice Model

In the choice model unhappy users, instead of complaining to an unsatisfactory service provider, turn to an alternative provider to get a better service. The money follows the choice, so that good providers gain resources, while poor providers lose resources. This gives all providers a strong incentive to improve their levels of service.

What are the assumptions concerning motivation implicit in the choice model? At first sight it would appear that the model is based on the assumption of egoistic motivations. Certainly, one of the reasons why providers might feel impelled to provide a good service is that it is in their self-interest to do so. If they do not provide an appropriate service, they will lose business and perhaps their livelihoods; if they do provide a service that users like, they will increase the resources available to them and hence will be able to improve their own standard of living.

However, self-interest could only be one of their motivations. In fact, this incentive structure should work whether providers are altruists, egoists, or a combination of both. Self-interested providers will want to attract users because their livelihoods and thus their self-interest depend on their staying in business. But altruistic ones will also want to stay in business so that they can continue to provide a service of benefit to users—an incentive that will be even more powerful if their altruism takes the form of wanting to do the best for their users as the users themselves perceive it. So altruists as well as egoists will want to provide services that benefit users.

It should be emphasized that, as with voice, this argument will apply only if the provider is a certain kind of altruist: one who wishes to fulfill the needs and wants of users as they themselves perceive them. More paternalistic altruists, who had their own perceptions of what would contribute best to a user's well-being and who were not overly concerned with users self-perceived concerns, would not necessarily be incentivized to behave appropriately in the quasi-market. For the incentives in this kind of market are to respond to the choices of users, and these choices will be driven by the users' own perceptions as to what constitutes quality, not by the perceptions of the providers. If the two differ, then the paternalistic provider will be frustrated by the market's operations and therefore not in a position to provide a good service—at least as the user would define it.

Could not this argument—that the incentive structure implicit in the choice model could appeal both to an egoist and to a (nonpaternalistic) altruist—be also applied to the other models, such as mistrust and voice? We have already seen that the mistrust model could incorporate incentives that appeal to altruists as well as egoists—though only so long as the service provider perceived the incentive structure as reinforcing, not controlling. However, even if it were so perceived, it would work as an incentive (or, more accurately, would be perceived as actually reinforcing) only if the provider had the same perception of what was desirable for users as those at the top. Again, the provider would have to be a specific kind of altruist, but in this case a paternalistic one whose paternalistic vision coincided with that of those running the system.

The paternalism criticism could not be applied to the voice model, which, as we have seen, would appeal to the same kinds of altruists as the choice model: nonpaternalists whose concerns were with the welfare of users as they—the users—expressed it. The problem with voice is that, as we have seen, it provides no incentives on its own for providers to improve service to users. For that it has to be coupled with another model such as mistrust or choice.

Just to finish the story, I should add that the Blair government, and its successor led by Gordon Brown, continued to apply the choice-and-competition model to health care and education. Evidence is beginning to emerge that it has been effective in improving quality at least in health care (Cooper, Gibbons, Jones, & McGuire, 2010). And at the time of writing, it seems unlikely that the subsequent coalition government led by David Cameron will revert to any of the other models in the immediate future.

■ THEORIES OF MOTIVATION

It should by now be apparent that almost any form of policy toward social service delivery has to incorporate some view as to what motivates people who work to deliver these services. It should also be apparent that many current forms of policy, including the models described above, contain fairly simplistic views of this motivation. As the contributions of other authors to this book show, there is now a growing literature on motivation providing theories that offer more sophisticated understandings of different kinds of behavior (see also Perry & Hondeghem, 2008). It is therefore worth asking how these theories can be mobilized to improve policy, especially that related to delivering social services.

We can illustrate how this might be done using two different models of caregiving motivation, articulated in this volume by Brown, Brown, and Preston, and by Mikulincer and Shaver. Both models hold that (a) the original evolutionary function of the caregiving system may have been to motivate parents to sacrifice and provide for their offspring; (b) parental caring and investment in the young are responses to offsprings' cues for need, such as immaturity, cries for help, and other signs of vulnerability; (c) the caregiving system has been elaborated, especially in human beings, to support acts of altruism directed not only toward offspring but toward others as well; and (d) threats to the perceived safety or security of those in a position to provide care can interfere with their altruistic decision making. (The essays in this volume by Numan and by Porges and Carter also stress the importance of safety for caregiving and examine the relevant neurophysiological underpinnings.) On this last point, Brown and Brown (2006) emphasize that from an evolutionary perspective helping others may incur certain risks to the self-preservation of the helper, including the risk of being exploited by those being helped. One way, they suggest, to reduce these risks is to direct help preferentially—to those with whom we share close social bonds based on mutual dependence.

The obvious prediction from these models is that we will feel altruistic motivations when we are with friends, relatives, or other people that we care about. When we think about social policy, then, it might make sense to ask whether altruistic motivation is possible to cultivate among strangers. One could infer from these new models of motivation that signs of need or vulnerability in others or feelings of interdependence could lead to altruistic motivation, even toward strangers, as long as the cues for need and vulnerability were genuine. An example of this may be reflected in the world-wide outpouring of support for victims in the recent earthquake in Haiti. Despite the absence of personal relationships with the victims, people contributed large sums of money, and some gave up their own jobs temporarily to travel to Haiti and work on a voluntary basis to help rebuild the country and provide medical services to victims. In this case, there were clear signs that need and vulnerability were genuine (no one questioned whether the earthquake happened), which may have prompted those with the ability to contribute to feel altruistically motivated toward the victims.

These theories, and their supporting data, are broadly convincing, though I would wish to interpret the idea of needing to minimize threats to safety and security as broadly as possible so as to include all forms of self-interested costs, including those that may not involve an immediate threat to safety and security, such as the expenditure of one's own money and the use of one's own time. However, the theories may need some modification to explain the phenomenon of "crowding out" (Deci & Ryan, 1985; Frey, 1999). Consider the well-known example of blood donation raised by Titmuss (1971/1997). He argued that introducing payment for blood into a system that previously relied upon altruistic donation would reduce both the quantity and the quality of the blood supplied. Yet such payments clearly reduce any threats to self-preservation and exploitation, at least when these are interpreted as including monetary costs; hence they should encourage more altruistic activity, not discourage it. Frey (1999) has made a similar argument with respect to the payment of volunteers. He claims that introducing payment for an activity that was previously provided voluntarily might diminish the amount of the activity undertaken. But payment should increase the self-interested benefit (or diminish the overall cost) to individuals undertaking the activity and therefore increase it.

To help resolve this kind of difficulty, elsewhere I have proposed a theory of altruistic motivation that draws attention to the possible positive benefits that may derive from incurring a personal sacrifice or a cost to one's self-interest(Le Grand, 2003/2006, Ch. 4). The central argument is that the sense of well-being that some individuals derive from altruistic acts depends, at least in part, positively on the cost to their self-interest of the acts concerned. So blood donors perceive themselves as making something of a sacrifice in giving blood, volunteers the same in volunteering their labor; and they derive well-being from the fact that they are making these sacrifices to help others. However, if they are paid for this sacrifice, the overall cost to them of the altruistic act is reduced and so is the well-being that they derive from the act. Hence, other things being equal, they will reduce their supply of blood or voluntary labor.

If this is correct, then the fact that there may be a price to be paid in terms of self-interest may make an altruistic act more likely to occur than if there was no cost. But would this hold regardless of the price to be paid? In particular, what if the cost in terms of self-interest is very high? Then it seems likely that, except perhaps for a few extraordinary individuals for whom the need for self-sacrifice is overwhelming, or for those who share very close social bonds with the target of the altruistic act, self-interest will dominate and the activity will be indeed be curtailed.

What are the implications of this nuanced view of human motivation for the models of service delivery? First, it offers possibilities for making the trust model more effective. For it suggests that caregiving motivations will be enhanced if, for instance, the cues indicating vulnerability or need are emphasized. This might argue for policy measures that increase the personal interaction between patients and doctors, for example, or between teachers and students. Examples might include longer consulting times in doctors' surgeries, smaller class sizes in schools, and breaking up large service organizations into smaller ones to reduce the gaps between higher management, frontline services, and the people they serve. All of these measures would increase personal contacts and interaction, thus allowing more time for the need and vulnerability cues to be observed, for states of mutual dependence to be recognized, and for social bonds to develop.

Similarly, there may be measures that could reduce some of the more threatening elements of the cues that indicate potential personal costs to caregiving activities—although, as noted above, some element of sacrifice may need to be retained. For instance, betrayal or exploitation is less likely to occur if both sides of the interaction or transaction can identify with each other—if they have common interests, share common perceptions, or see themselves as interdependent in some way. Although there is a checkered history of measures to persuade people with historic differences to identify with one another (blacks and whites in the southern United States, French and English speakers in Canada, and Protestants and Catholics in Northern Ireland come to mind), they do not always fail (as indeed some of those examples illustrate). And if they succeed, as well as having enormous benefits for the wider society, they may have the spin-off benefit of making it easier for the providers and users of social services to trust one another and thus provide or obtain, respectively, a better service.

However, even if we can succeed in enhancing the impact of cues of vulnerability or need while diminishing the impact of cues that apparently threaten safety, it seems unlikely that we can rely entirely upon the trust model to deliver services such as health care or education. Contrary to what much of Titmuss's (1971/1997) arguments seem to imply, we could not rely upon pure altruism to deliver our social services. The cues for vulnerability or need may be enhanced, but however powerful they are, it is only in very exceptional circumstances—such as the existence of close social bonds based on mutual dependence—that the drive to respond to these cues will completely overwhelm self-interested motivations. So, for instance, doctors, nurses, and teachers will need some level of pay for their activities, if only to meet the necessities of life; if in debt due their training, they will need a reasonable level of income to pay off the debt. More generally, those who work in hospitals and schools will have a self-interested desire to keep their institutions financially solvent, so as to preserve their jobs, their security, and their incomes. Unless channeled appropriately, the pursuit of that self-interest can lead to actions that have an adverse impact on the interests and well-being of users.

It will therefore be necessary, in addition to employing the enhanced trust model, to use models of social service delivery, such as the choice model, that rely at least in part upon self-interested incentives to improve quality. However, the caregiving analyses discussed above also offer some insights into the best way to apply those models. First, the level of self-interested incentives should not be set so high so as to eliminate all elements of personal sacrifice. So, for instance, the pay of doctors, nurses, or teachers working in public services could be set at lower levels than the full market rate operating in the private sector; then those professionals would be making a sacrifice through continuing to work in public service. Such a policy would not be uncontroversial and could lead to (and indeed, in the past, has led to) accusations of exploitation; however, it is where the logic of the analysis points (see Le Grand, 2003/2006, Ch. 4, for further discussion).

Second, there is a danger in such models that the motivations (self-interest and caregiving) may not be aligned. A classic example is the practice common in many countries where doctors who work in the public sector for a salary also undertake private work on a fee-for-service basis. Here the caregiving motivation is the principal driver for the work in the public sector, since doctors' incomes do not change no matter how much or how little work they do and no matter the quality of that work. (Of course, this may not be true if doctors' performance is monitored as under the mistrust model, but this practice is rare.) In contrast, the private-sector work may be principally motivated by self-interest, driven by the fee-for-service system. But there should also be some caregiving motivation at work here, although it may be partly crowded out by the reduction in the level of personal sacrifice implicit in the fee-for-service system. In the absence of strong bonds between doctors and their patients, the combination of motives under fee-for-service is likely to be stronger than the motivations in the public sector , and in consequence the private-sector work will tend to drive out the public-sector work. In this case, the only way for the public employer to resolve the situation is either to ban the physicians concerned from taking private work or to align incentives by introducing a fee-for-service system in the public sector as well—though perhaps at a lower rate than in the private sector to allow for a measure of sacrifice.

■ CONCLUSION

If any model of social service delivery is to work—that is, if it is to deliver high-quality services—it must be based on a proper understanding of the motivation of the people who work within the services. There must also be an awareness of the extent to which the implementation of the model itself affects motivation—whether, for instance it crowds in or crowds out altruistic or caregiving behavior.

New developments in theories of prosocial motivation, many of which are discussed in this book, offer an exciting opportunity for improving our models of delivering health care, education, and other social services. It is to be hoped that this essay has in a small way contributed to the process of exploiting that opportunity.

■ ACKNOWLEDGMENTS

I am very grateful to Stephanie Brown and Michael Brown for their most helpful comments on earlier versions of this paper.

■ REFERENCES

Bevan, G., & Hamblin, R. (2008). Hitting and missing targets by ambulance service for emergency calls: Effects of different systems of performance measurement within the UK. *Journal of the Royal Statistical Society Series A, 172*(1), 161–190.

Bevan, G., & Hood, C. (2006a). Have targets improved performance in the English NHS? *British Medical Journal, 332,* 419–422.

Bevan, G., & Hood, C. (2006b). What's measured is what matters: Targets and gaming in the English public health care system. *Public Administration, 84*(3), 517–538.

Brown S.L. and Brown R.M. (2006) 'Selective investment theory: recasting the functional significance of close relationships'. *Psychological Inquiry, 17*(1), 1–29.

ooper, Z., Gibbons, S., Jones, S., & McGuire, A. (2010). *"Does hospital competition save lives? Evidence from the English NHS patient choice reforms"* London School of Economics: LSE Health Working Paper Number 16, January.

Deci, E. L., & Ryan, R. M. (1985). *Intrinsic motivation and self-determination in human behaviour* New York, NY: Plenum Press.

Enthoven, A. (2007). An American Perspective [Afterword]. In Le Grand (2007), *The other invisible hand: Delivering public services through choice and competition.* Oxford, England: Princeton University Press.

Frey, B. (1999). *Economics as a science of human behaviour.* Boston, MA: Kluwer Academic.

Hirschman, A. (1970). *Exit, voice and loyalty.* Cambridge, MA: Havard University Press.

Le Grand, J. (2006). *Motivation, agency and public policy: Of knights and knaves, pawns and queens* [Revised], Oxford, England: Oxford University Press (Original work published 2003).

Le Grand, J. (2007). *The other invisible hand: Delivering public services through choice and competition.* Oxford, England: Princeton University Press.

Mayer, R., Davis, J., & Schoorman, F. (1995). An integrative model of organizational trust. *Academy of Management Review, 20,* 709–734.

Perry, J. L., & Hondeghem, A. (eds.) (2008). *Motivation in Public Management.* Oxford, England: Oxford University Press.

Propper, C., Sutton, M., Whitnall, C., & Windmeijer, F. (2008). Did "targets and terror" reduce waiting times in England for hospital care? *The B.E. Journal of Economic Analysis and Policy, 8*(2) (contributions), Article 5. Available at http://www.bepress.com/bejeap/vol8/iss2/art5

Titmuss, R. (1997). *The gift relationship.* London, England; Allen and Unwin (Original work published 1971).

Tomkins, C. (2001). Interdependencies, trust and information in relationships, alliances and networks. *Accounting Organisations and Society, 26,* 161–191.

◼ EPILOGUE

Too often we underestimate the power of a touch, a smile, a kind word, a listening ear, an honest compliment, or the smallest act of caring, all of which have the potential to turn a life around. (Leo Buscaglia)

Contributors to this volume have identified new developments in evolutionary biology, neuroscience, and the social sciences that help us affirm and better understand our capacity for engaging in acts of caring, small or heroic, that have the potential to turn lives around. Despite the dominance of self-interest accounts of human behavior, the essays in this volume should give pause to those who remain locked in the belief that prosocial behaviors are of little interest in their own right or are explained fully by self-regarding motivational constructs.

◼ RECAPITULATION

A number of important contributions and themes are evident in the essays. Mindful of Ellen Berscheid's advice (this volume), essayists have identified important properties of what she calls "caregiving love," being careful to differentiate caregiving behavior from its motivational underpinnings, and thus contributing to our understanding of the basic components of the caregiving motivational system.

Several essayists have noted that other-directed caring is part of our evolutionary legacy, likely derived from developments in mammalian neural circuitry specialized for parenting. Operating from this evolutionary vantage point, some contributors have extended or constructed models of the caregiving system that integrate neurophysiological and psychological mechanisms and provide a basis for understanding the boundary conditions of concern for others. These modelers, from diverse backgrounds, have converged on caregiver safety as an important cue for activating (or inhibiting) caregiving motivation, and on the importance of empathic concern in mediating caregiving behavior. And some essayists have dared to imagine what other social sciences—economics and political science in particular—might gain by using the new understanding of caregiving motivation revealed in the pages of this book to inform their disciplines and generate more realistic and humanistic social policies.

◼ UNFINISHED BUSINESS

As noted early in the volume (Brown, Brown, &Preston; Krebs), scientific interest in caregiving is rooted in ideas and controversies related to *altruism*, and so it is not surprising that nearly all of the essayists consider, in one form or another, altruistic behavior (giving that benefits the recipient at a cost to the donor), altruistic (selfless) motivation, or both. Over the years, many psychologists (though not all) have been skeptical of the existence of altruistically motivated caregiving, but for the most part it has enjoyed a particularly lofty status in religion and moral philosophy, and in the mind of the public. Crocker and Canevello (this volume) have even gone so far as to argue, with empirical justification, that unless caregiving is motivated by genuine concern for the well-being of others, it will (paradoxically) undermine self-interest.

But not all observers of human nature see altruism in a positive light, as evident in these words from the famous writer and political philosopher Ayn Rand (1960):

> Do not confuse altruism with kindness, good will, or respect for the rights of others. These are not primaries, but consequences, which, in fact, altruism makes impossible. . . . If any civilization is to survive, it is the morality of altruism that men have to reject.

Undoubtedly, some of the essays in our volume, if not the entire book, would have proved unsettling to Rand were she still alive. Its content reflects an emerging new, practical science of altruism, one that questions underlying assumptions about human nature and delineates the substrates that mediate "kindness," "good will," and perhaps even "respect for the rights of others." As such, our volume can be characterized as an attempt to deliberately "confuse altruism with kindness" in an effort to direct scientific attention to this elusive topic, a topic with the promise of new knowledge about the interpersonal universe. Still, a few of the essayists raise intriguing questions about unintended or unwanted consequences associated with caregiving motivation. For example, mechanisms that mediate caregiving behavior may also play a role in competition (Numan), psychopathology (Gruber & Keltner; Swain), and even suicide and homicide (Brown, Brown, & Preston).

As we move toward exploring a new scientific frontier of other-directed motivation, it will be important to attend to the costs as well as the benefits of caregiving, and find ways to facilitate genuine concern and care for others without leaving caregivers vulnerable to exploitation or making them feel excessively burdened, anxious, or depressed. However, doing so requires us to move beyond esoteric debates about the existence of altruism and its inherent goodness (or evil), in an effort toward finding solutions to those vexing social problems that require for their solution a genuine concern for the well-being of others.

▪ REFERENCES

Buscaglia, Leo. US author & lecturer (1925–1998) http://www.goodreads.com/author/quotes/27573.Leo_Buscaglia, accessed 6/12/11

Rand, A. (1960, February). Faith and Force: The Destroyers of the Modern World. A lecture delivered at Yale University. Published as a pamphlet by the Nathaniel Branden Institute (1967). Available at: http://freedomkeys.com/faithandforce.htm, accessed 6/12/2011.

■ INDEX

Page numbers followed by "*t*" indicate tables.